*Oracle Press*™

# Expert Oracle PL/SQL

*Oracle Press*™

# Expert Oracle PL/SQL

Ron Hardman
Michael McLaughlin

**McGraw-Hill**/Osborne

New York   Chicago   San Francisco
Lisbon   London   Madrid   Mexico City   Milan
New Delhi   San Juan   Seoul   Singapore   Sydney   Toronto

*The McGraw·Hill Companies*

**McGraw-Hill**/Osborne
2100 Powell Street, 10th Floor
Emeryville, California 94608
U.S.A.

To arrange bulk purchase discounts for sales promotions, premiums, or fund-raisers, please contact **McGraw-Hill/Osborne** at the above address.

## Expert Oracle PL/SQL

1234567890 CUS CUS 0198765

ISBN 0-07-226194-3

| | |
|---|---|
| **Acquisitions Editor**<br>Lisa McClain | **Copy Editor**<br>Mike McGee |
| **Project Manager**<br>Patty Mon | **Proofreader**<br>Paul Tyler |
| **Project Editor**<br>Claire Splan | **Composition & Illustration**<br>International Typesetting and Composition |
| **Acquisitions Coordinator**<br>Alex McDonald | **Series Design**<br>Jani Beckwith, Peter F. Hancik |
| **Technical Editor**<br>Cheryl Riniker | **Cover Design**<br>Damore Johann Design, Inc. |

This book was composed with Corel VENTURA™ Publisher.

To Susan—a wonderful wife, mother, and friend. You will forever amaze me.

—*Ron Hardman*

To Lisa—my constant, my wife and best friend; and Sarah, Joseph, Elise, Ian, Ariel, Callie, Nathan, Spencer, and Christianne—our terrific children. Thank you for your inspiration, patience, and sacrifice that made writing this book possible.

—*Michael McLaughlin*

# About the Authors

**Ron Hardman** is an application developer with Academy School District 20 in Colorado Springs, CO, and is founder of Peak Retrieval LLC, a company devoted to information retrieval technologies including Oracle Text. Prior to working at the school district, Ron was a Senior Principal Analyst at Oracle specializing in performance tuning, and was an Oracle Database Developer and Consultant with SAIC and Commerce One. He was given the Oracle ACE award by OTN in 2005, and is a frequent presenter on the topics of Information Retrieval, Oracle Text, and PL/SQL at conferences worldwide. Ron is coauthor of *Oracle Database 10g PL/SQL Programming*, and is a frequent contributor to the OTN forums.

**Michael McLaughlin** is a professor at BYU - Idaho in the Information Systems Department of the Business and Communication School and founder of TechTinker.com, a company focused on application development and development technologies. He worked at Oracle Corporation for over eight years in consulting, development, and support, working with the database, tools, and Oracle E-Business Suite. Prior to his tenure at Oracle Corporation, he worked as an Oracle developer, systems and business analyst, and DBA beginning with Oracle 6. He is a coauthor of *Oracle Database 10g PL/SQL Programming*. He presents at Oracle User Group meetings.

# About the Technical Editor

**Cheryl Riniker** is a Principal Support Engineer at Oracle Corporation and has worked at Oracle for over five years. She works with the financials modules of Oracle Applications and is an Oracle Certified Professional. She also performed the technical review for *Oracle Database 10g PL/SQL Programming*. She has worked as a developer, business analyst, and technical writer prior to working at Oracle.

# Contents at a Glance

## PART V
## PL/SQL Server Pages and Database Management

## PART VI
## Appendixes

# Contents

## PART I
## Advanced Concepts, Internals, and Debugging Concepts

PART III
# Optimizing PL/SQL Solutions

## PART VI
# Appendixes

# Acknowledgments

any thanks go to Lisa McClain and Alex McDonald at Osborne McGraw-Hill for their tireless work on this project. Claire Splan and Mike McGee, who efficiently moved this text through copyedit to production, helped to keep us on track. Thanks so much for your guidance. Cheryl Riniker, one of the best technical resources in Oracle Worldwide Support, provided invaluable feedback in her technical edit and review of the text.

Thanks to Omar Alonso, Mohammad Faisal, Garrett Kaminaga, and the rest of the Oracle Text development team for their feedback. Special mention goes to Barbara Boehmer who graciously allowed us to use her Levenshtein Distance function to demonstrate a new feature in Oracle 10g Release 2. Thanks to BYU-Idaho Information Systems Department and to Academy School District 20 IT and Administration for their support and feedback on this text. Finally, no acknowledgement would be complete without thanking the production department. Thank you so much for putting all of the pieces together, and for all of your hard work.

# Introduction

This book covers advanced topics related to PL/SQL, including many examples that you can use immediately in your own development. All examples are available online, either at www.OraclePress.com or at www.PLSQLBook.com. Simply download them to your computer, and run them according to the instructions provided.

Chapters are organized into six parts:

- Part 1: Advanced Concepts, Internals, and Debugging Concepts

- Part 2: Invoker's Rights, Java Libraries, and Object Patterns

- Part 3: Optimizing PL/SQL Solutions

- Part 4: Text Management Using PL/SQL

- Part 5: PL/SQL Server Pages and Database Management

- Part 6: Appendixes

Throughout the book you will notice sections titled "Why Would I Use This?" and "How Does That Work?" These are questions that we have when reading books all the time, but they all too often go unanswered. In the "Why Would I Use This?" sections we try to provide practical applications for the features we are discussing. If the uses are obvious, we do not include it. Where the use is not so plain, we add this section to spur some ideas for how you can take advantage of the feature(s).

The "How Does That Work?" sections are included because nearly every programmer we know has a desire to know more about how something functions than is practically necessary. We've added this section where we wanted to know. Please feel free to e-mail us at *Feedback@PLSQLBook.com* if you are curious about the internals of other features. We will consider adding it for future releases of the book.

# What This Book Is Not

To set your expectations appropriately, this book is not for beginners. It does not cover FOR loops, cursors, data types, or the structure of procedures, functions, or packages. If you are looking for this type of coverage, pick up our *Oracle 10g PL/SQL Programming* book published by Oracle Press, and then return to this title. *Oracle 10g PL/SQL Programming* covers beginning through advanced topics and prepares you for the subjects you'll find in *Expert Oracle PL/SQL*.

# Conventions

- Code examples are in COURIER.

- References to database objects or code snippits are in COURIER.

- Items of interest are in **BOLD** or are *ITALICIZED*.

- "Why Would I Use This?" and "How Does This Work?" sections are in separate text boxes.

# Examples

Each chapter is constructed to stand by itself. As a result, the examples are completely self-contained by chapter. If you want to run the examples for Chapter 10, download the ZIP file from www.OraclePress.com, or get the code from www.PLSQLBook.com, and begin with the creation of the user. To ensure all examples work in your environment, please run only the user creation script for that chapter and don't attempt to reuse a schema created from another chapter. The permissions are different from script to script. Also, if a README is present, please read it prior to running any scripts.

If you have any problems running any examples, please e-mail us at *Feedback@ PLSQLBook.com*. We will make every attempt to correct the problem quickly. If there is an error, please do send along a log file showing the message, as well as the following details about your environment:

- Database version

- Operating system

- Chapter

- Application server version (if it is a PSP problem)

# PART
## I

# Advanced Concepts, Internals, and Debugging Concepts

# CHAPTER
1

## Introduction to Advanced Concepts, Patterns, and Techniques

**ex·pert**
*Having, involving, or displaying special skill or knowledge derived from training or experience.*

—Miriam-Webster Online Dictionary

ive years of programming. This is the time it takes for most programmers to feel as if they've come of age as a professional. Traditional programming concepts are second nature, like driving a car or typing on a keyboard. Employers recognize this, often advertising jobs requiring *five* or more years' experience. Something happens around this time though. Passion for the craft either accelerates, driving its possessor to new heights, or it withers, causing year five to be the high-water mark of many careers.

Those that push through this five-year *breaking point* often come through with a renewed desire to learn. If you're reading this book, chances are you have a desire to push through and succeed, and are searching for knowledge that will help you do your job better, and make you more efficient.

Expert PL/SQL is for those who wish to accelerate their skills, and go beyond traditional PL/SQL programming. You may have just switched from another programming language, and want to delve more deeply into PL/SQL than other books do, or you may want to expand on the PL/SQL knowledge you already have. In this book, each chapter deals directly with tough questions, and introduces new concepts that you can apply to your current development projects.

This chapter foreshadows the rest of the book by covering the following topics:

- What it means to be an *expert*

- Who should read this book

- How examples are structured

- Oracle 10*g* Release 2 new features for PL/SQL

# What Is an *Expert?*

An expert programmer is someone others turn to for answers. They use their abilities to do more than build to spec. They influence every aspect of the development process, helping others who are on their way to becoming successful themselves. Being recognized as an expert is part skill and part attitude—and attitude is contagious.

Do you want to be an expert? In addition to reading this book, here are a few suggestions to increase your knowledge:

- Help others in your company. Offer short classes and target specific training needs you have observed.

- Monitor user forums and answer questions. Oracle's forum on OTN (http://otn.oracle.com/forums) is a good place to start. Metalink forums and those on www.OraFAQ.com are well attended, too. This is a great place to gain experience from other people's issues, and at the same time help them resolve problems they're having.

- Take note of problems that impact your organization, and find the solution. One difficulty every company seems to have is information overload. Terabytes of data—and no way to use most of it—is a problem you can help resolve. Warehouses of paper documents that could be digitally archived are a problem you can help resolve. (See Chapter 9.) Use these opportunities to improve your skills, while simultaneously improving the business.

Did you notice a common theme about these suggestions, aside from building your own success? They all help others succeed, too.

# 10g Release 2 New Features

One way to move toward expert status is to stay up-to-date on new features. It's tough to take advantage of enhancements if you do not know what they are! This section demonstrates many of the PL/SQL new features in Oracle 10g Release 2. Additions to existing functionality are also shown in various sections throughout the book so they won't be discussed in this chapter.

In this section, we cover the following new features:

- WRAP dynamically generated PL/SQL

- Conditional Compilation

- Asynchronous Commit

- Predictive Analysis

- Using UTL_MATCH to diff code

- Modifications to DBMS_OUTPUT

These new features are discussed in detail in the sections that follow.

# Obfuscation of PL/SQL Source Code

Pages 98–100 in the authors' *Oracle Database 10g PL/SQL Programming* book covered the PL/SQL Wrapper utility, showing how to hide source code by converting it to hexadecimal digits. The utility, found in $ORACLE_HOME/bin, is called WRAP. The drawback to using a command-line utility is that dynamically generated PL/SQL cannot be hidden.

Oracle 10g Release 2 adds an overloaded function and procedure to the DBMS_DDL supplied package. They are listed in Table 1-1.

To illustrate their use, we've created the following table to hold airport codes, regions, and countries:

```
-- Available online as part of wrap.sql
CREATE TABLE airport_list (
                    airport_id NUMBER(10) PRIMARY KEY,
                    airport_code VARCHAR2(10 CHAR) NOT NULL,
                    region VARCHAR2(30 CHAR) NOT NULL,
                    country VARCHAR2(30 CHAR) NOT NULL);
```

The following is a redacted list of data:

```
-- Available online as part of wrap.sql
INSERT INTO airport_list (airport_id, airport_code, region, country)
   VALUES (1, 'AKL', 'Auckland', 'NEW ZEALAND');
INSERT INTO airport_list (airport_id, airport_code, region, country)
   VALUES (2, 'BHE', 'Blenheim', 'NEW ZEALAND');
INSERT INTO airport_list (airport_id, airport_code, region, country)
   VALUES (3, 'CHC', 'Christchurch', 'NEW ZEALAND');
INSERT INTO airport_list (airport_id, airport_code, region, country)
   VALUES (4, 'CHT', 'Chatham Islands', 'NEW ZEALAND');
INSERT INTO airport_list (airport_id, airport_code, region, country)
   VALUES (5, 'DUD', 'Dunedin', 'NEW ZEALAND');
...
```

| Procedure/Function | Description |
| --- | --- |
| WRAP | Overloaded function that returns the wrapped PL/SQL source code when provided with the original source. |
| CREATE_WRAPPED | Procedure that wraps the source code provided as input. It's faster than using WRAP. |

**TABLE 1-1.** *WRAP*

## WRAP

Use the overloaded WRAP function with EXECUTE IMMEDIATE to create the wrapped code, as the following example illustrates:

```
-- Available online as part of wrap.sql
DECLARE
    v_procedure VARCHAR2(32767);
BEGIN
  v_procedure := 'CREATE OR REPLACE PROCEDURE wrap_test '
  ||'IS '
  ||'   v_airport_codes AIRPORT_LIST.AIRPORT_CODE%TYPE; '
  ||'  '
  ||'   CURSOR airport_cur IS '
  ||'      SELECT airport_code'
  ||'        FROM airport_list'
  ||'        ORDER BY airport_code;'
  ||'  '
  ||'BEGIN '
  ||'   FOR y IN airport_cur LOOP '
  ||'      DBMS_OUTPUT.PUT_LINE(''Airport Code: ''||y.airport_code);'
  ||'   END LOOP;'
  ||  'END;';

  EXECUTE IMMEDIATE DBMS_DDL.WRAP(v_procedure);
END;
/
```

To see the wrapped procedure, select the text from the USER_SOURCE view.

```
-- Available online as part of wrap.sql
SELECT text
  FROM user_source
 WHERE name = 'WRAP_TEST';
```

This shows the wrapped source as displayed next:

```
TEXT
------------------------------------------
PROCEDURE wrap_test wrapped
a000000
369
abcd
abcd
abcd
abcd
abcd
```

```
abcd
abcd
abcd
abcd
abcd
abcd
abcd
abcd
abcd
abcd
7
126 103
7ocFripnJzPMGnie8IGlP3gyt0Ywg1zQr54VfHRAEIlxkSMxHbTrPGA+fgyhXmOwh9KP3mV6
ue7N1Bu6yshPJJosBnUh7N3nKOJx09LhPITiEuVW2uCh7HQjVFwL7Ym6Hhaza+wvUDcACKoq
2WxWnMY5Dd2ncXZTZQ2Y5D3K34VpxqRjDtQTzcl8LG3Iwc2VQIViNCa6TxbjmQmL/zGkQRj8
AM+S7plFqrzRaV8LaHPHQT+v/0c1xSj8pR1dZi6z
```

## CREATE_WRAPPED

DBMS_DDL.CREATE_WRAPPED works in a similar way. The following example shows how it differs from the WRAP function.

```
-- Available online as part of wrap.sql
DECLARE
   v_procedure VARCHAR2(32767);
BEGIN
  v_procedure := 'CREATE OR REPLACE PROCEDURE create_wrapped_test '
  ||'IS '
  ||'   v_airport_codes AIRPORT_LIST.AIRPORT_CODE%TYPE; '
  ||' '
  ||'   CURSOR airport_cur IS '
  ||'      SELECT airport_code'
  ||'        FROM airport_list'
  ||'        ORDER BY airport_code;'
  ||' '
  ||'BEGIN '
  ||'   FOR y IN airport_cur LOOP '
  ||'      DBMS_OUTPUT.PUT_LINE(''Airport Code: ''||y.airport_code);'
  ||'   END LOOP;'
  ||  'END;';

  SYS.DBMS_DDL.CREATE_WRAPPED(v_procedure);
END;
/
```

The use of `EXECUTE IMMEDIATE` is not required. `USER_SOURCE` shows the wrapped source code once again.

```
TEXT
----------------------------------------
PROCEDURE create_wrapped_test wrapped
a000000
369
abcd
abcd
...
```

Execute the wrapped procedure to verify all works as expected:

```
-- Available online as part of wrap.sql
EXEC create_wrapped_test
```

This returns the following result:

```
Airport Code: AKL
Airport Code: BHE
Airport Code: CHC
Airport Code: CHT
Airport Code: DUD
Airport Code: GIS
...
```

Wrapping PL/SQL source is not so different using this method than it is using the `WRAP` binary. It is more flexible, however.

## Conditional Compilation

Conditional compilation allows you to write code containing version-specific features so that the post-processed code includes only the sections relevant to the database version the PL/SQL is written for. It uses `DBMS_DB_VERSION` and the following preprocessor control tokens:

- $ERROR

- $IF

- $THEN

- $ELSIF

- $ELSE

- $END

> ### Why Would I Use This?
> Now 10*g* Release 2 features can be included in application design where most needed, without waiting for the older releases of the data server to be desupported! While it was possible to mimic this previously in an IF-THEN statement, checking the version of the database, that IF-THEN statement was always included in the execution of the code. Now, the compiled version contains only the code that's relevant to the version where it will be run.

This feature is best explained through an example. The COMPILE_BY_VERSION procedure shown next uses predefined control tokens to tell Oracle the portion of code to evaluate prior to compilation:

```
-- Available online as part of compile_by_version.sql
CREATE OR REPLACE PROCEDURE compile_by_version
IS
BEGIN
    $IF DBMS_DB_VERSION.VER_LE_10_2
    $THEN
       DBMS_OUTPUT.PUT_LINE('10.2 and under');
    $ELSIF DBMS_DB_VERSION.VER_LE_10_1
    $THEN
       DBMS_OUTPUT.PUT_LINE('10.1 and under');
    $ELSE
       DBMS_OUTPUT.PUT_LINE('Not 10g');
    $END
END;
/
```

Take note that the $IF does not have an $END IF. Rather, it uses $END. This is obviously a departure from traditional IF-THEN-END IF syntax. The reason? END IF has a space in it; something that a control token cannot have. Use $END instead.

Now that the procedure is created, let's take a look at USER_SOURCE. The following SELECT gets the procedure text:

```
-- Available online as part of compile_by_version.sql
SET PAGES 9999
SELECT TEXT
FROM USER_SOURCE
WHERE NAME = 'COMPILE_BY_VERSION';
```

This returns the following:

```
TEXT
-------------------------------------------------
PROCEDURE compile_by_version
IS
BEGIN
    $IF DBMS_DB_VERSION.VER_LE_10_2
    $THEN
       DBMS_OUTPUT.PUT_LINE('10.2 and under');
    $ELSIF DBMS_DB_VERSION.VER_LE_10_1
    $THEN
       DBMS_OUTPUT.PUT_LINE('10.1 and under');
    $ELSE
       DBMS_OUTPUT.PUT_LINE('Not 10g');
    $END
END;
```

This is no different than the original! Instead of looking to USER | ALL | DBA_ SOURCE, use the DBMS_PREPROCESSOR.PRINT_POST_PROCESSED_SOURCE procedure to see the impact.

```
-- Available online as part of compile_by_version.sql
SET SERVEROUTPUT ON
BEGIN
    DBMS_PREPROCESSOR.PRINT_POST_PROCESSED_SOURCE (
        'PROCEDURE',
        'PLSQL',
        'COMPILE_BY_VERSION');
END;
/
```

This returns the following in our instance:

```
PROCEDURE compile_by_version
IS
BEGIN
    DBMS_OUTPUT.PUT_LINE('10.2 and under');
END;
```

**NOTE**
*The output may very well differ in your environment
if you're not running Oracle 10g Release 2.*

The $ is actually the preprocessor trigger character that tells Oracle what to process before completing compilation. ERROR, IF, THEN, ELSIF, ELSE, and END are already defined as control tokens.

## Asynchronous Commit

When a transaction is committed, Oracle writes the redo entry from memory (the Redo Buffer) to the Redo Log Files. Control is not returned to the client until this completes. Asynchronous commit allows you to return to the client without waiting for the redo to be written to disk.

Commit can use the options shown in Table 1-2.

To change COMMIT using these options, set either the COMMIT_WRITE parameter or specify the options during COMMIT. The following example sets the COMMIT_WRITE parameter:

```
SQL> conn / as sysdba
SQL> ALTER SYSTEM SET COMMIT_WRITE = NOWAIT;
```

Alternatively, specify the option(s) when issuing the COMMIT.

```
SQL> COMMIT NOWAIT;
```

The default is WAIT and IMMEDIATE, so modifying the COMMIT option as just shown results in the transaction being written to disk immediately, instead of waiting for confirmation prior to returning to the client.

## Data Mining—Using Predictive Analytics

Data mining is not new. Predictive analysis using the DBMS_PREDICTIVE_ ANALYTICS package is. The package is very straightforward, with only two procedures to examine current trends in existing data, and to predict future results based on patterns identified during package execution.

| Option | Description |
|---|---|
| BATCH | Write the transaction from the Redo Buffer to disk when capable, rather than on commit. |
| IMMEDIATE | Write the transaction from the Redo Buffer on commit. |
| NOWAIT | Do not wait for the redo to be written. Return to the client right away. |
| WAIT | Do not return to the client until the redo entry is written to disk. |

**TABLE 1-2.**    *Commit Options*

## Examining Current Data

The EXPLAIN procedure's structure is shown in Table 1-3.

To execute, pass the source table name to DATA_TABLE_NAME, and the column to explain to the EXPLAIN_COLUMN_NAME parameter. The EXPLAIN procedure looks at all columns in the source table, and analyzes their contents to determine whether a pattern of influence exists over the column being explained. When analysis is complete, the results for each column are printed in the result table. This table should not exist prior to the execution of DBMS_PREDICTIVE_ANALYTICS.

**NOTE**
*To run these examples, you must have the Data Mining option installed.*

The example used in this section starts with a table to hold student assessment data. Its structure is shown next:

```
-- Available online as part of predictive_analytics.sql
CREATE TABLE assessment (
                student_id NUMBER(10) PRIMARY KEY,
                performance NUMBER(10) NOT NULL,
                gender VARCHAR2(10) NOT NULL,
                ethnicity NUMBER(10) NOT NULL,
                age NUMBER(10) NOT NULL);
```

| | |
|---|---|
| DATA_TABLE_NAME | The name of the table that contains EXPLAIN_COLUMN_NAME. |
| EXPLAIN_COLUMN_NAME | The name of the column to be analyzed. |
| RESULT_TABLE_NAME | Table name to store the results of the procedure. The table name must be unique. |
| DATA_SCHEMA_NAME | The default is the current schema. If the table and column being analyzed are in another schema, provide the schema name here. |

**TABLE 1-3.** *Explain Procedure Parameters*

The sample data (not real!) includes test performance levels with typical disaggregations of gender, age, and ethnicity for third-graders. Ethnicity has five different ethnicities marked 1–5. The age range is eight through ten.

```
-- Available online as part of predictive_analytics.sql
INSERT INTO assessment
   VALUES (NULL, 3, 'M', 5, 10);
INSERT INTO assessment
   VALUES (NULL, 3, 'F', 5, 9);
INSERT INTO assessment
   VALUES (NULL, 2, 'F', 5, 9);
INSERT INTO assessment
   VALUES (NULL, 4, 'M', 5, 9);
INSERT INTO assessment
   VALUES (NULL, 4, 'M', 5, 9);
INSERT INTO assessment
   VALUES (NULL, 3, 'F', 5, 8);
INSERT INTO assessment
   VALUES (NULL, 3, 'M', 5, 9);
...
COMMIT;
```

A total of 1024 records are inserted into the assessment table when you run the `predictive_analytics.sql` script. As you would expect, the more data you have to analyze, the more precise the correlations will be. Outliers will have less impact when more records are present. For example, if only 64 records are in the assessment table, significant patterns will be difficult to determine, but improve the underlying data set, and relevant patterns begin to develop.

Execute the following to explain the `ASSESSMENT.PERFORMANCE` column:

```
-- Available online as part of predictive_analytics.sql
BEGIN
   DBMS_PREDICTIVE_ANALYTICS.EXPLAIN (
      'ASSESSMENT',
      'PERFORMANCE',
      'ASSESSMENT_ANALYSIS');
END;
/
```

`DBMS_PREDICTIVE_ANALYTICS.EXPLAIN` creates a table to store the output. We've named the table `ASSESSMENT_ANALYSIS`, but any valid table name will work. The tables, regardless of the name you provide, have the same structure. The table structure is shown next:

| Name | Null? | Type |
| --- | --- | --- |
| ATTRIBUTE_NAME | | VARCHAR2(40) |
| EXPLANATORY_VALUE | | NUMBER |
| RANK | | NUMBER |

The `ATTRIBUTE_NAME` column includes one record for each column in the analyzed table, less the column that they are being compared to. `EXPLANATORY_VALUE` is a number from 0 to 1 that ranks the ability of that column to explain the value of the target column. A value of 0 indicates that there is no correlation found, while a value of 1 indicates that the correlation is perfect. The higher the value is, the more the column can be relied upon to explain the value in the target column.

To see the results, select all three columns from the `ASSESSMENT_ANALYSIS` table.

```
-- Available online as part of predictive_analytics.sql
SET PAGES 9999
SELECT *
  FROM ASSESSMENT_ANALYSIS;
```

This results in the following:

```
ATTRIBUTE_NAME                              EXPLANATORY_VALUE        RANK
------------------------------------------- -----------------  ----------
GENDER                                               ,071302739          1
AGE                                                  ,059764092          2
ETHNICITY                                            ,037652922          3
STUDENT_ID                                                    0          4
```

So, with this sample set of data, gender is best able to explain performance, though it is by no means a perfect indicator. It is quite low in fact, turning in a dismal .07 explanatory value.

**NOTE**
*If you rerun this without dropping the `ASSESSMENT_
ANALYSIS` table, it will fail with the following:*

```
BEGIN
*
ERROR at line 1:
ORA-00955: name is already used by an existing object
ORA-06512: at "DMSYS.DBMS_PREDICTIVE_ANALYTICS", line 1100
ORA-06512: at line 2
```

*Drop the table prior to rerunning to avoid the error.*

## Predicting Future Results

It's pretty easy to find correlations between different types of data to help understand the results, but it's also possible to predict values with the same package. The `DBMS_PREDICTIVE_ANALYTICS.PREDICT` procedure has the parameters shown in Table 1-4.

| ACCURACY | Accuracy is an OUT parameter that returns the accuracy with which the prediction can be made. |
| DATA_TABLE_NAME | The name of the table being analyzed. |
| CASE_ID_COLUMN_NAME | This is generally the primary key, but can be any unique column. |
| RESULT_TABLE_NAME | The name of the table to create that will hold the results. |
| DATA_SCHEMA_NAME | The default is the current schema. To override the default, specify the name of the schema. |

**TABLE 1-4.** *Predict Procedure Parameters*

The same table and source data is used for this example, but a few additional records are added where the students have yet to take the assessment. Notice that the second column is NULL.

```
-- Available online as part of predictive_analytics.sql
INSERT INTO assessment
VALUES (NULL, NULL, 'M', 5, 9);
INSERT INTO assessment
VALUES (NULL, NULL, 'F', 5, 9);
INSERT INTO assessment
VALUES (NULL, NULL, 'F', 5, 9);
INSERT INTO assessment
VALUES (NULL, NULL, 'M', 2, 9);
INSERT INTO assessment
VALUES (NULL, NULL, 'M', 5, 9);
INSERT INTO assessment
VALUES (NULL, NULL, 'M', 5, 9);
INSERT INTO assessment
VALUES (NULL, NULL, 'M', 5, 8);
INSERT INTO assessment
VALUES (NULL, NULL, 'F', 5, 9);
INSERT INTO assessment
VALUES (NULL, NULL, 'M', 2, 9);
INSERT INTO assessment
VALUES (NULL, NULL, 'M', 4, 10);
INSERT INTO assessment
VALUES (NULL, NULL, 'F', 5, 9);
COMMIT;
```

Use DBMS_PREDICTIVE_ANALYTICS.PREDICT to predict the assessment values for these 11 students.

```
-- Available online as part of predictive_analytics.sql
SET SERVEROUTPUT ON
DECLARE
    v_predict_accuracy NUMBER(10);
BEGIN
    DBMS_PREDICTIVE_ANALYTICS.PREDICT (
        v_predict_accuracy,
        'ASSESSMENT',
        'STUDENT_ID',
        'PERFORMANCE',
        'ASSESSMENT_PREDICTION');
    DBMS_OUTPUT.PUT_LINE('*** Accuracy ***');
    DBMS_OUTPUT.PUT_LINE(v_predict_accuracy);
END;
/
```

This adds the prediction to the ASSESSMENT_PREDICTION table. Selecting from this table for the rows added earlier shows us where, statistically, we can expect the performance of each person to end up.

```
-- Available online as part of predictive_analytics.sql
SELECT * FROM
    ASSESSMENT_PREDICTION
    WHERE STUDENT_ID > 1024;
```

This returns the following data set:

```
STUDENT_ID PREDICTION PROBABILITY
---------- ---------- -----------
      1025          3  ,64883399
      1026          3  ,890236437
      1027          3  ,890236437
      1028          3  ,728349805
      1029          3  ,64883399
      1030          3  ,64883399
      1031          3  ,689166427
      1032          3  ,890236437
      1033          3  ,728349805
      1034          2  ,999986529
      1035          3  ,890236437
```

These students did not have any performance measure (the column is still NULL), but with a data set that is large enough, it's possible to predict performance based on patterns. In this case, student 1034 is likely to get a performance level of 2, whereas the other ten are likely to have a performance level of 3. We set no values to weight certain columns or values over others. This is determined by Oracle using DBMS_PREDICTIVE_ANALYTICS.

**TIP**
*As with any statistic, look beyond the numbers. Though it's possible, with enough data, to define certain macro trends with people (in this case, third-grade students), be careful not to apply those macro trends to the individual level. It's virtually impossible to determine, in advance, how a person will respond to events. To place artificial limitations on individuals based on predictive analysis allows this imprecise science to impact the outcome. It can limit potential, turning it into a self-fulfilling prophesy.*

## String Comparisons in PL/SQL

Oracle added the UTL_MATCH package in Version 10g Release 2 to compare strings. The four functions included in the package use different methods to compare a source string and destination string, and return an assessment of what it would take to turn the source into the destination string.

The functions are broken down into two categories. The categories are actually the algorithms employed to analyze the strings.

### Levenshtein Distance

The Levenshtein Distance (LD) algorithm, commonly called the Edit Distance (ED) algorithm, is the older of the two supported methods. It measures the distance between the source and destination strings. By distance, we're referring to the number of changes required to turn the source string into the destination string.

For example, the following two strings differ by one character:

```
'expresso', 'espresso'
```

Using the LD/ED algorithm, the distance is 1 since one character must change to make the first string match the second. The following function works for all supported releases. Thanks to Barbara Boehmer (of OTN forums fame) for graciously allowing us to use it in this chapter.

```
-- Available online as part of edit_distance.sql
CREATE OR REPLACE FUNCTION edit_distance
    (i_source_string IN VARCHAR2,
     i_target_string IN VARCHAR2)
```

```
      RETURN NUMBER
      DETERMINISTIC
AS
      v_length_of_source NUMBER := NVL (LENGTH (i_source_string), 0);
      v_length_of_target NUMBER := NVL (LENGTH (i_target_string), 0);

      TYPE mytabtype IS TABLE OF NUMBER
         INDEX BY BINARY_INTEGER;

      v_column_to_left mytabtype;
      v_current_column mytabtype;
      v_cost NUMBER := 0;
BEGIN
   IF v_length_of_source = 0 THEN
      RETURN v_length_of_target;
   ELSIF v_length_of_target = 0 THEN
      RETURN v_length_of_source;
   ELSE
      FOR j IN 0 .. v_length_of_target LOOP
         v_column_to_left(j) := j;
      END LOOP;
      FOR i IN 1.. v_length_of_source LOOP
         v_current_column(0) := i;
         FOR j IN 1 .. v_length_of_target LOOP
            IF SUBSTR (i_source_string, i, 1) =
               SUBSTR (i_target_string, j, 1)
               THEN v_cost := 0;
            ELSE v_cost := 1;
            END IF;
            v_current_column(j) := LEAST (v_current_column(j - 1) + 1,
                                 v_column_to_left(j) + 1,
                                 v_column_to_left(j - 1) + v_cost);
         END LOOP;
         FOR j IN 0 .. v_length_of_target LOOP
            v_column_to_left(j) := v_current_column(j);
         END LOOP;
      END LOOP;
   END IF;
   RETURN v_current_column(v_length_of_target);
END edit_distance;
/
```

Test this out by using the expresso/espresso example mentioned earlier.

-- **Available online as part of edit_distance.sql**
```
SELECT EDIT_DISTANCE('espresso', 'expresso') AS DISTANCE
FROM dual;
```

This returns a value of 1 as expected. This function performs essentially the same thing as the built-in UTL_MATCH.EDIT_DISTANCE function now available in Oracle 10g Release 2. To test this out, run the following:

-- Available online as part of edit_distance.sql
```
SELECT UTL_MATCH.EDIT_DISTANCE('espresso', 'expresso') AS DISTANCE
FROM dual;
```

This returns a value of 1 as well.

UTL_MATCH includes a second Edit Distance function that measures the similarity between strings. The return value is an integer between 0 and 100, where 0 indicates no similarity at all and 100 indicates a perfect match. This example tests out the similarity between expresso and espresso:

-- Available online as part of edit_distance.sql
```
SELECT UTL_MATCH.EDIT_DISTANCE_SIMILARITY(
    'expresso', 'espresso') AS DISTANCE
FROM dual;
```

This returns a value of 88 indicating that they are very much alike.

## Jaro-Winkler

The Jaro-Winkler algorithm is the second category of algorithms used in UTL_MATCH. These functions take the same two arguments, but instead of simply calculating the number of steps required to change the source string to the destination string, it determines how closely the two strings agree with each other. The algorithm also tries to take into account the possibility of a data entry error when determining similarity.

The following example uses the first Jaro-Winkler function, simply called JARO_WINKLER:

-- Available online as part of jaro_winkler.sql
```
SELECT UTL_MATCH.JARO_WINKLER(
    'expresso', 'espresso') AS AGREEMENT
FROM dual;
```

This returns the following value:

```
AGREEMENT
----------
 9,25E-001
```

This is the measure of agreement between the strings.

## How Does That Work?

The Jaro-Winkler algorithm tries to take into account some level of human error in the analysis of the data. The following calculation, discussed in a presentation by Dr. Adrian Esterman and John Bass on various name-matching techniques, shows how the Jaro-Winkler algorithm works.

$$JW = \left( \frac{1}{3} \bullet \frac{c}{s1} \right) + \left( \frac{1}{3} \bullet \frac{c}{s2} \right) + \left( \frac{1}{3} \bullet \frac{t}{c} \right)$$

Where:

- $c$ = The number of characters that match
- $s1$ = The length of the first string
- $s2$ = The length of the second string
- $t$ = The number of transpositions required

Just like Edit Distance, there is a similarity function. To run it, do the following:

```
-- Available online as part of jaro_winkler.sql
SELECT UTL_MATCH.JARO_WINKLER_SIMILARITY(
    'expresso', 'espresso') AS AGREEMENT
FROM dual;
```

The result is as follows:

```
AGREEMENT
----------
        92
```

Like `EDIT_DISTANCE_SIMILARITY`, the closer the return value is to 100, the closer the two strings are to each other.

# DBMS_OUTPUT.PUT_LINE

Of course, `DBMS_OUTPUT.PUT_LINE` is not new. It has been available for years to print lines to the screen as follows:

```
-- Available online as part of dbms_output.sql
SET SERVEROUTPUT ON
```

```
BEGIN
   DBMS_OUTPUT.PUT_LINE('PRINT ME');
END;
/
```

If you have used this procedure for anything but a 'Hello World' example though, you know about the 255-byte limitation with the procedure. The following example tries to print more than 255 bytes of text in Oracle 9i:

```
--Available online as part of dbms_output.sql
SET SERVEROUTPUT ON
DECLARE
   v_string VARCHAR2(500 CHAR);
BEGIN
   v_string := 'Five years of programming.  This is the time it '
                 ||'takes for most programmers to feel as if they''ve '
                 ||'come of age as a professional.  Traditional '
                 ||'programming concepts are second nature, like '
                 ||'driving a car or typing on a keyboard.  Employers '
                 ||'recognize this, often ...';
   DBMS_OUTPUT.PUT_LINE(v_string);
END;
/
```

It returns the following:

```
ERROR at line 1:
ORA-20000:  ORU-10028:  line length overflow, limit of 255 chars per line
```

The solution in prior releases was to use the SUBSTR function as follows:

```
--Available online as part of dbms_output.sql
SET SERVEROUTPUT ON
DECLARE
   v_string VARCHAR2(500 CHAR);
BEGIN
   v_string := 'Five years of programming.  This is the time it '
                 ||'takes for most programmers to feel as if they''ve '
                 ||'come of age as a professional.  Traditional '
                 ||'programming concepts are second nature, like '
                 ||'driving a car or typing on a keyboard.  Employers '
                 ||'recognize this, often ...';
   DBMS_OUTPUT.PUT_LINE(SUBSTR(v_string, 1, 255));
   DBMS_OUTPUT.PUT_LINE(SUBSTR(v_string, 256));
END;
/
```

This is not the most user-friendly way of handling this. Oracle 10*g* Release 2 lifts the 255-byte limitation. Run the same example in 10*g* Release 2.

```
--Available online as part of dbms_output.sql
SET SERVEROUTPUT ON
DECLARE
    v_string VARCHAR2(500 CHAR);
BEGIN
    v_string := 'Five years of programming.  This is the time it '
                ||'takes for most programmers to feel as if they''ve '
                ||'come of age as a professional.  Traditional '
                ||'programming concepts are second nature, like '
                ||'driving a car or typing on a keyboard.  Employers '
                ||'recognize this, often ...';
    DBMS_OUTPUT.PUT_LINE(v_string);
END;
/
```

This prints correctly and is a welcome sight for developers.

## Summary

In this chapter, we defined what an expert is, both from the standpoint of the level of knowledge a person has, and from the range of impact on both your organization and other workers that a person might have. Finally, we demonstrated some new features introduced in Oracle 10*g* Release 2 and showed how they can be leveraged immediately.

# CHAPTER
## 2

# PL/SQL Internals

ow does this work?! This is our number one question whenever we use any complex tool. Although each of the other chapters in this book answers this question for the features being covered, none answers the question for PL/SQL as a whole. That's the purpose of this chapter.

In this chapter, we discuss PL/SQL architecture, including

- Database architecture review

- The PL/SQL compiler, including a discussion of Diana

- Interpreted vs. native compilation

# A Database Architecture Primer

There's no way to fully understand PL/SQL architecture without a basic awareness of the database architecture and its role in processing user requests. In this section, we review the database components used with PL/SQL, including the instance, database structures, user and server processes, and how all of these pieces communicate with each other.

Figure 2-1 illustrates how a user request is processed for a *Dedicated Server Architecture*. The components shown are those directly involved with processing queries when configured for a dedicated server, such as that discussed in this section.

**NOTE**
*This is the 10,000-meter view of the database architecture. It's intended as a primer only. Many other memory structures and background processes are involved in processing, but aren't discussed here in detail. See the Oracle Database Concepts guide (available at http://otn.oracle.com) for information on additional database architectural components, and for differences when using shared server architecture.*

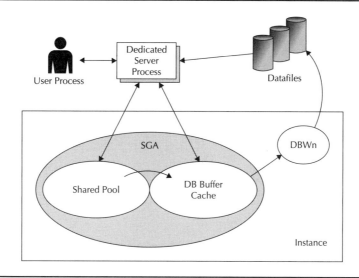

**FIGURE 2-1.**   *The database architecture*

## User and Server Processes

When an application (such as SQL*Plus) initiates a connection to the data server, the *User Process* requests a connection using SQL*Net. The LISTENER on the server picks up the request, and provides a *Dedicated Server Process* to handle it. Once this connection is made, the LISTENER is no longer used. In fact, the LISTENER can be stopped after a connection is made, and the User Process is still able to continue as if nothing happened.

To illustrate this, start a SQL*Plus session (for a local database, make sure to specify your net service name so the LISTENER is used).

```
>sqlplus plsql@rhdb
SQL*Plus: Release 10.1.0.3.0 - Production on Thu Jan 27 17:12:32 2005
Copyright (c) 1982, 2004, Oracle.  All rights reserved.
Enter password:
Connected to:
Oracle Database 10g Enterprise Edition Release 10.1.0.3.0 - Production
With the Partitioning, OLAP and Data Mining options
SQL>
```

Type the following:

```
SELECT SYSDATE
FROM dual;
```

Today's date is displayed. Keep the SQL*Plus window active, and then in another OS session window (the DOS or UNIX prompt), stop the `LISTENER`.

```
>lsnrctl
LSNRCTL> stop
```

Type the same query in your SQL*Plus window again.

```
SELECT SYSDATE
FROM dual;
```

The result is the same despite the `LISTENER` being stopped. The reason you could continue with your SQL*Plus session is that the `LISTENER` already completed its mission. It received the connection request, provided a dedicated server process for the connection, completed user authentication, and the connection was established.

Now quit SQL*Plus and attempt to reconnect. You should receive the following error:

```
ERROR:
ORA-12541: TNS:no listener
```

By disconnecting the SQL*Plus session, the Dedicated Server Process was released. On reconnect, the `LISTENER` is once again employed, but this time it's stopped.

**NOTE**
*Don't forget to restart your `LISTENER`! You can restart it from the command line by simply typing* `lsnrctl start`.

# The Process Global Area

The Process Global Area (PGA) memory is allocated by the operating system process to a single user connection. It can be used only by that session, and once the session is terminated, the space allocated to the PGA is returned to the operating system.

The PGA is used as a memory store for local variables, MCode (discussed later in this chapter), and other private system resources. In a dedicated server environment, the UGA (User Global Area that contains structures as global variables) is also part of the PGA. The UGA is discussed in greater detail in the section titled SGA (System Global Area).

Since Oracle 9*i*, Oracle has supported automatic memory management for the PGA. Set the parameter WORKAREA_SIZE_POLICY to AUTO, and Oracle makes certain the PGA does not exceed the value specified for PGA_AGGREGATE_TARGET. Of course, the WORKAREA_SIZE_POLICY parameter can always be set to MANUAL to allow for manual memory management.

Oracle 10*g* Enterprise Manager includes a PGA management screen, shown in Figure 2-2.

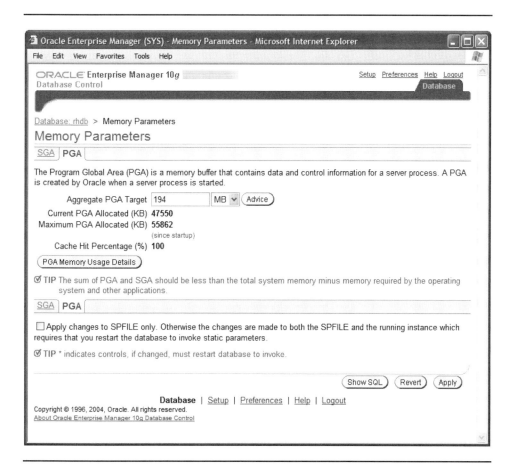

**FIGURE 2-2.** *PGA memory management in Enterprise Manager*

It's possible to modify PGA settings and monitor PGA usage in this screen. When using automatic memory management, very little needs to be done with regard to the PGA memory allocation.

# An Instance

When a SQL statement is sent by a User Process, it gets passed through the Dedicated Server Process to the Oracle instance. An Oracle *instance* is made up of memory structures and background processes.

## The System Global Area

The memory structures are included in a structure known as the System Global Area (SGA). One key memory region in the SGA that's involved with PL/SQL processing is the shared pool. When a SQL statement is passed to the instance, it's parsed, the syntax is checked, object availability and permissions are checked, and the execution plan is generated in a substructure of the shared pool.

Oracle 10*g* Enterprise Manager includes an SGA management screen, shown in Figure 2-3.

Automatic Shared Memory Management can be enabled here if you haven't already done so.

A second structure that's present when using MTS (shared server) is the UGA. The UGA contains session-specific information, but in a shared server environment it's in the SGA rather than the PGA. You must know how your environment is configured to determine whether your UGA is in the PGA or SGA.

**The Shared Pool**    The shared pool, as part of the SGA, is available to all users of the instance. This means that data and code in the shared pool are available for other users (with proper permissions) to access. Because of this, the memory used by one session's activity is not automatically cleared when the user disconnects. Anything cached in the shared pool must be aged out, or explicitly flushed, in order to clear it. It's also possible to pin code in memory so it won't be aged out.

The shared pool contains two main structures: the data dictionary cache and the library cache. What does the data dictionary cache store? Rows from the data dictionary of course. When the data dictionary is used, the rows are cached in the data dictionary cache inside the shared pool rather than being read into the database buffer cache. Since the data dictionary is Read-Only, there's no need to write from the data dictionary cache back to disk.

The library cache has more to do with PL/SQL processing than the data dictionary cache. It's the location where SQL statement text is parsed and validated prior

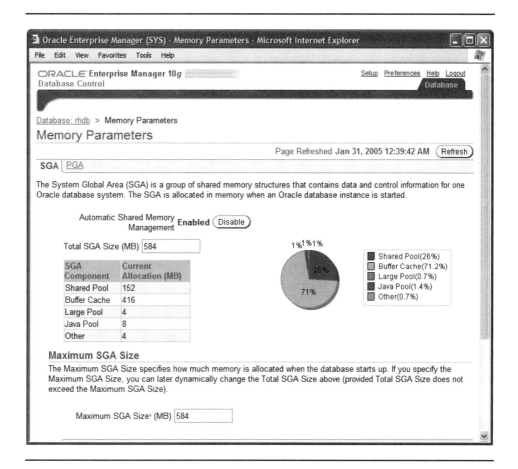

**FIGURE 2-3.** *SGA management in Enterprise Manager*

to execution. It contains a number of different namespaces, or libraries. Use the following SQL statement to determine the namespaces in the library cache:

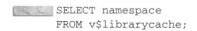

```
SELECT namespace
FROM v$librarycache;
```

The result of this SELECT in Oracle 10*g* is as follows:

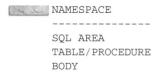

```
NAMESPACE
---------------
SQL AREA
TABLE/PROCEDURE
BODY
```

```
TRIGGER
INDEX
CLUSTER
OBJECT
PIPE
JAVA SOURCE
JAVA RESOURCE
JAVA DATA
```

The SQL AREA namespace is where the shared SQL is parsed and validated. When SQL is loaded to the library cache, it's aged out using an LRU (Least Recently Used) algorithm once no longer in use by the calling process.

**The User Global Area**    The User Global Area (UGA) is located in the PGA when using a dedicated server, and in the SGA when running MTS (shared server). To see the current size of the UGA, the following script can be used.

```
-- Available online as part of uga.sql
SELECT    SUBSTR (a.NAME, 9, 10) "Name",
            ROUND (SUM (b.VALUE) / 1024 / 1024,
                    1)
        || ' M' "Total UGA for all sessions"
    FROM v$statname a, v$sesstat b
   WHERE a.statistic# = b.statistic# AND a.NAME = 'session uga memory'
GROUP BY a.NAME;
```

This results in the following:

```
Name
-------------------------
Total UGA for all sessions
-------------------------
uga memory
10.7 M
```

Notice that this provides a total for all active sessions. When the database is configured as a dedicated server, each process gets its own PGA, and therefore its own UGA. The only way to determine the amount of memory allocated to the UGA is to determine the total for all processes.

## Background Processes

There are required and optional background processes. These processes are part of the instance, but aren't included in the SGA. One of the required processes is included in Figure 2-1, and is called *DB Writer (DBWn)*. Its job is to write dirty buffers to disk from the database buffer cache. Another important process for anyone connected to the data server is Process Monitor (PMON). PMON cleans up after us. For example, if we lose our connection to the data server, PMON ensures that our dedicated process does not hang out there forever waiting for us to return.

**NOTE**
*A common misconception is that DBWn is used to read and write data to the datafiles. Actually, it only writes the data. The server process is used to read the data from the datafiles to memory.*

## The Database

All too often the term "database" is used interchangeably with "instance." They are, in fact, unique. Where *instance* refers to the memory and background processes, *database* refers to the following physical files:

■ Data files

■ Control files

■ Redo Log files

If you come from a SQL Server or Sybase background, this may be a bit of a revelation since terminology differs from Oracle most drastically for those databases. It does make sense though! If you back up your database, are you backing up your memory? How about processes like DB Writer? Of course not! If all else fails, it's possible to get your database going as long as you have these three files. Archive logs would of course be handy, and would be required for point-in-time recovery. Your parameter files and Oracle binaries would be handy as well. They can be re-created/reinstalled with relative ease, however. Only the three files we mentioned are absolutely necessary.

# A PL/SQL Architecture Overview

When a PL/SQL program unit is passed to Oracle, it gets processed through a compiler. The compiler creates a syntax tree, passes it through an optimizer, and generates machine code that's stored in the database for execution at a later time. Oracle 9*i* introduced native compilation. Using native compilation, the code is converted to shared C libraries on the database host. Computation-intensive PL/SQL programs will notice an improvement in performance since little interpretation is required by Oracle in order to process the instructions.

Execution is performed in the PL/SQL engine with the assistance of the PL/SQL virtual machine and the SQL engine. When a program unit is called, code that is compiled as *interpreted* has its machine code (MCode) heap loaded into the SGA. The instructions are processed by the PL/SQL virtual machine which communicates with the RDBMS kernel. The PL/SQL engine carries out the instructions with the assistance of the SQL engine to help with the SQL statements.

If a program unit is compiled using native compilation, instead of the machine code heap being loaded to the SGA, the shared libraries are loaded to the PGA. The PL/SQL virtual machine is still required, though it does not need to do any interpretation of the code. The PL/SQL and SQL engines perform the same functions as with interpreted.

## Early vs. Late Binding

Late binding means that code is compiled at execution. Languages that use late binding are generally very flexible since modifications can be made up to and during compilation and execution.

Early binding means that code is compiled prior to execution. Namespaces are verified, permissions are checked, and all syntax is validated. This saves considerable time during execution since much of the work has already been completed. Oracle PL/SQL employs early binding.

# The PL/SQL Compiler

The PL/SQL compiler is an Oracle component that underwent significant changes in the 10*g* release. In particular, the code generator was replaced with a new-and-improved generator that is two to three times faster than its predecessor, according to Oracle benchmarks.

PL/SQL program units are compiled when they're created. The part that can be easily seen is the syntax and dependency check that's performed. If a dependent object doesn't exist, or is invalid, a compilation error message is returned.

There are a number of other steps performed during compilation, some of which you may not be aware of. This section shows the steps performed during compilation, including an overview of Diana (Descriptive Intermediate Attribute Notation for Ada) and the new code generator.

## Compilation Steps

The PL/SQL compiler processes source code through the three steps shown in Figure 2-4.

The syntax and semantic steps are considered the front-end of the compiler, while the code generator is the back-end.

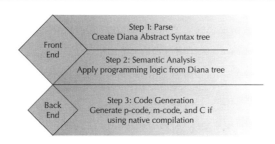

**FIGURE 2-4.**   *The PL/SQL compiler*

## The Compiler Front-End

The front end of the PL/SQL compiler includes the *parse* and *semantic steps*. Parse generates a code tree that is passed to the semantic analyzer which is responsible for determining dependencies based on the code tree, handling overloading, detecting object type inheritance, and so on.

**Step 1: Parse**     The primary function of the parse step is to generate Diana. Diana is an Abstract Syntax Tree (AST) that describes the program. Whenever a program is compiled, a Diana instance is created and saved to the database (there are some exceptions to this, which are discussed later in this section). It's used by the compiler for tasks like compiling dependent objects at runtime, and analyzing type and package specifications.

As you might have guessed from the name, Diana is drawn from the Ada programming language. Like Ada, Oracle PL/SQL uses a metanotation called IDL (Interface Descriptive Language) to define Diana. Oracle's variation of IDL is called FIDL (Function IDL).

Diana is a tree-structured abstract type that provides metadata about the code. Although the PL/SQL compiler is written in C, Diana has a few built-in PL/SQL packages that provide information to libraries and other structures that need to see it. One package name related to Diana is called ... DIANA. Another utility package is called DIUTIL. The DIUTIL package creation script called diutil.sql is located in the $ORACLE_HOME/rdbms/admin/ directory.

There are some limitations on PL/SQL object sizes related to Diana. The sizes limitations are not based on the number of lines of code, but rather the number of Diana nodes generated for the code. The limitations are shown in Table 2-1.

The approximation is based on an average of between five to ten nodes per line of PL/SQL. This can vary widely based on your code.

| Up to 7.3 | 2**14(16K) Diana nodes<br>Approximately 3,000 lines of code |
|---|---|
| 8.0 to 8*i* R2 | 2**15(32K) Diana nodes<br>Approximately 6,000 lines of code |
| 8*i* R3 and up | 2**26(64M) Diana nodes<br>Approximately 6,000,000 lines of code |

**TABLE 2-1.** *Diana Node Limitations*

How can the size of your code be checked? One way is to inspect the USER_OBJECT_SIZE view. This view returns the size based on the following tables:

```
IDL_CHAR$
IDL_SB4$
IDL_UB1$
IDL_UB2$
```

These tables hold the compiled code in the database. When the code is executed and loaded to memory, the size of the code loaded to the SGA can differ significantly. More on code generation is available later in this chapter in the section titled "Compiler Back-End."

To test the size stored in this view, look at the following example package:

```
-- Available online as part of diana_size.sql
CREATE OR REPLACE PACKAGE diana_size
AS
    PROCEDURE get_parsed_size(
        i_object_name IN VARCHAR2,
        cv_result IN OUT SYS_REFCURSOR);
END diana_size;
/

CREATE OR REPLACE PACKAGE BODY diana_size
AS
    PROCEDURE get_parsed_size(
        i_object_name IN VARCHAR2,

        cv_result IN OUT SYS_REFCURSOR)
    IS
```

```
    BEGIN
       OPEN cv_result FOR
       SELECT name, type, parsed_size
       FROM user_object_size
       WHERE name = i_object_name;

    END get_parsed_size;
END;
/
```

Pass the name of the object to the package and it uses a cursor variable to return the result set. Execute it as follows:

```
SQL> VARIABLE x REFCURSOR
SQL> EXEC diana_size.get_parsed_size('DIANA_SIZE', :x)

PL/SQL procedure successfully completed.

SQL> print x
```

The printout shows the following result:

```
NAME                           TYPE          PARSED_SIZE
------------------------------ ------------- -----------
DIANA_SIZE                     PACKAGE               320
DIANA_SIZE                     PACKAGE BODY            0
```

The package specification has a value for PARSED_SIZE, but the package body does not. The reason? Since release 7.2 of the data server, Diana that's generated for package and object type bodies is discarded after a successful compilation. As a result, the size for them is 0.

Oracle provides a little known/used script that can be used to examine the Diana. It's available in $ORACLE_HOME/rdbms/admin/dumpdian.sql. Use of this script depends on your release, so check the script header before running.

In addition to the creation of the Diana instance, the Parse step communicates with the RDBMS SQL parser to detect and include bind variables in the AST. The SQL parser is common to both PL/SQL and SQL*Plus, ensuring SQL syntax that's valid in SQL*Plus is also valid in PL/SQL.

One more important task that's performed during Parse has to do with the use of the WRAP utility. WRAP hides source code (it does not actually encrypt). It's completely unreadable by people, but Oracle of course has no problem with it. To WRAP the code, the Diana is written as a byte array to a flat file.

**Step 2: Semantic Analysis**    The Semantic Analysis step takes the AST generated during the Parse step as input. A few of the major tasks performed in this step are as follows:

- Perform name resolution (including function overloading)

- Build the type inheritance hierarchy

- Determine code dependencies

- Work with the RDBMS SQL parser to examine the SQL statement semantics

Since this step does not actually create code, its most critical function is to prepare the Diana instance for processing by the code generator. At the completion of this step, annotated AST is passed to the code generator.

## The Compiler Back-End
The front-end did a great deal of the mapping and analysis of the code tree. The PL/SQL compiler's back-end processes seek to generate and optimize the machine code that represents the PL/SQL object.

Figure 2-5 shows the flow through the compiler. The code generator step has three distinct subprocesses that work from the analyzed Diana instance for an object, and which result in optimized machine code.

Each section of the code generator is detailed in the next section.

**Step 3: Code Generation**    Oracle 10*g* introduced a new code generator that improves performance of certain PL/SQL programs by a factor of 2 over Oracle 9*i*, and a factor of 3 over Oracle 8 according to a number of performance tests made public by Oracle. The new code generator uses Diana and outputs MCode, but the transformation process is quite different from earlier releases.

In the first phase for the new code generator, the IL Generator (ILGEN) translates the Diana instance of a PL/SQL program to an intermediate language (IL) form. As discussed earlier, the Parse step creates a syntax tree called Diana when PL/SQL source code is compiled. The Diana instance is saved to the database before being transformed into IL.

The second phase introduces the local and global optimizers. The local optimizer takes a pass at the IL, removing many of the inefficiencies. Local optimization is a fast process that all PL/SQL objects must go through, but it's essential to improving the efficiency of the completed machine code. The global optimizer isn't nearly as fast. It occurs after local optimization, and processes it through routines that analyze the control flow and exception handling, and eliminates dead or redundant code. The goal of both of these optimizers is to improve the runtime performance of the final machine code.

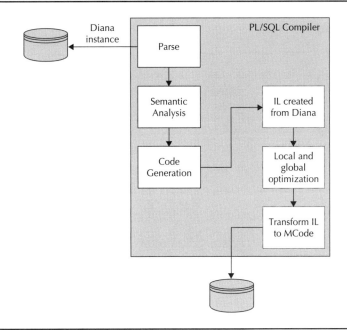

**FIGURE 2-5.**   *The compiler flow*

**TIP**
*Using the global optimizer, it's possible to improve
PL/SQL performance by a factor of 3 percent over
the Oracle 8 release.*

The third and final phase transforms the IL to MCode (compiled machine code).
The MCode is saved to the database, and is the code that gets run when a PL/SQL
program unit is executed. MCode is the language understood by the PL/SQL virtual
machine, which is discussed in detail in a few sections of this chapter.

## Interpreted vs. Native Compilation

As was just discussed in the last section, PL/SQL is transformed to MCode when
compiled. Execution of a PL/SQL object actually executes the MCode which must
be interpreted during runtime by the PL/SQL virtual machine. Oracle 9*i* introduced
the ability to compile PL/SQL into native C code. Native compilation (NCOMP)
creates shared libraries that are linked to Oracle, and at execution, performance is
much faster for computation-intensive code.

To see the current state of affairs in your environment, run the following **SELECT** command:

```
SELECT value
FROM v$parameter
WHERE name = 'plsql_code_type';
```

In our environment (which is set to the default settings), this returns the following result:

```
VALUE
------------
INTERPRETED
```

**NOTE**
*The* PLSQL_COMPILER_FLAGS *parameter is deprecated in Oracle 10g. If you're using Oracle 9i, check the value for* PLSQL_COMPILER_FLAGS.

Both interpreted and native compilation requires the same PL/SQL compiler steps outlined earlier. Each passes through the same three main phases, and in the end, MCode is stored in the database. The difference is that NCOMP also uses a certified C compiler to create shared C libraries.

### Execution: Interpreted

If interpreted compilation is used, the MCode heap is loaded to the SGA and interpreted by the PL/SQL virtual machine (PVM) at runtime. It's pinned in the SGA (shared pool) for the duration of the call. Once the call completes, and the MCode is no longer pinned, it's aged out of the shared pool.

### Execution: NCOMP

NCOMP libraries are loaded to the PGA at runtime. This removes the need to use SGA resources for the MCode, and prevents memory conflicts that can occur with interpreted compilation. These conflicts are not a major occurrence, but it is another reason to consider NCOMP. Using NCOMP, PL/SQL program constructs like LOOP, IF-THEN, and so on don't need to use the Byte Code Interpreter of the JVM, also improving performance.

**Why Would I Use This?**
You would use native compilation if your PL/SQL makes heavy use of PL/SQL programming constructs like loops. Typical candidates are those that perform complex calculations. Programs that are mostly SQL won't see the benefit. Keep in mind that native compilation takes longer than the default interpreted compilation since the shared libraries must be generated.

Beginning in Oracle 10g, the shared libraries are actually stored in the data dictionary, not just on the database server file system. Another major improvement is that native compilation now supports RACs (Real Application Clusters). Code can also be set to either native or interpreted by PL/SQL program unit (procedure, function, and so on). Historically, the *package* or *object type* spec and body had to be compiled in the same way. Oracle 10g supports separate compilation settings for the spec and body now, so it's possible to compile the spec as interpreted, and the body as native.

**TIP**
*Though there is great flexibility in compiling objects differently, be consistent. If you plan on using native compilation, we recommend you use it for all of your PL/SQL. It's much easier to maintain if you aren't switching back and forth, and you won't experience the negative performance side effects of interpreted and native code calling each other.*

# PL/SQL Virtual Machine

The PL/SQL virtual machine (PVM) is a memory-to-memory structure specifically designed for PL/SQL. When a program unit (PL/SQL stored object or anonymous block) whose code type is interpreted is executed, the PVM receives the MCode instructions, and interprets them for use in the local environment. It communicates the interpreted instructions to the RDBMS kernel. When using NCOMP, the PVM has to do less, but is still involved in the execution.

The PVM processes the set of instructions, and then interacts with the data server to complete the execution of the code. The PVM uses 12 registers for addressing program constructs. Table 2-2 lists the 12 registers currently in use:

**NOTE**
*There are actually 16 registers available. Only 12 are used currently.*

The addresses are made up of a register plus an offset. If you've ever been fortunate enough to see a PL/SQL Runtime Dump, these may look familiar to you. The dump writes the addresses to the file as register+offset. For example, FP+12 is the Frame Pointer with an offset of 12.

MCode contains byte-code instructions for the PVM. The byte-code is broken into 4K pages, with the last page being less than or equal to 4K. Byte-code is read by the byte-code interpreter of the PVM upon execution of the code. Since it gets the byte-code instructions from MCode, NCOMP code skips this step (since the MCode heap isn't loaded to the SGA).

| Register | Description |
| --- | --- |
| AP | Argument pointer |
| DL0 | Pointer to programs that are dependencies |
| DL1 | Pointer to instantiations of programs that are dependencies |
| DPF | Display frame |
| DS | Data segment |
| FP | Frame pointer |
| GF | Global frame |
| HS | Handle segment |
| PB_PC | Probe_PC |
| PC | Program counter |
| ST | State |
| TP | Temp stack pointer |
| TPM | Temp stack mark |

**TABLE 2-2.** *Registers*

The Oracle 10*g* PVM was modified to take advantage of the improvements made to the code generator. In particular, the local and global optimizers add additional instructions to the MCode to assist the PVM with execution.

# Summary

There's a lot more that goes into the compilation and execution of PL/SQL than meets the eye. Oracle has been very busy improving everything from parse through execution to make compilation steps more complete, and execution faster. To see how all of this fits into the discussion of high-performance PL/SQL, turn to Chapter 8.

# CHAPTER
## 3

Debugging PL/SQL
Applications

anaging PL/SQL code errors in the database requires planning and organization. You need a simple and consistent approach to the challenge of trapping, tracing, and identifying runtime errors. However, there is a distinct difference between managing errors in runtime code versus database trigger code.

**TIP**
*Oracle has also added a new DBMS_UTILITY .FORMAT_CALL_STACK function to Oracle 10g, which will be covered in this chapter. It allows custom formatting of call stacks.*

This chapter stands independent of the other chapters in the book. All of the content in it works in currently supported versions of the Oracle database except the

## Why Would I Use This?

We use debugging techniques to develop a consistent and flexible approach to debugging our PL/SQL programs. While we deliver consistent and carefully composed code, three people surprise us too often. They are the Applications DBAs, other programmers, and end-users.

Applications DBAs have on occasion done data maintenance that removes critical relationships, which cause our code to fail. We have found that careful attention to detail error handling ensures we can quickly identify where the data was hacked.

Other programmers sometimes fail to understand what stored packages are designed to accomplish and use the packages in unanticipated ways. One example is using an Application Programming Interface (API) for end-user individual updates as a component in their batch updating programs. If we embed debugging code that can be switched on with an optional formal parameter, our code can be quickly enabled to see how it may be misused or abused by other programs.

End-users find ways to do things that business rules seldom adequately anticipate. We plan for their misuse at all critical junctures by using debugging techniques.

Oracle 10*g* `DBMS_UTILITY.FORMAT_CALL_STACK`. In this chapter we will do the following:

- Introduce error-handling mechanisms
    - Differences between compile and runtime errors
    - Standard syntax for exception management
- Discuss the error stack and demonstrate stack management
    - Introduce and demonstrate error stack management
    - Introduce and demonstrate 10*g* new error stack formatting
- Discuss error management in database triggers

This chapter was developed to be read sequentially. You should consider browsing it, in order, before targeting a specific section.

# Introducing Error-Handling Mechanisms

Oracle exhibits two types of errors: compile time and runtime errors. You'll learn about the challenge of trapping, tracing, and identifying runtime errors in the next section.

## Differences Between Compile and Runtime Errors

Compile time exceptions or errors happen when you attempt to run your anonymous PL/SQL program or store a PL/SQL program as a stored function, procedure, or package. Compile time exceptions also occur when running SQL statements. Both of these types of errors are trapped and raised by one of two parsers. The SQL errors are caught by the SQL parser and the PL/SQL errors are caught by the PL/SQL parser.

The following `basic_error1.sql` script raises a PL/SQL parser error. You should make sure you cleaned your environment by running the `create_user` `.sql` statement.

-- **Available online as part of basic_error1.sql file.**

```
DECLARE

  -- Define local variable.
  my_string       VARCHAR2(1) := ' ';
  my_number       NUMBER;
```

```
BEGIN

  -- Attempt to assign a single white space to a number.
  my_number := TO_NUMBER(my_string);

END;
/
```

The following error appears when running the program:

-- **This is output from basic_error1.sql script.**

```
END;
*
ERROR at line 14:
ORA-06550: line 14, column 1:
PLS-00103: Encountered the symbol "END" when expecting one of the following:
. ( * % & = - + ; < / > at in is mod not rem
<an exponent (**)> <> or != or ~= >= <= <> and or like
between ||
The symbol ";" was substituted for "END" to continue.
```

The error means a punctuation element is missing from the program. In this case, line 10 does not have a statement-terminating semicolon, but the PL/SQL parser points to the next row in the program. The parser frequently points to the row beneath the actual syntax error. You can see the line numbers referenced by the error stack by typing the **LIST** command (only the first letter is really necessary to run it). If you listed the program, it would display the following:

```
 1  DECLARE
 2
 3    -- Define a single character variable length string.
 4    my_string           VARCHAR2(1) := ' ';
 5    my_number           NUMBER;
 6
 7  BEGIN
 8
 9    -- Attempt to assign a single white space to a number.
10    my_number := TO_NUMBER(my_string);
11
12* END;
```

If you added a SQL statement that references a nonexistent table before the line with the missing semicolon, you would still see the same error message about the missing semicolon. This is because the PL/SQL parser runs through the entire program before calling the SQL parser to check embedded SQL statements.

**TIP**
*PL/SQL syntax is always checked before SQL syntax.
Only when the PL/SQL syntax is semantically
correct will SQL syntax errors be shown when
attempting to run an anonymous or named block
PL/SQL program.*

Compile time errors are simply things you'll need to work through as you
write your PL/SQL code. There is, unfortunately, no way to build in compile time
debugging, so you're stuck with the PL/SQL parser. Runtime errors happen during
the execution phase of the PL/SQL program. The following is an example of a
runtime program causing an error condition:

```
-- Available online as part of basic_error2.sql file.
DECLARE

  -- Define local variable.
  my_string          VARCHAR2(1) := ' ';
  my_number          NUMBER;

BEGIN

  -- Attempt to assign a single white space to a number.
  my_number := TO_NUMBER(my_string);

END;
/
```

The program compiles fine but encounters a runtime execution when attempting
to use the TO_NUMBER function against a white space. The error raises the following
exception:

```
-- Available online as output from basic_error2.sql script.
DECLARE
*
ERROR at line 1:
ORA-06502: PL/SQL: numeric or value error: character to number
conversion
error
ORA-06512: at line 14
```

As a rule, the PL/SQL parser generally does a good job of finding the correct line
number for runtime exceptions. Runtime errors raise runtime exceptions. These
errors are the ones you want to trap, trace, and identify. In the next section, you'll
review the basic syntax for PL/SQL exception management.

# The Standard Syntax for Exception Management

As a beginning or experienced PL/SQL developer, you learned the PL/SQL block structure. This section is most likely a review for most PL/SQL programmers. The EXCEPTION block is the key for managing exceptions, while the DECLARE block is where you put user-defined exceptions. The BEGIN block is where your program encounters an error, raises an exception, and passes control to its local EXCEPTION block or an external PL/SQL EXCEPTION block.

Oracle provides a series of predefined exceptions in the STANDARD package. These are useful tools in your debugging of Oracle PL/SQL programs. All errors raised return a negative number. For example, the INVALID_CURSOR is raised by a value of –1001. The predefined exceptions are noted in Table 3-1.

| Exception | Error | Exception Raised When |
|-----------|-------|------------------------|
| ACCESS_INTO_NULL | ORA-06530 | You encounter this when attempting to access an uninitialized object. |
| CASE_NOT_FOUND | ORA-06592 | You encounter this when you have defined a CASE statement without an ELSE clause and none of the CASE statements meet the runtime condition. |
| COLLECTION_IS_NULL | ORA-06531 | You encounter this when attempting to access an uninitialized NESTED TABLE or VARRAY. |
| CURSOR_ALREADY_OPEN | ORA-06511 | You encounter this when attempting to open a cursor that is already open. |
| DUP_VAL_ON_INDEX | ORA-00001 | You encounter this when attempting to insert a duplicate value to a table's column when there is a unique index on it. |
| INVALID_CURSOR | ORA-01001 | You encounter this when attempting a disallowed operation on a cursor, like closing a closed cursor. |
| INVALID_NUMBER | ORA-01722 | You encounter this when attempting to assign something other than a number to a number or when the LIMIT clause of a bulk fetch returns a nonpositive number. |
| LOGIN_DENIED | ORA-01017 | You encounter this when attempting to log in with a program to an invalid username or password. |

**TABLE 3-1.** *Predefined Exceptions in the Standard Package*

| Exception | Error | Exception Raised When |
|---|---|---|
| NO_DATA_FOUND | ORA-01403 | You encounter this when attempting to use the SELECT-INTO structure and the statement returns a null value, when you attempt to access a deleted element in a nested table, or when you attempt to access an uninitialized element in an index-by table (now called an associative array in 10*g*). |
| NOT_LOGGED_ON | ORA-01012 | You encounter this when a program issues a database call and is not connected, which is typically after the instance has disconnected your session. |
| PROGRAM_ERROR | ORA-06501 | You encounter this all too often when an error occurs that Oracle has not yet formally trapped. This happens with a number of the Object features of the database. |
| ROWTYPE_MISMATCH | ORA-06504 | You encounter this when your cursor structure fails to agree with your PL/SQL cursor variable, or an actual cursor parameter differs from a formal cursor parameter. |
| SELF_IS_NULL | ORA-30625 | You encounter this error when you try to call an object type nonstatic member method in which an instance of the object type has not been initialized. |
| STORAGE_ERROR | ORA-06500 | You encounter this error when the SGA has run out of memory or been corrupted. |
| SUBSCRIPT_BEYOND_COUNT | ORA-06533 | You encounter this error when the space allocated to a NESTED TABLE or VARRAY is smaller than the subscript value used. |
| SUBSCRIPT_OUTSIDE_LIMIT | ORA-06532 | You encounter this error when you use an illegal index value to access a NESTED TABLE or VARRAY, which means a nonpositive integer. |
| SYS_INVALID_ROWID | ORA-01410 | You encounter this error when you try to convert a string into an invalid ROWID value. |
| TIMEOUT_ON_RESOURCE | ORA-00051 | You encounter this error when the database is unable to secure a lock to a resource. |

**TABLE 3-1.** *Predefined Exceptions in the Standard Package* (cont.)

| Exception | Error | Exception Raised When |
|---|---|---|
| TOO_MANY_ROWS | ORA-01422 | You encounter this when using the SELECT-INTO and the query returns more than one row. |
| VALUE_ERROR | ORA-06502 | You encounter this when you try to assign a variable into another variable that is too small to hold it. |
| ZERO_DIVIDE | ORA-01476 | You encounter this when you try to divide a number by zero. |

**TABLE 3-1.**  *Predefined Exceptions in the Standard Package* (cont.)

In conjunction with the predefined Oracle exceptions, Oracle provides two built-in functions. These are useful in managing errors in the EXCEPTION block of PL/SQL. They're displayed in Table 3-2.

You will use slightly modified examples of the prior program to demonstrate the basics of the EXCEPTION block. Both predefined Oracle and user-defined exceptions are used.

The following demonstrates the SELECT-INTO syntax and Oracle-predefined NO_DATA_FOUND exception with a white space literal value from a dummy table. The dummy table contains no rows to return with the query. This example is found in the basic_error3.sql script:

```
-- Available online as part of basic_error3.sql script.
-- Create a dummy table.
CREATE TABLE dummy
( dummy_value      VARCHAR2(1));

DECLARE

  -- Define local variable.
  my_string        VARCHAR2(1) := ' ';
  my_number        NUMBER;

BEGIN

  -- Select a white space into a local variable.
  SELECT ' ' INTO my_string FROM dummy;
```

```
  -- Attempt to assign a single white space to a number.
  my_number := TO_NUMBER(my_string);

EXCEPTION

  WHEN no_data_found THEN
    dbms_output.put_line('SELECT-INTO'||CHR(10)||SQLERRM);

END;
/
```

| Function | Oracle Predefined Errors | User-defined Errors |
|---|---|---|
| SQLCODE | Returns a negative number that maps to the Oracle predefined exceptions with one exception: the NO_DATA_ FOUND exception returns a positive one hundred. | Returns a positive one if there is no EXCEPTION_ INIT PRAGMA defined. If an EXCEPTION_INIT PRAGMA is defined, it returns a valid number in the range of negative 20001 to negative 20999. |
| SQLERRM | Is overloaded and performs as qualified: Returns the defined error code and message for a raised exception if no number is passed to it. Returns the actual number parameter as a negative integer and a non-Oracle exception message if a positive number is passed to it or a negative number that is not an Oracle predefined exception. Returns the actual number parameter as a negative integer and the Oracle defined message if a negative number for an Oracle predefined exception is passed. | Returns a one and a "User-Defined Exception" message if triggered by the **RAISE** command. Returns a valid integer in the range of negative 20001 to negative 20999 and a text message set by the RAISE_APPLICATION_ INFO function. |

**TABLE 3-2.** *Oracle's Two Built-In Functions*

The program returns the following output, which illustrates formatting standard Oracle predefined exceptions. The CHR(10) inserts a line return and provides a clean break between the program's and Oracle's predefined message:

```
-- Available online as part of basic_error3.sql script.
SELECT-INTO
ORA-01403: no data found
```

User-defined errors have two implementation directions. One is with a precompiler EXCEPTION_INIT instruction and the other is without it. The basic_error4.sql program demonstrates a user-defined exception without a precompiler directive:

```
-- Available online as part of basic_error4.sql script.
DECLARE

  -- Define local exception variable.
  my_error         EXCEPTION;
  my_number        NUMBER;

BEGIN

  -- Raise the exception.
  RAISE my_error;

EXCEPTION

  WHEN others THEN
    dbms_output.put_line('RAISE my_error'||CHR(10)
                    ||'SQLCODE ['||SQLCODE||']'||CHR(10)
                    ||'SQLERRM ['||SQLERRM||']');

END;
/
```

The program returns the following output, which illustrates formatting user-defined exceptions. The CHR(10) inserts a line return and provides a clean break between the program's SQLCODE and SQLERRM messages:

```
-- Available online as output from basic_error4.sql script.
RAISE my_error
SQLCODE [1]
SQLERRM [User-Defined Exception]
```

The following `basic_error5.sql` demonstrates a user-defined exception with a precompiler `EXCEPTION_INIT` instruction and `RAISE_APPLICATION_ERROR` function:

```
-- Available online as part of basic_error5.sql script.
DECLARE

  -- Define local exception variable.
  my_error            EXCEPTION;
  PRAGMA EXCEPTION_INIT(my_error,-20001);

BEGIN

  -- Raise the exception.
  RAISE my_error;

EXCEPTION

  WHEN my_error THEN
    dbms_output.put_line('RAISE my_error'||CHR(10)
                        ||'SQLCODE ['||SQLCODE||']'||CHR(10)
                        ||'SQLERRM ['||SQLERRM
                        ||'User defined error.]');

END;
/
```

The program returns the following output:

```
-- Available online as output from basic_error5.sql script.
RAISE my_error
SQLCODE [-20001]
SQLERRM [ORA-20001: User defined error.]
```

The benefit of the last example is a meaningful user error message that's assigned to the `EXCEPTION` block, allowing you to build a more robust approach to error trapping. As you'll see in subsequent sections, using RAISE to handle an exception allows the program to continue or abort based on your business logic. The alternative function, `RAISE_APPLICATION_INFO`, immediately causes the program to throw an exception and abort execution. Both have specific uses. `RAISE_APPLICATION_INFO` is useful to stop execution immediately and force a transaction rollback.

You have completed the basic introduction to exception management, which was most likely a review. The balance of the chapter will be devoted to examining approaches to exception management.

# Discussing the Error Stack and Demonstrating Stack Management

The error stack is the sequencing of errors from the triggering event to the calling block of code. PL/SQL throws an exception in the BEGIN block when a failure occurs and runs the code in its local EXCEPTION block. If the failure is in a nested or referenced PL/SQL block, it first runs a local EXCEPTION block before running the calling program unit's EXCEPTION block. It then continues running available EXCEPTION code blocks or returning errors to the error stack until it returns control to the outermost PL/SQL block.

When PL/SQL does not contain EXCEPTION blocks, you get a propagation of line number and error codes. In Oracle 10g, you can use an EXCEPTION block and the DBMS_UTILITIES package to get line number and error codes. The following illustration demonstrates the propagation of errors in PL/SQL programs:

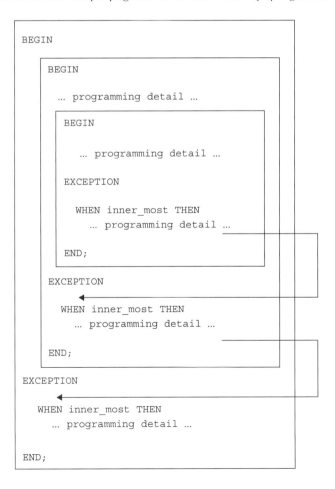

The error stack has been useful from Oracle 7 forward. There are two approaches to managing errors in PL/SQL and they depend on the application transaction control requirements. If you encounter an error that's fatal to the business logic of your application, you need to raise an exception. The exception should stop the business process and rollback the transaction to a state where the data is safe and consistent.

When the error is not fatal to your application business logic, you may choose to log the error in a table and allow the transaction to complete. If you opt for this scenario, you should also have a mechanism for recovering the original transaction state. This type of error management will be covered later in the chapter when you examine error management in database triggers.

The next two sections highlight management of the error stack in named PL/SQL blocks. First, we'll discuss how to manage error stacks within anonymous and named block PL/SQL units. Then, we'll show you the new formatting feature of Oracle 10*g*.

# Introducing and Demonstrating Error Stack Management

This section shows how to format error stack management around your code in Oracle 9*i*, which provides a number of tools for managing error stacks. The following demonstrates how to do this by:

- Building a standard error event management procedure

- Building a set of named PL/SQL stored procedures and functions

- Demonstrating a generated error stack

### Why Would I Use This?

We find that understanding the error stack is a shortcut to debugging our PL/SQL programs. Error stacks are often tricky because you have to figure out if you read them from top to bottom or bottom up. We find it handy to remember the top program triggered the error and the bottom program is where the error occurred. The triggering program is the last one executed or the one at the top. The error we need to fix is always at the bottom unless it is some dependent data corrupted by another program or user.

The error management procedure is found in the `error_management1.sql` script. The script creates a simple procedure that will be called from the `EXCEPTION` block in each of the named PL/SQL stored functions and procedures later in this section:

-- Available online as part of error_management1.sql script.

```
CREATE OR REPLACE PROCEDURE handle_errors
( object_name          IN       VARCHAR2
, module_name          IN       VARCHAR2 := NULL
, table_name           IN       VARCHAR2 := NULL
, sql_error_code       IN       NUMBER   := NULL
, sql_error_message    IN       VARCHAR2 := NULL
, user_error_message   IN       VARCHAR2 := NULL ) IS

  -- Define local exception variable.
  raised_error         EXCEPTION;

  -- Define a nested table to manage exceptions.
  TYPE error_stack IS TABLE OF VARCHAR2(80);

  -- Define a local nested table variable.
  errors               ERROR_STACK := error_stack();

  FUNCTION object_type
  ( object_name_in     IN       VARCHAR2 )
  RETURN VARCHAR2 IS

    -- Define default type.
    return_type        VARCHAR2(12) := 'Unidentified';

  BEGIN

    FOR i IN ( SELECT    object_type
                FROM     user_objects
                WHERE    object_name = object_name_in ) LOOP

      return_type := i.object_type;

    END LOOP;

    -- Return discovered or unknown type.
    RETURN return_type;

  END object_type;
```

```
BEGIN

  -- Extend and append to error stack.
  errors.EXTEND;
  errors(errors.COUNT) := object_type(object_name)||' ['||object_name||']';

  -- Check if module name not null and append to error.
  IF module_name IS NOT NULL THEN

    -- Extend and append to error stack.
    errors.EXTEND;
    errors(errors.COUNT) := 'Module Name: ['||module_name||']';

  END IF;

  -- Check if table name not null and append to error.
  IF table_name IS NOT NULL THEN

    -- Extend and append to error stack.
    errors.EXTEND;
    errors(errors.COUNT) := 'Table Name: ['||table_name||']';

  END IF;

  -- Check if SQLCODE not null and append to error.
  IF sql_error_code IS NOT NULL THEN

    -- Extend and append to error stack.
    errors.EXTEND;
    errors(errors.COUNT) := 'SQLCODE Value: ['||sql_error_code||']';

  END IF;

  -- Check if SQLERRM not null and append to error.
  IF sql_error_message IS NOT NULL THEN

    -- Extend and append to error stack.
    errors.EXTEND;
    errors(errors.COUNT) := 'SQLERRM Value: ['||sql_error_message||']';

  END IF;

  -- Check if user error message not null and append to error.
  IF user_error_message IS NOT NULL THEN

    -- Extend and append to error stack.
    errors.EXTEND;
    errors(errors.COUNT) := user_error_message;

  END IF;
```

```
   -- Print a line to break the error stack.
   errors.EXTEND;
   errors(errors.COUNT) := '---------------------------------------';

   -- Raise an exception.
   RAISE raised_error;

EXCEPTION

   WHEN raised_error THEN
     FOR i IN 1..errors.COUNT LOOP
       dbms_output.put_line(errors(i));
     END LOOP;
     RETURN;

END;
/
```

The stored procedure does the following:

- It defines a signature of a mandatory object_name and optional module_name, table_name, sql_error_code, sql_error_message, and user_error_message. All but the formal parameter sql_error_code are VARCHAR2 variables. When a signature contains many optional values, you generally will use positional referencing to submit actual parameter lists.

- It defines a raised_exception EXCEPTION variable.

- It defines an error_stack local nested table and a variable that implements the nested table type.

- It defines a local function that determines what the object type of the mandatory object_name parameter is. A default of UNIDENTIFIED is used when a null value is passed as the actual parameter.

- It extends physical space and assigns the object type to the error stack nested table.

- It uses an if-statement to determine if the optional variables are not null. If they are not null, it extends physical space and assigns the error to the error stack nested table.

- It raises the locally defined exception, which triggers the EXCEPTION code block. It then prints the contents of the error stack nested table.

Before testing the `handle_errors` procedure, you need to build a dummy table, as well as three procedures that illustrate error stack propagation. You build the dummy table with the following script:

**-- Available online as part of error_management1.sql script.**

```
-- Create a dummy table.
CREATE TABLE dummy
( dummy_value        VARCHAR2(1));
```

The following three procedures are built in descending order because of their dependencies. The `error_level1` procedure calls `error_level2` procedure, which then calls `error_level3` procedure. You can build these with the following:

**-- Available online as part of error_management1.sql script.**

```
CREATE OR REPLACE PROCEDURE error_level3 IS

  -- Define local variables for error stack management.
  local_object            VARCHAR2(30)  := 'ERROR_LEVEL3';
  local_module            VARCHAR2(30)  := 'MAIN';
  local_table             VARCHAR2(30)  :=  NULL;
  local_user_message      VARCHAR2(80)  :=  NULL;

BEGIN

  -- Insert a value too large for the column.
  INSERT INTO dummy VALUES (11);

EXCEPTION

  -- Raise exception by calling the handle_errors procedure.
  WHEN others THEN
    handle_errors( object_name => local_object
                 , module_name => local_module
                 , sql_error_code => SQLCODE
                 , sql_error_message => SQLERRM );
    RAISE;

END error_level3;
/
```

```
CREATE OR REPLACE PROCEDURE error_level2 IS

  -- Define local variables for error stack management.
  local_object          VARCHAR2(30) := 'ERROR_LEVEL2';
  local_module          VARCHAR2(30) := 'MAIN';
  local_table           VARCHAR2(30) :=  NULL;
  local_user_message    VARCHAR2(80) :=  NULL;

BEGIN

  -- Call next level.
  error_level3();

EXCEPTION

  -- Raise exception by calling the handle_errors procedure.
  WHEN others THEN
    handle_errors( object_name => local_object
                 , module_name => local_module
                 , sql_error_code => SQLCODE
                 , sql_error_message => SQLERRM );
    RAISE;

END error_level2;
/

CREATE OR REPLACE PROCEDURE error_level1 IS

  -- Define local variables for error stack management.
  local_object          VARCHAR2(30) := 'ERROR_LEVEL1';
  local_module          VARCHAR2(30) := 'MAIN';
  local_table           VARCHAR2(30) :=  NULL;
  local_user_message    VARCHAR2(80) :=  NULL;

BEGIN

  -- Call next level.
  error_level2();

EXCEPTION

  -- Raise exception by calling the handle_errors procedure.
  WHEN others THEN
    handle_errors( object_name => local_object
                 , module_name => local_module
                 , sql_error_code => SQLCODE
                 , sql_error_message => SQLERRM );
    RAISE;

END error_level1;
/
```

The stored procedures do the following:

- They define an `error_level3` procedure that attempts to insert a value too large for the column in the dummy table created earlier.

- They define an `error_level2` procedure that calls the `error_level2` procedure.

- They define an `error_level3` procedure that calls the `error_level3` procedure.

You can test the propagation of a formatted error stack by running the following test program:

-- **Available online as part of error_management1.sql script.**

```
-- Define an anonymous test block.
BEGIN

  -- Start the chain of calls.
  error_level1;

END;
/
```

You'll get the following formatted error stack from the test in Oracle 9*i* (Oracle 10*g* provides a different result):

-- **Available online as output of the error_management1.sql script.**

```
PROCEDURE [ERROR_LEVEL3]
Module Name: [MAIN]
SQLCODE Value: [-1401]
SQLERRM Value: [ORA-01401: inserted value too large for column]
----------------------------------------
PROCEDURE [ERROR_LEVEL2]
Module Name: [MAIN]
SQLCODE Value: [-1401]
SQLERRM Value: [ORA-01401: inserted value too large for column]
----------------------------------------
```

```
PROCEDURE [ERROR_LEVEL1]
Module Name: [MAIN]
SQLCODE Value: [-1401]
SQLERRM Value: [ORA-01401: inserted value too large for column]
----------------------------------------
BEGIN
*
ERROR at line 1:
ORA-01401: inserted value too large for column
ORA-06512: at "PLSQL.ERROR_LEVEL1", line 22
ORA-06512: at line 3
```

You have now covered how to format your error stack in PL/SQL to demonstrate an error trace through named procedures. The method does require a bit of effort but clearly illustrates to support staff the propagation path to trace, diagnose, and fix problems in the data or application code.

Losing visibility to the line number of the error is also problematic in Oracle 9*i*. Oracle 10*g* has a fix to prevent losing line-number visibility. In the next section, you will review the new features provided by Oracle 10*g* in the DBMS_UTILITY package that helps manage error stacks.

# Introducing and Demonstrating 10*g* New Error Stack Formatting

This section shows how to format error stack management with the new Oracle 10*g* DBMS_UTILITY around your code in Oracle 9*i*.

In the prior section, there was a user_error_message formal parameter in the handle_errors package that went unused. In Oracle 9*i*, you may use it for user error management or not use it at all. However, you will want a placeholder in your handle_errors procedure to manage the output from the DBMS_UTILITY package's FORMAT_ERROR_BACKTRACE procedure. The user_error_message formal parameter is a nice fit for that.

### Why Would I Use This?

We find formatting the 10*g* error stack offers us some flexibility in documenting and tracking error sequences. This is handy because sometimes we can't remember how we designed the program after it has been released to the customer.

The `handle_errors` procedure and dummy table remain the same in the following discussion. However, the three procedures illustrating exception propagation have changed slightly, as noted next:

-- **Available online as part of error_management2.sql script.**

```
CREATE OR REPLACE PROCEDURE error_level3 IS

  -- Define local variables for error stack management.
  local_object          VARCHAR2(30)  := 'ERROR_LEVEL3';
  local_module          VARCHAR2(30)  := 'MAIN';
  local_table           VARCHAR2(30)  :=  NULL;
  local_user_message    VARCHAR2(200) :=  NULL;

BEGIN

  -- Insert a value too large for the column.
  INSERT INTO dummy VALUES (11);

EXCEPTION

  -- Raise exception by calling the handle_errors procedure.
  WHEN others THEN
    handle_errors(object_name => local_object
              ,module_name => local_module
              ,sql_error_code => SQLCODE
              ,sql_error_message => SQLERRM
              ,user_error_message =>DBMS_UTILITY.FORMAT_ERROR_BACKTRACE);
    RAISE;

END error_level3;
/

CREATE OR REPLACE PROCEDURE error_level2 IS

  -- Define local variables for error stack management.
  local_object          VARCHAR2(30)  := 'ERROR_LEVEL2';
  local_module          VARCHAR2(30)  := 'MAIN';
  local_table           VARCHAR2(30)  :=  NULL;
  local_user_message    VARCHAR2(200) :=  NULL;

BEGIN

  -- Call next level.
  error_level3();
```

```
EXCEPTION

  -- Raise exception by calling the handle_errors procedure.
  WHEN others THEN
    handle_errors(object_name => local_object
                 ,module_name => local_module
                 ,sql_error_code => SQLCODE
                 ,sql_error_message => SQLERRM
                 ,user_error_message =>DBMS_UTILITY.FORMAT_ERROR_BACKTRACE);
    RAISE;

END error_level2;
/
CREATE OR REPLACE PROCEDURE error_level1 IS

  -- Define local variables for error stack management.
  local_object            VARCHAR2(30) := 'ERROR_LEVEL1';
  local_module            VARCHAR2(30) := 'MAIN';
  local_table             VARCHAR2(30) :=  NULL;
  local_user_message      VARCHAR2(200) :=  NULL;

BEGIN

  -- Call next level.
  error_level2();

EXCEPTION
  -- Raise exception by calling the handle_errors procedure.
  WHEN others THEN
    handle_errors(object_name => local_object
                 ,module_name => local_module
                 ,sql_error_code => SQLCODE
                 ,sql_error_message => SQLERRM
                 ,user_error_message =>DBMS_UTILITY.FORMAT_ERROR_BACKTRACE);
    RAISE;

END error_level1;
/
```

The stored procedures do the following:

■ They define an error_level3 procedure that attempts to insert a value too large for the column in the dummy table created earlier. In the EXCEPTION block, they use the DBMS_UTLITY.FORMAT_ERROR_ BACKTRACE procedure to capture the line number where the exception is raised.

■ They define an `error_level2` procedure that calls the `error_level2` procedure. It likewise uses the DBMS_UTILITY package to capture the line number where the exception is raised.

■ They define an `error_level3` procedure that calls the `error_level3` procedure. It likewise uses the DBMS_UTILITY package to capture the line number where the exception is raised.

You can test the propagation of a formatted error stack by running the following test program:

```
-- Available online as part of error_management2.sql script.

-- Define an anonymous test block.
BEGIN

  -- Start the chain of calls.
  error_level1;

END;
/
```

You should get the following formatted error stack from the test:

```
-- Available online as output of the error_management2.sql script.

PROCEDURE [ERROR_LEVEL3]
Module Name: [MAIN]
SQLCODE Value: [-12899]
SQLERRM Value: [ORA-12899: value too large for column
"PLSQL"."DUMMY"."DUMMY_VALUE" (actual: 2, maximum: 1)]
ORA-06512: at "PLSQL.ERROR_LEVEL3", line 12
---------------------------------------
PROCEDURE [ERROR_LEVEL2]
Module Name: [MAIN]
SQLCODE Value: [-12899]
SQLERRM Value: [ORA-12899: value too large for column
"PLSQL"."DUMMY"."DUMMY_VALUE" (actual: 2, maximum: 1)]
ORA-06512: at "PLSQL.ERROR_LEVEL3", line 23
ORA-06512: at "PLSQL.ERROR_LEVEL2", line 12
---------------------------------------
```

```
PROCEDURE [ERROR_LEVEL1]
Module Name: [MAIN]
SQLCODE Value: [-12899]
SQLERRM Value: [ORA-12899: value too large for column
"PLSQL"."DUMMY"."DUMMY_VALUE" (actual: 2, maximum: 1)]
ORA-06512: at "PLSQL.ERROR_LEVEL2", line 23
ORA-06512: at "PLSQL.ERROR_LEVEL1", line 12
--------------------------------------
BEGIN
*
ERROR at line 1:
ORA-12899: value too large for column "PLSQL"."DUMMY"."DUMMY_VALUE"
(actual: 2, maximum: 1)
ORA-06512: at "PLSQL.ERROR_LEVEL1", line 23
ORA-06512: at line 4
```

DBMS_UTILITY.FORMAT_ERROR_BACKTRACE now provides you with an effective tool to trace, diagnose, and fix problems in the data or application code. The only tedious part is linking the line numbers with the stored line number for the stored programs. This can be done by using the data dictionary.

For example, if you would like to find the source error that occurred at line 12 in the error_level3 procedure, the following query will provide the offending line of code:

```
COL line FORMAT 999
COL text FORMAT A60

SELECT    line
,         text
FROM      user_source
WHERE     name = 'ERROR_LEVEL3'
AND       line = 12;
```

The output shows the following:

```
LINE TEXT
---- ---------------------------------------
INSERT INTO dummy VALUES (11);
```

This new FORMAT_ERROR_BACKTRACE procedure in the DBMS_UTILITY package is a blessing when it comes to the quick identification of an error's location. Unfortunately, it does not appear to be something that can be back-ported into Oracle 9*i*.

You now know how to manage error stacks in Oracle 9*i* and 10*g* for standard transactional code. The next section examines how to map these techniques to database triggers.

# Error Management in Database Triggers

Database triggers are event-driven programs. If you're unfamiliar with database triggers, see Chapter 10.

Triggers are activated when a transactional program unit calls a database object, like a table or view. Database triggers may sometimes call other stored functions, procedures, and packages. When triggers call other stored objects, those program units cannot contain any transaction control language (TCL) commands, like **SAVEPOINT**, **ROLLBACK**, and **COMMIT**.

Database triggers have two behavioral patterns. One is for a critical error, which is similar to everything we covered in the previous examples. Another is for a non-critical error. A noncritical error may be a security or audit issue. These may include unauthorized updates to tables and views. When they happen, you should store the transaction data in a way that is transparent to the user or hacker executing the transaction. This requires a different approach to error stack management.

In lieu of raising exceptions, you'll store the data and transaction information into a set of database tables. This can be done by rewriting the `handle_errors` procedure to receive a serialized string of data and all user-defined error messages and then writing them to an auditing table. The best alternative is to define a table for the error information and another for the recoverable state, which is best stored in a CLOB data type.

# Summary

In this chapter, you explored PL/SQL exception handling and learned how to manage error propagation and stacks. You should be able to use the chapter's example code to build your own architecture in order to support internal applications.

# PART
# II

Invoker's Rights,
Java Libraries, and
Object Patterns

# CHAPTER
## 4

# Invoker's-Rights
# Architecture

anaging PL/SQL code libraries in the database requires planning and organization. Oracles 8*i* through Oracle 10*g* databases provide two options for organizing code libraries. The options are definer's-rights and invoker's-rights. This chapter discusses how you implement the invoker's-rights option.

Oracle has always had definer's-rights architecture as the default. Oracle 8*i* introduced invoker's-rights architecture. Many ERP/CRM database applications use invoker's-rights concepts. You can build robust applications with definer's-rights architecture when working with centralized data.

The Oracle Applications Suite uses definer's-right architecture to share common code components and manage internal component interfaces. Oracle applications use an architecture of grants and synonyms to manage their definer's-rights implementation. They use these because the data is distributed by subsystems in the same instance.

This chapter stands independent of others in the book because all of its content works in currently supported versions of the Oracle database. The following topics will be covered:

- Introducing definer's-right and invoker's-rights concepts

  - Definer's-right concepts

  - Invoker's-right concepts

- Understanding the architectures

  - Understanding definer's-right architecture

  - Understanding invoker's-right architecture

- Comparing and contrasting implementation strategies

## Why Would I Use This?

We use definer's-rights or invoker's-rights architecture to implement applications in the Oracle database. Definer's-rights architecture ensures we have control of all inserts, updates, and deletes against centralized data. Invoker's-rights architecture ensures we have control of all inserts, updates, and deletes against distributed data.

We increase control and organization when using definer's-rights or invoker's-rights architecture to build applications. Our applications become better organized and easier to user, support, and maintain. Accepting the default without understanding it can lead us to make critical errors that increase the complexity and support cost of our applications.

The focus is to introduce, compare and contrast, and demonstrate how to implement definer's-rights and invoker's-rights architectures in Oracle. Since this isn't a tutorial on the basics of using stored PL/SQL program units, you're encouraged to explore Chapters 8 through 10 in *Oracle 10g PL/SQL Programming* where all the features of stored program units are explored. Stored PL/SQL program units are standalone procedures and functions, packages, and triggers.

The demonstration of these concepts requires two user schemas. The `create_invoker_user.sql` script should be run before using any of the code for this chapter. This script creates, or drops and re-creates, the MYAPP user/schema and the PLSQL user/schema. You need to run it as the SYSTEM user/schema or with delegated DBA role permissions.

**NOTE**
*User and schema are synonymous, so for the sake of simplicity we'll use schema throughout the rest of the chapter.*

# Introducing Definer's-Rights and Invoker's-Rights Concepts

You choose to use definer's-rights or invoker's-rights when you define stored PL/SQL program units. PL/SQL programming units are, by default, definer's-rights programs. We'll now examine basic definer's-rights and invoker's-rights concepts.

## Definer's-Rights Concepts

Definer's-rights PL/SQL program units are executed with the privileges of the owner who defined them. This means any user with execution privileges may access objects with the privileges of the stored PL/SQL programming unit. All users with

**Why Would I Use This?**

We use definer's-rights when we know one of two things. Either we'll grant all external schemas the same execute privileges and have all our data in single tables, or our application already has developed a security system based on the connection or session information.

We find that Oracle Applications E-Business Suite deploys definer's-rights. We find it a powerful architecture, especially when deployed to include context-sensitive views that change based on the user's privileges. We recommend definer's-right for consolidated processing models.

execution privileges have the same access rights. This is the desired solution when all users touch the same data tables.

**TIP**
*A security system on the connection or session information enables you to provide limited or concurrent access to different sets of information from the same code base and database table sources.*

The definer's-rights pattern ensures you control access to all inserts, updates, and deletes against the same data through your stored PL/SQL programs. You achieve this by building or licensing application metadata and security programs like those found in ERP/CRM applications. Many ERP/CRM solutions use row-by-row database triggers to enforce user privileges. This is expensive because it increases the time to complete transactions. The triggers also function based on user-level security maintained in a set of application-tier metadata.

The trade-off is that the data is centralized and you avoid reconciliation of multiple data streams. The downside is that data volumes increase dramatically and throughput may degrade.

**NOTE**
*Oracle applications work with definer's rights and use an elaborate set of stored PL/SQL application metadata and shared libraries to achieve concurrency within a single schema—the APPS schema—and manage security in the APPLSYSPUB and APPLSYS schemas.*

You can see the utility of definer's-rights development by using the following PL/SQL package in the PLSQL schema. Make sure you're in the PLSQL schema by running the SQL*Plus command **SHOW USER**. Afterward, you should run the create_definer1.sql script to build this package:

-- Available online as part of create_definer1.sql file.

```
-- Create a DEFINER_RIGHTS package.
CREATE OR REPLACE PACKAGE definer_rights IS

  -- Define a GET_LITERAL function.
  FUNCTION get_literal
```

```
  ( literal VARCHAR2 )
  RETURN VARCHAR2;

END;
/

-- Create a DEFINER_RIGHTS package body.
CREATE OR REPLACE PACKAGE BODY definer_rights IS

  -- Define a GET_LITERAL function.
  FUNCTION get_literal
  ( literal VARCHAR2 )
  RETURN VARCHAR2 IS

  BEGIN

    -- Use an implicit for-loop to avoid declaring variables.
    FOR i IN (SELECT   literal
                FROM dual) LOOP

      -- Return the value.
      RETURN 'Called by ['||literal||']';

    END LOOP;

  END get_literal;

END definer_rights;
/
```

The script creates a stored PL/SQL package with the following characteristics:

- It defines a package `definer_rights` with a single function `get_literal`.

- It defines the `definer_rights` package body and implements a `get_literal` function. The function:

  - Takes a single formal parameter named `literal` of the `VARCHAR2` data type.

  - Uses a for-loop with an implicit cursor that uses the actual parameter value and the `DUAL` table.

  - Returns the value of the for-loop structure: the actual parameter value as a `VARCHAR2` data type.

After creating the package and package body, the `create_definer1.sql` script then grants `EXECUTE` privileges to the `MYAPP` schema, as shown next:

```
-- Available online as part of create_definer1.sql file.

-- Grant EXECUTE privileges to MYAPP schema.
GRANT EXECUTE ON definer_rights TO myapp;
```

You can test the definer package by running the following query in the `PLSQL` schema, which is the definer of the package:

```
SELECT    definer_rights.get_literal(USER)
FROM      dual;
```

You should see the following output:

```
DEFINER_RIGHTS.GET_LITERAL(USER)
------------------------------------
Called by [PLSQL]
```

After verifying that the locally stored PL/SQL package works in the `PLSQL` schema, connect to the `MYAPP` schema by using the following syntax:

```
CONN MYAPP/MYAPP
```

Verify you are in the correct schema by running the SQL*Plus command **SHOW USER**, which will display the following:

```
USER is "MYAPP"
```

You can test the definer's-rights package by running a similar query to the one you ran in the owning schema. You need to chain a user schema in front of a stored package, function, or procedure name. Also, when you chain a user to a package, you chain the package to a function or procedure defined in the package.

**NOTE**
*Chaining is the process of connecting schemas to stored programming units and objects. It's done by using the schema name and a period.*

You should check who you are at this point. Check if you're in the MYAPP schema by running the SQL*Plus command **SHOW USER**. Then, run the following query:

```
SELECT   plsql.definer_rights.get_literal(USER)
FROM     dual;
```

You'll see the following output:

```
PLSQL.DEFINER_RIGHTS.GET_LITERAL(USER)
--------------------------------------
Called by [MYAPP]
```

You have now queried from the public DUAL table with execute privileges against another schema's stored PL/SQL package. The create_definer2.sql script changes the dynamics of the problem slightly. It now creates and uses a table owned by the definer of the package. You should reconnect as the PLSQL user and use SQL*Plus to verify that you are the PLSQL user. Then, run the create_definer2.sql script to define a local_table in the PLSQL schema using the following:

```
-- Available online as part of create_definer2.sql file.

-- Create a local table.
CREATE TABLE local_table
( owner_name VARCHAR2(30 CHAR)
, user_name  VARCHAR2(30 CHAR) );
```

Then, build a modified definer_rights package as noted next:

```
-- This is found in the create_definer2.sql file.

-- Create a DEFINER_RIGHTS package.
CREATE OR REPLACE PACKAGE definer_rights IS

  -- Define a SET_DATA function.
  FUNCTION set_data
  ( user_in VARCHAR2 )
  RETURN BOOLEAN;

  -- Define a GET_DATA function.
  FUNCTION get_data
  ( user_in VARCHAR2 )
  RETURN VARCHAR2;

END;
/
```

```
-- Create a DEFINER_RIGHTS package body.
CREATE OR REPLACE PACKAGE BODY definer_rights IS

  -- Define a SET_DATA function.
  FUNCTION set_data
  ( user_in VARCHAR2 )
  RETURN BOOLEAN IS

    -- Define default return value.
    retval BOOLEAN := FALSE;

  BEGIN

    -- Use an implicit for-loop to avoid declaring variables.
    INSERT
    INTO      local_table
    VALUES
    ('PLSQL'
    , user_in );

    COMMIT;

    -- Reset return value.
    retval := TRUE;

    -- Return value.
    RETURN retval;

  END set_data;

  -- Define a GET_DATA function.
  FUNCTION get_data
  ( user_in VARCHAR2 )
  RETURN VARCHAR2 IS

  BEGIN

    -- Use an implicit for-loop to avoid declaring variables.
    FOR i IN (SELECT    user_in
              ,         owner_name
              ,         user_name
              FROM      local_table
              WHERE     user_name = user_in ) LOOP
```

```
      -- Return the value.
      RETURN 'Called by ['
      ||      user_in||']['||i.owner_name||']['||i.user_name||']';

   END LOOP;

  END get_data;

END definer_rights;
/
```

The script creates a stored PL/SQL package that provides the following features:

- It defines a package `definer_rights` with two functions: `get_data` and `set_data`.

- It defines a package body `definer_rights` with two functions: `get_data` and `set_data`. They do the following:

  - The `set_data` function inserts a row into the `local_table` table in the definer's schema, which is the `PLSQL` user.

  - The `get_data` function returns the actual parameter and two columns in the `local_table` table.

After rebuilding the `definer_rights` package, you can run the following anonymous block PL/SQL program as the `PLSQL` user to test it. The test is executed automatically for you from the `create_definer2.sql` file.

**-- Available online as part of `create_definer2.sql` file.**

```
-- Test the definer table from the definer schema.
BEGIN

  -- Call the function that inserts the user name.
  IF definer_rights.set_data(USER) THEN

    -- Use an implicit for-loop to avoid declaring variables.
    FOR i IN (SELECT   definer_rights.get_data(user) data
              FROM     dual ) LOOP

      -- Print the value returned.
      DBMS_OUTPUT.PUT_LINE(i.data);

    END LOOP;

  END IF;

END;
/
```

The script does the following:

- It uses an if-statement to manage the return value from the set_data function. It checks the Boolean return value of the set_data function. If true, it does the following:

  - It uses an implicit cursor for-loop against the DUAL table to manage the return value of the get_data function.

  - It uses DBMS_OUTPUT.PUT_LINE to print the results, using the index to manage the structure returned by the implicit cursor, which contains two column values.

The anonymous block PL/SQL program returns the following results, provided you ran it as the PLSQL user:

```
Called by [PLSQL][PLSQL][PLSQL]
```

The balance of create_definer2.sql truncates local_table and grants execute to the MYAPP user. Please check the earlier example in the chapter for the exact syntax. You can now check whether another user can update the PLSQL user's local_table when the package is configured as a definer's-right module.

You perform the test by connecting as the MYAPP user and running the following anonymous block PL/SQL program:

```
-- Available online as part of test_definer1.sql file.

-- Set SQL*Plus environment lost due to schema connection change.
SET SERVEROUTPUT ON SIZE 1000000

-- Anonymous block program to test definer_rights package.
BEGIN

  -- Call the function that inserts the user name.
  IF plsql.definer_rights.set_data(USER) THEN

    -- Use an implicit for-loop to avoid declaring variables.
    FOR i IN (SELECT   plsql.definer_rights.get_data(user) data
              FROM     dual ) loop

      -- Print the value returned.
      DBMS_OUTPUT.PUT_LINE(i.data);

    END LOOP;
  END IF;
END;
/
```

## Why Would I Use This?

We use invoker's-rights when we know that our data is distributed. Invoker's-rights architecture enables you to implement an inexpensive and simple solution by providing controlled access to distributed data.

We recommend invoker's-rights when you build distributed applications because it is a natural fit. We get the opportunity with invoker's-rights to isolate organizational data, which you can later aggregate into a corporate repository. We find evening batch programs and scheduled jobs the easiest solution to aggregate the data sources.

The script does what the prior test script did in the PLSQL schema. The only changes are the front chaining of plsql and the dot between the package and function names. The anonymous block PL/SQL program returns the following results, provided you ran it as the PLSQL user:

```
Called by [MYAPP][PLSQL][MYAPP]
```

**NOTE**
*If you did not see the following output, you may not have enabled SERVEROUTPUT when you changed the session state by connecting to MYAPP schema from the PLSQL schema. If you ran test_definer1 .sql, it sets SQL\*Plus SERVEROUTPUT for you.*

You've seen the fundamental concepts of a definer's-rights pattern, so next we'll cover the invoker's-rights pattern.

# Invoker's-Rights Concepts

Invoker's-rights PL/SQL program units are executed with the privileges of the current user, not the owner who defined them. This means your privileges to objects may differ between users. This is an ideal solution when different users update different tables.

You make a stored PL/SQL programming unit an invoker's-right object by using the AUTHID key word when defining the code. This is a bit tricky if you don't know the correct syntax, because some misleading error messages can be prompted. The rule of thumb is that you can only use AUTHID on schema-level programs. This means you use it to define stored functions, procedures, and packages.

**TIP**
*A package body is the implementation of the package. The package is the schema-level program, not the package body.*

You cannot define AUTHID for functions and procedures within the scope of a package. If you attempt this, you will raise the following error:

```
Errors for PACKAGE BODY DEFINER_RIGHTS:

LINE/COL ERROR
-------- ----------------------------------------------------------
7/10     PLS-00157: AUTHID only allowed on schema-level programs
```

The following is the correct syntax for invoker_right_clause for all schema-level PL/SQL programming units:

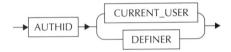

Use the create_invoker1.sql script to create an invoker's-rights package in the PLSQL schema. You should reconnect as the PLSQL user and use SQL*Plus to verify that you're the PLSQL user. Like the prior example, it depends on local_table being in the PLSQL schema but the script puts local_table back if it was dropped from the database. If you need to check the definition of the table, it's in the earlier definer's-rights section. You should now run the create_invoker1.sql script shown next:

**-- Available online as part of create_invoker1.sql file.**

```
-- Create an INVOKER_RIGHTS package.
CREATE OR REPLACE PACKAGE invoker_rights AUTHID CURRENT_USER IS

  -- Define a SET_DATA function.
  FUNCTION set_data
  ( user_in VARCHAR2 )
  RETURN BOOLEAN;

  -- Define a GET_DATA function.
  FUNCTION get_data
  ( user_in VARCHAR2 )
  RETURN VARCHAR2;

END;
/
```

```
-- Create an INVOKER_RIGHTS package body.
CREATE OR REPLACE PACKAGE BODY invoker_rights IS

  -- Define a SET_DATA function.
  FUNCTION set_data
  ( user_in VARCHAR2 )
  RETURN BOOLEAN AS

    -- Define default return value.
    retval BOOLEAN := FALSE;

  BEGIN

    -- Use an implicit for-loop to avoid declaring variables.
    INSERT
    INTO      local_table
    VALUES
    ('PLSQL'
    , user_in );

    COMMIT;

    -- Reset return value.
    retval := TRUE;

    -- Return value.
    RETURN retval;

  END set_data;

  -- Define a GET_DATA function.
  FUNCTION get_data
  ( user_in VARCHAR2 )
  RETURN VARCHAR2 AS

  BEGIN

    -- Use an implicit for-loop to avoid declaring variables.
    FOR i IN (SELECT    user_in
              ,         owner_name
              ,         user_name
              FROM      local_table
              WHERE     user_name = user_in ) LOOP
```

```
        -- Return the value.
        RETURN 'Called by ['
        ||      user_in||']['||i.owner_name||']['||i.user_name||']';

    END LOOP;

  END get_data;

END invoker_rights;
/
```

The script creates a stored PL/SQL package that provides the following features:

- It defines a package `invoker_rights` with two functions: `get_data` and `set_data`.

- It defines a package body `invoker_rights` with two functions: `get_data` and `set_data`. They do the following:

    - The `set_data` function inserts a row into the `local_table` table in the definer's schema, which is the `PLSQL` user.

    - The `get_data` function returns the actual parameter and two columns in the `local_table` table.

After building the `invoker_rights` package in the `PLSQL` schema, you can run the following anonymous block PL/SQL program in the `PLSQL` schema to test it:

**-- Available online as part of create_invoker1.sql file.**

```
-- Test the definer table from the definer schema.
BEGIN

  -- Call the function that inserts the user name.
  IF invoker_rights.set_data(USER) THEN

    -- Use an implicit for-loop to avoid declaring variables.
    FOR i IN (SELECT   invoker_rights.get_data(user) data
              FROM     dual ) LOOP

      -- Print the value returned.
      DBMS_OUTPUT.PUT_LINE(i.data);

    END LOOP;

  END IF;

END;
/
```

The script does the following:

- It uses an if-statement to manage the return value from the set_data function. It checks the Boolean return value of the set_data function. If true, it does the following:

  - It uses an implicit cursor for-loop against the DUAL table to manage the return value of the get_data function.

  - It uses DBMS_OUTPUT.PUT_LINE to print the results, using the index to manage the structure returned by the implicit cursor, which contains two column values.

The anonymous block PL/SQL program returns the following results, provided you ran it as the PLSQL user:

```
Called by [PLSQL][PLSQL][PLSQL]
```

The balance of create_invoker1.sql truncates local_table and grants execute to the MYAPP user. Please check the earlier example in the chapter for the exact syntax.

You can now check whether the other user can update the PLSQL user's local_table by connecting as the MYAPP user and running the following anonymous block PL/SQL program:

```
-- Available online as part of test_invoker1.sql file.

-- Anonymous block program to test invoker_rights package.
BEGIN

  -- Call the function that inserts the user name.
  IF plsql.invoker_rights.set_data(USER) THEN

    -- Use an implicit for-loop to avoid declaring variables.
    FOR i IN (SELECT   plsql.invoker_rights.get_data(user) data
              FROM     dual ) LOOP
```

```
    -- Print the value returned.
    DBMS_OUTPUT.PUT_LINE(i.data);

  END LOOP;

 END IF;

END;
/
```

The script does what the prior test script did in the PLSQL schema. The only changes are the front chaining of plsql and the dot between the package and function names. When you run the anonymous block PL/SQL program, it returns no results but raises the following exception:

```
BEGIN
*
ERROR at line 1:
ORA-00942: table or view does not exist
ORA-06512: at "PLSQL.INVOKER_RIGHTS", line 15
ORA-06512: at line 4
```

This exception is raised because the MYAPP user does not have privileges to write to the PLSQL schema's local_table object. Grant insert and select privileges on the PLSQL schema's local_table object to the MYAPP schema.

You've now learned the fundamental concepts of an invoker's-rights pattern. In the next section, we compare and contrast the definer's-right and invoker's-rights patterns.

# Understanding the Architectures

This section qualifies, compares, and contrasts the architectures. This demonstrates the benefits of a definer's-rights approach.

## Why Would I Use This?

We need to understand the benefits and disadvantages of both approaches to make a good architectural decision about which to use. As qualified earlier, we find definer's-rights a perfect fit for centralized code repositories and data when individual users see only conceptual views of the data. On the other hand, we find invoker's-rights an awesome tool for distributed applications and data sources. However, we need to tell you why we believe that. We explain why in this section.

# Understanding Definer's-Rights Architecture

The data in a definer's-rights architecture is sliced into pieces like salami. Each user only sees a slice of the whole. This is the most common approach. The following illustration shows the definer's-rights concept by allowing four users to see slices of information.

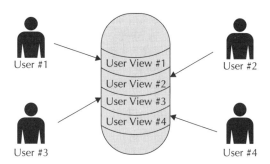

The definer's-rights pattern requires you to centralize your data in one schema. If you have different end users that should only see subsets of the data, you need to create some form of user security to segment what the end users see. A common approach is to use views based on session information. This requires (a) setting the CLIENT_INFO value on a connection to the database, and (b) building a striped view of a table.

The following section shows how the definer's-right architecture is implemented.

## Setting the CLIENT_INFO Value

Before beginning, this section assumes you'll do all testing of the CLIENT_INFO value in the PLSQL schema.

You use the DBMS_APPLICATION_INFO package to set the CLIENT_INFO value for a connection or session. The package has two procedures with slightly different signatures. The SET_CLIENT_INFO procedure uses an IN mode VARCHAR2, while the READ_CLIENT_INFO procedure uses an OUT mode VARCHAR2 variable as follows:

**Procedure Name and Signatures**

```
SET_CLIENT_INFO(client_info IN VARCHAR2)

READ_CLIENT_INFO(client_info OUT VARCHAR2)
```

The SET_CLIENT_INFO stores the information in the connections V$SESSION
.CLIENT_INFO column. The column is 64 characters in length. When using this
approach, you should develop an encoding schema to maximize the allotted space.
The following script illustrates setting and retrieving the CLIENT_INFO value in
PL/SQL. You should test it in both the PLSQL and MYAPP schemas.

**-- Available online as part of demo_client_info1.sql file.**

```
-- Anonymous block program to demonstrate DBMS_APPLICATION_INFO package.
DECLARE

  -- Declare a test variable.
  my_env VARCHAR2(1);

BEGIN

  -- Read CLIENT_INFO into a variable.
  DBMS_APPLICATION_INFO.READ_CLIENT_INFO(my_env);

  -- Print the current value of CLIENT_INFO.
  DBMS_OUTPUT.PUT_LINE('Read CLIENT_INFO value ['||my_env||'].');

  -- Display message.
  DBMS_OUTPUT.PUT_LINE('Set CLIENT_INFO to    [1].');

  -- Set the value to one.
  DBMS_APPLICATION_INFO.SET_CLIENT_INFO('1');

  -- Read CLIENT_INFO into a variable.
  DBMS_APPLICATION_INFO.READ_CLIENT_INFO(my_env);

  -- Print the current value of CLIENT_INFO.
  DBMS_OUTPUT.PUT_LINE('Read CLIENT_INFO value ['||my_env||'].');

END;
/
```

The script does three things:

- It reads the default or current setting of V$SESSION.CLIENT_INFO and
  prints it to the console.

- It sets the value of V$SESSION.CLIENT_INFO and prints it to the console.

- It reads the modified or current setting of V$SESSION.CLIENT_INFO and
  prints it to the console.

The script displays the following output in both the PLSQL and MYAPP schemas, provided you have not already set the value of CLIENT_INFO:

```
Read CLIENT_INFO value [].
Set CLIENT_INFO to      [1].
Read CLIENT_INFO value [1].
```

**NOTE**
*If you do not see a null value for V$SESSION*
*.CLIENT_INFO, disconnect and reconnect to the*
*SQL session.*

Unless you have altered the permissions of the user, any attempt to verify the contents of V$SESSION.CLIENT_INFO will fail and give you the following error:

```
FROM      V$SESSION
          *
ERROR at line 2:
ORA-00942: table or view does not exist
```

If you disconnect and reconnect as SYSTEM or as an authorized user with DBA privileges, you most likely won't see any values set in the CLIENT_INFO column of the V$SESSION view. If you have DBA privileges, you can see your setting by opening a new session with those privileges and querying the V$SESSION view.

An alternative approach is to use the SQL USERENV function and the dual table as shown in the demo_client_info2.sql script. This script sets CLIENT_INFO by executing the DBMS_APPLICATION_INFO.SET_CLIENT_INFO procedure in SQL and querying it with a select statement:

```
-- Available online as part of demo_client_info2.sql file.

-- Select the default value from V$SESSION.CLIENT_INFO.
SELECT   USERENV('CLIENT_INFO')
FROM     dual;

-- Execute the DBMS_APPLICATION_INFO package.
EXECUTE DBMS_APPLICATION_INFO.SET_CLIENT_INFO('1');

-- Select the overridden value from V$SESSION.CLIENT_INFO.
SELECT   USERENV('CLIENT_INFO')
FROM     dual;
```

The `demo_client_info2.sql` script does not require qualification. It displays the following output:

```
USERENV('CLIENT_INFO')
------------------------------------------------------------
<Null>

USERENV('CLIENT_INFO')
------------------------------------------------------------
1

USERENV('CLIENT_INFO')
------------------------------------------------------------
1
```

**TIP**
*The <Null> display is generated by using a SQL\*Plus command, SET NULL "<Null>", which is always helpful when debugging null value returns.*

You've learned how to set and retrieve the `CLIENT_INFO` value in PL/SQL and SQL. Now it's time to see how to implement a striped view of the data.

## Building a Striped View of a Table

Striped tables are quite straightforward once you know a couple of tricks and understand the publish-and-subscribe method (also known as an observer pattern in Object-Oriented (OO) programming).

The publish-and-subscribe pattern means that a program publishes an event and other programs may subscribe to read events. In the case of striped views, the view is the program. Users with privileges to read the view contents are subscribers.

There are two key tricks to these views: they must verify session information at runtime, and they are dynamic with two dependencies. One dependency is that the subscriber must set the `CLIENT_INFO` value in their session. Another is that the view must have a column that is a nonunique identifier for each stripe of the data.

You will use both the `MYAPP` and `PLSQL` schemas for this section. On that note, you should start connections in both the `MYAPP` and `PLSQL` schemas.

The `create_striped_view1.sql` script demonstrates a view with a nonunique identifier column, `striping_id`. You should note this column value is nonnumeric, but the following example *should be run in the PLSQL schema* and will demonstrate numeric resolution of the column value and `CLIENT_INFO` values:

```
-- Available online as part of create_striped_view1.sql file.

-- Drop shared table.
DROP TABLE shared_all;

-- Create shared table.
CREATE TABLE shared_all
( shared_id      NUMBER
, shared_text    VARCHAR2(20 CHAR)
, striping_id    VARCHAR2(10 CHAR));

-- Select the default value from V$SESSION.CLIENT_INFO.
CREATE OR REPLACE VIEW shared
  SELECT    shared_id
  ,         shared_text
  FROM      shared_all
  WHERE     NVL(TO_NUMBER(striping_id),0) =
             NVL(TO_NUMBER(SUBSTR(USERENV('CLIENT_INFO'),1,10)),0)

-- Insert a non-striped row.
INSERT
INTO      shared_all
VALUES
( 1,'One','');

-- Insert a striped row.
INSERT
INTO      shared_all
VALUES
( 2,'Two','1');

-- Insert a striped row.
INSERT
INTO      shared_all
VALUES
( 3,'Three','2');
```

The script does the following:

- It drops and creates a `shared_all` table, which is the shared data repository. `shared_all.striping_id` is the nonunique striping identifier.

- It creates a view `shared`, which publishes dynamic content based on the striping identifier. It does this by evaluating the contents of the `shared_all.striping_id` column with a null value function for data in the table and then joins that against a set of enclosing functions around a `USERENV` function. The latter does the following from the inside out:

  - It captures the `V$SESSION.CLIENT_INFO` value for the current session as a `VARCHAR2` with 64 characters.

- It uses the SUBSTR function to parse the first ten characters to a string.

- It uses the TO_NUMBER function to convert the parsed string to a number.

- It uses the NVL function to check whether the number is null or a value.

- It grants select, insert, update, and delete privileges on the striped view to the MYAPP schema.

- It seeds three values in the shared_all tables that meet different striping criteria.

- You may use the following select statement to view all values from the table:

```
COL shared_text FORMAT A11
COL shared_id   FORMAT A11

SELECT   *
FROM     shared_all;
```

It should show you the following results when run from the PLSQL schema:

```
SHARED_ID  SHARED_TEXT STRIPING_ID
---------- ----------- ---------------
        1 One         <Null>
        2 Two         1
        3 Three       2
```

You have now built the publishing side of the publish-and-subscribe pattern used for definer's-rights implementation. You should navigate to your other MYAPP schema session and run the following subscribing.sql script:

```
-- Available online as part of subscribing.sql file.

-- Drop synonym to the striped view.
DROP SYNONYM shared;

-- Create synonym to the striped view.
CREATE SYNONYM shared FOR plsql.shared;

-- Select the default value from V$SESSION.CLIENT_INFO.
SELECT   USERENV('CLIENT_INFO')
FROM     dual;
```

```
-- Format column value returns.
COL shared_id   FORMAT 990
COL shared_text FORMAT A20
COL userenv_col FORMAT A10

-- Select the non-striped values from the view.
SELECT    shared_id
,         shared_text
,         USERENV('CLIENT_INFO') userenv_col
FROM      shared;

-- Execute the DBMS_APPLICATION_INFO package.
EXECUTE DBMS_APPLICATION_INFO.SET_CLIENT_INFO('1');

COL shared_id   FORMAT 990
COL shared_text FORMAT A20
COL userenv_col FORMAT A10

-- Select the overridden value from V$SESSION.CLIENT_INFO.
SELECT    shared_id
,         shared_text
,         USERENV('CLIENT_INFO') userenv_col
FROM      shared;
```

The script does the following:

- It drops and creates a synonym to the striped `shared` view.

- It verifies that the session `CLIENT_INFO` value is null.

- It sets the `CLIENT_INFO` value to one.

- It formats the output to avoid running over the line length in SQL*Plus.

- It queries the striped `shared` view and current value of `CLIENT_INFO`. You can see that it maps to the second row of data inserted into the table.

**NOTE**
*If you have previously set your `CLIENT_INFO` value, you should unset it. Using the `EXECUTE dbms_application_info.set_client_ info(NULL)` statement resets your `CLIENT_INFO` value to the default null value.*

## Why Would I Use This?

You need to understand why striping is important, which is critical when using Oracle applications. We use striping to develop conceptual views that limit user access in a consolidated definer's-rights solution. As you will see, this technique enables you to build very powerful applications in a centralized format. We thank Oracle Applications Division for implementing this as their solution to multiple organizations in the same database.

You'll see the following output without setting the CLIENT_INFO value because the first row in the table is not striped:

```
SHARED_ID SHARED_TEXT          USERENV_CO
--------- -------------------- ----------
        1 One                  <Null>
```

The following output should appear after setting the CLIENT_INFO value, because the second row in the shared_all table has a nonunique striping identifier value equal to your CLIENT_INFO value:

```
SHARED_ID SHARED_TEXT          USERENV_CO
--------- -------------------- ----------
        2 Two                  1
```

**NOTE**
*Oracle applications are implemented using the definer's-rights architecture. There are multiple numeric values stored during a session connection. These maintain the striping for multiple organizations, multiple reporting currencies, and other aspects of the applications architecture.*

Another alternative to this implementation is to define the striped table as a number data type. This avoids the use of the TO_NUMBER function against the non-unique striping column in the shared view. You should build the view in the

PLSQL schema. Only the building of the view changes in create_striped_ view2.sql, and it now looks like this:

 -- **Available online as part of create_striped_view2.sql.**

```
-- Build a striped view.
CREATE OR REPLACE VIEW shared AS
  SELECT    shared_id
  ,         shared_text
  FROM      shared_all
  WHERE     NVL(striping_id,0) =
               NVL(TO_NUMBER(SUBSTR(USERENV('CLIENT_INFO'),1,10)),0);
```

**TIP**
*You can clear CLIENT_INFO by connecting to the same schema. For example, if you're connected as the MYAPP user and type **CONNECTION MYAPP/ MYAPP**, you'll clear the CLIENT_INFO value to enable retesting of this sample code.*

**NOTE**
*Oracle applications use the ORG_ID column in data tables with a suffix of _ALL to stripe subsystem data. Oracle implements striping like an old wagon wheel. Subsystems like accounts payable or general ledger are at the end of the spokes. The subsystems grant select, insert, update, and delete to the hub code repository. All interfaces between subsystems go through the hub code base, which manages all spoke subsystems.*

You've just learned how to build and implement a definer's-rights approach. You'll now do the same for the invoker's-rights approach.

# Understanding Invoker's-Rights Architecture
The data in invoker's-rights architecture may or may not be sliced into pieces. Invoker's-rights architecture provides two types of implementation strategies. One supports a distributed approach to data. The other supports a consolidated approach similar to the earlier discussion on striping tables to support definer's-rights architecture.

### Why Would I Use This?
You need to know how to use invoker's-rights architecture when working on distributed data applications. We use invoker's-rights architecture to ensure the integrity of distributed data while leveraging the same code repository. This architecture enables you to build powerful distributed applications.

Both implementation strategies share two common principles. Control resides in the data repository schemas to follow a common naming pattern, and control resides in the code repository to keep a single copy of application programs. The example you'll focus on is the distributed solution, because definer's-right is typically used for striping approaches.

Invoker's-rights architecture enables a complete distributed approach if you are unable to implement Oracle distributed systems because of distance, resources, or throughput. This is an inexpensive tool to accomplish distributed computing with the Oracle database.

Invoker's-rights architecture enables a single code repository to be shared across multiple data sets in the same database or in distributed databases. The following illustrates the invoker's-rights architecture:

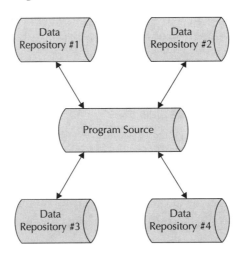

In the illustration, you have four data repositories that use a single code repository. The example code simplifies this architecture by using only one data repository, which will be the MYAPP schema. The code repository is the PLSQL schema.

The `create_invoker_package.sql` script builds a `data_store` sample table, which is a small package that enables a user to insert data into the target `data_store` table. You should run the following code in the PLSQL schema:

**-- Available online as part of create_striped_view2.sql.**

```
-- Create local table.
CREATE TABLE data_store
( data_id        NUMBER
, data_text      VARCHAR2(20 CHAR));

-- Create the data management package.
CREATE OR REPLACE PACKAGE data_management
AUTHID CURRENT_USER AS

  -- Define the insert_data procedure.
  PROCEDURE insert_data
  ( data_id      NUMBER
  , data_text    VARCHAR2);

END data_management;
/

-- Create the data management package body.
CREATE OR REPLACE PACKAGE BODY data_management AS

  -- Implement the insert_data procedure.
  PROCEDURE insert_data
  ( data_id      NUMBER
  , data_text    VARCHAR2) IS

  BEGIN

    -- Insert into the table.
    INSERT
    INTO      data_store
    VALUES
    ( data_id
    , data_text );

  END insert_data;

END data_management;
/

GRANT EXECUTE ON data_management TO MYAPP;
/
```

The script does the following:

- It drops and creates a local `data_store` table.

- It defines a `data_management` package that determines a single `insert_data` procedure.

- It defines a `data_management` package body that implements a single `insert_data` procedure.

- It grants execute on the `data_management` package to the `MYAPP` schema.

You have completed the setup of the code repository. Now you'll set up the data repository. Two or three steps can be used to set up the data repository. They are

1. Creating a synonym to point to the `PLSQL.DATA_MANAGEMENT` package

2. Creating a local table that uses the same name as the invoker's-rights schema or a different name

3. Building a view that matches the name of the target data table in the invoker's-rights schema if the table is implemented with a different name

You can use the following `create_invoker_data_store.sql` script to configure the `MYAPP` data store schema. You should run this now in your `MYAPP` schema:

**-- Available online as part of create_invoker_data_store.sql.**

```
CREATE SYNONYM data_management FOR plsql.data_management;

-- Create local table.
CREATE TABLE myapp_data_store
( data_id        NUMBER
, data_text      VARCHAR2(20 CHAR));

-- Create a local view that mirrors the code repository.
CREATE OR REPLACE VIEW data_store AS
SELECT    *
FROM      myapp_data_store;

-- Call the invoker's-right stored package.
EXECUTE data_management.insert_data(1,'One');
```

```
-- Use SQL*Plus to format the output.
COL data_text FORMAT A20

-- Query the local MYAPP_DATA_STORE table.
SELECT    data_id
,         data_text
FROM      myapp_data_store;
```

The script does the following:

- ■ It drops and creates a local synonym to the plsql.data_management package.

- ■ It defines a local myapp_data_store table, which differs from the name used in the invoker's-rights schema. This implementation requires a data_store view that matches the table implementation in the PLSQL schema.

- ■ It then executes the plsql.data_management.insert_data procedure. This inserts a row in the CURRENT_USER object myapp_data_store through the local data_store view.

- ■ It formats the myapp_data_store.data_text column and then queries the local table.

You should return the following output from the query:

```
  DATA_ID DATA_TEXT
---------- --------------------
        1 One
```

You have now completed the invoker's-right architecture. There are clearly some differences in organizing data. You'll now compare and contrast these two architectures.

# Comparing and Contrasting Implementation Strategies

The following summarizes definer's-rights and invoker's-rights architectures. You will review why one excels against the other in different scenarios. You should clearly see when and why you should use one over the other and in which scenarios.

## Definer's-Rights

The definer's-rights pattern ensures you control access to all inserts, updates, and deletes against the data through your stored PL/SQL programs. You achieve this by building or licensing application metadata and security programs, like those found in ERP/CRM applications. Many ERP/CRM solutions use row-by-row database triggers to enforce user privileges. This is expensive because it increases the time to complete transactions. It is also a tightly coupled solution from an Object-Oriented Analysis and Design (OOAD) perspective.

The triggers also function based on user-level security maintained in a set of application-tier metadata. Triggers may be in the centralized repository or in subsystem repositories. While more complex, positioning the data in distributed subsystems with grants to a code repository system is an alternative.

The data in definer's-rights architecture is sliced into pieces like salami. Each user only sees a slice of the whole. This is the most common approach. The natural problem that occurs is when the user needs to expand their slice of data.

Unless there is a robust application that supports functional application security and enables dynamically shifting views of data, the definer's-rights architecture is limited and hard to change. This is true because all permissions are centralized in the schema that controls the data and stored PL/SQL programming units.

## Invoker's-Rights

The invoker's-rights pattern ensures you control access to all inserts, updates, and deletes against the data through your stored PL/SQL programs. You achieve this by building all your code into a single repository. Any triggers can be specific to subordinate business units and managed on local instances or in external schemas.

The data in invoker's-rights architecture is like a buffet. Each subsystem that uses the code is left to work out its own implementation structure. This is a more loosely coupled approach to development, but has risks.

As you may have noticed, local tables are typically different names than the centralized table. This means that there can be a reconciliation of data in nonpeak operational hours. This provides you with some throughput advantages. At least it does if you have time in the evening batch processing window to consolidate data.

# Summary

You should consider implementing invoker's-rights architecture when you need to distribute data at a low cost and increase throughput, or when you need to provide implementation flexibility to groups within your organization. Alternatively, if you implement full ERP/CRM suites and can afford the tools, licenses, and overhead, you should consider implementing definer's-rights architecture.

# CHAPTER
# 5

## Extending PL/SQL
## with Java Libraries

xtending stored programs with Java is a very popular solution. PL/SQL is essential to the process of stored Java class libraries. PL/SQL wraps access to the Java class libraries, which means PL/SQL becomes the gate through which data moves to and from Java stored objects.

This chapter stands independent of others in the book since all its content works in currently supported versions of the Oracle database. We'll be covering the following topics:

- Java architecture in Oracle
- Oracle JDBC connection types
    - Client-side driver, or JDBC thin driver
    - Oracle call interface driver, or middle-tier thick driver
    - Oracle server-side internal driver, or server-tier thick driver
- Building Java class libraries in Oracle
    - Building internal server Java functions
    - Building internal server Java procedures
    - Building internal server Java objects
    - Troubleshooting Java class library build, load, drop, and use
- Mapping Oracle types

This chapter introduces you to the big picture of the Oracle Java architecture. After explaining the architecture, you'll see how to develop and extend Java components as application programming components.

### Why Would I Use This?
We'll use PL/SQL to interface between stored Java class libraries and other PL/SQL stored and anonymous block programs. We'll also map native and user-defined data types between Oracle and Java to write effective interfaces and support external Java Server Pages (JSPs).

# Java Architecture in Oracle

The Oracle 9*i* and 10*g* databases provide a robust architecture for developing server-side or internal Java programming components. Java components are Object-Oriented (OO) structures that fit naturally into Oracle's Object-Relational model. The component architecture is a library stack that contains

■ Platform-dependent operating systems, like UNIX, LINUX, and Microsoft Windows

■ Platform-dependent Oracle database management files and libraries

■ Oracle database instance Java Virtual Machine, which is platform independent

■ Java core class libraries, which are ported to various platforms

■ Oracle-supported Java Application Programming Interfaces (APIs), like SQLJ, JDBC, and JNDI

■ Oracle PL/SQL stored objects, which provide an interface between SQL and PL/SQL programs, as well as server-side Java classes

The Oracle and Java libraries store and manage application programs like a ubiquitous file system. Together they mask the structures and limitations of operating systems. Oracle libraries make storing, retrieving, and recovering files a standard process across many diverse platforms. The Java Virtual Machine (JVM) provides a standard environment where you can build well-documented OO programs. Oracle PL/SQL enables the development of wrapper packages to access Java libraries from other PL/SQL stored objects and SQL.

The architecture of the Oracle JVM is shown in the following illustration:

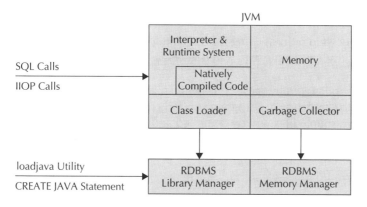

Oracle JVM uses two types of namespaces, the long name and short name. The long name is exactly as the class is named in Java. You can call stored Java programs by their native namespace. While the chapter examples are short and not placed into packages, you'll most likely put your Java programs into packages. The namespace for Java stored code includes the entire package hierarchy. When this is larger than 30 characters, Oracle uses a hashed namespace in the data dictionary views. Use the DBMS_JAVA package and LONGNAME function to get the full namespace. You can also use the DBMS_JAVA package and SHORTNAME function to get the short name.

The JVM enjoys automated storage management, which means you do not need to allocate and free memory explicitly. Also, Java is a strongly typed programming language like PL/SQL. The combination of strong typing and a garbage collector to manage memory provides a scalable and simplified environment like the PL/SQL runtime engine.

Both Java and PL/SQL are interpreted languages and they require Just-In-Time (JIT) compilation. Oracle 9*i* introduces native compilation for PL/SQL and Java programs. Native compilation enables Ahead-of-Time compilation. It changes PL/SQL and Java byte code into machine-executable programming code.

Native compilation speeds execution by eliminating JIT compilation delay. Unfortunately, it takes time to compile the interpreted languages programs into machine code. If you rarely change your code, the trade-off may be worth using native compilation.

There are three ways to put Oracle into the database instance. Your options are

1. A two-step process: (a) compiling the Java source file, <file_name> .java, with the javac executable to generate a Java byte code program, and (b) using the Oracle loadjava utility to put the file into the database instance.

2. A one-step process using the loadjava utility to compile and put the Java class file into the database instance.

3. A one-step process using Data Definition Language to build and compile the Java source file as a stored Java class.

There are occasionally parser problems in Oracle 9*i* R1 and using DDL commands to build the Java program can fail. These are fixed in 9*i* R2 and later versions. Java source files will be compiled and then loaded into the database instance with the loadjava utility in all examples.

**TIP**
*If you opt to use the one-step* loadjava *utility, please note you may encounter an ORA-29533 error for attempting to overwrite the file. The replace option in the* loadjava *utility does not work in some releases. Use* dropjava *with the* -user *option and the* <file_name>.class *before rerunning the* loadjava *utility.*

This chapter assumes you have a basic familiarity with Java. Basic familiarity means that you can compile and run Java programs. Sample command-line instructions are provided in the chapter examples, but Appendix D provides a basic tutorial as well as Java environment configuration instructions.

Java stored program units are like traditional PL/SQL program units. They are called with either definer's-rights or invoker's-rights access from a single session. There are differences between how Java works externally and internally within the Oracle database instance. The differences are qualified in the following:

- Execution control differs substantially from native Java. External to the Oracle instance, Java applications contain a main() method, which is invoked to run the program. Java programs internal to the instance do not contain a main() method. Java programs stored in an Oracle instance have two types of behaviors. They are

  - Java stored programs that serve as packages with functions and procedures are not instantiable classes. All variables and methods for these programs must be static, which means they act as class methods. This fixes their scope as mirrors of PL/SQL packages with functions and procedures. The coding syntax changes as does their accessibility to external Java applications.

  - Java stored programs that serve as object type body implementations can be instantiable classes. Variables and methods may be static and nonstatic. Unlike external Java classes, they cannot have overriding constructors, only a single default constructor. They are instantiated by implementing the SQLData interface defined in the JDBC2 API, and instantiation involves mapping data types between PL/SQL and Java.

- Java classes are stored in clear text, Java byte code, and compressed Java archives externally to the Oracle database instance. Oracle manages these as source, class, and resource Java objects. Schemas contain a JAVA$OPTIONS table, which can be accessed and configured by the DBMS_JAVA package, the SET_COMPILER_OPTION and RESET_COMPILER_OPTION procedures, or the GET_COMPILER_OPTION function.

- User interfaces are not supported for internal Java class files. This means there's no way to directly display to console or native sound device(s). Sound files can be manipulated from within Oracle, but they do not have access to the native sound devices. Oracle 10g differs slightly from Oracle 9i because it uses Java SDK 1.4.x, which supports Headless AWT.

- Internal Oracle Java class names are maintained in two forms. One is the short form that supports standard schema database objects and is limited to 30 characters. When a fully qualified package and class name exceeds the limit, Oracle automatically creates a hashed name as the class short name and stores the long name elsewhere.

- The standard Java `Class.forName()` isn't supported for internal Oracle Java classes. Oracle 9i and Oracle 10g support the use of multiple resolvers, which locate classes. You can get unexpected results from a search expecting one resolver that runs another.

- Operating resources are restricted. You can only alter these as the privileged user `SYSDBA`. Use the `DBMS_JAVA` package and `GRANT_PERMISSION` procedure to open operating resources like file IO.

- Java threading works differently for Oracle internal Java classes. The Oracle JVM uses a nonpreemptive threading model. This means that all threads run in a single operating system thread and the Oracle JVM merely switches contexts between threads. Switching context means that the Oracle JVM spawns one thread for a time slice and then another, in a round-robin fashion, until all threads complete.

**NOTE**
*The version of Oracle that you're using does dictate which version of the Java Software Development Kit you should use. For simplification, all examples were done using Java SDK 1.3.x, supported in Oracle 9i. They also work in Java SDK 1.4.x.*

The Oracle Java Developer's Guide lists two key error codes, but there are a number of others. Rather than list these error codes, we've included a troubleshooting section later in the chapter titled "Troubleshooting Java Class Library Build, Load, Drop, and Use."

Now that you've reviewed the key components of the Oracle Java architecture, in the next section we'll introduce you to the various JDBC drivers.

# Oracle JDBC Connection Types

Oracle implements the Java Database Connection (JDBC) in three ways in order to meet three different needs. These are the thin, thick, and default connections. Respectively, they map to the client-side driver, the call interface driver (or middle-tier driver), and the server-side (or internal) driver. In the next sections, you'll examine all three.

## The Client-Side Driver, or JDBC Thin Driver

The Oracle thin connection is probably the most used by Java applications, Java Server Pages (JSPs), and Enterprise Java Beans (EJBs). It provides many advantages to building code without directly accessing Oracle library files.

The advantages of the Oracle JDBC thin driver are numerous for external Java applications because it requires the least setup and configuration. First though, make sure your Java programming environment has access to the standard Java library and the Oracle JDBC library. You can set this up by configuring your CLASSPATH environment variable, which should include the Oracle `classes12` `.zip` Java archive file. You can find details about how to set these in Appendix D at the back of the book.

Unfortunately, you can't use the Oracle thin JDBC driver unless you've configured and started your database listener. You'll likewise need to provide the host name, listener port number, database name, and your user ID and password each time you spawn a connection to the database instance.

### Why Would I Use This?

You need to know what your options are when connecting Java programs to the Oracle database. When you know how they work, you're in a better position to select the correct JDBC driver to then connect your programs to the Oracle instance.

We find Java a very useful extension to the Oracle programming stack. Unfortunately, we also find it is critical to understand the nuances of your choices before matching a technology to a problem. We believe if you understand your Java options, you will make better choices of how to leverage Java in your applications.

**TIP**
*The Oracle client-side or thin driver returns a rather meaningless error message if the host name, listener port number, or database name is incorrect. In fact, it will report a 17002 error. This error is found in Oracle's implementation of the JDBC API. Appendix D demonstrates a clean mechanism to audit for the error.*

The uses of the Oracle JDBC thin driver are limited to external Java applications, JSPs, and EJBs. A multithreaded Java servlet is an example of a Java application that would implement an Oracle JDBC thin driver file. Oracle JDBC thin connections can be optimistic or pessimistic connections.

Optimistic connections are temporary connections transmitted using the Hypertext Transfer Protocol (HTTP), which are limited to a 15-second pipelined TCP socket connection. These are ideal for JSPs but resource-expensive because they must establish a connection for each communication.

Pessimistic connections are typically transmitted using a state-aware TCP socket that's open through the duration of the connection. Pessimistic connections are used by multithreaded Java servlets to create and maintain database connection pools. Java servlets can be implemented in two-tier or n-tier solutions, and avoid resource-expensive short-lived connections and disconnections across HTTP.

# The Oracle Call Interface Driver, or Middle-Tier Thick Driver

The Oracle call interface (OCI) driver is more tightly coupled with the Oracle C/C++ libraries than the Oracle JDBC thin driver. If you use the Oracle JDBC call interface (or middle-tier thick) driver, you'll need to ensure that the `PATH`, `CLASSPATH`, and `LD_LIBRARY_PATH` environment variables map to Oracle libraries. The libraries need to be on the same physical platform or map through a storage area network (SAN), like NFS in UNIX.

The OCI driver can maintain persistent connection pools through Java servlets. The performance of the OCI driver is often slower than the Oracle JDBC thin driver. As a rule, you'll have an easier configuration if you use the Oracle JDBC thin driver in your servlet. Also, you won't suffer performance degradation if you maintain active connection pools in your Java servlet.

## The Oracle Server-Side Internal Driver, or Server-Tier Thick Driver

The Oracle server-side internal driver is likewise tightly coupled with, and dependent on, the Oracle C/C++ libraries. Unfortunately, there's no other choice available to build Java programs as stored objects in the Oracle database.

The Oracle server-side internal driver uses the `defaultConnection()` method of the Connection class to connect to the database. This poses a bit of a testing problem if you want to test the Java program externally. It's best if you test the Java code in your development instance and avoid building a work-around.

Unlike the OCI driver, the server-side internal drive is faster than the Oracle JDBC thin driver. As you read the chapter and examine the code, you'll find that embedding Java in the Oracle database requires a few tricks and techniques.

The next section examines how to build and troubleshoot class libraries and instantiable Java stored objects.

# Building Java Class Libraries in Oracle

When you choose to build Java class libraries, you have two deployment choices. You can build call-interface driven (middle-tier) or server-side Java class libraries.

Call-interface libraries act like server-side includes to your Apache server. They must be replicated to all nodes of your Apache server and are managed within the structure of your web server load-balancing tool. These components act like external programs that call into the Oracle server and are better treated in Enterprise Java books.

### Why Would I Use This?

You need to know when a Java class belongs as an internal or external library. We find Java libraries deployed internally in the database have well-defined but narrow uses. Likewise, we find external libraries to be powerful components but less convenient than locally stored objects. You will need to understand these two technologies to make good deployment choices.

**NOTE**
*While call-interface driver or middle-tier Java class libraries are not directly covered, they do require direct reference in their path to the Oracle OCI libraries. The OCI libraries are in the Oracle Application Server but not on other web servers.*

Server-side Java class libraries are stored objects within the Oracle JVM, which is a subcomponent of the Oracle database. Server-side Java class libraries are the core theme of this chapter. In the next two sections, you'll learn how to build internal server Java functions and procedures.

**NOTE**
*If you're unfamiliar with configuring and testing a Java JDBC connection, please check Appendix D for instructions.*

Java programming ranges from simple to complex, but these examples should be straightforward. You have two core executables to run Java programs, which you'll use in the examples. They are

- **javac**   Compiles your text file Java programs into Java byte code
- **java**   Runs your compiled Java byte code programs

The file-naming convention in Java is case-sensitive so you should ensure you name files consistent with the web-based code example files. If you attempt to compile a Java file when the file name and class name are different, you'll receive an error. Also, the file extension for Java programs is a lowercase `.java`.

You'll now build a simple `HelloWorld1.java` file to make sure the balance of the examples works. If you're working in Microsoft Windows, please open a Command Prompt Window. If you're working in UNIX, please use a terminal window. The following is the code for `HelloWorld.java`:

`-- Available online as part of HelloWorld1.java file.`

```
// Class definition.
public class HelloWorld1
{
   // -------------------------------------------/
```

```
  // Static main to print Hello World.
  public static void main(String args[])
  {
    // Print the message to console.
    System.out.println("Hello World.");

  } // End of static main.

  // -------------------------------------------/

} // End of HelloWorld1 class.
```

Java text files are compiled by the following syntax:

`javac HelloWorld1.java`

Successful compilation does not return anything to the console. The lack of any message is a good thing. The way to verify whether or not you have a Java byte code file is to run the Microsoft Windows directory (**dir**) command or UNIX list (**ls**) command for files matching `HelloWorld1.*` in the present working directory. You should see two files displayed to the console:

`HelloWorld1.java`
`HelloWorld1.class`

After building the Java byte code compiled program, you can test its execution by doing the following:

`java HelloWorld1`

**NOTE**
*You do not provide the .class extension when running Java programs because it is assumed. Appending `.class` to the file name will raise the following exception: java.lang.NoClassDefFoundError: HelloWorld1/class.*

**TIP**
*You can also raise the java.lang .NoClassDefFoundError: HelloWorld1/class error if you do not have your present working directory in your PATH and CLASSPATH environment variables.*

You'll receive the following results:

```
Hello World.
```

The next section covers how you build server-side or internal server Java programming units. You'll learn how to build Java class files to support stored functions and procedures and how to wrap their existence in PL/SQL packages. The following two sections are sequential and the second section assumes you have worked through the first.

## Building Internal Server Java Functions

You build an internal server Java function by building a Java class file that will use the server-side internal or JDBC thick connection. As qualified earlier in the chapter, the JDBC thick connection depends on Oracle Call Interface (OCI) libraries. All OCI libraries are directly accessible from your Java class file when you've loaded it into the Oracle JVM.

Java internal or server-side class files are built and accessed by a three-step process. You use Java to build and compile the class file. Then, you use the Oracle `loadjava` utility to load the compiled class file into the server. Once built and loaded into the server, you build a PL/SQL wrapper to the Java class library.

The following assumes you have the correct `CLASSPATH` and `PATH` to use Java. If you are unable to compile or test the Java programs, it's possible your environment is configured incorrectly. As mentioned earlier, you should use Appendix D to ensure you have correctly configured your environment.

The example builds a Java class library with two methods. These methods are overloaded, which means they have different signatures or formal parameter lists. They each return a variable length character array or Java string. Both of the

### Why Would I Use This?

We use internal server Java functions for the same reasons we write PL/SQL functions, which is to process and return a result that does not involve Data Manipulation Language (DML) commands. Java functions have the ability to mirror PL/SQL functions and call external libraries to leverage Java Archive Repository (JAR) files.

This feature is very effective when we have an application written in Java and want to enable the development team to write their server-side code in the same language. We have found that enabling them to stay in Java minimizes errors.

overloaded methods will map to two overloaded PL/SQL functions that return
VARCHAR2 native Oracle data types. The code for `HelloWorld2.java` follows:

**-- Available online as part of HelloWorld2.java file.**

```java
// Oracle class imports.
import oracle.jdbc.driver.*;

// Class definition.
public class HelloWorld2
{
  // -----------------------------------------/

  // The Hello method.
  public static String hello()
  {
    // Call overloaded method with a null String.
    return "Hello World.";
  } // End of hello() method.

  // -----------------------------------------/

  // The hello method.
  public static String hello(String name)
  {
    // Call overloaded method with a null String.
    return "Hello " + name + ".";

  } // End of hello() method.

  // -----------------------------------------/

  // Static main to test instance outside of Oracle.
  public static void main(String args[])
  {
    // Print the return message to console.
    System.out.println(HelloWorld2.hello());

    // Print the return message to console.
    System.out.println(HelloWorld2.hello("Larry"));

  } // End of static main.

  // -----------------------------------------/

} // End of HelloWorld2 class.
```

The program does the following:

- It defines a single class with two `Hello()` class methods. The methods are overloaded, which means they have different signatures or formal parameter lists. They are both static methods because only static methods can be referenced by a PL/SQL wrapper package. Static methods do not require an instance of the class to run. They function much like a function in C or a PL/SQL stored package function.

- It defines a `main()` method, which you can use to test the program before loading it into the Oracle database instance. The `main()` method will be ignored when the class file is loaded into the Oracle instance. In the main method, both static `Hello()` and `Hello(String name)` methods are called and the result passed as an actual parameter to the console.

As a rule, you want to remove testing components like the `main()` method before loading them into the database. If they are left, they have no effect on the stored Java class library.

Use the following syntax to test the program with the Java utility:

```
java HelloWorld2
```

The following output will be displayed to the console:

```
Hello World.
Hello Larry.
```

If you have not built the `PLSQL` schema, please run the `create_user.sql` script now. When you have the `PLSQL` schema built, compile it with the `javac` utility, as covered earlier in the chapter. Once compiled you'll load it into the Oracle JVM with the `loadjava` utility as follows:

```
loadjava -r -f -o -user plsql/plsql HelloWorld2.class
```

**NOTE**
*On the Microsoft platform, you may get a message that states "The procedure entry point kpuhhalo could not be located in the dynamic link library OCI.dll." If you receive this error, it means you don't have %ORACLE_HOME\bin% in your PATH environment variable.*

The `loadjava` utility command loads the Java `HelloWorld2` class file into the Oracle JVM under the `PLSQL` schema. After loading the Java class file into the database, you'll need to build a PL/SQL wrapper to use it. The following `HelloWorld2.sql` script builds the package and package body as a wrapper to the Java class library:

-- Available online as part of **HelloWorld2.sql** file.

```
-- Create a PL/SQL wrapper package to a Java class file.
CREATE OR REPLACE PACKAGE hello_world2 AS

  -- Define a null argument function.
  FUNCTION hello
  RETURN VARCHAR2;

  -- Define a one argument function.
  FUNCTION hello
  ( who  VARCHAR2 )
  RETURN VARCHAR2;


END hello_world2;
/

-- Create a PL/SQL wrapper package to a Java class file.
CREATE OR REPLACE PACKAGE BODY hello_world2 AS

  -- Define a null argument function.
  FUNCTION hello
  RETURN VARCHAR2 IS
  LANGUAGE JAVA
  NAME 'HelloWorld2.Hello() return String';

  -- Define a null argument function.
  FUNCTION hello
  ( who  VARCHAR2 )
  RETURN VARCHAR2 IS
  LANGUAGE JAVA
  NAME 'HelloWorld2.Hello(java.lang.String) return String';

END hello_world2;
/
```

The script does the following:

- It creates a package with two overloaded `Hello` functions that return `VARCHAR2` data types. One is a null argument signature and the other has one formal parameter.

- It creates a package body with two overloaded `Hello` functions that implement a stored Java class file. The PL/SQL `NAME` keyword provides a reference to the stored Java class file and the return value. You must fully qualify formal parameters by using the complete package path to the defined class, like the `java.lang.String` reference. The return type can be shortened to String because Oracle understands it as the external data type.

You can verify all components are present to test by querying the `user_objects` view with the following:

-- **Available online as part of HelloWorld2.sql file.**

```
SELECT    object_name
,         object_type
,         status
FROM      user_objects
WHERE     object_name IN ('HelloWorld2','HELLO_WORLD2');
```

The script should output the following results:

-- **This output is generated from the online HelloWorld2.sql file.**

| OBJECT_NAME | OBJECT_TYPE | STATUS |
|---|---|---|
| HELLO_WORLD2 | PACKAGE | VALID |
| HELLO_WORLD2 | PACKAGE BODY | VALID |
| HelloWorld2 | JAVA CLASS | VALID |

If you did not get the same output, you'll need to see what step you may have skipped. Please do that before attempting to proceed. If you did get the same output, you can now test the Java class library in SQL and PL/SQL. You can test it in SQL with a query or in PL/SQL with the `DBMS_OUTPUT.PUT_LINE` statement. The following illustrates a SQL query of the wrapper, which uses the internal Java class file:

```
SELECT    hello_world2.hello('Paul McCartney')
FROM      dual;
```

The query will return the following results:

```
HELLO_WORLD2.HELLO('PAULMCCARTNEY')
-----------------------------------
Hello Paul McCartney.
```

You have now covered how to build Oracle database instance-stored Java class files that map methods to functions. The next section will examine how you build components to deliver procedure behavior.

# Building Internal Server Java Procedures

Building a procedure will follow very similar rules to building functions. PL/SQL procedures have an IN or IN and OUT mode. However, you cannot use an IN and OUT mode in PL/SQL when wrapping a Java method. If you attempt to define a package body with a procedure using IN and OUT modes, it will raise the following exception:

```
PLS-00235: the external type is not appropriate for the parameter
```

You'll now build an IN mode procedure as a wrapper to a Java class method. When you use Java methods in the context of a procedure, you return a void type from the Java method.

## Why Would I Use This?

We use internal server Java procedures for the same reasons we write PL/SQL procedures, which is to process result sets that may or may not return a result and which involve Data Manipulation Language (DML) commands. Java procedures have the ability to mirror PL/SQL procedures and call external libraries to leverage Java Archive Repository (JAR) files.

This feature is very effective when we have an application written in Java and want to enable the development team to write their server-side code in the same language. We have found that enabling them to stay in Java minimizes errors.

The following Java source file supports an IN mode PL/SQL procedure:

-- Available online as part of HelloWorld3.java file.

```java
// Oracle class imports.
import java.sql.*;
import oracle.jdbc.driver.*;

// Class definition.
public class HelloWorld3
{
  // Define the doDML() method.
  public static void doDML(String statement
                          ,String name) throws SQLException
  {
    // Define a connection for Oracle.
    Connection conn = new OracleDriver().defaultConnection();

    // Define and initialize a prepared statement.
    PreparedStatement ps = conn.prepareStatement(statement);

    // Assign the cursor return.
    ps.setString(1,name);
    ps.execute();

  } // End of the doDML() method.

  // -------------------------------------------/

  // Define the doDQL() method.
  public static String doDQL(String statement) throws SQLException
  {
    // Define and initialize a local return variable.
    String result = new String();

    // Define a connection for Oracle.
    Connection conn = new OracleDriver().defaultConnection();

    // Define and initialize a prepared statement.
    PreparedStatement ps = conn.prepareStatement(statement);

    // Execute a query.
    ResultSet rs = ps.executeQuery();
```

```
    // Use a while-loop even though only one row is returned.
    while (rs.next())
    {
      // Assign the cursor return.
      result = rs.getString(1);
    }

    // Return the user name.
    return result;

  } // End of the doDQL() method.

} // End of HelloWorld3 class.
```

The program does the following:

■ It defines a single class with two static methods. One method returns a void and the other returns a String, which maps to a VARCHAR2 data type. The methods do the following:

■ The myDML() method has a signature with two formal parameters. Both parameters are String data types. One takes the SQL statement and the second sends the data to be inserted. It creates a Connection and PreparedStatement with the first formal parameter. Then, it maps the second parameter to the SQL statement and executes the statement. This is the pattern for DML statements.

■ The myDQL() method has a signature with one formal parameter, which is the SQL query submitted as an actual parameter. It creates a Connection and PreparedStatement with the formal parameter. It returns a String, which is the return value for the last row fetched in the while-loop.

There is no main() method in the HelloWorld3.java class file. Including a main() method to test the program externally to the database would require changing the connection to a client-side or OCI driver. You can refer to Appendix D if you wish to build a test externally to the database instance.

Most likely, you have built the PLSQL schema, but if not, you should run the create_user.sql script now. When you have the PLSQL schema built, compile it with the javac utility as covered earlier in the chapter. Once compiled, you'll load it into the Oracle JVM with the loadjava utility using the following:

```
loadjava -r -f -o -user plsql/plsql HelloWorld2.class
```

The `loadjava` utility command loads the Java `HelloWorld3` class file into the Oracle JVM under the `PLSQL` schema. After loading the Java class file into the database, you'll need to build a `mytable` table and PL/SQL wrapper to use it.

The `mytable` table is built by using the following command:

**-- Available online as part of HelloWorld3.sql file.**

```
CREATE TABLE mytable (character VARCHAR2(100));
```

The following `HelloWorld3.sql` script builds the package and package body as a wrapper to the Java class library:

**-- Available online as part of HelloWorld3.sql file.**

```
-- Create a PL/SQL wrapper package to a Java class file.
CREATE OR REPLACE PACKAGE hello_world3 AS

  -- Define a single argument procedure.
  PROCEDURE doDML
  ( dml    VARCHAR2
  , input VARCHAR2 );

  -- Define a single argument function.
  FUNCTION doDQL
  ( dql    VARCHAR2 )
  RETURN  VARCHAR2;


END hello_world3;
/

-- Create a PL/SQL wrapper package to a Java class file.
CREATE OR REPLACE PACKAGE BODY hello_world3 AS

  -- Define a single argument procedure.
  PROCEDURE doDML
  ( dml    VARCHAR2
  , input VARCHAR2 ) IS
  LANGUAGE JAVA
  NAME 'HelloWorld3.doDML(java.lang.String,java.lang.String)';

  -- Define a single argument function.
  FUNCTION doDQL
  ( dql    VARCHAR2 )
  RETURN  VARCHAR2 IS
```

```
  LANGUAGE JAVA
  NAME 'HelloWorld3.doDQL(java.lang.String) return String';

END hello_world3;
/
```

The script does the following:

- It creates a package with one procedure and one function, which do the following:

  - The doDML procedure takes two formal parameters that are VARCHAR2 data types.

  - The doDQL function takes one formal parameter that is a VARCHAR2 and returns a VARCHAR2 data type.

- It creates a package body with the procedure and function mapped to Java class files and methods. The PL/SQL NAME keyword provides a reference to the stored Java class file and the return value. You must fully qualify formal parameters by using the complete package path to the defined class, like the java.lang.String reference.

You can verify that all components are present to test by querying the user_objects view with the following:

-- **Available online as part of HelloWorld3.sql file.**

```
SELECT    object_name
,         object_type
,         status
FROM      user_objects
WHERE     object_name IN ('HelloWorld3','HELLO_WORLD3');
```

The script should output the following results:

-- **This output is generated from the online HelloWorld3.sql file.**

```
OBJECT_NAME                     OBJECT_TYPE   STATUS
------------------------------- ------------- -------
HELLO_WORLD3                    PACKAGE       VALID
HELLO_WORLD3                    PACKAGE BODY  VALID
HelloWorld3                     JAVA CLASS    VALID
```

If you did not get the same output, you'll need to see what step you may have skipped. Please do this before attempting to proceed. If you did get the same output, you can now test the Java class library in SQL and PL/SQL. You can test it in SQL with a query or in PL/SQL with the `DBMS_OUTPUT.PUT_LINE` statement. The following illustrates a SQL query of the wrapper, which uses the internal Java class file:

```
SELECT    hello_world3.doDQL('SELECT character FROM mytable')
FROM      dual;
```

The query returns the following results:

```
HELLO_WORLD3.DODQL('SELECTCHARACTERFROMMYTABLE')
-----------------------------------
Bobby McGee
```

You've now covered how to build Oracle database instance-stored Java class files that map a Java method to a PL/SQL procedure. The next section discusses how to build real Java objects wrapped by PL/SQL object types.

# Building Internal Server Java Objects

The Java programming language is Object-Oriented (OO). In the previous examples, Java stored objects were used as static functions. The potential to use Java to accomplish significant OO computing models lies in the Oracle object features introduced in Oracle 9*i* Release 2. Beginning with that release, you can construct instances of object types and use them as objects. After you develop an understanding of

## Why Would I Use This?

We use internal server Java objects for the same reasons you use PL/SQL objects. Using Java as instantiable and threaded objects is where the value of using stored Java objects adds value once you understand how to use the `SQLData` interface. Java internal server objects have the ability to indirectly instantiate objects. The internal server Java objects are awkward to use for Java developers because they use external or indirect interfaces to effect communication.

This section illustrates how the `SQLData` interface is used and explains the concepts supporting it. We believe Java developers will find this feature useful but tricky to use at first. This section should help you jump-start your use of the feature.

implementing stored Java objects in this section, you can see how PL/SQL objects work in Chapter 6.

Server-side stored Java programs support full runtime object behaviors starting with Oracle 9*i*, as noted earlier. This means you can now design, develop, and implement natural Java applications beneath PL/SQL object type wrappers. These Java classes can have instance methods, which mean nonstatic methods. You may also use static methods for libraries.

The balance of the differences covered earlier in the chapter still applies. You build Java object libraries by writing the Java class file and SQL object type definition. Object type bodies are not defined when the object type implementation is written in a stored Java object.

The substantial difference between external Java and server internal Java objects is the way you construct an instance of the class. You do not directly instantiate the class file and cannot use overriding constructors in the Java class file. The `SQLData` interface is the key to instantiating stored Java objects. It enables instantiating the Java class by passing back and forth the parameter values. This enables a class to return a reference to a copy or instance of the class.

**TIP**
*There's no way to instantiate directly a default constructor when using a stored Java object class. You also cannot use overriding constructors. The* `SQLData` *interface allows you to pass values to an instantiated class based on known class scope instance variables. Instance variables are not static variables. These limits are imposed by the implementation of the* `SQLData` *interface.*

Implementing the `SQLData` interface is done by providing a variable definition and three concrete methods in your Java class file. The following are the components:

- A `String` data type named `sql_type`.

- A `getSQLTypeName()` method that returns a `String` data type.

- A `readSQL()` method that takes two formal parameters and returns a `void`. One formal parameter is a `SQLInput` that contains a stream. The other is a string that contains a data type name.

- A `writeSQL()` method that takes one formal parameter, which is a `SQLOutput` that contains a stream.

Details on implementing runtime Java classes will be illustrated in the following examples. The `HelloWorld4` Java class file is designed to work as an instantiable Java stored object type body. The source code for the class is:

-- **Available online as part of HelloWorld4.java file.**

```java
// Oracle class imports.
import java.sql.*;
import java.io.*;
import oracle.sql.*;
import oracle.jdbc.*;
import oracle.jdbc.oracore.*;

// Class definition.
public class HelloWorld4 implements SQLData
{
  // Define and initialize a private class name variable.
  private String className = new String("HelloWorld4.class");

  // Define a formal parameter signature variable.
  private String instanceName;

  // Define a private schema qualified name value.
  private String qualifiedName;

  // Define a class instance variable to support SQLData Interface.
  private String sql_type;

  // -------------------------------------------/

  // Define default constructor.
  public HelloWorld4()
  {
    // Define local String variables.
    String user = new String();

    // Use a try-catch block because of SQL statement.
    try
    {
      // Call a method of the inner class.

      user = getUserName();

    }
    catch (Exception e) {}
```

```java
  // Set the class instance variable.
  qualifiedName = user + "." + className;

} // End of default constructor.

// ------------------------------------------/

// Define a method to return a qualified name.
public String getQualifiedName() throws SQLException
{
  // Define and initialize a return variable.
  return this.qualifiedName + "." + instanceName;

} // End of getQualifiedName() method.

// ------------------------------------------/

// Define a method to return the database object name.
public String getSQLTypeName() throws SQLException
{
  // Returns the UDT map value or database object name.
  return sql_type;

} // End of getSQLTypeName() method.

// ------------------------------------------/

// Define getUserName() method to query the instance.
public String getUserName() throws SQLException
{
  // Define and initialize a local return variable.
  String userName = new String();

  // Define and initialize a query statement.
  String getDatabaseSQL = "SELECT user FROM dual";

  // Define a connection for Oracle.
  Connection conn = new OracleDriver().defaultConnection();

  // Define and initialize a prepared statement.
  PreparedStatement ps = conn.prepareStatement(getDatabaseSQL);

  // Execute a query.
  ResultSet rs = ps.executeQuery();
```

```
   // Use a while-loop even though only one row is returned.
   while (rs.next())
   {
   // Assign the cursor return.
     userName = rs.getString(1);
   }

   // Return the user name.
   return userName;

} // End of getUserName() method.

// -------------------------------------------/

// Implements readSQL() method from the SQLData interface.
public void readSQL(SQLInput stream, String typeName) throws SQLException
{
   // Define sql_type to read input and signal overloading signatures.
   sql_type = typeName;

   // Pass values into the class.
   instanceName = stream.readString();

} // End of readSQL() method.

// -------------------------------------------/

// Implements readSQL() method from the SQLData interface.
public void writeSQL(SQLOutput stream) throws SQLException
{
   // You pass a value back by using a stream function.
   // stream.writeString('variable_name');

} // End of readSQL() method.

} // End of HelloWorld4 class.
```

The Java class file does the following:

- It defines five key import statements. Make sure you use these as your starting point for stored Java object classes.

- It defines four String data type class instance variables. The className variable is defined and initialized but the instanceName and qualifiedName variables are only defined. The sql_type variable is also only defined, but that's how it should be done when using the SQLData interface. Also note that all four are private access level variables.

■ It defines a single class with a no argument constructor. This is typically called the default constructor. You'll see why it's important to note when you examine how to instantiate this object in PL/SQL. Within the default constructor, the qualifiedName variable is initialized. This is the only place where the variable can be assigned a value. It's implemented this way to demonstrate that the default constructor is executed.

■ It defines five methods. Two are unique to the test class and three are required to implement the SQLData interface. They do the following:

■ The getQualifiedName() method returns the this .qualifiedName variable, which is an instance variable for the class. If you were to attempt to reference a class-level variable in a Java stored class supporting a PL/SQL function and procedure wrappers, it would fail. The loadjava would raise an exception to prevent putting it into the database instance.

■ The getSQLTypeName() method implements a method from the SQLData interface and assigns a user defined type to a local variable. This enables the class to be managed within the scope of the Oracle JVM.

■ The getUserName() method queries the database for the current user of the stored Java class.

■ The readSQL() method manages the incoming stream to the Java stored object class. The example uses one direct mapping to illustrate the differences between two instantiated classes during testing.

■ The writeSQL() method manages the outgoing stream from the Java stored object class. The example requires no direct mapping of the outgoing stream but the syntax is there for your convenience. This is done because all variables are defined with private access. Private access variables are encapsulated by design and are available only through published methods.

If you have not built the PLSQL schema, please run the create_user.sql script now. When you have the PLSQL schema built, you can compile it with the javac utility as covered earlier in the chapter. However, there is an alternative syntax that enables you to load and compile against the Oracle JVM libraries. You can directly load a Java source, or text, file with the loadjava utility as follows:

```
loadjava -r -f -o -user plsql/plsql HelloWorld4.java
```

The loadjava utility command behaves slightly differently when you choose this option. It parses, stores the Java source as a text entry, and compiles the stored Java source into a Java byte stream in the Oracle JVM under the PLSQL schema.

**TIP**
*After loading the Java class file into the database this way, you won't be able to use the* `dropjava` *utility to remove the* `HelloWorld4.class` *file. Instead, use the* `dropjava` *utility to remove the* `HelloWorld4.java` *file, which also drops the* `HelloWorld4.class` *file.*

You'll need to build a SQL object type to wrap the Java stored object class. The following `HelloWorld4.sql` script builds the object type as a wrapper to the Java class object:

-- **Available online as part of HelloWorld4.sql file.**

```
-- Create a PL/SQL wrapper package to a Java class file.
CREATE OR REPLACE TYPE hello_world4 AS OBJECT
EXTERNAL NAME 'HelloWorld4' LANGUAGE JAVA
USING SQLData
( instanceName VARCHAR2(100) EXTERNAL NAME 'java.lang.String'
, CONSTRUCTOR FUNCTION hello_world4
  RETURN SELF AS RESULT
, MEMBER FUNCTION getQualifiedName
  RETURN VARCHAR2 AS LANGUAGE JAVA
  NAME 'HelloWorld4.getQualifiedName() return java.lang.String'
, MEMBER FUNCTION getSQLTypeName
  RETURN VARCHAR2 AS LANGUAGE JAVA
  NAME 'HelloWorld4.getSQLTypeName() return java.lang.String' )
INSTANTIABLE FINAL;
/
```

The SQL object type wrapper does the following:

■ It defines an object type using an external name that is the case-sensitive Java class name and the USING SQLData clause. The USING SQLData clause requires at least one variable with an external name that identifies the Java data type.

■ It defines a single constructor function that takes no arguments. If you provide an overriding constructor, it will not be used.

■ It defines two functions. One reads the instance qualifiedName value and another reads the SQLTypeName value.

**NOTE**
*Any attempt to use `SQLData` without a mapped type will raise an exception. If you want to instantiate a class and not pass any variables to it, you can designate a blank VARCHAR2(1) EXTERNAL NAME 'java.lang.String' in the wrapper. Then, you simply avoid defining the streams in the `SQLData` interface methods `readSQL` and `writeSQL` and pass a NULL argument when instantiating the PL/SQL wrapper in your PL/SQL programs.*

After you've defined the PL/SQL object type wrapper, you can see that both the object type and body have been registered in the Oracle instance metadata. You can see this by running the following query:

```
COL object_name FORMAT A30
COL object_type FORMAT A12
COL status      FORMAT A7

SELECT    object_name
,         object_type
,         status
FROM      user_objects
WHERE     object_name = 'HELLO_WORLD4';
```

The output, if you have run everything successfully, will be the following:

```
OBJECT_NAME                     OBJECT_TYPE  STATUS
------------------------------- ------------ -------
HELLO_WORLD4                    TYPE         VALID
HELLO_WORLD4                    TYPE BODY    VALID
```

If you use the `dropjava` utility at this point, you'll invalidate the TYPE BODY. Reloading the Java source file with the `loadjava` utility leaves the TYPE BODY in an invalid status. The first call to the object results in the following error:

```
-- Available online as part of HelloWorld4.sql script as qualified above.

DECLARE
*
ERROR at line 1:
ORA-29549: class PLSQL.HelloWorld4 has changed, Java session state cleared
ORA-06512: at "PLSQL.HELLO_WORLD4", line 0
ORA-06512: at line 10
```

A second call to the object results in success, but the Oracle instance metadata will still report that the `TYPE BODY` is invalid. The metadata report is incorrect, but you'll need to run an **ALTER** command to fix it. For example, you can use the following:

```
ALTER TYPE hello_world4 COMPILE BODY;
```

Now, you'll test this PL/SQL object type wrapper by instantiating two object instances with the following script:

```
-- Available online as part of HelloWorld4.sql file.

DECLARE

  -- Define and instantiate an object instance.
  my_obj1 hello_world4 := hello_world4('Adam');
  my_obj2 hello_world4 := hello_world4('Eve');

BEGIN

  -- Test class instance.
  dbms_output.put_line('Item #1: ['||my_obj1.getQualifiedName||']');
  dbms_output.put_line('Item #2: ['||my_obj2.getQualifiedName||']');
  dbms_output.put_line('Item #3: ['||my_obj1.getSQLTypeName||']');
  dbms_output.put_line('Item #4: ['||my_obj1.getSQLTypeName||']');

  -- Test metadata repository with DBMS_JAVA.
  dbms_output.put_line(
    'Item #5: ['||user||'.'||dbms_java.longname('HELLO_WORLD4')||']');

END;
/
```

You should see the following output displayed:

```
Item #1: [PLSQL.HelloWorld4.class.Adam]
Item #2: [PLSQL.HelloWorld4.class.Eve]
Item #3: [PLSQL.HELLO_WORLD4]
Item #4: [PLSQL.HELLO_WORLD4]
Item #5: [PLSQL.HELLO_WORLD4]
```

The `SQLData` interface allows you to pass a User Defined Type (UDT), which means you can use any defined user structure. If you debug the execution of the Java instance, you'll find that each invocation of the instance method actually reinstantiates the class instance.

The next section discusses troubleshooting the Java class library processes that build, load/drop, and use Java server stored object classes.

# Troubleshooting Java Class Library Build, Load, Drop, and Use

This section covers how to troubleshoot Java class libraries. Some of this becomes intuitive after a while but initially it is very tricky.

### Building, Loading, and Dropping Java Class Library Objects

When you build Java class libraries, you can encounter a number of problems. Many errors occur through simple syntax rule violations, but often the PATH or CLASSPATH environment variable excludes required Java libraries. You need to ensure that your PATH environment variable includes the Java SDK released with the Oracle database you're using. It's best if you research which Java class libraries you'll require and then source them into your CLASSPATH. The following illustrates the minimum for the examples used in this chapter by the operating system:

**WINDOWS**

```
C:> set PATH=%PATH%;C:%ORACLE_HOME%\jdk\bin
C:> set CLASSPATH=%CLASSPATH%;C:%ORACLE_HOME%\jdbc\lib\classes12.zip
```

If you want to use the JPublisher command-line tool, you need to add both of the following Java archive files:

```
%ORACLE_HOME%\sqlj\lib\translator.zip
%ORACLE_HOME%\sqlj\lib\runtime12.zip
```

### Why Would I Use This?

As we've worked with the advanced product stack in Oracle, helpful troubleshooting hints have saved us hours of time that might be spent banging away fruitlessly on the keyboard. We've found that Oracle server-side Java components have a number of errors that have led us astray. Therefore, we want to let you know what they are.

We find it frustrating to use Oracle features when the troubleshooting steps are spread across three to ten manuals. Too often these are not cross-referenced and are hard to find. We believe this section will save you hours of setup and configuration effort to make the examples work.

### UNIX

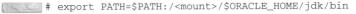
```
# export PATH=$PATH:/<mount>/$ORACLE_HOME/jdk/bin
# export CLASSPATH=$CLASSPATH:/<mount>/$ORACLE_HOME/jdbc/lib/classes12.zip
```

If you want to use the JPublisher command-line tool, you must add both of these Java archive files to your `CLASSPATH` environment variable:

```
$ORACLE_HOME/sqlj/lib/translator.zip
$ORACLE_HOME/sqlj/lib/runtime12.zip
```

Another potential problem in configuring Java archive access can be found in the `LD_LIBRARY_PATH` used in the `listener.ora` file. Check to make sure it's set as follows:

```
LD_LIBRARY_PATH=C:\oracle\ora92\lib;C:\oracle\ora92\jdbc\lib
```

You may also encounter an error like this, which says you cannot drop a Java class file directly from your database instance. The error is raised by running the `dropjava` utility with the following syntax:

```
C:> dropjava -u plsql/plsql HelloWorld4.class
```

The following error message should then appear:

```
Error while dropping class HelloWorld4
    ORA-29537: class or resource cannot be created or dropped directly
```

The reason for the error is that you used `loadjava` with the source file, `HelloWorld4.java`. Thus, you should use `dropjava` and the source file, which will delete the class and source file.

**NOTE**
*The behavior is generally consistent with this preceding description, but occasionally the command will work and delete both the source and class files from the Oracle JVM.*

The error signaling that you have excluded something from your `CLASSPATH` environment variable should appear as follows:

```
C:\>loadjava -r -f -o -user plsql/plsql HelloWorld4.class
errors   : class HelloWorld4
    ORA-29521: referenced name oracle/jdbc2/SQLData could not be found
    ORA-29521: referenced name oracle/jdbc2/SQLInput could not be found
    ORA-29521: referenced name oracle/jdbc2/SQLOutput could not be found
The following operations failed
    class HelloWorld4: resolution
exiting  : Failures occurred during processing
```

If you get an `ORA-29549` error, you're missing a Java archive reference. As noted early in the chapter, an `ORA-29549` error is also raised when the Java class is removed and replaced the first time it's called.

**TIP**
*If you replace your Java class files, make sure you call them once from the target schema to avoid users managing the Java session change.*

Now that you've reviewed the major issues with building, loading, and dropping Java stored object class files, let's examine some errors in the SQL and PL/SQL environment.

## Using Java Class Library Objects
When you use Java stored object classes, you should ensure you define only one constructor in the PL/SQL object type definition. The only constructor acted on by a PL/SQL object type wrapper is the default constructor.

**TIP**
*Avoid overriding constructors unless you plan to call them from other Java libraries wrapped as procedures and functions.*

An example of overriding constructors being ignored is found in the `HelloWorld4e.sql` script. The script references the `HelloWorld4.class` file addressed earlier in the chapter. `HelloWorld4e.sql` defines two constructors for the `HelloWorld4.class` file. One is a null argument constructor and the other is a single formal parameter argument. Since there's no duplicate constructor defined in the targeted class file, you would expect the following object type definition to fail:

-- **Available online as part of HelloWorld4.sql file.**

```
-- Create a PL/SQL wrapper package to a Java class file.
CREATE OR REPLACE TYPE hello_world4 AS OBJECT
EXTERNAL NAME 'HelloWorld4' LANGUAGE JAVA
USING SQLData
( instanceName VARCHAR2(100) EXTERNAL NAME 'java.lang.String'
, CONSTRUCTOR FUNCTION hello_world4
  RETURN SELF AS RESULT
, CONSTRUCTOR FUNCTION hello_world4
  ( instanceName VARCHAR2 )
  RETURN SELF AS RESULT
, MEMBER FUNCTION getQualifiedName
  RETURN VARCHAR2 AS LANGUAGE JAVA
  NAME 'HelloWorld4.getQualifiedName() return java.lang.String'
, MEMBER FUNCTION getSQLTypeName
  RETURN VARCHAR2 AS LANGUAGE JAVA
  NAME 'HelloWorld4.getSQLTypeName() return java.lang.String' )
INSTANTIABLE FINAL;

/
```

It does not fail, however, and instead succeeds to define a type that misrepresents the internal Java program's capabilities. You can run this test program found in the `HelloWorld4e.sql` script, which demonstrates that the type fails to support the overriding constructor:

-- **This is found in HelloWorld4e.sql file.**

```
DECLARE

  -- Define and instantiate an object instance.
  my_obj1 hello_world4 := hello_world4('Adam');
  my_obj2 hello_world4 := hello_world4('Eve');

  PROCEDURE write_debug
  ( number_in NUMBER
  , value_in  VARCHAR2 ) IS

  BEGIN

    INSERT INTO java_debug VALUES (number_in,value_in);

  END write_debug;
```

```
BEGIN

  -- Test class instance.
  dbms_output.put_line('Item #1: ['||my_obj1.getQualifiedName||']');
  write_debug(101,'Item #1 Completed');
  dbms_output.put_line('Item #2: ['||my_obj2.getQualifiedName||']');
  write_debug(102,'Item #2 Completed');
  dbms_output.put_line('Item #3: ['||my_obj1.getSQLTypeName||']');
  write_debug(103,'Item #3 Completed');
  dbms_output.put_line('Item #4: ['||my_obj1.getSQLTypeName||']');
  write_debug(104,'Item #4 Completed');

  -- Test metadata repository with DBMS_JAVA.
  dbms_output.put_line(
    'Item #5: ['||user||'.'||dbms_java.longname('HELLO_WORLD4')||']');

END;
/
```

This will send the following output to your console:

-- **This output is generated from the HelloWorld4e.sql file.**

```
DECLARE
*
ERROR at line 1:
ORA-06502: PL/SQL: numeric or value error
ORA-06512: at line 4
```

This would imply that the overriding constructor takes a single VARCHAR2 formal parameter and cannot support a VARCHAR2 value. The real issue is that the SQLData type is what is passed and it's managed as a SQLData type. As noted earlier, the methods used in the SQLData interface define how values are passed.

You may encounter many issues when first implementing stored Java object classes and thus may benefit from building a java_debug error management table like the following:

```
CREATE TABLE java_debug
( debug_number NUMBER
, debug_value VARCHAR2(4000) );
```

Adding the following method to your Java class files will enable you to write to the java_debug table:

```
// Define the debugLog() method.
public void debugLog(int debug_number
                     ,String debug_value) throws SQLException
{
  String statement = "INSERT INTO java_debug VALUES (?,?)";
```

```
    // Define a connection for Oracle.
    Connection conn = new OracleDriver().defaultConnection();

    // Define and initialize a prepared statement.
    PreparedStatement ps = conn.prepareStatement(statement);

    // Assign the cursor return.
    ps.setInt(1,debug_number);
    ps.setString(2,debug_value);
    ps.execute();

  } // End of the debugLog() method.
```

You have now covered the major issues with troubleshooting Java stored object classes. The next section summarizes the mapping of Oracle types to Java types.

# Mapping Oracle Types

Oracle maps all native types and User Defined Types (UDTs) to Java types. When you use SQLData you map individual components and structures. The following table notes how Oracle types map to Java types:

| SQL Data Types | Java Class Data Types |
|---|---|
| CHAR | oracle.sql.CHAR |
| LONG | java.lang.String |
| VARCHAR2 | java.lang.Byte |
| | java.lang.Short |
| | java.lang.Integer |
| | java.lang.Long |
| | java.lang.Float |
| | java.lang.Double |
| | java.lang.BigDecimal |
| | java.sql.Date |
| | java.sql.Time |
| | java.sql.Timestamp |
| | byte |
| | short |
| | int |
| | long |
| | float |
| | double |

| SQL Data Types | Java Class Data Types |
|---|---|
| DATE | oracle.sql.DATE<br>java.lang.String<br>java.sql.Date<br>java.sql.Time<br>java.sql.Timestamp |
| NUMBER | oracle.sql.NUMBER<br>java.lang.Byte<br>java.lang.Short<br>java.lang.Integer<br>java.lang.Long<br>java.lang.Float<br>java.lang.Double<br>java.lang.BigDecimal<br>byte<br>short<br>int<br>long<br>float<br>double |
| OPAQUE | oracle.sql.OPAQUE |
| RAW<br>LONG RAW | oracle.sql.RAW<br>byte[] |
| ROWID | oracle.sql.CHAR<br>oracle.sql.ROWID<br>java.lang.String |
| BFILE | oracle.sql.BFILE |
| BLOB | oracle.sql.BLOB<br>oracle.jdbc.Blob (JDK 1.1.*x*) |
| CLOB<br>NCLOB | oracle.sql.CLOB<br>oracle.jdbc.Clob (JDK 1.1.*x*) |
| OBJECT<br>Object types | oracle.sql.STRUCT<br>java.sql.Struct (JDK 1.1.*x*)<br>java.sql.SQLData<br>oracle.sql.ORAData |

| SQL Data Types | Java Class Data Types |
|---|---|
| REF<br>Reference types | oracle.sql.REF<br>java.sql.Ref (JDK 1.1.*x*)<br>oracle.sql.ORAData |
| TABLE<br>VARRAY<br>Nested table and types<br>VARRAY types | oracle.sql.ARRAY<br>java.sql.Array (JDK 1.1.*x*)<br>oracle.sql.ORAData |
| Any of the preceding<br>SQL types | oracle.sql.CustomDatum<br>oracle.sql.Datum |

Native types and UDTs can be used and managed by the SQLData conventions covered in the chapter. The Oracle JPublisher tool enables you to develop SQLData stubs and programs to use your UDTs.

# Summary

You should now have an understanding of how to implement and troubleshoot server-side or internal Java class libraries. With these skills, you can build robust solutions in Java, affording you a certain simplicity over using PL/SQL.

# CHAPTER
6

# Implementing
PL/SQL Objects

P L/SQL objects have become powerful in Oracle 9*i*. They enable you to develop object types as replacements to record types, build object views, and use transient objects to build a façade to hide the complexity of subsystems.

While PL/SQL object types were introduced in Oracle 8, you'll find they've grown up with the release of Oracle 9*i*. The Oracle 9*i* release presents a new face to leveraging object-oriented (OO) development practices within PL/SQL. In this chapter, you'll learn how to define and use PL/SQL objects in the database for a number of purposes. You'll review the basics, definitions, constructions, assignments, and record-type substitutions. After covering the basics, you'll explore limitations and uses beyond traditional data and record-type substitutions. You'll build a façade using transient objects to reduce the complexity of a subsystem of database tables.

This chapter stands independent of other chapters in the book. *It covers some material **only** available in Oracle 9i and later versions.* The façade pattern demonstrates static and member procedures. Member procedures are available in Oracle 9*i*. You'll learn about the following topics:

- Introducing object and object types

- Instantiating object types

- Extending PL/SQL object types to compound object types

- Using PL/SQL objects as data types within tables

- Using PL/SQL objects as object views

- Using PL/SQL object types as a subsystem façade

## Why Would I Use This?

We use transient objects to hide the complexity of our Entity Relationship Diagram (ERD) from Java developers. It provides our application developers with a higher view of components so they can better connect with them.

As developers, we know the benefits of hiding complexity with layers of programming code. Transient objects enable you to build views that have methods. We believe you can simplify your application development by building the stored programming code with the data views. Transient objects are the tool to accomplish this consolidation and it works well from the second release of Oracle 9*i* forward.

The focus is to demonstrate how to implement objects in Oracle. Since this isn't a tutorial on the basics of using objects, you're encouraged to explore Chapters 14 and 15 in *Oracle 10g PL/SQL Programming* where all features of objects, including inheritance, are discussed.

# Introducing Objects and Object Types

You see objects everywhere in Oracle products. Tables, views, stored packages, stored procedures, and so on, are all objects. Objects are likewise schema objects. This means they act similar to other schema objects, but their closest cousin is a stored package.

## What Is an Oracle Object?

An Oracle object type is a structure that is user-defined. The structure may be used as a user-defined type when building a table, passing a formal parameter, or returning a complex structure from a stored function. Like a stored package, an object has a specification and a body. The specification declares the structure of the object and the body provides the object type's implementation.

The specification defines the attributes, constructors, and member functions and procedures. The difference between stored packages and objects is syntax and the concept of a constructor. A constructor is a specialized function that enables a program to create an instance of an object type. Technically, an object type is the definition and implementation, while an object instance or object is a copy built by a constructor, which is then populated with one or more rows of data.

The syntax to build an object type specification is shown in Figure 6-1.

An object type may be defined as a structure and never instantiated or frequently instantiated. Instantiating an object type means to define it, and construct an instance of it.

**NOTE**
*If this is the first code you have run or you want to clean up your schema, please use the* create_ user.sql *script from the* SYSTEM *user or take the role of a privileged user with DBA privileges. This will create the* PLSQL *user and schema. After creating the user, log on as the* PLSQL *user.*

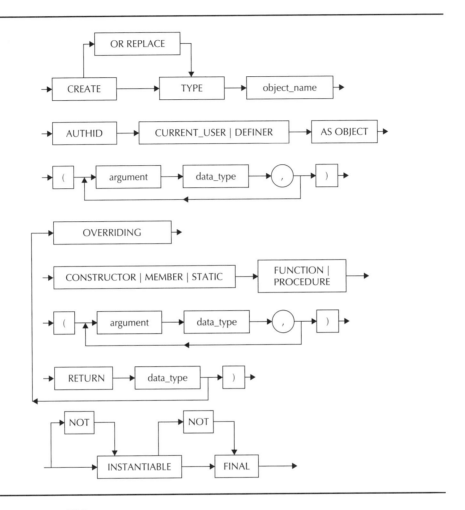

**FIGURE 6-1.** *Object type syntax*

A sample object type to illustrate the power of transient objects is defined in the following code sample:

-- **This is found in the `create_basic_object1.sql` file.**

```
CREATE OR REPLACE TYPE build_test
AUTHID CURRENT_USER IS OBJECT
( my_number NUMBER
, CONSTRUCTOR FUNCTION build_test
```

```
RETURN SELF AS RESULT
, CONSTRUCTOR FUNCTION build_test
( my_number NUMBER )
RETURN SELF AS RESULT
, MEMBER PROCEDURE print_instance_variable
, MAP MEMBER FUNCTION equals RETURN NUMBER )
INSTANTIABLE NOT FINAL;
/
```

The sample creates an object type with the following characteristics:

■ It defines an object type named `build_test`, using the CURRENT_USER permission. The CURRENT_USER designates the user calling the method.

■ It defines two constructors. One uses no arguments and the other uses a single argument constructor.

■ It defines a member procedure that acts on an instance of the object type. The member procedure takes no formal parameter.

■ It defines a MAP function, which returns the numeric instance variable. This compares the two numeric instance variables, which are the contents of the object instances. The MAP function is limited to comparing numbers and variable length strings and is generally only effective for single-element class instances.

**NOTE**
*Take careful note to make sure the name of the constructor function IS EQUAL to the name of the object type.*

The `build_test` object type specification shows you how to build a basic object. The generalized syntax for building an object type body is shown in Figure 6-2. The following shows you how to build the object type body:

**-- This is found in the create_basic_object1.sql file.**

```
CREATE OR REPLACE TYPE BODY build_test AS

  -- Define a null argument constructor.
  CONSTRUCTOR FUNCTION build_test
  RETURN SELF AS RESULT IS

    -- Define an instance variable.
    my_instance_number NUMBER := 0;
```

```
BEGIN

  -- Assign the local variable to the instance variable.
  SELF.my_number := my_instance_number;

  -- Return instance of the object type.
  RETURN;

END;

-- Define a single argument constructor.
CONSTRUCTOR FUNCTION build_test

( my_number NUMBER )
RETURN SELF AS RESULT IS

BEGIN

  -- Assign the actual parameter to instance variables.
  SELF.my_number := my_number;

  -- Return instance of the object type.
  RETURN;

END;

-- An object member procedure.
MEMBER PROCEDURE print_instance_variable IS

BEGIN

  -- Print the instance variable.
  DBMS_OUTPUT.PUT_LINE('Instance Variable ['||self.my_number||']');
END;

-- A comparison member procedure.
MAP MEMBER FUNCTION equals
RETURN NUMBER IS

BEGIN

  -- Return the instance variable.
  RETURN self.my_number;

END;

END;
/
```

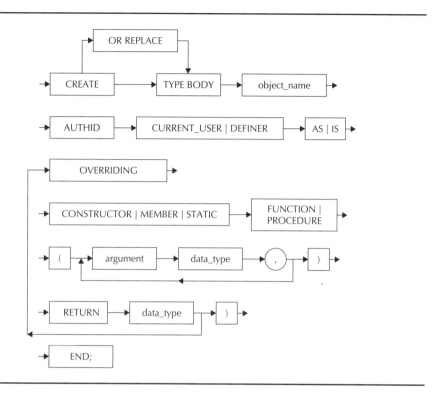

**FIGURE 6-2.** *Object type body syntax*

The sample creates an object type body that implements the object type specification. It has the following characteristics:

■ It defines a null argument constructor that defines a default local variable `my_instance_number` and initializes it to a value of zero. It assigns the `my_instance_number` instance variable `SELF.my_number`. This assignment is done with the reserved word `SELF`, a period and an object type instance variable. Just as periods separate package variables, periods separate `SELF` and an instance variable or method name. `SELF` references the current instance of any object type, which requires the object be instantiated. All constructors return a copy of the object type, which is known as an object instance or object.

- It defines a single argument constructor and assigns the actual parameter (or value passed as an argument) to the instance variable SELF.my_number. Like the null argument constructor, it returns an object instance.

- It defines a local null argument member procedure print_instance_number that prints to the console a message that includes the value of the instance variable.

- It defines a MAP member function. This is used to compare instances of classes.

**NOTE**
*The MAP member function can only return a scalar type of CHAR, DATE, NUMBER, and VARCHAR2. Also, you can have only one MAP or ORDER function in any object type. If you attempt to define both, the object type specification will raise a PLS-00154 error, which states that "An object type may have only 1 MAP or 1 ORDER method."*

The benefit of a MAP member function is limited. It is limited because you can test for equality only when a single number identifies the class. This only works well when you write wrapper classes mapping primitive data types, like NUMBER, to a meaningful user-friendly description. Writing a wrapper class is like creating new application metadata (data about data or data describing data). This type of metadata works like that found in the definition of DBA_OBJECTS or USER_OBJECTS views. These views convert known numeric values to user-friendly object descriptions, like TABLE, VIEW, PACKAGE, PACKAGE BODY, and so on.

The ORDER member function is typically presented as a means to sequence object instances in ascending or descending order. You can use it that way, but as a rule it is not very useful in that role. If you want to use it to order object instances, the ORDER member function takes a parameter of the object type and typically returns one of the following:

- A negative 1 if the actual parameter is greater than the current instance

- A positive 1 if the actual parameter is less than the current instance

- A zero if they are equal

### Why Would I Use This?

We use ORDER member function to mimic the traditional Java programming language equals method. As an OO programmer, the ORDER member function intuitively tells us how to compare object instances. We've borrowed this technique from the Java programming language, where the equals method takes a single formal parameter of an instance of the object type. We use the comparison method to evaluate whether two object instances are equal by applying object type internally-known rules.

We believe the ORDER member function is a terrific solution to a shortfall in a single hierarchical model provided in the Java programming language as the equals method. We believe it will simplify your runtime comparison of transient objects.

The ORDER member function must return a number data type and cannot return a Boolean data type. You can leverage this by using the traditional C programming language pattern for building numeric Boolean values, with zero for false and one for true. The following is a new object type specification using the ORDER member function as a true comparison method:

-- **This is found in the create_basic_object2.sql file.**

```
CREATE OR REPLACE TYPE build_test
AUTHID CURRENT_USER IS OBJECT
( my_number NUMBER
, my_name   VARCHAR2(20 CHAR)
, CONSTRUCTOR FUNCTION build_test
RETURN SELF AS RESULT
, CONSTRUCTOR FUNCTION build_test
( my_number NUMBER
, my_name   VARCHAR2 )
RETURN SELF AS RESULT
, MEMBER PROCEDURE print_instance_variable
, ORDER MEMBER FUNCTION equals
( my_class BUILD_TEST ) RETURN NUMBER )
INSTANTIABLE NOT FINAL;
/
```

The sample creates an object type with the following characteristics:

- It defines an object type named `build_test` using the `CURRENT_USER` permission. `CURRENT_USER` designates the user calling the method. This object type is more than a mere wrapper to a numeric primitive.

- It defines two constructors. One uses no arguments and the other uses a two-argument constructor.

- It defines a member procedure that acts on an instance of the object type. The member procedure takes two formal parameters.

- It defines an order function, which acts as the equivalent to an `equals` method in the Java programming language. The order function returns a variable that enables the contents of one object to be seen as equal to another.

Implementing the object type is displayed in the following code:

**-- This is found in the create_basic_object2.sql file.**

```
CREATE OR REPLACE TYPE BODY build_test AS

  -- Define a null argument constructor.
  CONSTRUCTOR FUNCTION build_test
  RETURN SELF AS RESULT IS

    -- Define an instance variable.
    my_instance_number NUMBER := 0;
    my_instance_name   VARCHAR2(20 CHAR) := '';

  BEGIN

    -- Assign the local variable to the instance variable.
    SELF.my_number := my_instance_number;
    SELF.my_name := my_instance_name;

    -- Return instance of the object type.
    RETURN;

  END;

  -- Define a single argument constructor.
  CONSTRUCTOR FUNCTION build_test
  ( my_number NUMBER
  , my_name   VARCHAR2 )
  RETURN SELF AS RESULT IS
```

```
BEGIN

  -- Assign the parameters to instance variables.
  SELF.my_number := my_number;
  SELF.my_name := my_name;

  -- Return instance of the object type.
  RETURN;

END;

-- An object member procedure.
MEMBER PROCEDURE print_instance_variable IS

BEGIN

  -- Print the instance variable.
  DBMS_OUTPUT.PUT_LINE('Instance Number ['||SELF.my_number||']');
  DBMS_OUTPUT.PUT_LINE('Instance Name   ['||SELF.my_name||']');

END;

-- A sequencing member procedure.
ORDER MEMBER FUNCTION equals
( my_class BUILD_TEST )
RETURN NUMBER IS

  -- Define default return values.
  false_value NUMBER := 0;
  true_value  NUMBER := 1;

BEGIN

  -- Determine value to return.
  IF SELF.my_number = my_class.my_number AND
     SELF.my_name = my_class.my_name      THEN

    -- Return True they are equal.
    RETURN true_value;

  ELSE

    -- Return False they are unequal.
    RETURN false_value;
```

```
      END IF;

   END;

END;
/
```

The sample creates an object type body with the following characteristics:

- It defines a null argument constructor that defines a default local variable my_instance_number and my_instance_name and initializes them to a value of zero and null respectively. It assigns the my_instance_number instance variable SELF.my_number and my_instance_name instance variable SELF.my_name. All constructors return a copy of the object type, which is known as an object instance or object.

- It defines a two-argument constructor and assigns the actual parameters (or values passed as arguments) to the instance variables SELF.my_number and SELF.my_name. Like the null argument constructor, it returns an object instance.

- It defines a local null argument member procedure print_instance_ number that prints to console a message that includes the value of the instance variables.

- It defines an ORDER member function. This is used to compare instances of classes and is a true corollary to the equals method implemented in Java.

You should be aware that you could define any number of constructor functions, member functions, or member procedures in any object type. The general overloading rules are the same for object type methods as package functions and procedures.

**TIP**
*You can use PRAGMA guarantees, but they will restrict effective use of transitive object types.*

In this section, you learned how to define object types. Now let's look at how to use them in programs and tables.

# Instantiating Object Types

Using the `build_test` object type, you'll see how to declare local variables as user-defined object types and instantiate them. The basics of declaring an anonymous block PL/SQL variable do not change. You declare the variable by creating a variable name and assigning the variable a data type. The following example uses the `build_test` user-defined object type created by the `create_basic_object2.sql` script. It's used because the ORDER member function is the only true OO comparison process provided unless you write your own member function.

**TIP**
*You should leverage the ORDER member function as the equivalent to the Java equals method because it will be easier to enforce as a coding practice. As you noticed in the build_test object type, the ORDER member function is named equals.*

Instantiating a variable is like initializing a variable except with one difference. When you initialize a variable, you assign the right-hand variable of the same type to the left-hand target. Instantiating an object type, you must call the constructor and provide actual parameters if required by the constructor function. The `test_basic_object1.sql` script allows you to verify that the MAP member function works for numeric values. The following example program demonstrates constructing, using, and comparing two instances of the `build_test` object type:

```
-- This is found in the test_basic_object2.sql file.

DECLARE

  -- Declare and initialize two instances.
  my_object_1 BUILD_TEST := build_test;
  my_object_2 BUILD_TEST := build_test(1,'My Object');

BEGIN

  -- Print formatting header.
  DBMS_OUTPUT.PUT_LINE('============================');

  -- Print formatting header.
  DBMS_OUTPUT.PUT_LINE('My Object 1 is:');
  DBMS_OUTPUT.PUT_LINE('--------------------------');
```

```
   -- Call object method.
   my_object_1.print_instance_variable;

   -- Print formatting header.
   DBMS_OUTPUT.PUT_LINE('--------------------------');
   DBMS_OUTPUT.PUT_LINE('My Object 2 is:');
   DBMS_OUTPUT.PUT_LINE('--------------------------');

   -- Call object method.
   my_object_2.print_instance_variable;

   -- Print formatting header.
   DBMS_OUTPUT.PUT_LINE('--------------------------');
   DBMS_OUTPUT.PUT_LINE('Test Object Equality:');
   DBMS_OUTPUT.PUT_LINE('--------------------------');

   -- Use an if then else to audit equality.
   IF my_object_1.equals(my_object_2) = 1 THEN
     DBMS_OUTPUT.PUT_LINE('They are equal.');
   ELSE
     DBMS_OUTPUT.PUT_LINE('They are unequal.');
   END IF;

   -- Print formatting header.
   DBMS_OUTPUT.PUT_LINE('===========================');

END;
/
```

The sample program uses the `build_test` object type. It does the following:

■ It defines, initializes, and assigns two instances of the `build_test` object type. It uses the null argument constructor to build the first instance. Then, it passes actual parameter values to the two-argument constructor to build the second instance of the `build_test` object type. Based on the default value set in the definition of the `build_test` object type, these are not equal.

■ It uses the DBMS_OUTPUT package to print a formatting header.

■ It calls the no argument `build_test` object type member procedure `print_instance_number` for the first instance of the object type. The call appears much like it would if you called a package procedure. The difference is subtle but important. When you call a package procedure, the stored name of the package precedes the procedure name. When you call an object type procedure, you use the instance name instead of the object type name before the member procedure name. The reason is that the object type member procedure acts on the instance data because its scope is the instance of an object.

■ It compares the two object instances of the `build_test` object type. They are found unequal.

The following illustrates the output from the `test_basic_object2.sql` program:

-- **Running the test_basic_object2.sql script generates this.**

```
===========================
My Object 1 is:
---------------------------
Instance Number [0]
Instance Name   []
---------------------------
My Object 2 is:
---------------------------
Instance Number [1]
Instance Name    [My Object]
---------------------------
Test Object Equality:
---------------------------
They are unequal.
===========================
```

At this point, you'll see the values of the instances differ based on their constructors. They are separate address spaces and memory units held in the SGA memory of Oracle. They each have a context only in the scope of the local anonymous block program.

You've seen how to define, instantiate, and access the contents of objects, and noted that object types define behavior that can then be mapped to objects in SGA memory. Next, you'll explore using object types in lieu of record types.

# Extending PL/SQL Object Types to Compound Object Types

You'll build a couple of new object types for this section. The code for it can be found online as `create_sample_object1.sql` and `create_sample_object2.sql` files. These programs create the `NAME_OBJECT` and `CONTACT_OBJECT` object types. They are both presented as `FINAL` object types, which mean they cannot be subclasses. This is a preferred solution since changes to a super class may result in subclass type evolution. Subclass type evolution means that when a super class changes, you must cascade those changes to all subclasses of the super class.

**TIP**
*As a rule, object types are easier to use by aggregation methods than by inheritance. You should examine alternatives to any business need that requires you to inherit from an object type because of subclass type evolution demands.*

The class model illustrating how to employ object types uses an OO programming façade pattern. It's shown in Figure 6-3.

## Why Would I Use This?

We use façade patterns to organize and simplify access to data. As mentioned, the façade pattern uses the concept of aggregation to hide levels of complexity. As an OO developer, we know this without being hindered by all the complexities of the issue. We wish that OO programming actually said this in English, instead of hiding the details. While it takes us a bit more time to apply patterns during software development, it builds layered programming APIs with PL/SQL stored packages that require less time to maintain.

We believe the façade pattern in PL/SQL has been used for years in package design and application and that mapping it to transient objects will be straightforward with these examples. You should find the approach similar to your package development approach but with a twist. You now have the ability to build views with methods because that's what transient objects really are.

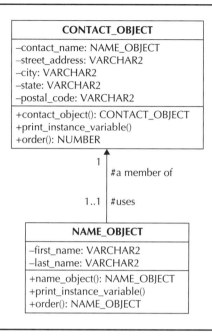

**FIGURE 6-3.** *The UML static diagram*

The user-defined object type is a NAME_OBJECT, which creates a structure of first_name and last_name. The structure gives us a single item to manage, which is an example of hiding the complexity or abstracting the details. The create_sample_object1.sql script builds the NAME_OBJECT object type. When built, you can display the structure by using the SQL*Plus **DESCRIBE** command. The following is the output from the **DESCRIBE** command after running the script:

```
-- Built by running the create_sample_object1.sql script generates this.
```

```
Name                                      Null?    Type
----------------------------------------- -------- --------------------
 FIRST_NAME                                         VARCHAR2(20 CHAR)
 LAST_NAME                                          VARCHAR2(20 CHAR)

METHOD
------
 FINAL CONSTRUCTOR FUNCTION NAME_OBJECT RETURNS SELF AS RESULT
```

```
METHOD
------
FINAL CONSTRUCTOR FUNCTION NAME_OBJECT RETURNS SELF AS RESULT
Argument Name                    Type                    In/Out Default?
-----------------------------    ---------------------   ------ --------
FIRST_NAME                       VARCHAR2                IN
LAST_NAME                        VARCHAR2                IN
MEMBER PROCEDURE PRINT_INSTANCE_VARIABLE

METHOD
------
ORDER MEMBER FUNCTION EQUALS RETURNS NUMBER
Argument Name                    Type                    In/Out Default?
-----------------------------    ---------------------   ------ --------
MY_CLASS                         NAME_OBJECT            IN
```

If you would like to test the NAME_OBJECT object type, you can use the test_
sample_object1.sql script. After building the user-defined type, you can build
the CONTACT_OBJECT object type that uses the NAME_OBJECT as a data type for
an attribute. When user-defined objects begin using other user-defined object types,
they are called compound or complex object types. The reason they label them as
complex is because you begin chaining object type and attributes with dot notation,
as you'll see later in the "Using PL/SQL Object Types as a Subsystem Façade" section.
The following demonstrates defining the complex object type specification and
body:

-- **This is found in the create_sample_object2.sql script.**

```
-- Define an object type.
CREATE OR REPLACE TYPE contact_object
AUTHID CURRENT_USER IS OBJECT
( contact_name    NAME_OBJECT
, street_address VARCHAR2(20 CHAR)
, city            VARCHAR2(14 CHAR)
, state           VARCHAR2(2 CHAR)
, postal_code     VARCHAR2(5 CHAR)
, CONSTRUCTOR FUNCTION contact_object
RETURN SELF AS RESULT
, CONSTRUCTOR FUNCTION contact_object
( contact_name    NAME_OBJECT
, street_address VARCHAR2
, city            VARCHAR2
, state           VARCHAR2
, postal_code     VARCHAR2 )
```

```
RETURN SELF AS RESULT
, CONSTRUCTOR FUNCTION contact_object
( first_name     VARCHAR2
, last_name      VARCHAR2
, street_address VARCHAR2
, city           VARCHAR2
, state          VARCHAR2
, postal_code    VARCHAR2 )
RETURN SELF AS RESULT
, MEMBER PROCEDURE print_instance_variable
, ORDER MEMBER FUNCTION equals
( my_class CONTACT_OBJECT ) RETURN NUMBER )
INSTANTIABLE NOT FINAL;
/


-- Build the object type body.
CREATE OR REPLACE TYPE BODY contact_object AS

  -- Define a null argument constructor.
  CONSTRUCTOR FUNCTION contact_object
  RETURN SELF AS RESULT IS

    -- Define an instance variable.
    first_name     VARCHAR2(20 CHAR) := NULL;
    last_name      VARCHAR2(20 CHAR) := NULL;
    street_address VARCHAR2(20 CHAR) := NULL;
    city           VARCHAR2(14 CHAR) := NULL;
    state          VARCHAR2(2 CHAR)  := NULL;
    postal_code    VARCHAR2(5 CHAR)  := NULL;

  BEGIN

    -- Assign the local variable to the instance variable.
    SELF.contact_name := name_object(first_name,last_name);
    SELF.street_address := street_address;
    SELF.city := city;
    SELF.state := state;
    SELF.postal_code := postal_code;

    -- Return an instance of the object type.
    RETURN;

  END;
```

```
-- Define a compound object type argument constructor.
CONSTRUCTOR FUNCTION contact_object
( contact_name    NAME_OBJECT
, street_address VARCHAR2
, city           VARCHAR2
, state          VARCHAR2
, postal_code    VARCHAR2 )
RETURN SELF AS RESULT IS

BEGIN

  -- Assign the parameters to instance variables.
  SELF.contact_name := contact_name;
  SELF.street_address := street_address;
  SELF.city := city;
  SELF.state := state;
  SELF.postal_code := postal_code;

  -- Return an instance of the object type.
  RETURN;

END;

-- Define a compound object type argument constructor.
CONSTRUCTOR FUNCTION contact_object
( first_name     VARCHAR2
, last_name      VARCHAR2
, street_address VARCHAR2
, city           VARCHAR2
, state          VARCHAR2
, postal_code    VARCHAR2 )
RETURN SELF AS RESULT IS

BEGIN
  -- Assign the parameters to instance variables.
  SELF.contact_name := name_object(first_name,last_name);
  SELF.street_address := street_address;
  SELF.city := city;
  SELF.state := state;
  SELF.postal_code := postal_code;

  -- Return an instance of the object type.
  RETURN;

END;

-- An object member procedure.
MEMBER PROCEDURE print_instance_variable IS
```

```
BEGIN

  -- Print the instance variables from the embedded object type.
  SELF.contact_name.print_instance_variable;

  -- Print a formatting line.
  DBMS_OUTPUT.PUT_LINE('-------------------------------');

  -- Print all elements, using attribute chaining for nested object types.
  DBMS_OUTPUT.PUT_LINE('First Name    : '||SELF.contact_name.first_name);
  DBMS_OUTPUT.PUT_LINE('Last Name     : '||SELF.contact_name.last_name);
  DBMS_OUTPUT.PUT_LINE('Street Address: '||SELF.street_address);
  DBMS_OUTPUT.PUT_LINE('City          : '||SELF.city);
  DBMS_OUTPUT.PUT_LINE('State         : '||SELF.state);
  DBMS_OUTPUT.PUT_LINE('Postal Code   : '||SELF.postal_code);

END;

-- A sequencing member procedure.
ORDER MEMBER FUNCTION equals
( my_class CONTACT_OBJECT )
RETURN NUMBER IS

  -- Define default return values.
  false_value NUMBER := 0;
  true_value  NUMBER := 1;

BEGIN

  -- Determine value to return.
  IF SELF.contact_name.equals(my_class.contact_name) = true_value AND
     SELF.street_address = my_class.street_address AND
     SELF.city = my_class.city AND
     SELF.state = my_class.state AND
     SELF.postal_code = my_class.postal_code THEN

    -- Return True they are equal.
    RETURN true_value;

  ELSE

    -- Return False they are unequal.
    RETURN false_value;

  END IF;

END;

END;
/
```

**Why Would I Use This?**

We use overloaded constructors in OO programming to support business rules that would call an instance of an object type differently. The technique enables us to build a more flexible design.

We can't imagine how you'd ever write effective programs without the overloading of methods. The same can be said for construction of object instances. We simply need the flexibility and Oracle delivered it beginning with Oracle 9*i*.

The CONTACT_OBJECT implements the UML static diagram using an instance of NAME_OBJECT as an instance attribute. The reason for using an encapsulated or nested user-defined object type is to highlight the concepts of attribute chaining and encapsulation. Attribute chaining involves using a sequence of dot notations between object references, nested object references, and attributes or methods. Encapsulation involves hiding complexity by using an interface.

There are three types of constructors in the CONTACT_OBJECT object type body. One is a no argument constructor and the other two use multiple attribute constructors. Any of the constructors may be called to build an instance of the object type. The following explains what is done in the object type constructors and methods:

- It defines three constructors that do the following:

  - The null argument constructor declares all elements necessary to build an instance of the indirect attributes for the nested NAME_OBJECT and direct attributes for CONTACT_OBJECT. These variables are defined in the declaration section of the constructor method and are local in scope. All of these are initialized as null values. They are then assigned to the instance variables referenced by the SELF-parameter, which is the keyword used to designate an instance. Using SELF, a dot and attribute name references an instance variable.

  - The second constructor uses a nested user-defined NAME_OBJECT and four other direct attributes. The actual parameters are then assigned to instance variables referenced by the SELF-parameter, as discussed previously.

■ The third constructor uses direct variables of native Oracle 9*i* data types. In the constructor's execution section, a nested NAME_OBJECT is built with a call to its constructor before assigning it to the instance variable of the NAME_OBJECT user-defined type. The other actual parameters are then assigned to instance variables by the SELF-parameter, as discussed previously.

■ It defines a print_instance_variable method that describes the contents of the object type. First, it calls the print_instance_ variable member procedure of the nested NAME_OBJECT object. Second, it uses the DBMS_OUTPUT package to print a formatting line to break the printed content of the nested object from the native attributes of CONTACT_OBJECT. Third, it uses the DBMS_OUTPUT package to print the native attributes. Attribute chaining is used to print the nested attributes of the NAME_OBJECT instance.

■ It defines a compare member function that enables the object to check for other objects that share equivalent definition and values. Within the IF-THEN-ELSE statement, the nested NAME_OBJECT is validated by a call to its own compare member function.

You can validate its effectiveness by using the following:

```
-- This is found in the test_sample_object2.sql file.

DECLARE

  -- Declare and initialize two instances.
  my_object_1 CONTACT_OBJECT := contact_object(
                          'David'
                         ,'Crockett'
                         ,'1 Alamo Square'
                         ,'San Antonio'
                         ,'TX'
                         ,'78202');

  my_object_2 CONTACT_OBJECT := contact_object(
                          name_object('Santiago','Bowie')
                         ,'1 Alamo Square'
                         ,'San Antonio'
                         ,'TX'
                         ,'78202');
```

```
BEGIN
… removed from text to save space …
END;
/
```

The sample program uses the CONTACT_OBJECT object type. It is very similar to the test programs used previously. The only substantive difference lies in the method of constructing instances of the CONTACT_OBJECT object type. The constructors do the following:

- The first construction of an instance of CONTACT_OBJECT uses direct attributes. Each of these attributes uses a standard Oracle 9*i* data types. The complexity of mapping the first_name and last_name attributes to the nested NAME_OBJECT is done within the constructor. You worked through the constructor earlier in the chapter.

- The second construction of an instance of CONTACT_OBJECT uses both a user-defined nested NAME_OBJECT and direct attributes. It does this by building an instance of NAME_OBJECT within the constructor statement for CONTACT_OBJECT. This approach does not mask the complexity of the elements that belong in a NAME_OBJECT instance, but it illustrates how you do it.

The following displays the results of the test program:

**-- The following is the output of test_sample_object2.sql file.**

```
===============================
My Object 1 is:
-------------------------------
Name [Bowie, Santiago]
-------------------------------
First Name    : David
Last Name     : Crockett
Street Address: 1 Alamo Square
City          : San Antonio
State         : TX
Postal Code   : 78202
-------------------------------
My Object 2 is:
-------------------------------
Name [Santiago, Bowie]
-------------------------------
First Name    : Santiago
Last Name     : Bowie
Street Address: 1 Alamo Square
```

```
City         : San Antonio
State        : TX
Postal Code  : 78202
-------------------------------
Test Object Equality:
-------------------------------
They are unequal.
===============================
```

Notice from the output that the objects are not equal. The NAME_OBJECT order member function found the difference. It did so because the CONTACT_OBJECT order member function used the nested object order member method. You can check the CONTACT_OBJECT object type body code for the order member function to find out how it did so. For your convenience, it uses an IF-THEN-ELSE statement to call the NAME_OBJECT order member function, which finds inequality between the two objects.

If you wrote the CONTACT_OBJECT, you would not need to know how the NAME_OBJECT resolved equality or inequality. You would only need to know how to call the nested object type's order member function. This is the essence of hiding complexity. While hiding complexity, it shows you how cohesive and loosely coupling behavior simplifies working with subsystems.

You have experimented with building object types and compound object types, and the examples have shown you several approaches used in building object constructors. In the next section, we'll develop more ideas based on this as we explore the façade pattern hiding the complexity of our data model.

**NOTE**
*While object types appear as mirrors to traditional record types in PL/SQL programming units, there are a couple of key differences. One is that object types need to be constructed before being assigned. The other is linked to Oracle 9i, where record types are no longer mutually assignable structures. If you attempt to assign a record structure to an object, you'll prompt an ORA-00382 error message. The error message text states that it's "an expression of wrong type."*

# Using PL/SQL Object Types as a Subsystem Façade

Let's continue uncovering the concept of object types by venturing into an OO façade development pattern. This section shows you how to design and implement a façade. You'll learn how object types are basic building blocks and critical to managing rows of data. You'll learn how to build collections of object types as the building blocks for data sets. In the end, it will be concluded that collections do not support constructors unless they are encapsulated as member attributes in a user-defined object type.

The first step to understanding a façade pattern is to look at the subsystem. We'll use an address book model to examine this. The following Entity Relationship Diagram (ERD) shown in Figure 6-4 displays a typical address book model.

The CONTACT table is the topmost parent in the subsystem. Any row in the CONTACT table may have one or more rows in either the ADDRESS or TELEPHONE tables. Likewise, the ADDRESS table may have one or more rows in the STREET_ADDRESS table. In each of these four relationships, you have a primary key column and foreign key column. The CONTACT, ADDRESS, and TELEPHONE tables all have subtypes within their structures, which means not all problem resolutions can be achieved with nonprocedural SQL.

You're probably familiar with the model and solution approaches to the problem. In Oracle databases, this would be an opportunity to write a collection of stored packages to provide an API to your user-interface programmer. There are problems with writing a collection of stored packages to build an API. For example, here are a few key dilemmas:

- APIs continue to grow over time.

- Naming conventions and purposes used in the API erode over time and duplication can occur.

- Scope and control of the APIs become difficult to manage and control during releases.

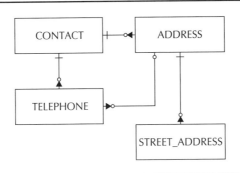

**FIGURE 6-4.** *An address book ERD*

**Why Would I Use This?**

We use a façade pattern and the invoker's-rights paradigm to eliminate direct access to data and provide a pseudo package level access to my objects. Here's where we get the huge benefit of invoker's-rights patterns in programming code.

We can know write objects that provide views to distributed data but a consistent approach to how those views are used. Likewise, we can use overloading to build methods that service our distributed data.

Many of these problems occur because some programmers would prefer to write their own direct access code rather than learn how to leverage the existing code. Some of this can be managed by using invoker's-rights patterns, as discussed in Chapter 4. Moreover, common application code is stored in the same schema that owns direct access to insert, update, and delete privileges on data. The question is how to fix that.

This approach leaves development teams without a direct access route to the data. The diagram shown in Figure 6-5 is an example of a façade pattern for an address book.

While space constrains a full implementation, we'll now examine the components to provide a standard interface to one (and a collection of) telephone row(s). The first step is to build a `telephone_object`. Before running the following file, you should run `create_tables.sql` to build and seed data tables. The following code provides the object type specification:

```
-- This is found in the create_telephone_objects.sql file.

-- Create the telephone object.
CREATE OR REPLACE TYPE telephone_object
AS OBJECT
( telephone_id          NUMBER
, contact_id            NUMBER
, address_id            NUMBER
, telephone_type        NUMBER
, country_code          VARCHAR2(3 CHAR)
, area_code             VARCHAR2(6 CHAR)
, telephone_number      VARCHAR2(10 CHAR)
, CONSTRUCTOR FUNCTION telephone_object
```

```
( telephone_id          NUMBER
, contact_id            NUMBER
, address_id            NUMBER
, telephone_type        NUMBER
, country_code          VARCHAR2
, area_code             VARCHAR2
, telephone_number      VARCHAR2 )
RETURN SELF AS RESULT
, CONSTRUCTOR FUNCTION telephone_object
( telephone_id          NUMBER     )
RETURN SELF AS RESULT
, MEMBER FUNCTION get_telephone_number
( telephone_id          NUMBER )
RETURN VARCHAR2
, MEMBER PROCEDURE delete_telephone_object
, STATIC PROCEDURE delete_telephone_object
( telephone_id          NUMBER )
, MEMBER PROCEDURE insert_telephone_object
, STATIC PROCEDURE insert_telephone_object
( telephone_id          NUMBER
, contact_id            NUMBER
, address_id            NUMBER
, telephone_type        NUMBER
, country_code          VARCHAR2
, area_code             VARCHAR2
, telephone_number      VARCHAR2 )
, MEMBER PROCEDURE update_telephone_object
, STATIC PROCEDURE update_telephone_object
( telephone_id          NUMBER
, country_code          VARCHAR2
, area_code             VARCHAR2
, telephone_number      VARCHAR2 )
, MEMBER PROCEDURE print_telephone_number
, MEMBER PROCEDURE print_telephone_object
, ORDER MEMBER FUNCTION equals
( class_in TELEPHONE_OBJECT )
RETURN NUMBER )
INSTANTIABLE NOT FINAL;
/
```

The object type implements all the attributes and methods found in the UML static diagram depicting the façade pattern. One constructor takes a `telephone_id` argument. It uses the argument to query and return a row from the database into your transient object. Therefore, a constructor provides the select method. Insert, update, and delete member procedures provide all data manipulation access to the database table. Static versions of the procedure enable invoking the object methods without instantiating an object. Member versions of the procedures enable using

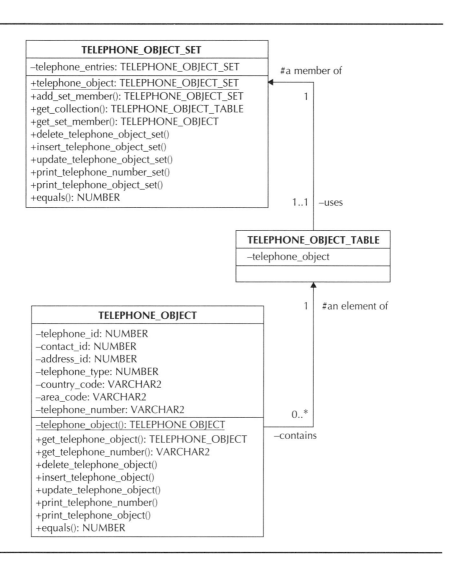

**FIGURE 6-5.**   *The UML static class diagram*

the object methods without passing formal arguments. Formal arguments are unnecessary because any instance of the class contains a copy of all current attributes.

The table need no longer provide grants externally from the schema since the object type now controls access. This is the first level of any façade pattern implemented against a database.

The implementation of the object type body is shown in the following:

-- This is found in the create_telephone_objects.sql file.

```
CREATE OR REPLACE TYPE BODY telephone_object AS
  -- ------------------------------------------------------------

  -- Define a complete attribute constructor.
  CONSTRUCTOR FUNCTION telephone_object
  ( telephone_id        NUMBER
  , contact_id          NUMBER
  , address_id          NUMBER
  , telephone_type      NUMBER
  , country_code        VARCHAR2
  , area_code           VARCHAR2
  , telephone_number    VARCHAR2 )
  RETURN SELF AS RESULT IS

  BEGIN

    -- Map and assign the column values to object attributes.
    SELF.telephone_id := telephone_id;
    SELF.contact_id := contact_id;
    SELF.address_id := address_id;
    SELF.telephone_type := telephone_type;
    SELF.country_code := country_code;
    SELF.area_code := area_code;
    SELF.telephone_number := telephone_number;

    -- Return an instance of the object type.
    RETURN;

  END;

  -- ------------------------------------------------------------

  -- Define a unique key attribute constructor.
  CONSTRUCTOR FUNCTION telephone_object
  ( telephone_id        NUMBER )
  RETURN SELF AS RESULT IS
```

```
  -- Define a cursor to get set elements.
  CURSOR get_telephone
  ( telephone_id_in IN NUMBER ) IS
    SELECT    *
    FROM      telephone
    WHERE     telephone_id = telephone_id_in;

BEGIN

  -- Use a for-loop to traverse the cursor.
  FOR i IN get_telephone(telephone_id) LOOP

    -- Map and assign the column values to object attributes.
    SELF.telephone_id := i.telephone_id;
    SELF.contact_id := i.contact_id;
    SELF.address_id := i.address_id;
    SELF.telephone_type := i.telephone_type;
    SELF.country_code := i.country_code;
    SELF.area_code := i.area_code;
    SELF.telephone_number := i.telephone_number;

  END LOOP;

  -- Return an instance of the object type.
  RETURN;

END;


  -- ------------------------------------------------------------

-- Define a function to build a telephone number.
MEMBER FUNCTION get_telephone_number
( telephone_id        NUMBER ) RETURN VARCHAR2 IS

  -- Define a return variable.
  retval     VARCHAR2(22 CHAR);

  -- Define a cursor to get telephone number.
  CURSOR get_telephone
  ( telephone_id_in IN NUMBER ) IS
    SELECT    country_code
    ,         area_code
    ,         telephone_number
    FROM      telephone
    WHERE     telephone_id = telephone_id_in;
```

```
BEGIN

  -- Query using a FOR-LOOP to ensure a null is returned when
  -- no row is found.
  FOR i IN get_telephone(telephone_id) LOOP

    retval :=
      '[('||i.area_code||') '||i.telephone_number||']';

  END LOOP;

  -- Solely to illustrate a null print return.
  IF retval IS NULL THEN

    retval := '[]';

  END IF;

  -- Return variable length string.
  RETURN retval;

END;
-- ------------------------------------------------------------

-- Define a procedure to delete a telephone object.
MEMBER PROCEDURE delete_telephone_object IS

  -- Define variable for DML statement.
  statement VARCHAR2(4000 CHAR);

BEGIN

  -- Build DML statement for Native Dynamic SQL (NDS).
  statement := 'DELETE '
            || 'FROM     telephone '
            || 'WHERE    telephone_id = '''
            ||  SELF.telephone_id||'''';

  -- Use Native Dynamic SQL to execute DML statement.
  EXECUTE IMMEDIATE statement;

END;

-- ------------------------------------------------------------
```

```
-- Define a procedure to delete a telephone object.
STATIC PROCEDURE delete_telephone_object
( telephone_id        NUMBER ) IS

  -- Define variable for DML statement.
  statement VARCHAR2(4000 CHAR);

BEGIN

  -- Build DML statement for Native Dynamic SQL (NDS).
  statement := 'DELETE '
            || 'FROM     telephone '
            || 'WHERE    telephone_id = '''
            ||  telephone_id||'''';

  -- Use Native Dynamic SQL to execute DML statement.
  EXECUTE IMMEDIATE statement;

END;

-- -----------------------------------------------------------

-- Define a procedure to insert a telephone object.
MEMBER PROCEDURE insert_telephone_object IS

BEGIN

  -- Use a static statement.
  INSERT
  INTO     telephone
  VALUES
  ( SELF.telephone_id
  , SELF.contact_id
  , SELF.address_id
  , SELF.telephone_type
  , SELF.country_code
  , SELF.area_code
  , SELF.telephone_number);

END;

-- -----------------------------------------------------------

-- Define a static procedure to insert a telephone object.
STATIC PROCEDURE insert_telephone_object
( telephone_id        NUMBER
, contact_id          NUMBER
, address_id          NUMBER
```

```
, telephone_type      NUMBER
, country_code        VARCHAR2
, area_code           VARCHAR2
, telephone_number    VARCHAR2 ) IS

BEGIN

  -- Use a static statement.
  INSERT
  INTO      telephone
  VALUES
  ( telephone_id
  , contact_id
  , address_id
  , telephone_type
  , country_code
  , area_code
  , telephone_number);

END;


-- ----------------------------------------------------------

-- Define a procedure to update a telephone object.
MEMBER PROCEDURE update_telephone_object IS

  -- Define variable for DML statement.
  statement VARCHAR2(4000 CHAR);

BEGIN

  -- Build DML statement for Native Dynamic SQL (NDS).
  statement := 'UPDATE    telephone '
            || 'SET       country_code = '''
            ||               SELF.country_code||''''
            || ',         area_code = '''
            ||               SELF.area_code||''''
            || ',         telephone_number = '''
            ||               SELF.telephone_number||''''
            || 'WHERE     telephone_id = '
            ||               SELF.telephone_id;

  -- Use Native Dynamic SQL (NDS) to execute DML statement.
  EXECUTE IMMEDIATE statement;
```

```
  COMMIT;

END;

-- -------------------------------------------------------------

-- Define a static procedure to update a telephone object.
STATIC PROCEDURE update_telephone_object
( telephone_id        NUMBER
, country_code        VARCHAR2
, area_code           VARCHAR2
, telephone_number    VARCHAR2 ) IS

  -- Define variable for DML statement.
  statement VARCHAR2(4000 CHAR);

BEGIN

  -- Build DML statement for Native Dynamic SQL (NDS).
  statement := 'UPDATE    telephone '
            || 'SET       country_code = '''
            ||                country_code||''''
            || ',         area_code = '''
            ||                area_code||''''
            || ',         telephone_number = '''
            ||                telephone_number||''''
            || 'WHERE     telephone_id = '
            ||                telephone_id;

  -- Use Native Dynamic SQL (NDS) to execute DML statement.
  EXECUTE IMMEDIATE statement;

  COMMIT;

END;

-- -------------------------------------------------------------

-- Member procedure to print the formatted object.
MEMBER PROCEDURE print_telephone_number IS
```

```
BEGIN

  -- Print formatted telephone number.
  DBMS_OUTPUT.PUT_LINE('Telephone '
  ||                    '[('||SELF.area_code||') '
  ||                    SELF.telephone_number||']');

END;

-- -----------------------------------------------------------

-- Member procedure to print the elements of the object.
MEMBER PROCEDURE print_telephone_object IS

BEGIN

  -- Print object attributes.
  DBMS_OUTPUT.PUT_LINE('SELF.TELEPHONE_ID     ['
  ||                    SELF.telephone_id||']');
  DBMS_OUTPUT.PUT_LINE('SELF.CONTACT_ID       ['
  ||                    SELF.contact_id||']');
  DBMS_OUTPUT.PUT_LINE('SELF.ADDRESS_ID       ['
  ||                    SELF.address_id||']');
  DBMS_OUTPUT.PUT_LINE('SELF.TELEPHONE_TYPE   ['
  ||                    SELF.telephone_type||']');
  DBMS_OUTPUT.PUT_LINE('SELF.COUNTRY_CODE     ['
  ||                    SELF.country_code||']');
  DBMS_OUTPUT.PUT_LINE('SELF.AREA_CODE        ['
  ||                    SELF.area_code||']');
  DBMS_OUTPUT.PUT_LINE('SELF.TELEPHONE_NUMBER ['
  ||                    SELF.telephone_number||']');

END;

-- -----------------------------------------------------------

-- A method to check for equality of object instances.
ORDER MEMBER FUNCTION equals
( class_in TELEPHONE_OBJECT )
RETURN NUMBER IS

  -- Define default return values.
  false_value NUMBER := 0;
  true_value  NUMBER := 1;
```

```
BEGIN

  -- Compare all elements in the object.
  IF SELF.telephone_id = class_in.telephone_id AND
     SELF.contact_id = class_in.contact_id AND
     SELF.address_id = class_in.address_id AND
     SELF.telephone_type = class_in.telephone_type AND
     SELF.country_code = class_in.country_code AND
     SELF.area_code = class_in.area_code AND
     SELF.telephone_number = class_in.telephone_number THEN

    -- Return True they are equal.
    RETURN true_value;

  ELSE

    -- Return False they are unequal.
    RETURN false_value;

  END IF;

END;


  -- -----------------------------------------------------------

END;
/
```

The following discusses the implementation of constructor functions, and member procedures and functions:

- It defines two constructors that do the following:

  - The first constructor uses direct variables of native Oracle 9*i* data types. It has a complete list of all direct attributes for a telephone_object. It assigns the actual parameters to instance variables for a TELEPHONE_ OBJECT object type. Then, it returns a complete object instance.

  - The second constructor uses a primary key value for the telephone table as the single formal parameter. It defines an explicit cursor with a single formal parameter. It uses a cursor for-loop to read the record into explicit assignments to all instance variables. Then, it returns a complete object instance.

- It defines a member function, `get_telephone_number`, that takes a single formal parameter, which should be the primary key value for the `telephone` table. It defines a return value as a variable length string and does not assign a default value. It defines an explicit cursor that takes a single formal parameter, which should likewise be the primary key value for the `telephone` table. It uses a for-loop to retrieve the `telephone` table row, and then formats and assigns it to the local return value variable. Afterward, it checks to determine if the return value is a null value, and if so, it assigns it a value. Then, it returns the formatted telephone number.

- It defines a member procedure `delete_telephone_object` that takes no formal parameter because it uses an instance variable. The instance variable is the primary key value for the `telephone` table. In the declaration section, the member procedure defines a variable length statement variable string. The execution section dynamically builds the statement using Native Dynamic SQL (NDS) and executes the statement.

- It defines a static procedure `delete_telephone_object` that takes a single formal parameter, which should be the primary key value for the `telephone` table. In the declaration section, the static procedure defines a variable length statement variable string. The execution section dynamically builds the statement using Native Dynamic SQL (NDS) and executes the statement.

- It defines a member procedure `insert_telephone_object` that takes no formal parameters. It uses a static `INSERT` statement to insert the instance variables to the `telephone` table attributes.

- It defines a static procedure `insert_telephone_object` that takes seven formal parameters. It uses a static `INSERT` statement to insert the actual parameter values into the table.

- It defines a member procedure `update_telephone_object` that takes no formal parameters. It uses four instance variables to update the target table. One is the primary key value for the `telephone` table. The other three represent the `country_code`, `area_code`, and `telephone_ number` columns of the table. These are the key values that would be updated for a contacts telephone number. In the declaration section, it defines a variable length statement string. The execution section dynamically builds the statement variable using Native Dynamic SQL (NDS) and executes the statement.

■ It defines a static procedure `update_telephone_object` that takes four formal parameters. One is the primary key value for the `telephone` table. The other three represent the `country_code`, `area_code`, and `telephone_number` columns of the table. These are the key values that would be updated for a contacts telephone number. In the declaration section, it defines a variable length statement string. The execution section dynamically builds the statement variable using Native Dynamic SQL (NDS) and executes the statement.

■ It defines a member procedure `print_telephone_number` that prints to the console a formatted telephone number using the `DBMS_OUTPUT` package.

■ It defines a member procedure `print_telephone_object` that prints the contents of a `telephone_object` instance using the `DBMS_OUTPUT` package.

■ It defines an `ORDER` member function, `equals`, to check equality of one object against another.

**TIP**
*Writing an `equals` method is a recommended practice in OO programming. Using the `ORDER` member function as the `equals` function is the best solution for coding standards.*

The `telephone_object` object type and body have illustrated how you can build a real-world row façade and Data Manipulation Language (DML) interface to a database table. This is a beginning but not an end. You'll now examine the steps involved in building and working with the construction of an object type that uses a collection as an attribute.

Take the next step by creating a table of `telephone_object`. This is done with the following command:

```
-- This is found in the create_telephone_objects.sql file.

CREATE OR REPLACE TYPE telephone_object_table
AS TABLE OF telephone_object;
/
```

You now have a `telephone_object` table, or standard Oracle 9*i* collection. Collections are easy to use because they act as a densely populated list or set, which means they have an index from one to the maximum number of items in the list. Once you've initialized a collection, you can pass it by reference. Passing by reference means you can move the contents of the list from one programming scope to another. For example, you can initialize a collection in an anonymous block PL/SQL programming unit and move it to a stored procedure to add elements, or rows, and return the modified list.

The downside of an Oracle 9*i* collection is that it does not have an object constructor. If you could implement a constructor, you could pass a nonunique foreign key value and return a set of `telephone_object` objects. You're extending the concept used in the `telephone_object` constructor where you took a primary key argument to build an object type instance for a row in the `telephone` table. If a table collection had a constructor, you could pass a nonunique subtype key and return a set of `telephone_object` objects. Unfortunately, it doesn't.

**NOTE**
*Objects built with table collections have a quirk. The table size is fixed at the instantiation of the object and acts as an array. You can only change the size by extracting the collection from the object type, extending its size, adding a member to the collection, and reassigning the revised collection to the instance of the collection. This is done within the scope of a member procedure.*

### Why Would I Use This?

While we can't build a constructor for table collections, we can build an object type that uses the collection as an argument. This enables us to build an object collection with methods. We came across some syntax and scope challenges getting this working, but with the following examples you should be able to write it without problems.

We believe dynamic collections make transient objects tremendously useful for bulk processing. Also, you can write overloaded methods to support both individual and bulk processing models. This requires a bit more work than the examples we have provided but not much. We think you'll find the approach very useful in making objects server interactive and batch processing models simultaneously.

The next example shows you how to overcome these challenges and implement the next layer in a façade pattern. In the following, you'll find an object specification for an object type that uses a `telephone_object_table` as an instance attribute:

-- **This is found in the create_telephone_objects.sql file.**

```
CREATE OR REPLACE TYPE telephone_object_set
AS OBJECT
  ( telephone_entries     TELEPHONE_OBJECT_TABLE
  , set_size              NUMBER
, CONSTRUCTOR FUNCTION telephone_object_set
  ( telephone_entries     TELEPHONE_OBJECT_TABLE )
  RETURN SELF AS RESULT
, CONSTRUCTOR FUNCTION telephone_object_set
  ( contact_id            NUMBER    )
  RETURN SELF AS RESULT
, MEMBER PROCEDURE add_set_member
  ( telephone             TELEPHONE_OBJECT )
, MEMBER FUNCTION get_collection
  RETURN TELEPHONE_OBJECT_TABLE
, MEMBER FUNCTION get_set_member
  ( telephone_id          NUMBER    )
  RETURN TELEPHONE_OBJECT
, MEMBER PROCEDURE delete_telephone_object_set
  ( contact_id          NUMBER )
, MEMBER PROCEDURE insert_telephone_object_set
  ( telephone_table       TELEPHONE_OBJECT_TABLE )
, MEMBER PROCEDURE update_telephone_object_set
  ( telephone_entries     TELEPHONE_OBJECT_TABLE )
, MEMBER PROCEDURE print_telephone_number_set
, MEMBER PROCEDURE print_telephone_object_set
, ORDER MEMBER FUNCTION equals
  ( class_in TELEPHONE_OBJECT_SET )
  RETURN NUMBER )
INSTANTIABLE NOT FINAL;
/
```

The object type implements all the attributes and methods found in the UML static diagram depicting the compound object. It acts as the next level in the façade pattern and hides the complexity of the `telephone_object` object type.

Because many syntax issues and approaches generally aren't well documented, you should see the complete `telephone_object_set` object type body. This approach ensures you have a full implementation copy as a desk reference to leverage when developing your own façade patterns. The following shows the `telephone_object_set` object type body:

-- **This is found in the `create_telephone_objects.sql` file.**

```
CREATE OR REPLACE TYPE BODY telephone_object_set AS

  -- ------------------------------------------------------------

  -- Construct using a table collection.
  CONSTRUCTOR FUNCTION telephone_object_set
  ( telephone_entries  TELEPHONE_OBJECT_TABLE )
  RETURN SELF AS RESULT IS

  BEGIN

    -- Construct an instance of the telephone_object_set.
    SELF.telephone_entries := telephone_entries;

    -- Assign the size value to an instance variable.
    SELF.set_size := telephone_entries.LAST;

    -- Return an instance of the telephone_object_set.
    RETURN;

  END;

  -- ------------------------------------------------------------

  -- Construct using a subtype key in a table.
  CONSTRUCTOR FUNCTION telephone_object_set
  ( contact_id         NUMBER )
  RETURN SELF AS RESULT IS

    -- Define a local counter variable.
    c PLS_INTEGER := 1;

    -- Define an object structure.
    telephone TELEPHONE_OBJECT;

    -- Define and initialize the object collection.
    telephones TELEPHONE_OBJECT_TABLE := telephone_object_table();

    -- Define a cursor to get set elements.
    CURSOR get_telephone
    ( contact_id_in IN NUMBER) IS
      SELECT   telephone_id
```

```
      FROM     telephone
      WHERE    contact_id = contact_id_in;

BEGIN

  -- Use a for-loop to traverse the cursor.
  FOR i IN get_telephone(contact_id) LOOP

    -- Construct an instance of telephone_object.
    telephone := telephone_object(i.telephone_id);

    -- Allot space to the collection.
    telephones.EXTEND;

    -- Assign an element to the collection.
    -- ---------------------------------------------------------
    --   The index value for the collection may be a PLS_INTEGER
    --   but cannot be the for-loop counter variable "i". If you
    --   attempt to use the for-loop counter variable, you will
    --   raise an ORA-00382 error, which is an "expression of
    --   wrong type" message.
    -- ---------------------------------------------------------
    telephones(c) := telephone;

    -- Increment the counter.
    c := c + 1;

  END LOOP;

  -- Instantiate the object with the table collection.
  SELF.telephone_entries := telephones;

  -- Assign the size value to an instance variable.
  SELF.set_size := telephones.LAST;

  -- Return the object instance.
  RETURN;

END;


-- -------------------------------------------------------------

-- Add a member to the object collection of the instance.
MEMBER PROCEDURE add_set_member
( telephone          TELEPHONE_OBJECT ) IS
```

```
BEGIN

  -- Extend the local collection size.
  SELF.telephone_entries.EXTEND;

  -- Assign a new element.
  -- ----------------------------------------
  --   When the Oracle 9i Collection API EXTEND
  --   method is called, the size of the table
  --   collection is incremented by one.
  -- ----------------------------------------
  SELF.telephone_entries(SELF.telephone_entries.LAST) := telephone;

  -- Increment the known size of the collection.
  SELF.set_size := SELF.set_size + 1;

END;

-- ----------------------------------------------------------

-- Function to convert the object to a collection.
MEMBER FUNCTION get_collection
RETURN TELEPHONE_OBJECT_TABLE IS

BEGIN

  -- Return a table collection.
  RETURN SELF.telephone_entries;

END;

-- ----------------------------------------------------------

-- A method to get a set member value.
MEMBER FUNCTION get_set_member
( telephone_id         NUMBER   )
RETURN TELEPHONE_OBJECT IS

  -- Define a local counter variable.
  c PLS_INTEGER := 1;

  -- Define a object structure.
  telephone TELEPHONE_OBJECT;
```

```
BEGIN

  -- Use a for-loop to read through the set elements.
  FOR i IN 1..SELF.telephone_entries.LAST LOOP

    -- Check if set member is a match.
    IF SELF.telephone_entries(c).telephone_id = telephone_id THEN

      -- Assign object instance to object member.
      telephone := SELF.telephone_entries(c);

    END IF;

    -- Increment counter.
    c := c + 1;

  END LOOP;

  -- Return an instance of telephone.
  RETURN telephone;

END;

-- -----------------------------------------------------------

-- Member procedure to delete a set of telephone objects.
MEMBER PROCEDURE delete_telephone_object_set
( contact_id          NUMBER ) IS

  -- Define a local TELEPHONE_OBJECT variable.
  telephone           TELEPHONE_OBJECT;

  -- Define and initialize the object collection.
  telephones TELEPHONE_OBJECT_TABLE := telephone_object_table();

  -- Define a cursor to get set elements.
  CURSOR get_telephone
  ( contact_id_in IN NUMBER) IS
    SELECT   telephone_id
    FROM     telephone
    WHERE    contact_id = contact_id_in;

BEGIN

  -- Use a for-loop to read through the set elements.
  FOR i IN get_telephone(contact_id) LOOP
```

```
   -- Initialize an object instance.
   telephone := telephone_object(i.telephone_id);

   -- Access the method of the object type.
   telephone.delete_telephone_object;

 END LOOP;

END;


-- ------------------------------------------------------------

-- Member procedure to insert a set of telephone objects.
MEMBER PROCEDURE insert_telephone_object_set
( telephone_table     TELEPHONE_OBJECT_TABLE ) IS

BEGIN

 -- Loop through the initialized set.
 FOR i IN 1..SELF.TELEPHONE_ENTRIES.LAST LOOP

   -- Call the TELEPHONE_OBJECT method.
   SELF.telephone_entries(i).insert_telephone_object;

 END LOOP;

END;


-- ------------------------------------------------------------

-- Member procedure to update a set of telephone objects.
MEMBER PROCEDURE update_telephone_object_set
( telephone_entries    TELEPHONE_OBJECT_TABLE ) IS

BEGIN

 -- Loop through the initialized set.
 FOR i IN 1..SELF.TELEPHONE_ENTRIES.LAST LOOP

   -- Call the TELEPHONE_OBJECT method.
   SELF.telephone_entries(i).update_telephone_object;

 END LOOP;

END;


-- ------------------------------------------------------------
```

```sql
-- Member procedure to print the contents of the set.
MEMBER PROCEDURE print_telephone_object_set IS

BEGIN

  -- Print a double line break.
  DBMS_OUTPUT.PUT_LINE(
    '======================================');

  -- Use a for-loop to traverse the cursor.
  FOR i IN 1..SELF.telephone_entries.LAST LOOP

    -- Print a line break in-between return sets.
    IF i <> 1 THEN
      DBMS_OUTPUT.PUT_LINE(
        '--------------------------------------');
    END IF;

    -- Call the telephone_object print procedure.
    SELF.telephone_entries(i).print_telephone_object;

  END LOOP;

  -- Print a double line break.
  DBMS_OUTPUT.PUT_LINE(
    '======================================');

END;

-- ------------------------------------------------------------

-- Member procedure to print the phone numbers of the set.
MEMBER PROCEDURE print_telephone_number_set IS

BEGIN

  -- Print a double line break.
  DBMS_OUTPUT.PUT_LINE(
    '======================================');

  -- Use a for-loop to traverse the cursor.
  FOR i IN 1..SELF.telephone_entries.LAST LOOP
```

```
    -- Print a line break in-between return sets.
    IF i <> 1 THEN
      DBMS_OUTPUT.PUT_LINE(
        '--------------------------------------');
    END IF;

    -- Call the telephone_object print procedure.

    SELF.telephone_entries(i).print_telephone_number;

  END LOOP;

  -- Print a double line break.
  DBMS_OUTPUT.PUT_LINE(
    '======================================');

END;

-- ----------------------------------------------------------

-- Define a comparison function for a collection set object.
ORDER MEMBER FUNCTION equals
( class_in TELEPHONE_OBJECT_SET )
RETURN NUMBER IS

  -- Define return variable.
  retval      NUMBER := 1;

  -- Define default return values.
  false_value NUMBER := 0;
  true_value  NUMBER := 1;

  -- Define local instances of telephone objects.
  telephones_1 TELEPHONE_OBJECT_TABLE := telephone_object_table();
  telephones_2 TELEPHONE_OBJECT_TABLE := telephone_object_table();

BEGIN

  -- Assign set members to a table of objects.
  telephones_1 := SELF.get_collection;

  -- Assign set members to a table of objects.
  telephones_2 := class_in.get_collection;

  -- Loop through the initialized set.
  FOR i IN 1..SELF.TELEPHONE_ENTRIES.LAST LOOP
```

```
   -- Call the TELEPHONE_OBJECT method.
   IF telephones_1(i).equals(telephones_2(i)) = 1 THEN

     -- Assign a false value and exit loop.
     retval := false_value;

     -- Exit loop because one unequal element fails.
     EXIT;

   END IF;

 END LOOP;

 -- Return a default true numeric value.
 RETURN retval;

END;

END;
/
```

The following discusses the implementation of constructor functions, and member procedures and functions:

- It defines two constructors that do the following:

    - The first constructor uses a single table collection of the user-defined `telephone_object_table`. The execution section assigns the actual parameter to the table collection and sets the `set_size` instance variable to the number of elements in `telephone_object_table`. Then, it returns an instance of the `telephone_object_set` object type.

    - The second constructor uses a subtype key value for the `telephone` table as the single formal parameter. The declaration section defines a counter, a `telephone_object`, and `telephone_object_table` variable, and initializes the table collection as a null collection. Then, an explicit cursor is defined that returns a set of telephone rows. The explicit cursor uses one formal parameter. The execution section uses a cursor for-loop to read the records into the local table collection and assigns the collection to the instance. Then, it assigns the size of the table collection to the `set_size` instance variable and returns the object instance.

■ It defines a member procedure, `add_set_member`, which takes a single formal parameter—in this case, a `telephone_object` object type. In the declaration section, it defines a local table collection and initializes it as a null collection. In the execution section, a special syntax is used to assign the contents of the instance collection to the local variable. It uses the `SELF`, which is a reserved word for the instance and dot notation to another member function of the object type, to access and assign the contents of the object instance to the local table collection. It then uses the Oracle 9*i* Collection API to increase the size of the collection and assign the new object member to the collection. Afterward, it assigns the larger collection to the instance and increments the `set_size` instance variable. Note: This procedure is an important concept because it demonstrates how to increment an object type based on a table collection.

■ It defines a member function, `get_collection`, which enables external access to the `telephone_entries` table collection. It is also used by the `add_set_member` to demonstrate internal reference. The function simply returns an instance variable externally.

■ It defines the `delete_telephone_object_set`, `insert_telephone_object_set`, and `update_telephone_object_set` member procedures. They demonstrate techniques to call to the aggregation object type, `telephone_object`, and its methods. This demonstrates the layering of abstraction or hiding of complexity in the façade pattern.

■ It defines two other member procedures that demonstrate calls to nested object types. These are the `print_telephone_object_set` and `print_telephone_number_set` member procedures.

■ It defines an object type comparison member function, which is the `ORDER` member function you saw earlier in the chapter. It demonstrates iterative calls comparing the members of the `telephone_entries` variable by calling the `telephone_object` comparison member function. Access to the two functions is provided by the `telephone_object_set.get_collection` member function.

You've now completed a tour through the utility of transitive objects available in Oracle 9*i*. While this has illustrated the building blocks of a façade pattern, it's hoped that major syntax nuances and techniques have been effectively illustrated. The question you should have is, "Does it work?"

The following program enables you to test the `telephone_object_set` object type used in the façade pattern:

-- **This is found in the test_telephone_objects.sql file.**

```
DECLARE

  -- Define a counter variable.
  c            NUMBER := 1;

  -- Define and initialize as a null collection.
  telephones    TELEPHONE_OBJECT_TABLE := telephone_object_table();

  -- Define an object type using a collection.
  telephone_set TELEPHONE_OBJECT_SET;

BEGIN

  -- Extend the collection to add an element.
  telephones.EXTEND;

  -- Add an element.
  telephones(c) := TELEPHONE_OBJECT( 2001, 2001, 2001, 1006
                               ,'001','650','555-7890');

  -- Demonstrate the telephone_object print method.
  telephones(c).print_telephone_number;

  -- Increment the counter.
  c := c + 1;

  -- Extend the collection to add an element.
  telephones.EXTEND;

  DBMS_OUTPUT.PUT_LINE('Call Add Method.');

  -- Add an element.
  telephones(c) := TELEPHONE_OBJECT( 2001, 2001, 2001, 1006
                               ,'001','650','555-0987');

  -- Build a collection object with the constructor.
  telephone_set := telephone_object_set(telephones);

  -- Print message about what is being done with the object.
  DBMS_OUTPUT.PUT_LINE('What is there after construction?');
```

```
-- Print the contents of the collection object.
telephone_set.print_telephone_object_set;

-- Print message about what is being done with the object.
DBMS_OUTPUT.PUT_LINE('What is there after the add_set_member call?');

-- Use the method to increment the collection object.
telephone_set.add_set_member(
  TELEPHONE_OBJECT( 2001, 2001, 2001, 1006
                 ,'001','650','444-0987'));

-- Print the contents of the collection object.
telephone_set.print_telephone_number_set;

END;
/
```

The test program does the following:

- It defines a counter variable, a table collection variable, and a complex object type using an element of a collection variable. It also initializes the counter and collection as a null element collection.

- It extends the collection and constructs and assigns two elements to the collection. Then, it uses the collection as the actual parameter to construct an instance of the telephone_object_set complex object type. After it builds the object, it calls the object instance method print_telephone_object_set, which in turn calls the encapsulated telephone_object .print_telephone_object member method to print the elements.

- It then calls telephone_object_set.add_set_member by building an anonymous instance of telephone_object as the actual parameter.

## Why Would I Use This?

We wrote both telephone_object_set and telephone_object object instances to demonstrate the façade pattern since we believe they show you how they hide the details and encapsulated telephone_object object type. Also, we used the telephone_object_set object type to show how we mask complexity, make internal calls to base object type methods, and act on elements of an internal collection.

We also believe you'll see the benefit of using overloaded methods to support both interactive and bulk processing models in your code. The extensibility of these concepts should empower you to write great code.

This actually extends the internal collection of the object instance and adds the new member as discussed previously.

- It finally calls the `telephone_object_set.print_telephone_number_set` method, which calls the encapsulated `telephone_object.print_telephone_number` member method to print the numbers in the internal collection.

**NOTE**
*Anonymous class instances can be built and passed as actual parameters by calling the constructor as a function. This mechanism differs from Java where you need to use the reserved word NEW to build an anonymous instance of the class.*

The following is the output from the testing script. It shows what's there after the initial construction with two elements and after calling the `add_set_member` function. It produces the following output:

```
-- This is the output from the test_collection_object.sql file.

==========================================
SELF.TELEPHONE_ID       [2001]
SELF.CONTACT_ID         [2001]
SELF.ADDRESS_ID         [2001]
SELF.TELEPHONE_TYPE     [1006]
SELF.COUNTRY_CODE       [001]
SELF.AREA_CODE          [650]
SELF.TELEPHONE_NUMBER   [555-7890]
------------------------------------------
SELF.TELEPHONE_ID       [2001]
SELF.CONTACT_ID         [2001]
SELF.ADDRESS_ID         [2001]
SELF.TELEPHONE_TYPE     [1006]
SELF.COUNTRY_CODE       [001]
SELF.AREA_CODE          [650]
SELF.TELEPHONE_NUMBER   [555-0987]
==========================================
What is there after the add_set_member call?
==========================================
Telephone [(650) 555-7890]
------------------------------------------
Telephone [(650) 555-0987]
------------------------------------------
Telephone [(650) 444-0987]
==========================================
```

You have now seen how to use Oracle 9*i* transitive objects to build a façade to hide the complexity of an ERD model. There are a couple of cautions you should be aware of when using these techniques. Caution One is to carefully watch your object scope. Caution Two is to learn how to build wrappers around the initialization and extension of collections.

## Summary

You should now have a substantive knowledge of Oracle 9*i* object types, with enough skills to begin developing your own object types and employing a façade pattern in your database application design.

# PART
## III

# Optimizing
# PL/SQL Solutions

# CHAPTER
# 7

# Threading
# PL/SQL Execution

hreading PL/SQL code may be a new or old idea to you. If threading PL/SQL is a new idea, you'll find a complete solution in this chapter. If threading PL/SQL execution is an old idea, you'll learn techniques to control execution and the Oracle 10g migration strategy outside of the DBMS_JOB built-in package.

Oracle 7 through Oracle 9i provided two ways to create parallel PL/SQL execution. One is the building of a shell script to control execution. The other is the use of the DBMS_JOB package. The DBMS_JOB built-in package enables you to submit parallel or concurrent jobs within the native SQL environment. Unfortunately, Oracle 10g replaces DBMS_JOB with the DBMS_SCHEDULER built-in package and a disclaimer that DBMS_JOB is solely provided for backward compatibility. It appears that "solely provided" means that DBMS_JOB is no longer used by Oracle 10g internal components and customers who rely on it need to find new alternatives.

**TIP**
*If you check $ORACLE_HOME/rdbms/admin/ dbms_job.sql, you will find Oracle's disclaimer that DBMS_JOB is deprecated and is only provided for backward compatibility. As you read the balance of the chapter, you'll realize you should start migrating now because DBMS_JOB will cease to exist in some future version of the Oracle database.*

### Why Would I Use This?

We use parallel execution when optimizing batch processing and to support database maintenance tasks, which enables us to minimize their execution time. When we have large amounts of data to process in small time windows, using a single thread of execution is often impossible.

While PL/SQL is not natively threaded like Java, it provides all the tools we need to write parallel programs. We use the DBMS_PIPE command to create and manage pipes. The pipes mimic traditional operating system primitives like semaphores. They enable us to build threaded programming models. We find parallel execution the only solution to some large-scale batch processing problems.

This chapter stands independent of others in the book since all of its content works in currently supported versions of the Oracle database. However, the DBMS_JOB package will be discontinued in a future release. The following topics will be explored:

- The concept of, and components for, parallel PL/SQL
  - Introduction and discussion of the DBMS_JOB package
  - Introduction and discussion of DBMS_ALERT and DBMS_PIPE
  - Introduction and discussion of threading concepts for parallel programs
- Demonstration on how to build a parallel PL/SQL application
  - Demonstration of a thread-of-control
  - Demonstration of threads-of-execution
  - Demonstration of parallel execution

The focus of this chapter is to discuss and demonstrate how to create parallel PL/SQL program units. The control and execution of the PL/SQL program unit are the focus of the discussion.

You'll need to run the create_user.sql script for this chapter before attempting to run any of the sample programs. In fact, it's best to run it now.

# Introducing Parallel PL/SQL Concepts and Components

You write PL/SQL programs to support one of two processing models: Online Transaction Processing (OLTP) and batch processing. Each processing model has different behaviors.

OLTP is characterized by small transactions that support end-user access to data. The small transactions need to happen quickly because an end-user is waiting on their completion. The time-bound nature of OLTP is called soft real-time processing. Threading or parallel concurrent programming is appropriate for OLTP solutions when it can shorten the response time to the end-user.

Batch processing is characterized by sets of bulk processing steps that update data or migrate and configure data warehouses. Batch processing typically takes a few minutes to a few hours of computer time because it involves complex and sequenced changes to data. The time sensitivity of batch processing is driven by the available machine resources and degree of concurrency achievable against physical machine resources. Concurrent processing through threading is very advantageous in reducing runtime requirements for batch processing.

Oracle provides several built-in packages you can use to create a threaded PL/SQL execution. Unfortunately, PL/SQL is not natively threaded and requires a close attention to details.

# Introducing and Demonstrating the DBMS_JOB Package

The DBMS_JOB package provides you with the ability to process data in the background and concurrently, and eliminates the need to manage concurrency from external operating system programs, like shell scripts.

DBMS_JOB relies on the Coordinator Job Queue (CJQ) to manage background processing. There were three configuration environment variables in your Oracle 7 and Oracle 8 init.ora files. One was deprecated in Oracle 8*i* and another was deprecated in Oracle 9*i*. The JOB_QUEUE_INTERVAL parameter has been replaced by the INTERNAL ONLY _JOB_QUEUE_INTERVAL parameter as noted in the following, which is prefaced with an underscore.

**TIP**
*The future direction of Oracle is Oracle Streams, which is an advanced feature of Oracle Advanced Queuing.*

**NOTE**
*Oracle INTERNAL ONLY parameters should be avoided unless their use is directed by Oracle Support Services. Some published works use these parameters, which are now deprecated.*

## Why Would I Use This?

We use the DBMS_JOB package to build PL/SQL parallel execution, which has been around from Oracle 7 through Oracle 10g. We recommend it if you're currently running in Oracle 9*i* since it's your only choice. It's also best to develop an external Java Servlet to replace it in Oracle 10g since DBMS_JOB is moving toward deprecation by Oracle.

The original DBMS_JOB init.ora parameters are noted in the following table, along with their deprecation and version.

| Parameter | Description |
|---|---|
| JOB_QUEUE_PROCESSES | The JOB_QUEUE_PROCESSES parameter sets the degree of concurrency supported by the CJQ. The valid range is a value between 0 and 1000 and the default value is 10. The CJQ will spawn these dynamically as follows:<br><br>ora_{ ORACLE_SID }_snp0<br>...<br>ora_{ ORACLE_SID }_snp36 |
| JOB_QUEUE_INTERVAL | The JOB_QUEUE_INTERVAL parameter is the wake-up interval to check the job queue for newly submitted jobs. The default setting of 60 seconds is generally fine for most environments. JOB_QUEUE_INTERVAL is *deprecated in Oracle 9i* and replaced with an Oracle INTERNAL ONLY _JOB_QUEUE_INTERVAL parameter, which Oracle says should not be used except in conjunction with Oracle Support Services. The INTERNAL ONLY parameter supports an **alter** command against a system in Oracle 9*i* and 10*g*. |
| JOB_QUEUE_KEEP_CONNECTIONS | The JOB_QUEUE_KEEP_CONNECTIONS parameter should generally be set as TRUE, which enables permanent connections to be established and reused. If this is FALSE, you would continuously disconnect and reconnect, which consumes resources unnecessarily. Oracle 8*i* deprecated the JOB_QUEUE_KEEP_CONNECTIONS parameter and manages it dynamically. |

You can check the default value of JOB_QUEUE_PROCESSES by querying the v$parameter view as follows:

```
COL name FORMAT A20
COL value FORMAT A10
SELECT    name
,                   value
FROM      v$parameter
WHERE     name = 'job_queue_processes';
```

**NOTE**
*Oracle 9i and Oracle 10g won't natively enable you to read the public V$PARAMETER synonym. You must have your DBA grant you those permissions from the SYS account.*

You should see the following output unless you or your DBA have overridden the default value for job_queue_processes:

```
NAME                 VALUE
-------------------- ----------
job_queue_processes  10
```

If you don't have at least a value of ten concurrent jobs, please use the following to alter your system:

```
ALTER SYSTEM SET job_queue_processes = 10;
```

You can create a small table, sequence, and package that enable you to test the DBMS_JOB package, as noted next:

```
-- This is found in the create_job1.sql file.

-- Create a result table.
CREATE TABLE result
( result_id    NUMBER
, submit       DATE
, process      DATE
, result_value NUMBER );
```

```
-- Create a sequence for the result table.
CREATE SEQUENCE result_s1
INCREMENT BY     1
START WITH       1
ORDER;

-- Create a package that shows a clock difference.
CREATE OR REPLACE PACKAGE sample_job1 IS

  -- Define a function with default values.
  FUNCTION add_loop
  ( minimum      NUMBER := 1
  , maximum      NUMBER := 10000000 )
  RETURN NUMBER;

  -- Define a procedure to display results.
  PROCEDURE display_results
  ( submit_date DATE
  , minimum      NUMBER := NULL
  , maximum      NUMBER := NULL );

END sample_job1;
/

-- Create a package that shows a clock difference.
CREATE OR REPLACE PACKAGE BODY sample_job1 IS

  -- Define a function with default values.
  FUNCTION add_loop
  ( minimum NUMBER := 1
  , maximum NUMBER := 10000000 )
  RETURN NUMBER IS

    -- Declare local variable.
    retval NUMBER := 0;

  BEGIN

    -- Loop from the minimum to maximum.
    FOR i IN minimum..maximum LOOP
```

```
   -- Check if the loop index is equal to the maximum value.
   IF maximum = i THEN

     -- Assign the value.
     retval := i;

   END IF;

 END LOOP;

 -- Return value.
 RETURN retval;

END add_loop;

-- Define a procedure to display results.
PROCEDURE display_results
( submit_date DATE
, minimum       NUMBER := NULL
, maximum       NUMBER := NULL ) IS

 -- Set current time.
 current_date DATE := SYSDATE;

 -- Calculate the value.
 calculated_value NUMBER := sample_job1.add_loop;

BEGIN

 -- Manage return value.

 INSERT
 INTO      result
 VALUES
 ( result_s1.nextval
 , submit_date

 , SYSDATE
 , calculated_value );

END display_results;

END sample_job1;
/
```

The `create_job1.sql` script creates a table, sequence, and package with the following characteristics:

- It defines a `result` table that allows the `DBMS_JOB` submitted job to leave a marker of what it did.

- It defines a `result_s1` sequence used to populate the primary key of the sample result table.

- It defines a `sample_job1` package that contains an `add_loop` function and `display_results` procedure. They do the following:

  - The `add_loop` function takes the `minimum` and `maximum` formal parameters, which have default values. The function runs a long running loop. You may need to override the default values to get a difference between the submitted and inserted times or speed sample execution.

  - The `display_results` procedure takes a `submit_date`, and `minimum` and `maximum` formal parameters. The latter two have default values of NULL, which makes them optional actual parameters.

The `DBMS_JOB.SUBMIT` procedure enables you to submit jobs to the Coordinator Job Queue (CJQ). It has the following list of formal parameters:

```
PROCEDURE SUBMIT
   Argument Name    Type              In/Out Default?
   ---------------  ----------------  ------ --------
   JOB              BINARY_INTEGER    OUT
   WHAT             VARCHAR2          IN
   NEXT_DATE        DATE              IN     DEFAULT
   INTERVAL         VARCHAR2          IN     DEFAULT
   NO_PARSE         BOOLEAN           IN     DEFAULT
   INSTANCE         BINARY_INTEGER    IN     DEFAULT
   FORCE            BOOLEAN           IN     DEFAULT
```

Only the first two parameters are required. We can accept the default values for the optional formal parameters. The first formal parameter `job` has an OUT mode, which requires its execution to be within the scope of a PL/SQL or OCI program unit.

The following anonymous block PL/SQL program enables you to test the `DBMS_JOB.SUBMIT` procedure:

```
-- This is found in the create_job1.sql file.
DECLARE

  -- Record the job number.
  job_out PLS_INTEGER;
```

```
BEGIN

  -- Submit the job for immediate execution.
  DBMS_JOB.SUBMIT( JOB => job_out
                 , WHAT => 'sample_job1.display_results(SYSDATE);' );

  -- DBMS_JOB.SUBMIT requires a COMMIT to signal complete submission.
  COMMIT;

  -- Print the job number.
  DBMS_OUTPUT.PUT_LINE('The job is: ['||job_out||']');

END;
/
```

The anonymous block PL/SQL program does the following:

- It submits the `sample_job1.display_results` procedure with a single actual parameter of `SYSDATE`.

- It uses a `COMMIT` statement to signal completion of the `DBMS_JOB.SUBMIT` procedure. If you don't use an explicit `COMMIT` statement in the calling program, the job will be implicitly rolled back.

- It prints the returned job number from the `DBMS_JOB.SUBMIT` procedure.

You can use the following formatting and query to see the pending results:

```
-- This is found in the create_job1.sql file.
COL date1 FORMAT A20
COL date2 FORMAT A20

-- Query result table.
SELECT    result_id
,         TO_CHAR(submit,'DD-MON-YY HH24:MI:SSSS') date1
,         TO_CHAR(process,'DD-MON-YY HH24:MI:SSSS') date2
,         result_value
FROM      result;
```

While your `result_id` and date values will differ, they will display the following formatted results:

```
RESULT_ID DATE1                     DATE2                   RESULT_VALUE
--------- -------------------- -------------------- ------------
       81 27-FEB-05 10:42:3131 27-FEB-05 10:42:3535    10000000
```

Note that the submission date is slightly sooner than the job execution. The delay is structured in `sample_job1.display_results` by calling the `sample_job1.add_loop` function before inserting the record in the `result` table.

There are several other functions and procedures in the `DBMS_JOB` package. They aren't covered here because all you need to see is how to start a job to work with parallel PL/SQL programming constructs. You now know how to build a stored procedure that can be used by the `DBMS_JOB` package and how to submit it with `DBMS_JOB.SUBMIT`.

# Introducing, Comparing, and Contrasting DBMS_PIPE and DBMS_ALERT

The `DBMS_PIPE` and `DBMS_ALERT` packages enable intersession communication, which is necessary to effect threaded execution. `DBMS_PIPE` is the only way to effectively manage threads because the publish-and-subscribe paradigm adopted by `DBMS_ALERT` can result in missing signals between threads.

While this is not a tutorial on `DBMS_PIPE` or `DBMS_ALERT`, you should understand their basic architectures. The following walks you through the fundamental architectures. Then, you can compare and contrast the two approaches to supporting threaded programs.

## Why Would I Use This?

We use `DBMS_PIPE` and `DBMS_ALERT` packages to communicate between different sessions of a database. You need to know how they work so you can guarantee synchronization between your threaded or concurrent PL/SQL programs.

`DBMS_PIPE` provides your PL/SQL development environment with structures that mimic operating system semaphores. `DBMS_PIPE` creates and manages the content of pipes in the Oracle SGA. It is the only effective way to communicate between different sessions of the database without writing data to tables.

**NOTE**
*A full tutorial is found in* Oracle Database 10g PL/SQL Programming. *DBMS_ALERT and DBMS_PIPE are covered in Chapter 11.*

The DBMS_PIPE architecture is very much like a UNIX pipe, which is a First-In-First-Out (FIFO) queue. FIFO queues are effective tools for reading and writing data between multiple programs without creating shared memory segments. DBMS_PIPE provides a natural shared memory structure because it uses the Oracle Shared Global Area (SGA) to write and then read data through the pipe. You may elect to implement DBMS_PIPE as a private (single user only) or public (instance only) structure. As a rule, threaded programs run with the same privileges and a private pipe is adequate to support PL/SQL concurrent programs.

The DBMS_PIPE architecture can be represented as shown in Figure 7-1. It shows that a program in one session writes to a local buffer and transfers to a private-named pipe. The contents remain in the private pipe until read by another session. When the other session reads the private pipe, it transfers the contents to a local buffer to access them in a PL/SQL program unit.

After FIFO, DBMS_PIPE queues are read, and the contents are removed. This can cause a problem in concurrent program execution because DBMS_PIPE is used as the resource gate. A resource gate controls access to critical resources, like operating system semaphores. The intersession pipes managed by DBMS_PIPE act

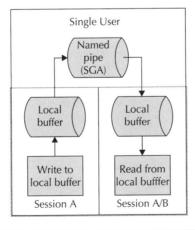

**FIGURE 7-1.** *Private or public pipe write-and-read operation*

like operating system semaphores with a twist. Semaphores act as gates to critical resources. They have an on and off state, whereas DBMS_PIPE pipes are written to a FIFO queue. The FIFO queue is emptied as read, which causes the semaphore pipe to disappear. Thread control is lost when the semaphore pipes disappear. Managing queued semaphores requires you to lock, read, and rewrite the queue contents until all pipe members of value sets are complete and the thread-of-control signals their release. Gates will be covered in more detail in the next section of this chapter.

The DBMS_ALERT architecture is more robust as a prefabricated publish-and-subscribe component because it implements the polling daemon and event triggers. Unfortunately, there is no effective way to gauge reading a published DBMS_ALERT and only the last published event is maintained.

Using DBMS_ALERT would not provide the necessary controls to manage threaded programs where three or more threads run concurrently. You need to use DBMS_PIPE to build robust threaded programs, but you can implement a two-thread only architecture with DBMS_ALERT.

# Introducing and Discussing Threading Concepts for Parallel Programs

You write threaded programs by applying a pattern. The pattern requires that you coordinate activities between the different threads. The generalized threading pattern defines a thread-of-control that starts and manages threads-of-execution. The thread-of-control makes sure all or none of the threads complete and commit their work.

## Why Would I Use This?

You need to know how parallel programs work in order to build them in the Oracle database. If you don't understand the architecture of something well, you'll make mistakes, which means having to rework and rewrite code. That's why it's best to get it right the first time.

The thread-of-control is the master of all concurrently executed threads. It starts, stops and manages all threads. It is the control unit that sets and unsets pipes that synchronize thread execution. You need to understand how to make this work. We know once you see the technique in a simple example that you can build robust threaded PL/SQL programming applications.

The transaction concept of all or nothing is defined by the term *ACID-compliant transactions*. ACID is an acronym for:

- **Atomic**   All or nothing happens.

- **Consistent**   The results from serial execution are the same as those from concurrent execution.

- **Isolated**   All results are hidden until committed.

- **Durable**   Once written, all changes are permanent.

ACID-compliant transactions have all of these properties. In PL/SQL, this means that all commits are executed at synchronizing events. You manage the synchronizing events by using paired resources, like named pipes.

In languages like Java, threading is natively part of the language. PL/SQL does not natively support threading and requires much the same effort as POSIX threads in C and C++. The sequencing requires a lock and a list, which can be a FIFO queue as delivered in the DBMS_PIPE package.

You must define a minimum of three pairs of pipes for optimistic models in which failures won't occur. Four pairs of pipes are required for a real-world model where errors arise. This is called a pessimistic model. In this example, there are four pairs of pipes defined as the USER name (PLSQL) followed by a dollar sign ($) and their functional name:

| Named FIFO Queue | Named FIFO Queue for Lock |
| --- | --- |
| PLSQL$THREAD_ABORT | PLSQL$THREAD_ABORT_LOCK |
| PLSQL$THREAD_COMMIT | PLSQL$THREAD_COMMIT_LOCK |
| PLSQL$THREAD_COMPLETE | PLSQL$THREAD_COMPLETE_LOCK |
| PLSQL$THREAD_REGISTER | PLSQL$THREAD_REGISTER_LOCK |

The lock-named pipe is required to prevent more than one thread from reading the FIFO queue simultaneously. Threads can write at any time to the named pipes that are FIFO queues. However, you must restrict threads-of-execution from concurrent reading of the PLSQL$THREAD_COMMIT_LOCK pipe. The reason for this limitation is that DBMS_PIPE must be read serially. You use locking named pipes to control read access to the pipes that contain lists of data. The locking pipes guarantee that the list is a complete FIFO queue and not a partial list being read by another thread.

Now that you've completed the introduction to threaded programming, let's move on to the next section which demonstrates how to build a threaded PL/SQL program.

# Demonstrating How to Build a Parallel PL/SQL Application

Once you've worked through building the framework for threaded PL/SQL execution, you'll then build a PL/SQL threaded program. The framework includes building DBMS_PIPE named pipes and a wrapper package to write-to and read-from the named pipes.

You'll build named pipes and modules to write-to and read-from named pipes. The following discussion demonstrates these concepts. Run the following create_thread_pipes.sql script to build the DBMS_PIPE named pipes:

```
-- This is found in the create_thread_pipes.sql file.
DECLARE

  -- Function output variable.
  retval INTEGER;

BEGIN

  -- Define a private pipe.
  retval := DBMS_PIPE.CREATE_PIPE('PLSQL$THREAD_ABORT'
                                  , 20000 );

  -- Define a private pipe.
  retval := DBMS_PIPE.CREATE_PIPE('PLSQL$THREAD_ABORT_LOCK'
                                  , 1 );
```

## Why Would I Use This?

You need to see how all the pieces fit together into a parallel solution. The first piece is how to effectively use DBMS_PIPE to build pipes. We provide a wrapper package that enables you to write-to and read-from the named pipes. We hope this jump-starts your use of the parallel PL/SQL programming techniques.

```
-- Define a private pipe.
retval := DBMS_PIPE.CREATE_PIPE('PLSQL$THREAD_COMMIT'
                               , 20000 );

-- Define a private pipe.
retval := DBMS_PIPE.CREATE_PIPE('PLSQL$THREAD_COMMIT_LOCK'
                               , 1 );

-- Define a private pipe.
retval := DBMS_PIPE.CREATE_PIPE('PLSQL$THREAD_COMPLETE'
                               , 20000 );

-- Define a private pipe.
retval := DBMS_PIPE.CREATE_PIPE('PLSQL$THREAD_COMPLETE_LOCK'
                               , 1 );

-- Define a private pipe.
retval := DBMS_PIPE.CREATE_PIPE('PLSQL$THREAD_REGISTER'
                               , 20000 );

-- Define a private pipe.
retval := DBMS_PIPE.CREATE_PIPE('PLSQL$THREAD_REGISTER_LOCK'
                               , 1 );

-- Print the retval status.
IF (retval = 0) THEN
  DBMS_OUTPUT.PUT_LINE('THREAD_PIPES are created.');
END IF;

EXCEPTION

-- Raise generic exception.
WHEN others THEN
  DBMS_OUTPUT.PUT_LINE(SQLERRM);
  RETURN;

END;
/
```

The program created eight DBMS_PIPE named pipes with a maximum of 20,000 entries for each data list pipe and one item each for lock pipes. The program raises an exception if an error occurs. Otherwise, you should see the following output:

```
THREAD_PIPES are created.
```

After you've created the DBMS_PIPE named pipes, you need to create wrapper packages to write-to and read-from the named pipes. The following create_wrapper.sql script provides you with that code:

```sql
-- This is found in the create_wrapper.sql file.

-- Create package specification.
CREATE OR REPLACE PACKAGE messenger IS

  -- Define function specification.
  FUNCTION send_message
    (user_name        VARCHAR2
    ,message_in       VARCHAR2
    ,pipe_name        VARCHAR2 )
    RETURN INTEGER;

  -- Define function specification.
  FUNCTION receive_message
    (user_name        VARCHAR2
    ,message_out      VARCHAR2
    ,pipe_name        VARCHAR2 )
    RETURN VARCHAR2;

END messenger;
/

-- Create package body.
CREATE OR REPLACE PACKAGE BODY messenger IS

  -- Define local package function to return user name.
  FUNCTION get_user
    RETURN VARCHAR2 IS

  BEGIN

    -- Use a cursor for-loop to get user name.
    FOR i IN (SELECT user FROM dual) LOOP

      -- Return the user.
      return i.user;

    END LOOP;
```

```
END get_user;

-- Implement package function defined in specification.
FUNCTION send_message
  (user_name      VARCHAR2
  ,message_in     VARCHAR2
  ,pipe_name      VARCHAR2 )
  RETURN INTEGER IS

  -- Define variable for target.
  target_pipe    VARCHAR2(100 CHAR);

BEGIN

  -- Purge local pipe content.
  DBMS_PIPE.RESET_BUFFER;

  -- Declare the target for a message.
  target_pipe := UPPER(user_name) || '$'
              || UPPER(pipe_name);

  -- Use the procedure to put a message in the local buffer.
  DBMS_PIPE.PACK_MESSAGE(message_in);

  -- Send message, success is a zero return value.
  IF (DBMS_PIPE.send_message(target_pipe) = 0) THEN

    -- Message sent, so return 0.
    RETURN 0;

  ELSE

    -- Message not sent, so return 1.
    RETURN 1;

  END IF;

END send_message;

-- Implement package function defined in specification.
FUNCTION receive_message
  (user_name      VARCHAR2
  ,message_out    VARCHAR2
  ,pipe_name      VARCHAR2 )
  RETURN VARCHAR2 IS
```

```
      -- Define variable for target mailbox.
      message          VARCHAR2(4000 CHAR) :=  NULL;
      target_pipe      VARCHAR2(100 CHAR);
      timeout          INTEGER := 0;
      return_code      INTEGER;

   BEGIN

      -- Purge local pipe content.
      DBMS_PIPE.RESET_BUFFER;

      -- Declare the target for a pipe.
      target_pipe := UPPER(user_name) || '$'
                  || UPPER(pipe_name);

      -- Use the procedure to put a message in the local buffer.
      return_code := DBMS_PIPE.receive_message(target_pipe,timeout);

      -- Evaluate and process return code.
      CASE return_code
        WHEN 0 THEN

          -- Read the message into a variable.
          DBMS_PIPE.UNPACK_MESSAGE(message);

        WHEN 1 THEN

          -- Assign message.
          message := 'The message pipe is empty.';

        WHEN 2 THEN

          -- Assign message.
          message := 'The message is too large for variable.';

        WHEN 3 THEN

          -- Assign message.
          message := 'An interrupt occurred, contact the DBA.';

      END CASE;

      -- Return the message.
      RETURN message;

   END receive_message;

END messenger;
/
```

The script builds a PL/SQL package that does the following:

- It creates a messenger package type with two public functions: one is send_message and the other is receive_message.

- It creates a messenger package body with one local function and two public functions. The get_user function returns the current user name to match against the DBMS_PIPE named pipes. The send_message and receive_message functions implement the logic to read-from and write-to named pipes. The internal functions do the following:

  - They define a local function that uses a query against the dual table to return the current user name.

  - They define a function that takes three formal parameters, a username, message, and a message box. The first actual parameter should be the current user. The second actual parameter should be the message that's written to the named pipe. The third actual parameter should be the name of the DBMS_PIPE named pipe. Internally, the function resets the local buffer, and then packs and sends a message.

  - They define a function that takes three formal parameters, a username, message, and message box. The first actual parameter should be the current user. The second actual parameter should be the message that's read from the named pipe. The third actual parameter should be the name of the DBMS_PIPE named pipe. Internally, the function resets the local buffer, and then unpacks and reads a message. It returns the following values dependent on what is found in the DBMS_PIPE named pipe:

    - **Returns a 0**  If a message is read from the DBMS_PIPE named pipe

    - **Returns a 1**  If the DBMS_PIPE named pipe is empty

    - **Returns a 2**  If the DBMS_PIPE named pipe is too small for the attempted message to fit into it

    - **Returns a 3**  If a system interrupt occurred, which is a problem for a DBA to troubleshoot

By running the preceding code examples, you've established the necessary framework to support threaded PL/SQL execution. You can examine three components to see how to build parallel PL/SQL applications. The three components are

- The thread-of-control organizes and synchronizes thread execution.

- Threads-of-execution run concurrently under the direction of the thread-of-control and signaling between DBMS_PIPE named pipes.

- Testing concurrent or parallel program execution is done with the DBMS_JOB package.

The next three sections cover these components. You should follow them through sequentially.

## Demonstrating a Thread-of-Control

A thread-of-control should invoke, manage, and signal threads-of-execution to complete processing. You'll now build a sample thread-of-control as a PL/SQL package. The sample thread-of-control uses the following:

- A user-defined attribute object type managing arguments

- A user-defined attribute_table collection of attribute object types enabling collections of the attribute object

- A user-defined attributes_object object type to manage collections of attribute_table types

- A user-defined attributes_table collection of attribute object types enabling collections of the attributes object

- A user-defined job_table collection of NUMBER data types

- A user-defined jobs_object object type to manage collections of the jobs_table object

- A package to manage the thread-of-control

**Why Would I Use This?**
You need to know how to control and synchronize threads-of-execution. If a threaded program fails to control and synchronize execution, it may corrupt data using concurrent or parallel programs.

We know the example to implement threaded PL/SQL programs is non-trivial because it contains a number of concepts. You should find that we cover each in sequence, including the full code to build the supplemental structures required to support the examples.

The syntax to build all of the thread-of-control components is found in the `create_thread_of_control.sql` script. Each segment of the program will be addressed so you'll have a complete set of the sample code in the book. It will be covered in three segments:

- Building the attributes collection
- Building the job collection
- Building the thread-of-control package

## Building the Attributes Collection

You build the attributes collection by starting with the smallest unit, which is an attribute that may be a `VARCHAR2` or `NUMBER` data type. Layers of access and utility are built on this basic structure and culminate in an `attributes_table` collection. The `attributes_table` collection contains a list of potential attributes for dynamic thread submission.

**Why Would I Use This?**
You need to know how to build a structure to pass lists of variables in a package that dynamically submits threads with different actual parameters. If this section is a challenge, you should review Chapter 6 for coverage of PL/SQL object types.

We use these to enable the passing of a list of argument parameters to our threaded program. There are a couple of other ways to do it, but we find this the most scalable and robust.

The `attribute` object type defines and implements an object wrapper containing an `attribute_type`, `attribute_number`, and `attribute_varchar2` structure. Only the fundamental utility of the objects are covered after programming units, and you're directed to Chapter 4 for broader coverage on objects. The `attribute` object type is qualified next:

-- **This is found in the create_thread_of_control.sql file.**

```sql
CREATE OR REPLACE TYPE attribute_object AS OBJECT
( attribute_type     VARCHAR2(12)
, attribute_number   VARCHAR2(38)
, attribute_varchar2 VARCHAR2(100)
, CONSTRUCTOR FUNCTION attribute_object
  ( attribute_type   VARCHAR2
  , attribute_value  VARCHAR2 ) RETURN SELF AS RESULT
, MEMBER FUNCTION get_type RETURN VARCHAR2
, MEMBER FUNCTION get_number RETURN NUMBER
, MEMBER FUNCTION get_varchar2 RETURN VARCHAR2
, MEMBER FUNCTION to_varchar2 RETURN VARCHAR2
, ORDER MEMBER FUNCTION equals
  ( class_in         ATTRIBUTE_OBJECT ) RETURN NUMBER )
INSTANTIABLE FINAL;
/

CREATE OR REPLACE TYPE BODY attribute_object AS

  CONSTRUCTOR FUNCTION attribute_object
  ( attribute_type   VARCHAR2
  , attribute_value VARCHAR2 ) RETURN SELF AS RESULT IS

  BEGIN

    -- Assign the type to the instance attribute.
    SELF.attribute_type := attribute_type;

    -- Check the type and build the variable type.
    IF SELF.attribute_type = 'NUMBER' THEN

      SELF.attribute_number := attribute_value;
      SELF.attribute_varchar2 := NULL;

    ELSIF SELF.attribute_type = 'VARCHAR2' THEN

      SELF.attribute_number := 0;
      SELF.attribute_varchar2 := attribute_value;

    END IF;
```

```
    -- Return instance.
    RETURN;

END;

-- Member function to return attribute type.
MEMBER FUNCTION get_type RETURN VARCHAR2 IS

BEGIN

  -- Return the size of the collection.
  RETURN SELF.attribute_type;

END;

-- Member function to return attribute NUMBER.
MEMBER FUNCTION get_number RETURN NUMBER IS

BEGIN

  -- Return the element of the collection.
  RETURN SELF.attribute_number;

END;

-- Member function to return attribute VARCHAR2.
MEMBER FUNCTION get_varchar2 RETURN VARCHAR2 IS

BEGIN

  -- Return the element of the collection.
  RETURN SELF.attribute_varchar2;

END;

-- Member function to return attribute VARCHAR2.
MEMBER FUNCTION to_varchar2 RETURN VARCHAR2 IS

BEGIN

  IF SELF.attribute_number IS NULL THEN

    -- Return the element of the collection.
    RETURN SELF.attribute_varchar2;
```

```
    ELSE

      -- Return the element of the collection.
      RETURN SELF.attribute_number;

    END IF;

  END;

  -- A method to check for equality of object instances.
  ORDER MEMBER FUNCTION equals
  ( class_in ATTRIBUTE_OBJECT )
  RETURN NUMBER IS

    -- Define default return values.
    false_value NUMBER := 0;
    true_value  NUMBER := 1;

  BEGIN

    -- Compare all elements in the object.
    IF SELF.attribute_type = class_in.attribute_type AND
      SELF.attribute_number = class_in.attribute_number AND
      SELF.attribute_varchar2 = class_in.attribute_varchar2 THEN

      -- Return True they are equal.
      RETURN true_value;

    ELSE

      -- Return False they are unequal.
      RETURN false_value;

    END IF;

  END;

END;
/
```

The `attribute_object` object type defines and implements the following methods:

- A constructor that takes two arguments: `attribute_type` and `attribute_value`. Note that both of these variables are `VARCHAR2` data types. They could also be defined as overriding constructors with an `attribute_type` of `VARCHAR2` and `attribute_value` of `NUMBER`.

■ A member function `get_type` that the actual parameter sent to the formal `attribute_type` parameter. It can be either `VARCHAR2` or `NUMBER`.

■ A member function `get_number` that returns the `attribute_value` when it's `NUMBER`.

■ A member function `get_varchar2` that returns the `attribute_value` when it's `VARCHAR2`.

■ A member function `to_varchar2` that converts and returns the structure to a `VARCHAR2` variable.

■ An order member function `equals` that compares two object type instances and returns a zero for false and one for true.

After defining and implementing the `attribute_object` object, you define a collection of the `attribute_object` object type. To do so, use the following syntax:

```
-- This is found in the create_thread_of_control.sql file.
CREATE OR REPLACE TYPE attribute_table
  AS TABLE OF ATTRIBUTE_OBJECT;
/
```

These building blocks enable you to build an object to manage collections of `attribute` objects. You can manage these collections with the `attributes_object` object type and body covered in the following:

```
-- This is found in the create_thread_of_control.sql file.

CREATE OR REPLACE TYPE attributes_object AS OBJECT
( attribute_list    ATTRIBUTE_TABLE
, CONSTRUCTOR FUNCTION attributes_object RETURN SELF AS RESULT
, CONSTRUCTOR FUNCTION attributes_object
  ( attribute_in    ATTRIBUTE_OBJECT ) RETURN SELF AS RESULT
, CONSTRUCTOR FUNCTION attributes_object
  ( attribute_list  ATTRIBUTE_TABLE ) RETURN SELF AS RESULT
, MEMBER PROCEDURE add_item
  ( attribute_in    ATTRIBUTE_OBJECT )
, MEMBER FUNCTION count RETURN NUMBER
, MEMBER PROCEDURE delete_item
  ( index_value     NUMBER )
, MEMBER PROCEDURE delete_item
  ( index_start     NUMBER
  , index_end       NUMBER )
, MEMBER FUNCTION limit RETURN NUMBER
```

```
, MEMBER FUNCTION get_attribute_list RETURN ATTRIBUTE_TABLE
, MEMBER FUNCTION to_varchar2 RETURN VARCHAR2
, ORDER MEMBER FUNCTION equals
  ( class_in         ATTRIBUTES_OBJECT ) RETURN NUMBER )
INSTANTIABLE FINAL;
/

CREATE OR REPLACE TYPE BODY attributes_object AS

  -- Constructor to build a null collection.
  CONSTRUCTOR FUNCTION attributes_object RETURN SELF AS RESULT IS

  BEGIN

    -- Define collection variable.
    SELF.attribute_list  := attribute_table();

    -- Return instance.
    RETURN;

  END;

  -- Constructor to build a collection with an initial value.
  CONSTRUCTOR FUNCTION attributes_object
  ( attribute_in    ATTRIBUTE_OBJECT ) RETURN SELF AS RESULT IS

  BEGIN

    -- Initialize the instance variable.
    SELF.attribute_list := attribute_table(attribute_in);

    -- Return instance.
    RETURN;

  END;

  -- Constructor to build a collection with an initial collection.
  CONSTRUCTOR FUNCTION attributes_object
  ( attribute_list  ATTRIBUTE_TABLE ) RETURN SELF AS RESULT IS

  BEGIN

    -- Assign an existing collection to the instance collection.
    SELF.attribute_list := attribute_list;

    -- Return instance.
    RETURN;

  END;
```

```
-- Member procedure to add to the internal collection.
MEMBER PROCEDURE add_item
( attribute_in    ATTRIBUTE_OBJECT ) IS

  -- Define and initialize collection
  attribute_list ATTRIBUTE_TABLE := attribute_table();

BEGIN

  -- Extend the instance collection space by one.
  SELF.attribute_list.EXTEND;

  -- Assign the new value.
  SELF.attribute_list(SELF.attribute_list.LAST) := attribute_in;

END;

-- Member function to return size of internal collection.
MEMBER FUNCTION count RETURN NUMBER IS

BEGIN

  -- Return the size of the collection.
  RETURN SELF.attribute_list.COUNT;

END;

-- Member function to return size of internal collection.
MEMBER PROCEDURE delete_item
( index_value    NUMBER ) IS

  -- Declare a local counter variable.
  counter        NUMBER := 1;

  -- Define and initialize a local collection.
  attribute_list  ATTRIBUTE_TABLE := attribute_table();

BEGIN

  -- Check for valid index value.
  IF SELF.attribute_list.EXISTS(index_value) THEN

    -- Delete element.
    SELF.attribute_list.DELETE(index_value);

    -- Allocate space to the local collection.
    attribute_list.EXTEND(SELF.attribute_list.COUNT);
```

```
        -- Copy contents to a re-indexed collection.
        FOR i IN SELF.attribute_list.FIRST..SELF.attribute_list.LAST LOOP

          -- Check if index value exists.
          IF SELF.attribute_list.EXISTS(i) THEN

            -- Assign a value to the reindexed collection.
            attribute_list(counter) := SELF.attribute_list(i);

            -- Increment the local counter.
            counter := counter + 1;

          END IF;

        END LOOP;

      END IF;

      -- Assign the re-indexed collection to the instance collection.
      SELF.attribute_list := attribute_list;

  END;

  -- Member function to return size of internal collection.
  MEMBER PROCEDURE delete_item
  ( index_start    NUMBER
  , index_end      NUMBER ) IS

    -- Declare a local counter variable.
    counter        NUMBER := 1;

    -- Define and initialize a local collection.
    attribute_list  ATTRIBUTE_TABLE := attribute_table();

  BEGIN

    -- Check starting index is less than the ending index.
    IF index_start >= index_end THEN

      RAISE_APPLICATION_ERROR(-20000,
        'Starting index is larger than ending index');

    END IF;

    -- Check for a valid index.
    IF SELF.attribute_list.EXISTS(index_start) AND
       SELF.attribute_list.EXISTS(index_end) THEN
```

```
        -- Delete element.
        SELF.attribute_list.DELETE(index_start,index_end);

        -- Allocate space to the local collection.
        attribute_list.EXTEND(SELF.attribute_list.COUNT);

        -- Copy contents to a re-indexed collection.
        FOR i IN SELF.attribute_list.FIRST..SELF.attribute_list.LAST LOOP

          -- Check if index value exists.
          IF SELF.attribute_list.EXISTS(i) THEN

            -- Assign a value to the re-indexed collection.
            attribute_list(counter) := SELF.attribute_list(i);

            -- Increment the local counter.
            counter := counter + 1;

          END IF;

        END LOOP;

      END IF;

      -- Assign the re-indexed collection to the instance collection.
      SELF.attribute_list := attribute_list;

  END;

  -- Member function to return size of internal collection.
  MEMBER FUNCTION limit RETURN NUMBER IS

  BEGIN

    -- Return the size of the collection.
    RETURN SELF.attribute_list.COUNT;

  END;

  -- Member function to return the internal collection.
  MEMBER FUNCTION get_attribute_list
  RETURN ATTRIBUTE_TABLE IS

  BEGIN

    -- Return a table collection.
    RETURN SELF.attribute_list;

  END;
```

```
-- Member function to return attribute VARCHAR2.
MEMBER FUNCTION to_varchar2 RETURN VARCHAR2 IS

  -- List the attributes.
  list            VARCHAR2(4000);

BEGIN

  -- Read and serialize values.
  FOR i IN 1..SELF.attribute_list.COUNT LOOP

    IF i = 1 THEN

      -- Assign values.
      list :=
        '['||i||'] ['||SELF.attribute_list(i).to_varchar2||']'||CHR(10);

    ELSIF i = SELF.attribute_list.COUNT THEN

      -- Assign values.
      list := list ||
        '['||i||'] ['||SELF.attribute_list(i).to_varchar2||']';

    ELSE

      -- Assign values.
      list := list ||
        '['||i||'] ['||SELF.attribute_list(i).to_varchar2||']'||CHR(10);

    END IF;

  END LOOP;

  -- Return the size of the collection.
  RETURN list;

END;

-- Order method to compare current instance with another.
ORDER MEMBER FUNCTION equals
( class_in ATTRIBUTES_OBJECT ) RETURN NUMBER IS

  -- Define return variable.
  retval          NUMBER := 1;

  -- Define default return values.
  false_value     NUMBER := 0;
  true_value      NUMBER := 1;
```

```
   -- Define local instances of telephone objects.
   attributes_1    ATTRIBUTE_TABLE := attribute_table();
   attributes_2    ATTRIBUTE_TABLE := attribute_table();

  BEGIN

    -- Assign set members to a table of objects.
    attributes_1 := SELF.get_attribute_list;

    -- Assign set members to a table of objects.
    attributes_2 := class_in.get_attribute_list;

    -- Loop through the initialized set.
    FOR i IN 1..attributes_1.LAST LOOP

      -- Call the JOBS_OBJECT method.
      IF attributes_1(i) = attributes_2(i) THEN

        -- Assign a false value and exit loop.
        retval := false_value;

        -- Exit loop because one unequal element fails.
        EXIT;

      END IF;

    END LOOP;

    -- Return a default true numeric value.
    RETURN retval;

  END;

END;
/
```

The `attributes_object` object type defines and implements the following methods:

- Three constructors:

    - A constructor that takes no arguments, and which builds a null collection.

    - A constructor that takes a single formal parameter of an `attribute_object` to build a single element collection.

    - A constructor that takes a single formal parameter of an `attribute_table` to build an object instance containing that collection.

- A member procedure `add_item` that takes an `attribute_object` instance and adds it to the internal collection.

- A member procedure `delete_item` that takes an index value and deletes an `attribute_object` instance from the collection. It then reorders the collection to ensure that the index values are sequential or densely populated.

- A member procedure `delete_item` that takes a beginning and ending index value and deletes the set of `attribute_object` instances from the collection. It then reorders the collection to ensure that the index values are sequential or densely populated.

- A member procedure `limit` that returns a `NUMBER` that maps to the `COUNT` of the internal nested table collection.

- A member procedure `get_attribute_list` that returns an `attribute_table` collection equal to the contents of the internal collection.

- A member function `to_varchar2` that converts and returns the structure to a `VARCHAR2` variable. The function uses `attribute_object.to_varchar2` to concatenate and return values of the collection.

- An order member function `equals` that compares two object type instances and returns a zero for false and one for true.

After defining and implementing the `attributes_object` object, you define a collection of the `attributes_object` object type. To do so, use the following syntax:

```
-- This is found in the create_thread_of_control.sql file.
CREATE OR REPLACE TYPE attributes_table
  AS TABLE OF ATTRIBUTES_OBJECT;
/
```

The `attributes_table` provides a structure that enables you to pass a list of arguments for threads to the `thread_of_control` package. You will also need to track and manage a list of jobs, which is the list of your threads. The `job_table` and `jobs_objects` enable you to do so and are covered in the next section.

## Building the Job Collection

The first component builds the `job_table` nested table collection of `NUMBER`. This object is used to manage our collection of parallel job numbers. While you can implement this as a record type in a PL/SQL package, you should consider using a database object type as better documented and easier to support as an application programming interface.

**Why Would I Use This?**
You need to know how to build a structure to maintain and pass lists of job numbers in the package that dynamically submits threads with different actual parameters. This documents a structure in the schema that contains a list of numbers.

We find it useful to use Oracle object types for these in lieu of record types and collections implemented as package global structures. You should review Chapter 6 for our reasoning in making this recommendation.

The syntax to build the `job_table` nested table collection of `NUMBER` is next but should not be run outside the context of the `create_thread_of_control` `.sql` script:

```
-- This is found in the create_thread_of_control.sql file.
CREATE OR REPLACE TYPE job_table AS TABLE OF NUMBER;
/
```

**NOTE**
*If you attempt to run the re-creation of the `job_table` type, you will raise an ORA-02303 because there are dependent objects.*

The user-defined object type is written to enable instantiation of an object that can be passed by reference or value in the thread-of-control package. The wrapper object type has three overriding constructors and several methods to manage adding, deleting, sizing, and comparing instances of the object type.

**TIP**
*You pass by references using the NO COPY option. Unfortunately, the NO COPY option is a hint and does not guarantee a pass by reference. However, the IN OUT mode combination to a procedure does mimic a pass by reference.*

The user-defined wrapper object type is shown next:

-- This is found in the create_thread_of_control.sql file.

```
CREATE OR REPLACE TYPE jobs_object AS OBJECT
( job_list          JOB_TABLE
, CONSTRUCTOR FUNCTION jobs_object RETURN SELF AS RESULT
, CONSTRUCTOR FUNCTION jobs_object
  ( job_number       NUMBER ) RETURN SELF AS RESULT
, CONSTRUCTOR FUNCTION jobs_object
  ( job_list_in      JOB_TABLE ) RETURN SELF AS RESULT
, MEMBER PROCEDURE add_item
  ( job_number       NUMBER )
, MEMBER FUNCTION count RETURN NUMBER
, MEMBER PROCEDURE delete_item
  ( index_value      NUMBER )
, MEMBER PROCEDURE delete_item
  ( index_start      NUMBER
  , index_end        NUMBER )
, MEMBER FUNCTION limit RETURN NUMBER
, MEMBER FUNCTION get_job_list RETURN JOB_TABLE
, ORDER MEMBER FUNCTION equals
  ( class_in         JOBS_OBJECT ) RETURN NUMBER )
INSTANTIABLE FINAL;
/

CREATE OR REPLACE TYPE BODY jobs_object AS

  -- Constructor to build a null collection.
  CONSTRUCTOR FUNCTION jobs_object RETURN SELF AS RESULT IS

    -- Define collection variable.
    job_list        JOB_TABLE := job_table();

  BEGIN

    -- Return instance.
    RETURN;

  END;

  -- Constructor to build a collection with an initial value.
  CONSTRUCTOR FUNCTION jobs_object
  ( job_number       NUMBER ) RETURN SELF AS RESULT IS
```

```
BEGIN

  -- Initialize the instance variable.
  SELF.job_list := job_table(job_number);

  -- Return instance.
  RETURN;

END;

-- Constructor to build a collection with an initial collection.
CONSTRUCTOR FUNCTION jobs_object
( job_list_in    JOB_TABLE ) RETURN SELF AS RESULT IS

BEGIN

  -- Assign an existing collection to the instance collection.
  SELF.job_list := job_list_in;

  -- Return instance.
  RETURN;

END;

-- Member procedure to add to the internal collection.
MEMBER PROCEDURE add_item
( job_number    NUMBER ) IS

  -- Define and initialize collection
  job_list JOB_TABLE := JOB_TABLE();

BEGIN

  -- Extend the instance collection space by one.
  SELF.job_list.EXTEND;

  -- Assign the new value.
  SELF.job_list(SELF.job_list.LAST) := job_number;

END;

-- Member function to return size of internal collection.
MEMBER FUNCTION count RETURN NUMBER IS
```

```
BEGIN

  -- Return the size of the collection.
  RETURN SELF.job_list.COUNT;

END;

-- Member function to return size of internal collection.
MEMBER PROCEDURE delete_item
( index_value     NUMBER ) IS

  -- Declare a local counter variable.
  counter         NUMBER := 1;

  -- Define and initialize a local collection.
  job_list        JOB_TABLE := job_table();

BEGIN

  -- Check for valid index value.
  IF SELF.job_list.EXISTS(index_value) THEN

    -- Delete element.
    SELF.job_list.DELETE(index_value);

    -- Allocate space to the local collection.
    job_list.EXTEND(SELF.job_list.COUNT);

    -- Copy contents to a re-indexed collection.
    FOR i IN SELF.job_list.FIRST..SELF.job_list.LAST LOOP

      -- Check if index value exists.
      IF SELF.job_list.EXISTS(i) THEN

        -- Assign a value to the re-indexed collection.
        job_list(counter) := SELF.job_list(i);

        -- Increment the local counter.
        counter := counter + 1;

      END IF;

    END LOOP;

  END IF;
```

```
                      (

      -- Assign the re-indexed collection to the instance collection.
      SELF.job_list := job_list;

END;

-- Member function to return size of internal collection.
MEMBER PROCEDURE delete_item
( index_start     NUMBER
, index_end       NUMBER ) IS

   -- Declare a local counter variable.
   counter         NUMBER := 1;

   -- Define and initialize a local collection.
   job_list        JOB_TABLE := job_table();

BEGIN

   -- Check starting index is less than the ending index.
   IF index_start >= index_end THEN

      RAISE_APPLICATION_ERROR(-20000,
        'Starting index is larger than ending index');

   END IF;

   -- Check for a valid index.
   IF SELF.job_list.EXISTS(index_start) AND
      SELF.job_list.EXISTS(index_end) THEN

      -- Delete element.
      SELF.job_list.DELETE(index_start,index_end);

      -- Allocate space to the local collection.
      job_list.EXTEND(SELF.job_list.COUNT);

      -- Copy contents to a re-indexed collection.
      FOR i IN SELF.job_list.FIRST..SELF.job_list.LAST LOOP

         -- Check if index value exists.
         IF SELF.job_list.EXISTS(i) THEN

            -- Assign a value to the re-indexed collection.
            job_list(counter) := SELF.job_list(i);
```

```
      -- Increment the local counter.
      counter := counter + 1;

    END IF;

  END LOOP;

END IF;

-- Assign the re-indexed collection to the instance collection.
SELF.job_list := job_list;

END;

-- Member function to return size of internal collection.
MEMBER FUNCTION limit RETURN NUMBER IS

BEGIN

-- Return the size of the collection.
RETURN SELF.job_list.COUNT;

END;

-- Member function to return the internal collection.
MEMBER FUNCTION get_job_list
RETURN JOB_TABLE IS

BEGIN

-- Return a table collection.
RETURN SELF.job_list;

END;

-- Order method to compare current instance with another.
ORDER MEMBER FUNCTION equals
( class_in JOBS_OBJECT ) RETURN NUMBER IS

-- Define return variable.
retval          NUMBER := 1;

-- Define default return values.
false_value     NUMBER := 0;
true_value      NUMBER := 1;
```

```
   -- Define local instances of telephone objects.
   jobs_1        JOB_TABLE := job_table();
   jobs_2        JOB_TABLE := job_table();

 BEGIN

   -- Assign set members to a table of objects.
   jobs_1 := SELF.get_job_list;

   -- Assign set members to a table of objects.
   jobs_2 := class_in.get_job_list;

   -- Loop through the initialized set.
   FOR i IN 1..jobs_1.LAST LOOP

     -- Call the JOBS_OBJECT method.
     IF jobs_1(i) = jobs_2(i) THEN

       -- Assign a false value and exit loop.
       retval := false_value;

       -- Exit loop because one unequal element fails.
       EXIT;

     END IF;

   END LOOP;

   -- Return a default true numeric value.
   RETURN retval;

 END;

END;
/
```

The user-defined object type defines the following behaviors:

- It creates an instantiable object type that cannot be subclassed. The object type contains the following:

    - It has three overriding constructors, which are

        - A null argument constructor that returns an object with an empty job_table collection.

- A single argument constructor of a NUMBER data type, which adds a number to the existing internal job_table collection and returns the modified object instance.

- A single argument constructor of a job_list user-defined nested table collection. A job_table collection type is passed as the formal parameter to construct an instance of jobs_object.

■ An add_item procedure that adds an element to the internal job_list collection. The add_item procedure takes a single number and adds it to the internal job_table collection.

■ A count member function that returns the number of elements in the internal job_list collection. The count function acts as a wrapper to the native collection API count function, which is only available within the scope of the object type.

■ An overloaded delete_item member procedure that deletes an element based on an index value or a range of index values. The overloaded procedures manage the deletion of one or more elements and re-indexing of the nested table to eliminate gaps in the sequence so the internal collection is always densely populated. "Densely populated" means that the numeric index values of the collection are sequential. This is accomplished by:

- Defining a local nested table collection.

- Allocating space to the local nested table collection equal to the reduced size of the internal nested table collection.

- Using dual counters in a for-loop to sequence the index values contiguously.

- Assigning the re-indexed nested table collection to the internal nested table collection.

■ A limit member function that returns the number of elements in the internal job_list collection. The limit function acts as a wrapper to the native collection API count function, which is only available within the scope of the object type.

■ A get_job_list member function that returns a copy of the internal job_list collection.

■ An order member function equals that compares copies of the wrapper object type class. The comparison is done by looping through the indexed values of the collection, which requires that each be densely populated to use a simple for-loop.

> ## Why Would I Use This?
> You should know how to organize functions and procedures, marshal dynamic argument lists, submit jobs, and monitor job completion. We have built the `thread_of_control` package to demonstrate these concepts.
>
> You will find all the basic components there for parallel PL/SQL programming. The examples we have provided demonstrate large-grain control, which is typically done with semaphores or in POSIX C++ with mutex variables. Fine-grain control is called interthread communication and is done by coordinating directly between executing threads. If you choose to implement interthread communication you can use the DBMS_PIPE package to manage named pipes by calling it from your threads-of-execution.

You can use these object types to contain, maintain, and pass instances of the object through the `thread_of_control` package.

## Building the Thread-of-Control Package

The `thread_of_control` package and package body provide you with a complete code example of threading the execution of PL/SQL programs. You may extend it to include interthread communication with other pipe submissions, but unfortunately space does not allow that example.

The following defines the `thread_of_control` package specification:

```
-- This is found in the create_thread_of_control.sql file.
CREATE OR REPLACE PACKAGE thread_of_control IS

  -- Define a job message type.
  TYPE job_message IS TABLE OF VARCHAR2(100);

  -- Define standard exceptions.
  complete_failed       EXCEPTION;
  lock_failed           EXCEPTION;
  send_failed           EXCEPTION;
  submit_failed         EXCEPTION;
  receive_failed        EXCEPTION;
  rewrite_failed        EXCEPTION;
  rewrite_lock_failed   EXCEPTION;
```

```
-- Define the PRAGMA for user-defined exceptions.
PRAGMA EXCEPTION_INIT(complete_failed,-200001);
PRAGMA EXCEPTION_INIT(lock_failed,-200002);
PRAGMA EXCEPTION_INIT(send_failed,-200003);
PRAGMA EXCEPTION_INIT(submit_failed,-200004);
PRAGMA EXCEPTION_INIT(receive_failed,-200005);
PRAGMA EXCEPTION_INIT(rewrite_failed,-200006);
PRAGMA EXCEPTION_INIT(rewrite_lock_failed,-200007);

-- Define manage_threads function specification.
FUNCTION manage_threads
  ( user_name      IN VARCHAR2
  , program_name   IN VARCHAR2
  , attributes     IN ATTRIBUTES_TABLE
  , run_threads    IN NUMBER := 1 )
  RETURN BOOLEAN;

END thread_of_control;
/
```

The `thread_of_control` package does the following:

- It defines seven user-defined exceptions that are used in the package body.

- It defines a `manage_threads` function, which is the only schema-level function or procedure that is accessible. It acts as a façade pattern to the `thread_of_control` package.

The package body is implemented as follows:

```
-- This is found in the create_thread_of_control.sql file.
CREATE OR REPLACE PACKAGE BODY thread_of_control IS

  -- Define a package variable.
  locked       VARCHAR2(4)   := 'LOCK';

  -- Define forward references to alphabetize local units.
  PROCEDURE register_threads
    ( user_name      IN     VARCHAR2
    , program_name   IN     VARCHAR2
    , attributes     IN     ATTRIBUTES_TABLE
    , job_list       IN OUT JOBS_OBJECT
    , run_threads    IN     NUMBER := 1 );

  FUNCTION send_message
    ( user_name      VARCHAR2
    , message_in     VARCHAR2
    , pipe_name      VARCHAR2 ) RETURN INTEGER;
```

```
FUNCTION receive_message
  ( user_name     VARCHAR2
  , pipe_name     VARCHAR2 ) RETURN VARCHAR2;

PROCEDURE wait;

-- Define complete_threads function.
PROCEDURE complete_threads
  ( user_name      IN     VARCHAR2
  , program_name   IN     VARCHAR2
  , job_list       IN OUT JOBS_OBJECT
  , global_commit  IN OUT BOOLEAN ) IS

  -- Define local variables.
  message          VARCHAR2(4000);

  -- Define structures to hold contents of named pipe.
  job_message_list JOB_MESSAGE := job_message();

BEGIN

  -- Set the lock.
  IF (thread_of_control.receive_message
        ( user_name
        ,'THREAD_REGISTER_LOCK' ) = locked ) THEN

    -- Read complete list.
    FOR i IN 1..job_list.LIMIT LOOP

      -- Assign the message.
      message := thread_of_control.receive_message
                   ( user_name
                   ,'THREAD_REGISTER');

      -- Check for status of threads.
      IF (program_name = SUBSTR(message,1,INSTR(message,'[',1,1) - 1))
      THEN

        -- Extend collection.
        job_message_list.EXTEND;

        -- Assign the message to the list.
        job_message_list(i) := message;

        -- Check if all threads are complete.
        IF job_message_list.COUNT = job_list.LIMIT THEN

          -- Update thread object type as complete.
          global_commit := TRUE;

        END IF;
```

```
      -- Check for a partial completion of threads.
      ELSIF    job_message_list.COUNT < job_list.LIMIT
      AND      ( message = 'The message pipe is empty.'
      OR         message = 'The message is too large for variable.'
      OR         message = 'An interrupt occurred, contact the DBA.' )
      THEN

        -- Loop thru what has been read and write it back to the pipe.
        FOR j IN 1..job_message_list.COUNT LOOP

          -- Check re-registering of threads in the pipe.
          IF (thread_of_control.send_message
                ( user_name
                , job_message_list(j)
                ,'THREAD_REGISTER' ) != 0) THEN

            -- Raise exception.
            RAISE rewrite_failed;

          END IF;

        END LOOP;

        -- Set the lock.
        IF (thread_of_control.send_message
              ( user_name
              , locked
              ,'THREAD_REGISTER_LOCK' ) != 0) THEN

          -- Raise exception.
          RAISE rewrite_lock_failed;

        END IF;

      END IF;

    END LOOP;

    -- Verify that all threads have completed.
    IF job_list.LIMIT != job_message_list.COUNT THEN

      -- Raise exception.
      RAISE rewrite_failed;

    END IF;

  END IF;

EXCEPTION
```

```
    WHEN complete_failed THEN
      DBMS_OUTPUT.PUT_LINE('Complete failed: ['||SQLERRM||']');
      RETURN;

    WHEN rewrite_failed THEN
      DBMS_OUTPUT.PUT_LINE('Rewrite ['||message||
                           '] failed: ['||SQLERRM||']');
      RETURN;

    WHEN rewrite_lock_failed THEN
      DBMS_OUTPUT.PUT_LINE('Rewrite lock ['||message||
                           '_LOCK ] failed: ['||SQLERRM||']');
      RETURN;

END complete_threads;

-- Define manage_threads function.
FUNCTION manage_threads
  ( user_name    IN VARCHAR2
  , program_name IN VARCHAR2
  , attributes   IN ATTRIBUTES_TABLE
  , run_threads  IN NUMBER := 1)
  RETURN BOOLEAN IS

-- Define a process complete Boolean variable.
process_complete  BOOLEAN := FALSE;
retval            BOOLEAN := FALSE;

-- Define collection job set.
job_set         JOB_TABLE := job_table();

-- Define collection variable.
job_list        JOBS_OBJECT := jobs_object();

BEGIN

  -- If one thread fails, all should fail.
  thread_of_control.register_threads( user_name
                                    , program_name
                                    , attributes
                                    , job_list
                                    , run_threads );

  IF job_list.LIMIT > 0 THEN

    -- Assign the object's internal collection to a local variable.
    job_set := job_list.get_job_list;

  END IF;
```

```
    FOR i IN 1..attributes.COUNT LOOP

      IF job_list.LIMIT > 0 THEN

        -- Commit job submissions.
        COMMIT;

        -- Loop until all threads are complete.
        WHILE NOT process_complete LOOP

          -- Wait before checking or rechecking.
          wait;

          -- Check if all threads are complete.
          complete_threads ( user_name
                           , program_name
                           , job_list
                           , process_complete );

          -- Check if global commit has happened.
          IF process_complete THEN

            -- Exit the while loop.
            EXIT;

          END IF;

        END LOOP;

      END IF;

      -- Return a Boolean completion of true.
      retval := TRUE;

    END LOOP;

  -- Return result.
  RETURN retval;

END manage_threads;

-- Implement package function defined in specification.
FUNCTION receive_message
  ( user_name      VARCHAR2
  , pipe_name      VARCHAR2 )
  RETURN VARCHAR2 IS

  -- Define variable for target mailbox.
  message        VARCHAR2(4000 CHAR) :=  NULL;
  target_pipe    VARCHAR2(100 CHAR);
```

```
   timeout          INTEGER := 0;
   return_code      INTEGER;

BEGIN

  -- Purge local pipe content.
  DBMS_PIPE.RESET_BUFFER;

  -- Declare the target for a pipe.
  target_pipe := UPPER(user_name) || '$'
             || UPPER(pipe_name);

  -- Use the procedure to put a message in the local buffer.
  return_code := DBMS_PIPE.receive_message(target_pipe,timeout);

  -- Evaluate and process return code.
  CASE return_code
    WHEN 0 THEN

      -- Read the message into a variable.
      DBMS_PIPE.UNPACK_MESSAGE(message);

    WHEN 1 THEN

    -- Assign message.
    message := 'The message pipe is empty.';

    WHEN 2 THEN

    -- Assign message.
    message := 'The message is too large for variable.';

    WHEN 3 THEN

    -- Assign message.
    message := 'An interrupt occurred, contact the DBA.';

  END CASE;

  -- Return the message.
  RETURN message;

END receive_message;

-- Define register_threads function.
PROCEDURE register_threads
  ( user_name     IN     VARCHAR2
  , program_name  IN     VARCHAR2
```

```
, attributes    IN     ATTRIBUTES_TABLE
, job_list      IN OUT JOBS_OBJECT
, run_threads   IN     NUMBER := 1 ) IS

-- Define argument list.
arguments       VARCHAR2(4000);

-- Define a variable to hold the job number.
job_number      NUMBER;

-- Define a variable to hold dynamic what execution.
job_what        VARCHAR2(100);

FUNCTION parse_arguments
( attributes    IN     ATTRIBUTES_OBJECT )
RETURN VARCHAR2 IS

  -- Define a local variable to manage the argument list.
  args            VARCHAR2(4000);

  -- Define an attribute object table.
  attribute_list ATTRIBUTE_TABLE := attributes.get_attribute_list;

BEGIN

  -- Loop through the attribute list.
  FOR i IN 1..attribute_list.LAST LOOP

    -- Check if the attribute is a number.
    IF attribute_list(i).get_type = 'NUMBER' THEN

      -- Check if the first argument.
      IF i = 1 THEN

        -- Write to the argument list.
        args := args||attribute_list(i).get_number;

      ELSE

        -- Write to the argument list.
        args := args||','||attribute_list(i).get_number;

      END IF;

    ELSIF attribute_list(i).get_type = 'STRING' THEN

      -- Check if the first argument.
      IF i = 1 THEN
```

```
            -- Write to the argument list.
            args := args||''''||attribute_list(i).get_varchar2||'''';

         ELSE

            -- Write to the argument list.
            args := args||','''||attribute_list(i).get_varchar2||'''';

         END IF;

      END IF;

    END LOOP;

    -- Return argument list as a VARCHAR2.

    RETURN args;

  END;

BEGIN

  -- Run threads with different formal parameter signatures.
  FOR i IN 1..attributes.COUNT LOOP

    -- Parse the argument list.
    arguments := parse_arguments(attributes(i));

    -- Run threads with identical formal parameter signatures.
    FOR j IN 1..run_threads LOOP

      -- Define thread name.
      job_what := program_name||'['||i||'] ['||j||']';

      -- Submit the job for immediate execution.
      DBMS_JOB.SUBMIT( JOB => job_number
                     , WHAT => program_name||'('||arguments||');');

      -- Validate a job number is returned from DBMS_JOB.SUBMIT.
      IF job_number IS NOT NULL THEN

        -- Add the thread to the job list.
        job_list.add_item(job_number);

      ELSE

        -- Raise exception.
        RAISE submit_failed;

      END IF;
```

```
      -- Register thread.
      IF (thread_of_control.send_message( user_name
                                        , job_what
                                        ,'THREAD_REGISTER' ) != 0) THEN

        -- Raise exception.
        RAISE send_failed;

      END IF;

    END LOOP;

    -- Set the lock.
    IF (thread_of_control.send_message( user_name
                                      , locked
                                      ,'THREAD_REGISTER_LOCK' ) != 0) THEN

      -- Raise exception.
      RAISE lock_failed;

    END IF;

  END LOOP;

EXCEPTION

  WHEN send_failed OR lock_failed THEN
    DBMS_OUTPUT.PUT_LINE('Write failed: ['||SQLERRM||']');
    RETURN;

END register_threads;

-- Implement local function.
FUNCTION send_message
  ( user_name       VARCHAR2
  , message_in      VARCHAR2
  , pipe_name       VARCHAR2 )
  RETURN INTEGER IS

  -- Define variable for target.
  target_pipe     VARCHAR2(100 CHAR);

BEGIN

  -- Purge local pipe content.
  DBMS_PIPE.RESET_BUFFER;

  -- Declare the target for a message.
  target_pipe := UPPER(user_name) || '$'
              || UPPER(pipe_name);
```

```
   -- Use the procedure to put a message in the local buffer.
   DBMS_PIPE.PACK_MESSAGE(message_in);

   -- Send message, success is a zero return value.
   IF (DBMS_PIPE.send_message(target_pipe) = 0) THEN

     -- Message sent, so return 0.
     RETURN 0;

   ELSE

     -- Message not sent, so return 1.
     RETURN 1;

   END IF;

 END send_message;

 -- Define wait function specification.
 PROCEDURE wait IS

 BEGIN

   -- Pause program in a loop.
   FOR i IN 1..10000000 LOOP

     NULL;

   END LOOP;

 END wait;

END thread_of_control;
/
```

The `thread_of_control` package body does the following:

- It defines a package scope variable, `locked`, as a string literal.

- It uses forward referencing to enable the alphabetical ordering of functions and procedures.

- It defines a local `complete_threads` procedure, which verifies that *all of the threads* have signaled completion. Also, it ensures that when it has read the pipe it replaces it for the next attempt.

■ It defines the `manage_threads` procedure, which is the thread-of-control. This procedure registers threads by calling the `register_threads` procedure, and completes processing by calling the `complete_threads` procedure.

■ It defines a local `receive_message` function that implements the code demonstrated earlier in the chapter. The `receive_message` function reads the pipes between sessions.

■ It defines a local `register_threads` procedure. The `register_threads` procedure submits threads using the `DBMS_JOBS` package and writes to intersession pipes using the local `send_message` procedure. Also, it contains a procedure local function that parses the argument list to marshal actual job submission.

■ It defines a local `send_message` function that implements the code demonstrated earlier in the chapter. The `send_message` function writes to the intersession pipe.

The package demonstrates all required components to implement a threaded PL/SQL execution. Next, you'll see how to use the `thread_of_control` package.

# Demonstrating Threads-of-Execution

Having built the necessary components to support threaded PL/SQL, this section will demonstrate how to test the components. You will now work through the validation of the parallel programming model.

The process of verifying you can submit a threaded program consists of three steps, shown next:

■ Building a target thread table

■ Building a stored procedure to call from your test program

■ Building a test program to submit two concurrent threads

**Why Would I Use This?**

Seeing the construction of a complete concurrent or parallel program will help you implement and troubleshoot your own parallel programs faster. We hope the example provides you with a clear pattern to successfully build your own testing environment.

You build the table as follows:

-- **This is found in the create_threading_objects.sql file.**

```
CREATE TABLE thread
( thread_id          NUMBER
, value_start        NUMBER
, value_end          NUMBER
, date_created        DATE
, date_updated        DATE );
```

After building the table, populate it with data. The program used to populate it in this example is shown next:

-- **This is found in the create_threading_objects.sql file.**

```
DECLARE

  -- Define index-by tables (9i) or associative arrays (10g).
  TYPE number_table IS TABLE OF NUMBER
    INDEX BY BINARY_INTEGER;
  TYPE date_table IS TABLE OF DATE
    INDEX BY BINARY_INTEGER;

  -- Define and initialize a static date.
  date_value      DATE := SYSDATE;

  -- Define three variables of NUMBER_TABLE.
  number1          NUMBER_TABLE;
  number2          NUMBER_TABLE;
  number3          NUMBER_TABLE;
  date1            DATE_TABLE;
  date2            DATE_TABLE;

BEGIN

  -- Initialize the index-by table.
  FOR i IN 1..1000000 LOOP

    number1(i) := i;
    number2(i) := 1;
    number3(i) := 100;
    date1(i) := date_value;
    date2(i) := date_value;

  END LOOP;
```

```
  -- Use a bulk insert.
  FORALL i IN 1..1000000
    INSERT
    INTO        thread
    VALUES (number1(i),number2(i),number3(i),date1(i),date2(i));

  -- Commit the inserts.
  COMMIT;

END;
/
```

The threaded program will have a target stored program. You should use a stored procedure as the target program. Build the stored procedure as follows:

-- **This is found in the create_threading_objects.sql file.**

```
CREATE OR REPLACE PROCEDURE threaded_program
( value_start_in     NUMBER
, value_end_in       NUMBER
, value_new_in       NUMBER ) IS

BEGIN

  -- Update rows.
  UPDATE    thread
  SET       value_end = value_new_in
  ,         date_updated = SYSDATE
  WHERE     thread_id BETWEEN value_start_in AND value_end_in;

END;
/
```

As you can see, the sample threaded_program stored procedure is simple and takes three arguments. It updates a range of rows in the target table.

The program to submit two threads to the thread_of_control package uses the object types defined earlier to marshal variables for submission. The thread-of-execution is used by the threaded_program procedure, which is submitted in parallel by the following anonymous block PL/SQL program:

-- **This is found in the create_threading_objects.sql file.**

```
DECLARE

  -- Define and initialize thread of execution variables.
  user_name         VARCHAR2(30) := USER;
```

```
program_name      VARCHAR2(30) := 'THREADED_PROGRAM';
attribute_count   NUMBER := 3;

-- Define an ATTRIBUTES_OBJECT variable.
attribute         ATTRIBUTES_OBJECT;

-- Define the number of threads.
threads           NUMBER := 2;

-- Define collection types.
attribute_list    ATTRIBUTE_TABLE := attribute_table();
attributes_list   ATTRIBUTES_TABLE := attributes_table();

BEGIN

-- Allocate space to the collections.
attribute_list.EXTEND(attribute_count);
attributes_list.EXTEND(threads);

-- Use a for-loop to populate two threads of execution.
FOR i IN 1..2 LOOP

  IF i = 1 THEN

    -- Initialize argument components.
    attribute_list(1) := attribute_object('NUMBER',1);
    attribute_list(2) := attribute_object('NUMBER',100);
    attribute_list(3) := attribute_object('NUMBER',333);

  ELSIF i = 2 THEN

    -- Initialize argument components.
    attribute_list(1) := attribute_object('NUMBER',201);
    attribute_list(2) := attribute_object('NUMBER',300);
    attribute_list(3) := attribute_object('NUMBER',444);

  END IF;

  -- Construct an instance of attributes.
  attribute := attributes_object(attribute_list);

  -- Assign element to collection.
  attributes_list(i) := attribute;

  dbms_output.put_line('--------------------------');
  dbms_output.put_line(attributes_list(i).to_varchar2);
  dbms_output.put_line('--------------------------');

END LOOP;
```

```
-- Submit the threads.
IF THREAD_OF_CONTROL.MANAGE_THREADS( user_name
                                   , program_name
                                   , attributes_list ) THEN

  NULL;

END IF;

END;
/
```

The script builds a PL/SQL package that does the following:

- It defines in the declaration section local variables, including variables with user-defined object and collection types. It initializes all collection variables.

- It extends two collections, initializes values, and populates an attribute_ table and attributes_table collection. It calls the thread_of_ control.manage_threads procedure. The thread_of_control .manage_threads procedure starts, manages, and completes a thread-of-execution for each list of argument values.

Now that you've seen how to stage and execute a parallel PL/SQL program, let's see the execution documented.

## Demonstrating Parallel Execution

You can test these programs by running the create_thread_of_control.sql, create_threading_objects.sql, and verify_threaded_execution .sql scripts. The last script executes the following query, which shows that the two programs updated these row sets.

```
-- This is found in the verify_threaded_execution.sql file.

COL thread_id    FORMAT 9,999 HEADING 'Thread ID'
COL value_start  FORMAT 9,999 HEADING 'Value|Start'
COL value_end    FORMAT 9,999 HEADING 'Value|End'
COL created      FORMAT A20   HEADING 'Created'
COL updated      FORMAT A20   HEADING 'Updated'

-- Check results of threaded submission.
SELECT    thread_id
,         value_start
,         value_end
```

```
,          TO_CHAR(date_created,'DD-MON-YY HH24:MI:SS') created
,          TO_CHAR(date_updated,'DD-MON-YY HH24:MI:SS') updated
FROM       thread
WHERE      thread_id BETWEEN  99 AND 102
OR         thread_id BETWEEN 199 AND 202;
```

It shows the following output:

```
          Value  Value
Thread ID Start  End Created              Updated
--------- ------ --- -------------------- --------------------
       99      1 333 04-APR-05 20:21:34   04-APR-05 20:22:20
      100      1 333 04-APR-05 20:21:34   04-APR-05 20:22:20
      101      1 100 04-APR-05 20:21:34   04-APR-05 20:21:34
      102      1 100 04-APR-05 20:21:34   04-APR-05 20:21:34
      199      1 100 04-APR-05 20:21:34   04-APR-05 20:21:34
      200      1 100 04-APR-05 20:21:34   04-APR-05 20:21:34
      201      1 444 04-APR-05 20:21:34   04-APR-05 20:22:20
      202      1 444 04-APR-05 20:21:34   04-APR-05 20:22:20
```

You have now seen how to demonstrate parallel PL/SQL program execution. You should also have the knowledge to extend these parallel functionalities to your own environment.

# Summary

You've learned why DBMS_JOB and DBMS_PIPE enable you to build and run parallel or concurrent PL/SQL program units. You also explored the issues of control and sequencing required of the thread-of-control and threads-of-execution.

# CHAPTER
## 8

## High Performance
## PL/SQL

uning is a task that relies on an understanding of both code and database design. As a result, it can be one of the most difficult tasks for a developer or DBA to undertake. It can also be one of the most enjoyable and lucrative specialties. In this chapter, we focus on PL/SQL performance. In particular, the following topics are covered:

- Changes to Oracle 10*g* that impact performance

- SQL tuning techniques

- Ways to collect performance information for PL/SQL

- Native compilation

We use the following table for most of the examples in this chapter:

```
-- Available online as part of seed_data.sql
CREATE TABLE person (
                    PERSON_ID NUMBER(10),
                    FIRST_NAME VARCHAR2(20 CHAR),
                    LAST_NAME VARCHAR2(20 CHAR),
                    AGE NUMBER(10),
                    GENDER VARCHAR2(1 CHAR),
                    DOB TIMESTAMP,
                    HAIR_COLOR VARCHAR2(20),
                    EYE_COLOR VARCHAR2(20),
                    BIO VARCHAR2(50 CHAR),
                    ACTIVITY_ID NUMBER(10),
                    REFERRED_BY NUMBER(10));
```

To actually show how to write for performance, we populate this table with almost 4.8 million records. The following anonymous block does this:

```
-- Available online as part of seed_data.sql
DECLARE
  v_age PERSON.AGE%TYPE;
  v_birth_date PERSON.DOB%TYPE;
  v_month_shift NUMBER(10);
  v_person_id PERSON.PERSON_ID%TYPE := 1;
  v_gender PERSON.GENDER%TYPE := 'M';
  v_first_name PERSON.FIRST_NAME%TYPE := 'Hodge';
  v_last_name PERSON.LAST_NAME%TYPE := 'Podge';
  v_activity_id ACTIVITY.ACTIVITY_ID%TYPE;
  v_hair_color PERSON.HAIR_COLOR%TYPE := 'BROWN';
  v_eye_color PERSON.EYE_COLOR%TYPE := 'BLUE';
```

```
BEGIN
  FOR y IN 1..200000
    LOOP
    FOR x IN 1..2
      LOOP
      FOR z IN 1..12
        LOOP
        -- Includes ages 31 - 42
        v_age := 30 + z;

        -- Set the value to deduct from today's date to determine the bday
        v_month_shift := v_age * - 12;

        -- Determine the bday based on today's date and the age
        v_birth_date := ADD_MONTHS(systimestamp, v_age * - 12);

        -- Person_ID must be unique
        v_person_id := v_person_id + 1;

        -- Pick random activities
        v_activity_id := ROUND(DBMS_RANDOM.VALUE(1, 12), 0);

        INSERT INTO person
        VALUES (v_person_id, v_first_name || v_person_id, v_last_name
              || v_person_id,
              v_age, v_gender, v_birth_date, v_hair_color, v_eye_color,
              'bio text for a person '|| v_age ||' years old',
              v_activity_id, v_person_id - 1);
      END LOOP;

      -- change gender and name so 1/2 of entries are female
      v_gender := 'F';
      v_first_name := 'Hither';
      v_last_name := 'Yonder';
      v_hair_color := 'BLONDE';
      v_eye_color := 'BROWN';

      COMMIT;
    END LOOP;
  END LOOP;
EXCEPTION
  WHEN OTHERS
  THEN
      DBMS_OUTPUT.PUT_LINE(DBMS_UTILITY.FORMAT_ERROR_STACK);
END;
/
```

Run the `create_user.sql` and `seed_data.sql` scripts to set up the other examples in this chapter.

**NOTE**
*Depending on the size of your machine and the resources available, you may have to reduce the number of iterations in the loop. Simply drop the value in the first FOR loop to a manageable size for your environment.*

# PL/SQL Optimization in Oracle 10*g*

We discussed the new compiler, and optimization enhancements that were made to it, in Chapter 2. At compile time, the compiler analyzes the source code, and depending on the `PLSQL_OPTIMIZE_LEVEL` parameter value, it makes adjustments to the MCode that improves the performance. We don't have to do anything to take advantage of this enhancement. Take a look at the default `PLSQL_OPTIMIZE_SETTING` in your 10*g* environment.

```
SQL> show parameter plsql_optimize_level
```

This shows the following unless someone has changed the value:

```
NAME                                 TYPE        VALUE
------------------------------------ ----------- ------------
plsql_optimize_level                 integer     2
```

The default value is `2`. If compilation time is excessive, change the parameter value to `1`, but keep in mind that this impacts how thorough the optimization is.

Optimization occurs during the code generation phase, the third and final phase of PL/SQL compilation. For more information about the three phases of compilation, see Chapter 2. Three main steps make up the code generation phase. They're shown in Figure 8-1.

If you're running a version of Oracle prior to 10*g*, note that the compilation, and code generation in particular, is different. If you are upgrading to 10*g* from an earlier release, you will notice faster execution times because of the optimizer changes without making a single change to your code.

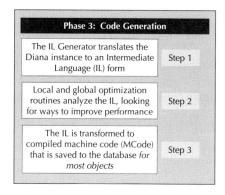

**FIGURE 8-1.**   *Code generation*

# SQL Tuning Review

Since most performance problems with PL/SQL objects are related to the SQL contained in them, any PL/SQL tuning discussion would be incomplete without covering it. We'll focus on the basics of SQL trace, indexes, and statistics. We won't cover all aspects of tuning SQL as it is beyond the scope of this book, and would require far more than this section to do it justice. Instead, we review some of the basic, yet most overlooked ways to improve the performance of your SQL.

Let's use a very basic example to start with, and then work our way toward a solution. The following simple SELECT statement takes far too long to run:

```
-- Available online as part of tune_sql.sql
SET TIMING ON SERVEROUTPUT ON
DECLARE
    v_count NUMBER(10);
BEGIN
    SELECT COUNT(rowid)
    INTO v_count
    FROM person
    WHERE gender = 'F'
    AND activity_id = '11'
    AND hair_color = 'BLONDE'
    AND age = 34
    AND eye_color = 'BROWN';
    DBMS_OUTPUT.PUT_LINE(v_count);
END;
/
```

This returns the following time on our instance:

```
Elapsed: 00:00:22.17
```

Over 22 seconds. That isn't what we'd consider a good time. It's a simple request. Obviously, it's oversimplified, but that's intentional. It's not necessarily the most complex code that becomes the bottleneck. Even simple code can put the brakes on an otherwise well-tuned application.

## Tracing and TKPROF

SQL_TRACE is the first place we generally start when tuning application code. To enable it, either set SQL_TRACE = TRUE in the parameter file (or spfile), or set it for the session as follows:

```
ALTER SESSION SET SQL_TRACE = TRUE;
```

With tracing enabled, run the anonymous block again.

```
-- Available online as part of tune_sql.sql
DECLARE
    v_count NUMBER(10);
BEGIN
    SELECT COUNT(rowid)
    INTO v_count
    FROM person
    WHERE gender = 'F'
    AND activity_id = '11'
    AND hair_color = 'BLONDE'
    AND age = 34
    AND eye_color = 'BROWN';
    DBMS_OUTPUT.PUT_LINE(v_count);
END;
/
```

Turn tracing off with the following command:

```
ALTER SESSION SET SQL_TRACE = FALSE;
```

**NOTE**
*We could have used DBMS_TRACE to enable tracing as well, but for our purposes, SQL_TRACE is an easier approach.*

The trace file can be found in the `user_dump_dest` directory. This location is found by running the following query:

```
SELECT value
FROM v$parameter
WHERE name = 'user_dump_dest';
```

While it's possible to use the raw trace, Oracle provides the TKPROF utility that formats the output for performance, and makes it a little easier to read. We'll use the following syntax to format the trace:

```
tkprof <<tracefile>> <<outputfile>> explain=plsql/oracle \
sort=<<exeela,prsela,fchela>>
```

**NOTE**
*The "\\" at the end of the first line allows us to continue the command on a second line in UNIX. Without it, a carriage return would run `tkprof` prematurely.*

The sort options allow us to order the contents of the file so it's easier to find what we're looking for. In this case, we're sorting first by execution time, second by parse time, and third by fetch time.

Passing our trace name and file name that we want for our output, we see the following at the top of our file:

```
-- Available online as part of book_trace.txt
 SELECT COUNT(ROWID)
FROM
 PERSON WHERE GENDER = 'F' AND ACTIVITY_ID = '11' AND HAIR_COLOR = 'BLONDE'
 AND AGE = 34 AND EYE_COLOR = 'BROWN'

call     count       cpu    elapsed       disk      query    current        rows
------- ------  -------- ---------- ---------- ---------- ---------- ----------
Parse        1      0.00       0.00          0          0          0           0
Execute      1      0.00       0.00          0          0          0           0
Fetch        1      2.12      21.76      43308      72078          0           1
------- ------  -------- ---------- ---------- ---------- ---------- ----------
total        3      2.12      21.76      43308      72078          0           1

Misses in library cache during parse: 0
Optimizer mode: ALL_ROWS
Parsing user id: 55  (PLSQL)   (recursive depth: 1)

Rows     Row Source Operation
------- ---------------------------------------------------
      1   SORT AGGREGATE (cr=72078 pr=43308 pw=0 time=21766662 us)
  36090     TABLE ACCESS FULL PERSON (cr=72078 pr=43308 pw=0 time=17142403 us)
```

```
Rows      Execution Plan
-------   -------------------------------------------------
      0   SELECT STATEMENT    MODE: ALL_ROWS
      1     SORT (AGGREGATE)
  36090       TABLE ACCESS (FULL) OF 'PERSON' (TABLE)
```

This tells us the following:

- The INTO is gone from the statement. The SQL is shown separate from the PL/SQL.

- Of PARSE, EXECUTE, and FETCH, FETCH took the longest.

- There was only one PARSE, EXECUTE, and FETCH, as shown in the COUNT column.

- The large gap between CPU and ELAPSED times points to something other than the processing power of the machine as being the issue.

- The execution plan shows that there was a full-table scan performed on the PERSON table.

The following section is found at the bottom of the trace file, and shows the total time taken by the SQL:

```
OVERALL TOTALS FOR ALL RECURSIVE STATEMENTS
call     count      cpu    elapsed       disk      query    current       rows
-------  -----  --------  ---------  ---------  ---------  ---------  ---------
Parse        2     0.00       0.00          0          0          0          0
Execute      2     0.00       0.00          0          0          0          0
Fetch        2     2.12      21.76      43308      72080          0          2
-------  -----  --------  ---------  ---------  ---------  ---------  ---------
total        6     2.12      21.76      43308      72080          0          2
```

So, the total time represented in the trace is 21.76 seconds of the total 22.17 seconds shown at the command line.

So, what's the problem? The full scan over this many records is the obvious answer.

## Indexes

To stop the full-table scan, we need to look at creating an index. To see which column to index, look at the WHERE clause. In this case, the WHERE clause is using the GENDER, ACTIVITY_ID, HAIR_COLOR, AGE, and EYE_COLOR columns.

These columns have low cardinality (not very many distinct values). Let's create the index and see what happens.

-- **Available online as part of tune_sql.sql**
```
 CREATE INDEX person_idx
ON person(gender,
          activity_id,
          hair_color,
          age,
          eye_color);
```

Once created, rerun the anonymous block with TIMING turned on and tracing enabled.

-- **Available online as part of tune_sql.sql**
```
SET TIMING ON SERVEROUTPUT ON
ALTER SESSION SET SQL_TRACE = TRUE;
DECLARE
    v_count NUMBER(10);
BEGIN
    SELECT COUNT(rowid)
    INTO v_count
    FROM person
    WHERE gender = 'F'
    AND activity_id = '11'
    AND hair_color = 'BLONDE'
    AND age = 34
    AND eye_color = 'BROWN';
    DBMS_OUTPUT.PUT_LINE(v_count);
END;
/
ALTER SESSION SET SQL_TRACE = FALSE;
```

This shows that the time to execute improved significantly.

```
Elapsed: 00:00:00.34
```

Now it's 0.34 seconds, down from 22.17 seconds. Not a bad improvement! The TKPROF'd trace shows the following:

```
SELECT COUNT(ROWID)
FROM
 PERSON WHERE GENDER = 'F' AND ACTIVITY_ID = '11' AND HAIR_COLOR = 'BLONDE'
```

```
    AND AGE = 34 AND EYE_COLOR = 'BROWN'

call     count      cpu    elapsed      disk      query    current       rows
------- ------ -------- ---------- ---------- ---------- ---------- ----------
Parse        1     0.00       0.00          0          0          0          0
Execute      1     0.00       0.00          0          0          0          0
Fetch        1     0.00       0.00          0         16          0          1
------- ------ -------- ---------- ---------- ---------- ---------- ----------
total        3     0.00       0.00          0         16          0          1

Misses in library cache during parse: 0
Optimizer mode: ALL_ROWS
Parsing user id: 55  (PLSQL)   (recursive depth: 1)


Rows     Row Source Operation
------- ---------------------------------------------------
      1  SORT AGGREGATE (cr=16 pr=0 pw=0 time=8887 us)
  36090   BITMAP CONVERSION TO ROWIDS (cr=16 pr=0 pw=0 time=117 us)
     25    BITMAP INDEX SINGLE VALUE PERSON_IDX (cr=16 pr=0 pw=0 time=1104
us)(object id 51175)


Rows     Execution Plan
------- ---------------------------------------------------
      0  SELECT STATEMENT   MODE: ALL_ROWS
      1   SORT (AGGREGATE)
  36090   BITMAP CONVERSION (TO ROWIDS)
     25    BITMAP INDEX (SINGLE VALUE) OF 'PERSON_IDX' (INDEX (BITMAP))
```

It used the new index, and the FETCH time no longer registers for the trace.

## The CBO and Statistics

Even with the correct indexes in place, it's possible that Oracle won't choose to use them. The Cost-Based Optimizer (CBO) is used to determine the quickest way to complete the requested task. If a SELECT statement queries a table with no indexes on the columns in the WHERE clause, Oracle performs a full-table scan. This was shown at the beginning of this section before any indexes were created. If an index

### Why Would I Use This?

Use bitmap indexes where the cardinality is low, as in the case of the GENDER, ACTIVITY_ID, HAIR_COLOR, AGE, and EYE_COLOR columns in our example. Applications that see primarily SELECT statements, such as DSS or Data Warehouse systems, will see the greatest benefit. If there are fewer than a couple hundred distinct values in a table, consider using a bitmap index over the traditional b-tree index.

exists, Oracle determines the estimated cost associated with various execution plans, and chooses the one that's lowest.

A full-table scan is bad all the time, correct?
Answer: No.

Remember, Oracle calculates the cost of many execution plans, and chooses the lowest cost among them. Consider the following:

```
SELECT systimestamp
FROM dual;
```

This does a full-table scan, of course. But since there's a single record in dual, who would index that? The same question arises regarding other queries against tables with a small number of records. It all comes down to cost.

So, how does Oracle get the cost then? It uses statistics generated on tables and indexes to determine the most efficient way to access the required information.

To show you what we mean, let's use a utility available on Metalink called SQLT (search on SQLT and you'll find references to it). It was written by Carlos Sierra from Oracle, and although other utilities are available, we're still partial to this tool. Provided with the SQL statement, we receive a report that tells us what the CBO is looking at, including the cost for each line of the execution plan, as well as object information that shows when statistics were last gathered, and the sample size used to estimate them. The following shows a SELECT statement we can use:

```
--Available online as sql.txt
SELECT p1.first_name||' '||p1.last_name, a.activity_name
FROM person p1, activity a
WHERE p1.activity_id = a.activity_id
AND p1.person_id IN (SELECT p2.referred_by
                     FROM person p2
                     WHERE p2.dob = p1.dob);
```

**TIP**
*If you try SQLT, use the sql.txt file in the online code. It's formatted correctly for use with SQLT.*

As mentioned earlier, one of the things SQLT reports is the line-by-line cost in the execution plan. It appears as follows in our instance:

```
-- Available online as part of SQLT_RONHARDMAN-L_ORCL_S0001.TXT
    OPERATION                        COST        CARDINALITY
```

```
------------------------------ ------------ --------------
  SELECT STATEMENT ..............69593            1
   HASH JOIN ....................69593            1
  . HASH JOIN (RIGHT SEMI) ....   69589           1
  .. TABLE ACCESS (FULL) PERSON...16014        4567295
  .. TABLE ACCESS (FULL) PERSON...16003        4567295
  . TABLE ACCESS (FULL) ACTIVITY..    3           13
```

Examine these from the inside out (start with TABLE ACCESS (**FULL**) PERSON in this case) since the numbers are cumulative. The two full-table scans of the PERSON table have a cost of 16014 and 16003. The full scan of the ACTIVITY table only has a cost of 3. The reason? Start by looking at what each table contains. This is shown in the next section of the report.

-- **Available online as part of SQLT_RONHARDMAN-L_BOOK_S0001.TXT**

| TBL | TABLE_NAME | NUM_ROWS (ACTUAL) |
| --- | --- | --- |
| 01 | ACTIVITY | 13 |
| 02 | PERSON | 4800001 |

So, the ACTIVITY table has 13 records and the PERSON table has 4,800,001. So, the cost associated with the full scan of the PERSON table is much greater than that of the ACTIVITY table, of course. Knowing this, let's not invest any effort into getting rid of the full scan on ACTIVITY. Instead, let's focus on the other two.

We know from looking at this report that there are no indexes on the PERSON table. Adding indexes for the columns in the WHERE clause should help. Notice also that we can change the query to get rid of the subquery, adding the PERSON table to the FROM clause a second time and joining the PERSON table to itself as follows:

```
SELECT p1.first_name||' '||p1.last_name, a.activity_name
  FROM person p1, activity a, person p2
 WHERE p1.activity_id = a.activity_id
 AND p1.person_id = p2.referred_by
 AND p1.dob = p2.dob;
```

Eliminating the subquery used to have a greater impact in earlier releases. Notice that the execution plan shown earlier created VIEW VW_SQ_1, which effectively does the same thing.

Finally, we can check to see when statistics were last gathered for all of the objects touched by the query. The LAST_ANALYZED column in ALL|DBA|USER_TABLES and ALL|DBA|USER_INDEXES shows the last time statistics were collected for the objects. SQLT reports this in a section titled MAIN CBO STATS. If they are stale, run DBMS_STATS to make them current.

> **Why Would I Use This?**
> We use tools like SQLT when SQL Trace and TKPROF yield results that do not
> point to the problem. The SQL statement does not actually execute, so we can
> use this for any SQL statement without worrying about rolling back any changes.
> It provides a method to iteratively tune a statement, seeing the impact of changes
> immediately. In short, we use tools like this when they will save time. Other
> tools, many of them with more information, are available for you to use, so
> research them and give them a try.

### DBMS_STATS

The DBMS_STATS package provides procedures to gather statistics for a specific
table, index, schema, or the whole database. To gather statistics for the PLSQL
schema, run the following:

```
EXEC DBMS_STATS.GATHER_SCHEMA_STATS('PLSQL');
```

After this completes, query the LAST_ANALYZED column in the USER_TABLES
view to see that the date is made current:

```
COLUMN table_name FORMAT A15
COLUMN last_analyzed FORMAT A15
SELECT table_name, last_analyzed
FROM user_tables
WHERE table_name = 'PERSON';
```

This shows the following in our instance:

```
TABLE_NAME      LAST_ANALYZED
--------------- ---------------
PERSON          01-MAY-05
```

With correct statistics, the CBO can more accurately calculate the cost.

# Finding PL/SQL Performance Problems

The first part of this chapter focused on SQL performance, and rightly so. Most
problems with PL/SQL can be traced back to the SQL used as part of PL/SQL
programs. If you've discovered that SQL is not the problem though, use the tools
provided by Oracle to uncover ways to improve PL/SQL.

Named blocks can take advantage of compile-time warnings. These are not fatal errors that prevent the execution of code should a warning be returned. Instead, they are informational messages that try to point developers to problems that they can expect during runtime.

PL/SQL Profiler provides a way to track PL/SQL object execution. It delivers feedback about program flow, showing how code is treated during execution. This different view of the program can often highlight the problem more easily than simply staring at the source code.

# Compiler Warnings

Warning messages can be any of the following:

■ **All**   This includes all available warning conditions and messages.

■ **Performance**   Only performance-related warnings are returned.

■ **Informational**   This flags code that may not be useful to the program, and which can be moved or corrected. The condition is not performance-related and won't generate an error. It's intended to assist developers in making code more maintainable.

■ **Severe**   Problems identified as severe indicate there may be a problem with code logic.

■ **Specific error**   This warning can be specific to an error message.

Of particular interest for this chapter is the Performance warning.

To enable the warnings, specify one of the preceding categories for either the current session or the instance. If specific warnings are more critical than others for you, it's possible to configure a warning to be treated as an error, preventing the successful compilation of the program unit.

### Parameter—PLSQL_WARNINGS

One way to ensure that a warning is regarded as an error is to use the PLSQL_WARNINGS parameter. To see what it's currently set at in your environment, type the following:

```
-- Available online as part of compiler_warnings.sql
SHOW PARAMETER PLSQL_WARNINGS
```

This shows the following in our environment:

```
NAME_COL_PLUS_SHOW_PARAM
------------------------
TYPE
-----------
VALUE_COL_PLUS_SHOW_PARAM
------------------------
plsql_warnings
string
DISABLE:ALL
```

To set this in our init.ora file, the syntax would be

```
PLSQL_WARNINGS='ENABLE:PERFORMANCE', 'ENABLE:SEVERE'
```

We actually prefer to set this from the SQL prompt. To do so, type the following (this must be done as SYSDBA).

```
-- Available online as part of compiler_warnings.sql
ALTER SYSTEM SET PLSQL_WARNINGS='ENABLE:PERFORMANCE', 'ENABLE:SEVERE';
```

To see the change, use SHOW PARAMETER again.

```
-- Available online as part of compiler_warnings.sql
SHOW PARAMETER PLSQL_WARNINGS
```

This returns

```
NAME_COL_PLUS_SHOW_PARAM
--------------------------------------------------------
TYPE
-----------
VALUE_COL_PLUS_SHOW_PARAM
--------------------------------------------------------
plsql_warnings
string
DISABLE:INFORMATIONAL, ENABLE:PERFORMANCE, ENABLE:SEVERE
```

To test this, we'll change the anonymous block used earlier in the chapter to populate the PERSON table to a stored procedure and compile it. The procedure is as follows:

```
-- Available online as part of compiler_warnings.sql
CREATE OR REPLACE PROCEDURE seed_data
```

```
IS
   v_age PERSON.AGE%TYPE;
   v_birth_date PERSON.DOB%TYPE;
   v_month_shift NUMBER(10);
   v_person_id PERSON.PERSON_ID%TYPE := 1;
   v_gender PERSON.GENDER%TYPE := 'M';
   v_first_name PERSON.FIRST_NAME%TYPE := 'Hodge';
   v_last_name PERSON.LAST_NAME%TYPE := 'Podge';
   v_activity_id ACTIVITY.ACTIVITY_ID%TYPE;
   v_hair_color PERSON.HAIR_COLOR%TYPE := 'BROWN';
   v_eye_color PERSON.EYE_COLOR%TYPE := 'BLUE';
BEGIN
  FOR y IN 1..200000
    LOOP
    FOR x IN 1..2
      LOOP
      FOR z IN 1..12
        LOOP
        -- Includes ages 31 - 42
        v_age := 30 + z;

        -- Set the value to deduct from today's date to determine the bday
        v_month_shift := v_age * - 12;

        -- Determine the bday based on today's date and the age
        v_birth_date := ADD_MONTHS(systimestamp, v_age * - 12);

        -- Person_ID must be unique
        v_person_id := v_person_id + 1;

        -- Pick random activities
        v_activity_id := ROUND(DBMS_RANDOM.VALUE(1, 12), 0);

        INSERT INTO person
        VALUES (v_person_id, v_first_name || v_person_id, v_last_name
                || v_person_id,
                v_age, v_gender, v_birth_date, v_hair_color, v_eye_color,
                'bio text for a person '|| v_age ||' years old',
                v_activity_id, v_person_id - 1);
      END LOOP;

      -- change gender and name so 1/2 of entries are female
      v_gender := 'F';
      v_first_name := 'Hither';
      v_last_name := 'Yonder';
      v_hair_color := 'BLONDE';
      v_eye_color := 'BROWN';
```

```
         COMMIT;
      END LOOP;
   END LOOP;
EXCEPTION
   WHEN OTHERS
   THEN
      DBMS_OUTPUT.PUT_LINE(DBMS_UTILITY.FORMAT_ERROR_STACK);
END;
/
```

Running this returns the following:

```
SP2-0804: Procedure created with compilation warnings
```

To see the warnings, type

```
SQL> show errors
LINE/COL ERROR
-------- -------------------------------------------------------
36/46    PLW-07202: bind type would result in conversion away
         from column type
37/20    PLW-07202: bind type would result in conversion away
         from column type
39/44    PLW-07202: bind type would result in conversion away
         from column type
```

So, it identified performance-related issues in the procedure. The procedure is still valid. Query the status from the USER_OBJECTS view.

```
-- Available online as part of compiler_warnings.sql
COL object_name FORMAT A30
COL status FORMAT A10
SELECT object_name, status
  FROM user_objects
  WHERE object_name = 'SEED_DATA';


OBJECT_NAME                    STATUS
------------------------------ -------
SEED_DATA                      VALID
```

If we deemed this issue so major that we believed it shouldn't compile, we could change it as follows:

```
-- Available online as part of compiler_warnings.sql
ALTER PROCEDURE seed_data COMPILE PLSQL_WARNINGS='ERROR:07202';
```

Now, a check of the USER_OBJECTS view shows that the object is marked as invalid:

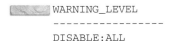 `-- Available online as part of compiler_warnings.sql`

```
COL object_name FORMAT A30
COL status FORMAT A10
SELECT object_name, status
  FROM user_objects
  WHERE object_name = 'SEED_DATA';


OBJECT_NAME                      STATUS
------------------------------   ---------
SEED_DATA                        INVALID
```

To disable the warning level again, type the following:

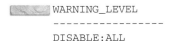 `-- Available online as part of compiler_warnings.sql`

```
ALTER SYSTEM SET PLSQL_WARNINGS='DISABLE:ALL';
```

## Package—DBMS_WARNING

The DBMS_WARNING package provides the same functionality as the PLSQL_WARNINGS parameter. The warning levels are identical. In fact, if PLSQL_WARNINGS is set, the warning level for DBMS_WARNING reflects it. To see the current setting, run the following:

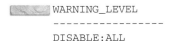 `-- Available online as part of compiler_warnings.sql`

```
SELECT DBMS_WARNING.GET_WARNING_SETTING_STRING() WARNING_LEVEL
FROM dual;
```

This shows the following in our instance:

`WARNING_LEVEL`

```
-----------------
DISABLE:ALL
```

 **NOTE**
*If you did not DISABLE:ALL for PLSQL_WARNINGS, your warning levels will still reflect those set in the last section.*

To set the warning level for the current session, call DBMS_WARNING.SET_WARNING_SETTING_STRING.

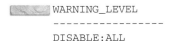 `-- Available online as part of compiler_warnings.sql`

```
CALL DBMS_WARNING.SET_WARNING_SETTING_STRING('ENABLE:ALL', 'SESSION');
```

A check of the warning level reflects this:

```
WARNING_LEVEL
-------------
ENABLE:ALL
```

Recompile the SEED_DATA procedure shown earlier, and the warning message is displayed.

```
-- Available online as part of compiler_warnings.sql
SQL> alter procedure seed_data compile;
SP2-0805: Procedure altered with compilation warnings
```

SHOW ERRORS reflects the same message shown earlier:

```
SQL> show errors
LINE/COL ERROR
-------- --------------------------------------------------------
36/46    PLW-07202: bind type would result in conversion away
         from column type
37/20    PLW-07202: bind type would result in conversion away
         from column type
39/44    PLW-07202: bind type would result in conversion away
         from column type
```

Line 36 is the INSERT statement. The problem is the three concatenated values in the INSERT, which is the reason for the three warning messages. The following simplifies the INSERT by moving the concatenation to a separate variable:

```
-- Available online as part of compiler_warnings.sql
CREATE OR REPLACE PROCEDURE seed_data
IS
...
   v_first_name PERSON.FIRST_NAME%TYPE := 'Hodge';
   v_first_name2 PERSON.FIRST_NAME%TYPE;
   v_last_name PERSON.LAST_NAME%TYPE := 'Podge';
   v_last_name2 PERSON.LAST_NAME%TYPE;
...
 BEGIN
...
        -- Set first_name, last_name, and bio values
        v_first_name2 := v_first_name||v_person_id;
        v_last_name2 := v_last_name||v_person_id;
```

```
            INSERT INTO person
            VALUES (v_person_id, v_first_name2, v_last_name2,
                    v_age, v_gender, v_birth_date,
                    'bio text',
                    v_activity_id, v_person_id - 1);
...
END;
/
```

Disable the warnings before continuing by typing the following:

```
CALL DBMS_WARNING.SET_WARNING_SETTING_STRING('DISABLE:ALL', 'SESSION');
```

# PL/SQL Profiler

When the problem is not as obvious as it was in the last section, DBMS_PROFILER can help track down the bottleneck. DBMS_PROFILER records code runs in a table so progress can be tracked over time. The purpose of Profiler is to gather information about a run, adjust the code to improve it, and then run it again with Profiler enabled.

## Setup

Although the DBMS_PROFILER package is already present, additional tables and PL/SQL objects might need to be created, depending on your particular uses. DBMS_PROFILER keeps run information in memory for the duration of a user's session. If the collected data should be stored persistently, it must be flushed to Profiler tables. These tables do not exist by default. They are created by the script $ORACLE_HOME/rdbms/admin/proftab.sql. To create the tables, log in to the PLSQL schema created as part of this chapter, and then run the proftab.sql script.

```
SQL> @?/rdbms/admin/proftab.sql
```

This creates the following three tables:

- PLSQL_PROFILER_DATA

- PLSQL_PROFILER_UNITS

- PLSQL_PROFILER_RUNS

To get the most out of Profiler, we suggest running the script $ORACLE_HOME/plsql/demo/profrep.sql. This script creates reporting utilities to use with Profiler. While it's possible to use Profiler without this, we'd strongly encourage you to set these utilities up. To do so, connect as the PLSQL user created in this chapter, and run

```
SQL> @?/plsql/demo/profrep.sql
```

| Name | Type | Description |
|------|------|-------------|
| FLUSH_DATA | Procedure and function | Writes data to the tables created by `?/rdbms/admin/proftab.sql` |
| GET_VERSION | Procedure | Retrieves the version of DBMS_PROFILER |
| INTERNAL_VERSION_CHECK | Function | Provides a compatibility check between DBMS_PROFILER and the data server |
| PAUSE_PROFILER | Procedure and function | Temporarily stalls data collection. Use RESUME_PROFILER to restart. |
| RESUME_PROFILER | Procedure and function | Starts data collection after it has been paused using PAUSE_PROFILER. |
| START_PROFILER | Two procedures and two functions | Starts collecting data. |
| STOP_PROFILER | Procedure and function | Stops collecting data. |

**TABLE 8-1.**  *DBMS_PROFILER Package Components*

## DBMS_PROFILER

The DBMS_PROFILER package contains the components shown in Table 8-1.

We use the DBMS_PROFILER.START_PROFILER and DBMS_PROFILER.STOP_PROFILER procedures more than any other. We'll use them in a minute to create a profile for the following PL/SQL function:

```
-- Available online as part of profiler.sql
CREATE OR REPLACE FUNCTION encrypt_password (
   i_password IN VARCHAR2)
   RETURN VARCHAR2
IS
   v_ciphertext RAW(500);
   v_deciphered VARCHAR2(500 CHAR);
```

```
      v_plaintext RAW(200) := UTL_I18N.STRING_TO_RAW(
                                        i_password,
                                        'AL32UTF8');
      v_type BINARY_INTEGER := DBMS_CRYPTO.AES_CBC_PKCS5;
      v_key RAW(128) := UTL_I18N.STRING_TO_RAW(
               DBMS_CRYPTO.RANDOMBYTES(16),  --generates 128 bit key..128/8
               'AL32UTF8');
BEGIN
   v_ciphertext := DBMS_CRYPTO.ENCRYPT(v_plaintext,
                                       v_type,
                                       v_key);

   RETURN v_ciphertext;
EXCEPTION
   WHEN OTHERS
   THEN
      DBMS_OUTPUT.PUT_LINE(DBMS_UTILITY.FORMAT_ERROR_STACK);
END;
/
```

**NOTE**
*For more information on DBMS_CRYPTO used here,*
*see Chapter 12.*

This function returns an encrypted string when passed plain text. For the sake of this example we're using a small table defined as follows:

```
-- Available online as part of profiler.sql
CREATE TABLE users (
   ID NUMBER(10) PRIMARY KEY,
   USERNAME VARCHAR2(20),
   PASSWORD VARCHAR2(500));

CREATE SEQUENCE user_seq
START WITH 1
INCREMENT BY 1;

BEGIN
   FOR y IN 1..10000
   LOOP
     INSERT INTO users (id, username, password)
       VALUES (user_seq.NEXTVAL,
               DBMS_RANDOM.STRING('A', 20),
               DBMS_RANDOM.STRING('A', 10));
   END LOOP;
```

```
COMMIT;
EXCEPTION
   WHEN OTHERS
   THEN
      DBMS_OUTPUT.PUT_LINE(DBMS_UTILITY.FORMAT_ERROR_STACK);
END;
/
```

We'll now use the PL/SQL Profiler to see what's happening during the execution of the ENCRYPT_PASSWORD function.

The first thing we'll do is start Profiler as follows:

**-- Available online as part of profiler.sql**
```
EXEC DBMS_PROFILER.START_PROFILER('encrypt')
```

This enables Profiler, so the next step is to run the ENCRYPT_PASSWORD function we created earlier.

**-- Available online as part of profiler.sql**
```
DECLARE
   v_new_password USERS.PASSWORD%TYPE;

   CURSOR password_cur
   IS
      SELECT *
      FROM users;
BEGIN
   FOR y IN password_cur
   LOOP
      v_new_password := ENCRYPT_PASSWORD(y.password);

      UPDATE users
      SET password = v_new_password
      WHERE id = y.id;
   END LOOP;
EXCEPTION
   WHEN OTHERS
   THEN
      DBMS_OUTPUT.PUT_LINE(DBMS_UTILITY.FORMAT_ERROR_STACK);
END;
/
```

When this returns, stop Profiler as follows:

**-- Available online as part of profiler.sql**
```
EXEC DBMS_PROFILER.STOP_PROFILER
```

Oracle provides a couple of scripts that can be used to view the Profiler output. One summary script can be found at $ORACLE_HOME/plsql/demo/profsum.sql. Set your terminal to a width of 120 for best viewing and then run the following:

```
SET PAGES 9999 LINESIZE 120 SERVEROUTPUT ON
spool profsum.log
@?/plsql/demo/profsum.sql
spool off
```

The following are a couple sections of interest in this report. First, the total execution time is shown as:

```
-- profsum.log created by running profsum.sql
GRAND_TOTAL
-----------
      2.16
```

Next, a summary breakdown of that time is provided.

```
-- Available online as part of profsum.log
UNIT_OWNER
--------------------------------
UNIT_NAME                          SECONDS    PERCENTAGE
--------------------------------   ---------  ----------
<anonymous>
<anonymous>                           2.01       93.13

PLSQL
ENCRYPT_PASSWORD                       .12        5.44

XDB
DBMS_XDBZ0                              .03        1.43
```

The majority of the time is spent outside of the ENCRYPT_PASSWORD function running miscellaneous routines, so there's little we can do alone in that function to improve the performance, other than to change what it is calling.

The report then goes on to break down the total time by the program unit being called. The most detailed section of this particular report is the trace, part of which is shown next:

```
-- Available online as part of profsum.log
===================================trace info===================================
==========Results for run #2 made on 01-MAG-05 17:28:12 ====================
```

```
(encrypt) Run total time:     30.05 seconds
Unit #1: <anonymous>.<anonymous> - Total time:        .00 seconds
Unit #2: <anonymous>.<anonymous> - Total time:        .00 seconds
Unit #3: <anonymous>.<anonymous> - Total time:       1.90 seconds
Unit #4: PLSQL.ENCRYPT_PASSWORD - Total time:         .12 seconds
1          0    ,02895099              FUNCTION encrypt_password (
2                                          i_password IN VARCHAR2)
3                                          RETURN VARCHAR2
4                                      IS
5                                          v_ciphertext RAW(500);
6                                          v_deciphered VARCHAR2(500 CHAR);
7     10.000   ,01156565  ,00000115     v_plaintext RAW(200) :=
                                             UTL_I18N.STRING_TO_RAW(
8                                                    i_password,
9                                                    'AL32UTF8');
10    10.000   ,00713332  ,00000071     v_type BINARY_INTEGER :=
                                             DBMS_CRYPTO.AES_CBC_PKCS5;
11    10.000   ,02857003  ,00000285     v_key RAW(128) :=
                                             UTL_I18N.STRING_TO_RAW(
12                                            DBMS_CRYPTO.RANDOMBYTES(16),
13                                                    'AL32UTF8');
14                                      BEGIN
15    10.000   ,01398390  ,00000139     v_ciphertext :=
                                             DBMS_CRYPTO.ENCRYPT(
                                                 v_plaintext,
16                                                   v_type,
17                                                   v_key);
18    10.000   ,01018302  ,00000101     RETURN v_ciphertext;
19                                      EXCEPTION
20                                          WHEN OTHERS
21                                          THEN
22         0    0                            DBMS_OUTPUT.PUT_LINE(
                                             DBMS_UTILITY.FORMAT_ERROR_STACK);
23    10.000   ,01728639  ,00000172   END
Unit #5: <anonymous>.<anonymous> - Total time:        .00 seconds
Unit #6: XDB.DBMS_XDBZ0 - Total time:                 .03 seconds
Unit #7: <anonymous>.<anonymous> - Total time:        .00 seconds
Unit #8: <anonymous>.<anonymous> - Total time:        .00 seconds
Unit #9: <anonymous>.<anonymous> - Total time:        .00 seconds
...
```

This line-by-line breakdown helps to focus on the problem even further.

# Native Compilation

Chapter 2 discussed the compilation process for interpreted code and touched briefly on the differences involved with native compilation. As a recap, the traditional approach to compilation is interpreted. MCode is stored with the Diana and is interpreted at runtime. Native compilation, on the other hand, does this work in advance. Instead of simply storing the MCode and Diana, C library files are generated during compilation. This means that during execution, no interpretation is necessary.

This can significantly improve the performance of PL/SQL, but it does not really do anything for code that is heavy in SQL. The reason: native compilation deals with PL/SQL, not SQL access to data.

The following example loops through 100 million times, evaluating each iteration against a constant, and then prints out text if the value is matched:

```
--Available online as part of native_compilation.sql
CREATE OR REPLACE PROCEDURE NATIVE_COM
IS
    v_area NUMBER(30);
    v_time NUMBER(30);

BEGIN

    v_time := DBMS_UTILITY.GET_TIME;
    FOR v_radius IN 1..100000000
    LOOP

      IF v_radius = 432000
      THEN
        DBMS_OUTPUT.PUT_LINE('We''ve reached the approximate radius of the sun');
        DBMS_OUTPUT.PUT_LINE('Though I doubt anyone has visited to');
        DBMS_OUTPUT.PUT_LINE('measure for sure');
      END IF;
    END LOOP;
    v_time := (DBMS_UTILITY.GET_TIME - v_time)/100;
    DBMS_OUTPUT.PUT_LINE(v_time);
END;
/
```

Using interpreted mode the time to execute this procedure is

```
Elapsed: 00:00:09.09
```

### Why Would I Use This?

Native compilation is great for applications that perform heavy calculations without going to the database. Code that uses PL/SQL constructs such as LOOP or IF-THEN will notice an improvement. Virtually any code that is not centered around accessing data in the database will notice an improvement.

Perform the following steps to enable native compilation with Oracle 10*g*:

1. Add a directory location for the `plsql_native_library_dir` parameter.

2. Restart the instance.

3. Alter the `plsql_code_type` parameter to NATIVE for either the session or the system.

4. Recompile all PL/SQL code.

By switching to native compilation, performance of the `NATIVE_COM` procedure improved dramatically.

```
ALTER SYSTEM SET PLSQL_CODE_TYPE='NATIVE';
ALTER PROCEDURE NATIVE_COM COMPILE;
EXEC NATIVE_COM
```

Now the procedure completes in the following time:

```
Elapsed: 00:00:02.26
```

# Performance Tuning Strategy

A user has reported a performance problem to you. What do you do? The following checklist can be used in most situations to troubleshoot the problem.

### Trace the Application

It is quite difficult to fix a problem before the source of the problem is identified. Since the biggest culprit of most performance problems is SQL, start by tracing the application using `SQL_TRACE`. Alternatively, use the Statspack utility or ADDM (available in 10*g*) to identify the poorly performing SQL. Make sure to run trace using binds and waits (level 12).

**TIP**
*Make certain you have `MAX_DUMP_FILE_SIZE` set to a large enough value to accommodate the raw trace file. These files can grow quickly, and if the parameter value is not high enough, the trace file will be truncated and won't show the problem.*

# SQL Steps

If you discover the problem is with PL/SQL and not SQL, skip to the next section titled "PL/SQL Steps." For problem SQL, follow this action plan:

## Determine the Number of Executions

If you notice that the number of executions is through the roof, stop! See what's calling the code. It may simply be an errant process or an out-of-control loop. Fix this and your problem may be resolved. If the executions are legitimate, find out why so many executions are required and see if they can be reduced through a change to the code.

## Look for Wait Events

Look at your top SQL statement in the TKPROF output. If the problem is in EXECUTE, and there is a large difference between CPU and ELAPSED times, then look at the wait events. An indicator is also a huge number in the DISK column. If this is the case, then the likely wait event is db file sequential read, and your explain plan will likely show the problem. Resolutions vary from proper indexing to changing the SQL statement to avoid going to disk. Other wait events can impact the problem as well, so be sure to examine both the wait event overview provided in the TKPROF, and the raw trace.

## Find Code That Can Benefit from Bind Variables

This is less of a problem now than in older releases, but there are sometimes opportunities for replacing constants with variables. If you find statements that are repeated simply because a value changes, see if a bind variable can be used in its place.

## Find Columns That Should Be Indexed

Examine the `WHERE` clause of the poorly performing SQL and determine where indexes may help. Create them in your test instance and verify that the performance is better. Now, weigh the improvement against the cost of having the index on that table. Tables that are modified frequently by DML incur a cost associated with maintaining indexes. Though your `SELECT` might be faster, `INSERTS`, `UPDATES`, and `DELETES` will now be slower. Weigh the benefit against the cost to make sure it is worthwhile.

## Verify That Statistics Are Current

If the indexes are there, but they are not being used, verify that the statistics are current. To do this, query the `ALL|DBA|USER_TABLES` and `ALL|DBA|USER_INDEXES` views. The column `LAST_ANALYZED` tells when statistics were last gathered for that object. When in doubt, gather statistics (use DBMS_STATS.GATHER_ SCHEMA_STATS or DBMS_STATS.GATHER_TABLE_STATS and DBMS_STATS .GATHER_INDEX_STATS). An ESTIMATE_PERCENT of 10 percent will be sufficient in most cases. When in doubt, gather statistics and recheck.

### Check Initialization Parameters

Verify that your parameter settings are as they should be. For example, the parameter optimizer_index_cost_adj impacts how the CBO weighs the cost of a full-table scan against the use of an index.

### Determine Whether the SQL Can Be Improved

Ultimately, the SQL may need to be rewritten. See if an inline view would work instead of that subquery in the WHERE clause, or if a function call might work better than that 20,000 line SQL statement with nested queries everywhere you look. (You laugh, but we had the privilege once of tuning a query in excess of 25,000 lines. It happens.)

Also, check to see if bulk processing would help. If you're repeatedly using the same SQL, save yourself time and do it in bulk.

# PL/SQL Steps

These steps work for most PL/SQL. Every application is different, however, so use what is appropriate for your environment.

### Check the SQL

We have to bring up SQL once again since it's the culprit most of the time. If your SQL trace does not show the problem with SQL, make sure you're looking at the right trace file. Also, examine the bottom of the raw trace file to see if it was truncated. It should show a message indicating that the MAX_DUMP_FILE_SIZE was exceeded.

### Look for Patterns

Can the problem be reproduced at will, or is it something that happens sporadically or only at certain times? If it can't be reproduced at will, check for contention. It may be that it's waiting for an object that's locked at certain times. If it can be reproduced at particular times of the day, see what else is happening on the system. It may simply be a resource conflict. This is an excellent time to turn your attention to Statspack or ADDM output.

### Run Profiler

Assuming the problem is in fact with the PL/SQL, use Profiler to collect as much information about the processing of the code as possible. Examine the output for those areas that can be tuned, and study the logic closely to see if it's optimal. If possible, run the code on a test box by itself, providing bind values taken from the trace. If you only notice small things that can be changed, modify them one or two at a time, and then rerun them using Profiler.

### Consider Native Compilation

If the time is spent in PL/SQL rather than SQL, consider using native compilation. Oracle currently recommends using native compilation for all of your code, or none of it, since there are performance implications with natively compiled code calling interpreted. This recommendation may change down the road, so check with Oracle on their current stance.

# Summary

In this chapter, we discussed the new optimizer, building on the discussion started in Chapter 2. We reviewed SQL performance-tuning techniques, including SQL_ TRACE and TKPROF, discussed the cost-based optimizer and statistics gathering, and demonstrated Oracle's compile-time performance warnings. We also showed how the PL/SQL Profiler can be used to generate output for tuning PL/SQL.

# PART
# IV

# Text Management
# Using PL/SQL

# CHAPTER
## 9

# Introduction to
# Information Retrieval

he SQL **SELECT** command is used to retrieve data from the database. For improved results, built-in functions can be employed, or operators such as `LIKE` or `BETWEEN` might be used. This type of search is considered data retrieval since this is essentially a dumb query. By "dumb query" we're referring to SQL's inability to determine what a document is about in order to provide the most relevant documents to the end user. It takes a query term as input and spits back out all documents that contain that term regardless of meaning.

Information Retrieval (IR), on the other hand, uses ranking algorithms to determine how relevant a document is to the search criteria. It provides the ability to manage data, and make sense of it. IR systems can determine what a document is about and, depending on the model used, return a result that does not contain any of the terms searched, but is still related to the topic of the keywords.

This chapter focuses on Oracle's IR solution called Oracle Text, and how PL/SQL can take advantage of this powerful component of the database. We cover the following:

- IR (from a computer science perspective)

- Oracle Text features overview

- Theme and gist generation using PL/SQL

- Keyword highlighting

- `WORLD_LEXER` use

- `CONTAINS` and `CATSEARCH` query processing

- Creating a document search page using PL/SQL Server Pages (PSPs)

We also create a few different types of IR applications to demonstrate some of the best features of Oracle Text. Be sure to download the code and documents posted online in order to get the most out of this chapter.

# Information Retrieval Overview

June 25, 1994. You now have data. Can you act on it? If we store that date in the database, and then search on the date, it returns the record. But what good is it when the date isn't in context? This is simply data retrieval.

December 18, 2003 is the date Larry Ellison married Melanie Craft. You now have information. If you're a business owner who makes a five-year anniversary pendant, you now have relevant information for your marketing department so they can plan their mailings prior to their five-year anniversary (I'm not suggesting that

**Why Would I Use This?**

In any organization, information is second only to people in importance. Without accurate IR systems, for-profit companies cannot compete. Without accurate IR systems, nonprofit organizations cannot effectively fulfill their charters. Without accurate and efficient IR systems, government agencies have a difficult time piecing together data to help protect their citizens. IR is wholly relevant to your organization.

you do!). If you're a friend or relative, you can send them a card. Whatever your relationship to them, or whatever your business, you now have enough information to act on the data.

So, what differentiates information from data?

Data with meaning applied is information. The aim of an IR application is to help determine the meaning of a document, rank results of queries in order of relevance, and present the results to the end user in a way that's useful. (See Figure 9-1.)

# IR Models

IR systems are only as good as the models they are based on. The type of model chosen depends largely on the business problem being addressed. For example, an online library system will likely require a different model than an e-mail repository search. In the book *Modern Information Retrieval* (Addison Wesley, 1999) by Ricardo Baeza-Yates and Berthier Ribeiro-Neto, the authors present three classic IR models (outlined in Table 9-1), which most others are based on.

Most IR systems use a hybrid based on one or more of these classic models. We say one or more because it's possible to have multiple implementation types with IR software where the model is customized to the business problem being addressed.

# Text Processing

*Tokens* are generally words, but may be a combination of words or characters. They are used for searching, categorization, classification, and theme extraction. The most useful type of token is a noun since it provides meaning to whatever sentence or document it is a part of.

---

Information = Data + Meaning

---

**FIGURE 9-1.** *The IR formula*

| Model | Structure | Description |
|---|---|---|
| Boolean | Based on set theory | Is there a matching word or string in the document or isn't there? This is very similar to a basic SELECT with a where clause. There is no interpretation in the basic model, and it's more data retrieval than IR. |
| Probabilistic | Based on probability ranking | When a query is submitted, documents are deemed either *probably* relevant or *probably* irrelevant. Those determined to be relevant to the intent of the query are returned in ranked order. |
| Vector | Algebraic design | The vector model assumes that relevant results may not be returned with the Boolean model, so weights are assigned to other possible matches that aren't exact matches to the query. This involves some interpretation of both query and document source to determine relevance. |

**TABLE 9-1.** *Classic IR Models*

Using a lexical approach to term extraction, documents can be broken into *tokens* for efficient search and retrieval. Western languages use white space to delimit words, terms, or tokens. IR indexing operations use this white space to differentiate one term from the next. Asian languages such as Japanese, Korean, or Chinese have no white-space delimiter, and are therefore much harder to parse.

Take the following sentence:

"The quick brown fox jumps over the lazy dog."

This sentence would be broken into the following tokens:

```
THE
QUICK
BROWN
FOX
JUMPS
OVER
LAZY
DOG
```

## Improving Relevance with Stopwords

Since IR systems are focused on relevance, it does no good to index and store tokens such as THE. Words like THE, OF, AND, and so on don't improve relevance, and in fact hurt performance. These kinds of words are referred to as stopwords or noise words, and most IR solutions can filter them out. Filtering out the stopwords, the token list is reduced to:

```
QUICK
BROWN
FOX
JUMPS
OVER
LAZY
DOG
```

Though stopwords have been removed, many of the tokens do not help much. The terms QUICK and LAZY mean very little without the nouns they are describing. The terms FOX and DOG (both nouns), however, provide a glimpse into what the text document is about. Nouns provide a higher degree of relevance than other sentence structures, and are used in many IR systems to extract the *theme* or *gist* of documents without manual intervention.

## Increasing the IR Vocabulary

Adding a thesaurus relates tokens to their synonyms, so searching on any of the synonyms retrieves the document containing the similar token. Using our *quick brown fox* example, a search on PUPPY would not normally return a positive result since the term does not exist in the source document. If a thesaurus were used that listed PUPPY as synonymous with DOG, the record would be returned.

# Queries

IR systems obviously require some ability to query the text that was indexed. The query method depends largely on the storage mechanism used. Relational databases use SQL to interact with the database, so SQL is used to perform the retrieval. Other systems are created to work with different standards, such as the Z39.50 protocol, discussed in greater detail later and in supplementary material.

For relational databases, the way the query is written depends on the following:

- The business problem being solved

- The quality and type of information already known

- The interface being used
- The user's ability to convert conceptual queries to logical queries

When we look under the covers of a simple keyword query, the true complexity can be seen. Take the following query *conceptualization*:

*We want to find all documents in a library system of more than 100,000 works that are related to the defense of the United States, and the government's role in it. This library includes everything from important U.S. Government documents to biographies of military generals, so this is likely a common theme. For our purpose, we need to know those documents drafted in the early years of the U.S. Government that are related to defense, and in particular, those that are part of the government's charter.*

This is a fairly simple request, yet converting this conceptual view of the query to the SQL query that accesses the database has a few issues:

1. *Defense* can be expressed in a number of ways without using the term itself. How can documents be included where the term *protection* is used instead of defense, for example?

2. Early documents sometimes spell the word defense as *defence*. We would hate to miss those!

3. A full list of documents from this library includes biographies and other types of documents we don't wish to see.

So, how can this be handled?

## Ranking

One part of the solution is to rank results by relevance. The ranking algorithm used depends on the model chosen (remember the "IR Models" section earlier in this chapter?). If a Boolean model is used, the search would fail to find documents that use "defence" rather than "defense." The probabilistic model would work well for this application, as would the vector model.

For vector modeling (arguably the most frequently used base model today), index terms are weighted to allow for partial matching. Complete matches are returned with a higher degree of relevance than those where only a portion of the search string was found. There is frequently a way to set a threshold *score* that must be met for the results to be returned. With the vector model, a search that includes nine keywords returns results based on relevance to those keywords. If eight of those terms are found in a document, it would be ranked higher than one in which only three of the terms were found.

## How Does That Work?

The vector model determines the document relevance by finding the similarity between the user query and the indexed document. In their book *Modern Information Retrieval*, Richardo Baeza-Yates and Berthier Ribeiro-Neto show how relevance is determined using t-dimensional vectors. The crux of the calculation is that by finding the cosine of the angle between the document and query vectors, the relevance is determined. The calculation is as follows:

$$sim(d_j, q) = \frac{\vec{d_j} \bullet \vec{q}}{|\vec{d_j}| \times |\vec{q}|}$$

Where $d_j$ is the document, $q$ is the query, $|d_j|$ is the norm of the document, and $|q|$ is the static norm of the query.

Going back to the defense example, the following string might provide us with a good list of documents to examine:

```
defense defence protection safety guard security secure
military militia
```

The results would be ranked according to the frequency with which the terms appeared in the document.

How would you describe this query? Clumsy, cumbersome, and useless comes to mind. What end user is going to pull out the thesaurus every time they need to enter keywords into a search window? In addition, there's no classification done to know anything about the documents returned except that one or more of the keywords is included.

Relevance ranking is important, but it is only one piece of an IR query solution.

## Thesaurus

Most IR solutions provide the user/programmer with the ability to add a thesaurus. A thesaurus can automatically match defense to defence, protection, safety, guard, security, and secure, and match military to militia. This reduces the earlier query to:

```
defense military
```

Much better!

Most solutions provide the ability to use a basic thesaurus, or add a custom thesaurus with an expanded list of terms. The list of terms is now manageable, though the results still include too many documents that have low relevance.

### Classification and Clustering

The process of clustering documents into classes then makes it possible to provide groupings for the end user rather than a simple list of documents to scan through. When documents are grouped together based on common traits, it's possible to look at an initial document list and restrict the results further to find *similar documents*.

For the defense example, we can query on the terms defense and military, and then when the results are returned showing the U.S. Constitution, we can find all documents with a similar classification, thereby eliminating those that aren't classified the same way. This result might return the Bill of Rights (the first ten amendments to the U.S. Constitution) and the remaining amendments to the Constitution.

# Intro to Oracle Text

If there's one component that has gone through significant naming and configuration changes with Oracle, it's Oracle Text. The timeline in Figure 9-2 shows the migration from SQL*TextRetrieval to the present-day Oracle Text configuration.

As illustrated in the timeline, Oracle Text is included in all currently supported versions of the Standard and Enterprise Editions of the database. There is no separate license requirement anymore. In fact, beginning in Oracle 9*i* it became a default, requiring that you unselect it if you didn't want it.

Oracle Text is installed in the CTXSYS schema. Make certain you unlock and provide a password to this schema after database creation. Built-in packages and object types are created during the install that help create and maintain Oracle Text structures. Refer to Appendix B for a list of supplied packages and some examples of the most frequently used procedures and functions.

**NOTE**
*The examples for this chapter require careful setup. Take note of the following:*

■ *The* create_user.sql *script creates a user called* plsql. *Do not change this name as it is hard-coded in some of the example scripts.*

■ *The* create_user.sql *script creates an Oracle directory. This can be any directory on your database server, but it must be created prior to running the user creation script.*

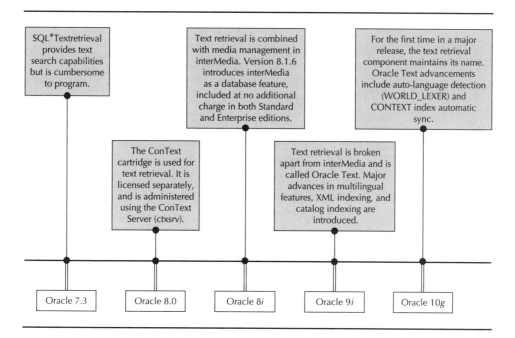

**FIGURE 9-2.** *The Oracle Text timeline*

- *Copy the files in* Chapter9/code/files *to the Oracle directory location. These are the documents that are indexed later.*

- *To run the PL/SQL Server Page example application, you must have a web server configured with access to the* plsql *schema. We recommend creating a DAD connection using Oracle Application Server 10*g.

Refer to the README.txt included in the code directory for additional setup information.

## Oracle Text and IR

The models discussed earlier are related to pure IR solutions. IR is for unstructured data, so its marriage to the relational database where structure is king is enough to make any therapist cringe. As the old saying goes, opposites attract, and the relational database/IR combination is no exception. The success of the relational database has brought about the need for the traditionally structured RDBMS to support unstructured data.

Oracle Text, depending on the configuration, supports a modified version of all three models. You will see, through examples in this section, attributes of each of the models, as well as some unique features not yet discussed.

## Features Overview

Oracle Text is Oracle's IR solution, providing all of the IR features (and more) discussed earlier. Four index types address nearly every business problem imaginable. Some highlights are

- The default filter used to process documents recognizes and extracts text from more than 150 different document types.

- The foreign language lexers that break text into tokens are unsurpassed in the industry, and excel at indexing Asian non–white space delimited text.

- Search features include stoplists to remove noise words, thesauri for expanding the search vocabulary, storage preferences that are critical when working with large amounts of data, and the ability to create concatenated datastores for indexing multiple columns.

**NOTE**
*Features vary quite a bit between releases of Oracle. All features discussed here are valid for Oracle 9i and Oracle 10g unless otherwise noted.*

## Index Creation

Oracle Text indexes are structured completely different than other indexes in Oracle. The INDEXTYPE in the CREATE INDEX statement determines which one of the four available Text indexes it is. Depending on the INDEXTYPE, additional parameters such as STOPLIST, WORDLIST, STORAGE, LEXER, and DATASTORE are available.

Figure 9-3 shows the different parameters that are involved in the index creation process for a CONTEXT index. The same process is followed by other indexes with a few differences. For a list of differences, refer to the *Oracle Text Reference* guide provided on OTN (http://otn.oracle.com).

Note where the parameters come into the indexing process, and how they work together to create the Text index. The following sections discuss each of these parameters in detail, and show how to create and/or modify them.

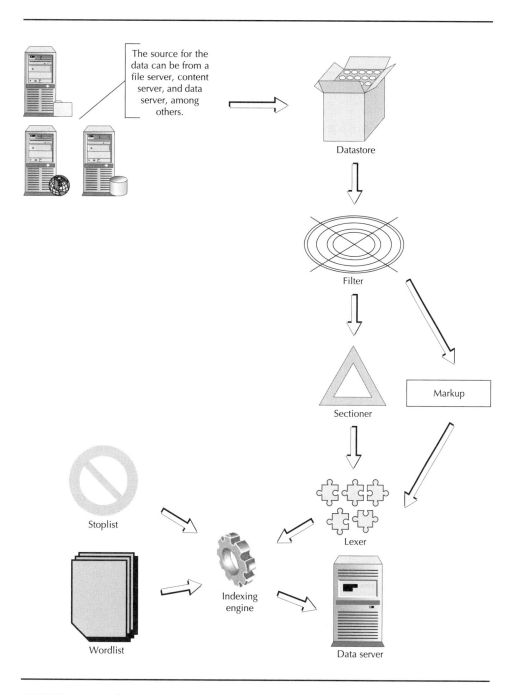

**FIGURE 9-3.** *The index creation process*

### Datastore

The Datastore preference tells Oracle how source data is structured. The default datastore is called DIRECT_DATASTORE and is used for most indexing operations. A URL_DATASTORE is used when the data source can be located via URL. Should you wish to index two data sources using a single index, a concatenated datastore is required.

To create a concatenated datastore, MULTI_COLUMN_DATASTORE is specified during preference creation as follows:

**--Available online as part of create_text_indexes.sql**

```
BEGIN
    CTX_DDL.CREATE_PREFERENCE(
        'EXPERT_CONCAT_DATASTORE',
        'MULTI_COLUMN_DATASTORE');
    CTX_DDL.SET_ATTRIBUTE(
        'EXPERT_CONCAT_DATASTORE',
        'columns',
        'TITLE, SHORT_DESCRIPTION');
END;
/
```

This example creates a Datastore named EXPERT_CONCAT_DATASTORE of type MULTI_COLUMN_DATASTORE. The columns included are TITLE and SHORT_DESCRIPTION. No table or index is specified at this time. That is done during index creation.

### Filter

The default filter for index creation is the INSO filter which Oracle licenses from Stellent Corporation (it's included with Oracle at no additional charge). In Oracle Database version 10.1.0.4 Oracle stopped including the INSO filter, and began bundling Verity® KeyView® Export©, developed by Verity, Inc. The Verity filter is now the default filter for Oracle Database 10.1.0.4 and up. Using either the INSO or Verity filter, Oracle Text can extract the text from more than 150 different document types. The filter allows text to be indexed the same way regardless of the type of source document. If you wish, it's possible to create a custom filter using USER_FILTER.

**TIP**
*If you are indexing HTML only, specify*
*CTXSYS.NULL_FILTER as a parameter for*
*the index.*

## Sectioner

The sectioner breaks the text apart from the document markup. The text is passed to the lexer to be broken into tokens while the markup is stored for section searching. Using section groups it's possible to search *within* a particular document section, such as text between tags in an XML document. The use of a section group is demonstrated later in this chapter when discussing the CONTEXT index.

## Lexers

Recall from our earlier discussion about text processing that token generation is the key to search, classification, categorization, and generating the theme or gist of a document. Lexers are the way Oracle generates these tokens. Table 9-2 lists the available lexers.

| Lexer Name | Description |
|---|---|
| BASIC_LEXER | Used for most languages employing a white space delimiter to separate terms. |
| CHINESE_VGRAM_LEXER | This lexer is included in all currently supported versions of the data server, and is used to pull tokens from Chinese text. |
| CHINESE_LEXER | CHINESE_LEXER is much more reliable than CHINESE_VGRAM_LEXER. Use this lexer if you have a choice. |
| KOREAN_LEXER | Breaks Korean text into tokens. This lexer is available in all currently supported versions of the data server. |
| KOREAN_MORPH_LEXER | KOREAN_MORPH_LEXER is the recommended lexer for tokenizing Korean text. |
| JAPANESE_VGRAM_LEXER | This lexer is included in all currently supported versions of the data server, and is used to pull tokens from Japanese text. |
| JAPANESE_LEXER | This lexer, introduced in Oracle 9i, provides better results than the older JAPANESE_VGRAM_LEXER. |

**TABLE 9-2.** *Types of Lexers*

| Lexer Name | Description |
|---|---|
| USER_LEXER | Didn't find a lexer that supports your language? USER_LEXER provides a way to create a language-specific lexer. |
| MULTI_LEXER | Available in all supported releases of the Oracle data server, MULTI_LEXER makes it possible to store text in many languages in the database, and use the correct language-specific lexer for each row. |
|  | To use it, lexers for each supported language must be created. They are then added as sublexers to MULTI_LEXER. The table being indexed must have a language column, and each record must have a value in it that tells Oracle the language of the text in that record. |
| WORLD_LEXER | Similar to MULTI_LEXER in that it supports indexing text in multiple languages in the same table and column. Not available until Oracle 10*g*, WORLD_LEXER can detect the language being indexed, removing the need to explicitly state each record's language in a column. It is less flexible than MULTI_LEXER though. |

**TABLE 9-2.** *Types of Lexers* (cont.)

The following example requires BASIC_LEXER only. It is created using the following syntax:

```
-- Available online as part of create_text_indexes.sql

BEGIN
   CTX_DDL.CREATE_PREFERENCE('EXPERT_LEXER', 'BASIC_LEXER');
   CTX_DDL.SET_ATTRIBUTE('EXPERT_LEXER', 'INDEX_THEMES', 'YES');
   CTX_DDL.SET_ATTRIBUTE('EXPERT_LEXER', 'THEME_LANGUAGE', 'ENGLISH');
END;
/
```

BASIC_LEXER is named EXPERT_LEXER. The only nonstandard attributes required for the example is the generation of themes. This lexer creation generates themes for all the indexes that use this lexer (more than one index can use a lexer). The themes are being generated for English text.

**TIP**
*For an in-depth discussion of lexers, refer to the*
Oracle Text Application Developer's Guide
*available on OTN.*

**Globalization and Lexers**   Table 9-2 included global lexers. The first, called
`MULTI_LEXER`, relies on a language column in the source table to specify the type
of lexer to use. As it indexes, the language value is compared to sublexer language
identifiers, and the correct one is used. If there's no match, the default lexer is used.

Oracle 10*g* introduces `WORLD_LEXER`. It works with Unicode, but does so in a
way that's completely different than `MULTI_LEXER`. Each character, regardless of
language, is actually one or more stored codepoints. What you actually see rendered
on your screen is called a glyph: a character representation of the codepoint. `WORLD_`
`LEXER` looks at the codepoints to determine whether the text being indexed is an
Arabic character/term, Asian character/term (Chinese, Japanese, Korean, and so on),
or other white-space delimited term. Figure 9-4 illustrates the process.

As is shown in the figure, Asian characters (which are not white-space delimited)
are broken into overlapping sections, two characters at a time. Note we said *characters*
this time, not *codepoints*. Characters can be made up of one or more codepoints,
so when two characters are extracted as a token, there may in fact be more than two
codepoints.

## How Does That Work?

Every Unicode character is made up of codepoints. Oracle provides a built-in
SQL function called UNISTR that can help convert codepoints to glyphs. The
following example converts the codepoints used in Figure 9-4:

```
-- Available online as part of unistr.sql

SELECT UNISTR('\0045\0078\0070\0065\0072\0074')
       ||' '||
       UNISTR('\0050\004C\002F\0053\0051\004C')
FROM dual;
```

The concatenation operator is used here for formatting. It's possible to
string together multiple strings of codepoints in a single line with UNISTR.

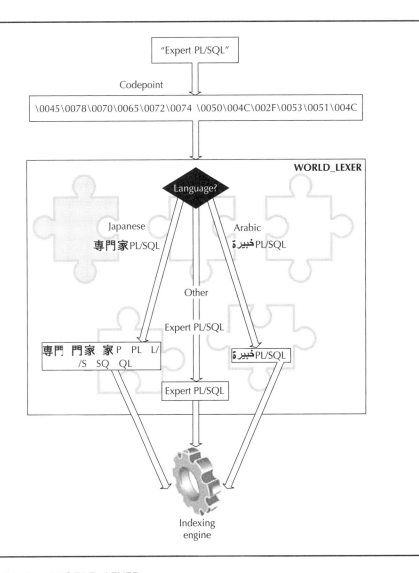

**FIGURE 9-4.** *WORLD_LEXER*

Arabic languages are white-space delimited, so the white space is used to distinguish one term from another. In addition to breaking the text apart, some additional normalization takes place.

All other languages are assumed to be white-space delimited. No additional processing is done, and features such as theme and gist creation are not possible.

The following example creates a WORLD_LEXER:

 --**Available online as part of create_text_indexes.sql**

```
BEGIN
   CTX_DDL.CREATE_PREFERENCE('EXPERT_WORLD_LEXER', 'WORLD_LEXER');
END;
/
```

No language-specific features are available since no language-specific lexers are used.

## Wordlists

Use a wordlist to enable fuzzy and stemming searches. Prefix and substrings can also be included to improve wildcard query performance.

The only type of wordlist available is BASIC_WORDLIST. The following script creates a wordlist called EXPERT_WORDLIST and sets a number of attributes:

--**Available online as part of create_text_indexes.sql**

```
BEGIN
   CTX_DDL.CREATE_PREFERENCE('EXPERT_WORDLIST', 'BASIC_WORDLIST');
   CTX_DDL.SET_ATTRIBUTE('EXPERT_WORDLIST', 'FUZZY_MATCH', 'ENGLISH');
   CTX_DDL.SET_ATTRIBUTE('EXPERT_WORDLIST', 'FUZZY_SCORE', '0');
   CTX_DDL.SET_ATTRIBUTE('EXPERT_WORDLIST', 'PREFIX_INDEX', 'TRUE');
   CTX_DDL.SET_ATTRIBUTE('EXPERT_WORDLIST', 'PREFIX_MIN_LENGTH', '2');
   CTX_DDL.SET_ATTRIBUTE('EXPERT_WORDLIST', 'PREFIX_MAX_LENGTH', '5');
   CTX_DDL.SET_ATTRIBUTE('EXPERT_WORDLIST', 'SUBSTRING_INDEX', 'TRUE');
   CTX_DDL.SET_ATTRIBUTE('EXPERT_WORDLIST', 'STEMMER', 'ENGLISH');
END;
/
```

If this wordlist is specified during index creation, fuzzy and stemming are possible with English. In addition, tokens created by the lexer include prefix and substring tokens to improve wildcard query performance.

**NOTE**
*Including prefix and substring tokens adds overhead. Weigh the cost of the indexing operation and additional overhead against the performance gain you see with searches.*

## Stoplists

If you look up the word THE in an index of the book *War and Peace*, would you find it? Of course not, because it's completely useless to index such a word. It doesn't help at all when trying to determine relevance. With this in mind, Oracle Text lets you include stoplists in the index creation to prevent the extraction of noise words. As was described in the IR section titled "Improving Relevance with Stopwords," terms such as THE, OF, AND, and so on are examples of noise words.

While Oracle provides a default stoplist called DEFAULT_STOPLIST, it's possible to create your own. The CTX_DDL.CREATE_STOPLIST procedure creates the stoplist. CTX_DDL.ADD_STOPWORD adds words to either the DEFAULT_STOPLIST or a custom one.

The following example creates a custom stoplist called EXPERT_STOPLIST:

**--Available online as part of create_text_indexes.sql**

```
BEGIN
  CTX_DDL.CREATE_STOPLIST ('EXPERT_STOPLIST','BASIC_STOPLIST');
...
  CTX_DDL.ADD_STOPWORD('EXPERT_STOPLIST','shall');
...
  CTX_DDL.ADD_STOPWORD('EXPERT_STOPLIST','with');
  CTX_DDL.ADD_STOPWORD('EXPERT_STOPLIST','would');
END;
/
```

This creates a custom stoplist, and includes words such as shall that aren't included in DEFAULT_STOPLIST. If you find other terms that need to be added, this can be done at any time using CTX_DDL.ADD_STOPWORD.

## Storage Preference

The DR$ tables shown in Table 9-3 are created with CONTEXT indexes. Other indexes use a subset of these tables, and are shown in the index-specific discussions later in this chapter.

### Why Would I Use This?

While we could have used the CTX_DDL.ADD_STOPWORD procedure to modify the default stoplist, we chose to create a custom stoplist. We don't recommend making changes to DEFAULT_STOPLIST (or any seeded preference) that aren't applicable to all Text indexes. The use of a custom stoplist provides flexibility for all applications sharing the same database.

| Table Name | Description |
|---|---|
| DR$ *index_name*$I | Contains token information. After indexing, tokens can be seen in the TOKEN_TEXT column. |
| DR$ *index_name*$K | Index Organized Table (IOT) used to map information about documents to their ROWIDs. It's referred to as the *keymap* table. |
| DR$ *index_name*$N | Negative list table where documents are marked for deletion. |
| DR$ *index_name*$P | Substring table for the index. |
| DR$ *index_name*$R | ROWIDs are stored in this table. |

**TABLE 9-3.** *Oracle Text* DR$ *Tables*

These tables are created automatically during the indexing process. While no intervention in the creation routine is required, a STORAGE preference can be used to direct how each table is stored.

The following preference defines storage for the $I, $K, and $R tables, as well as the index.

--**Available online as part of create_text_indexes.sql**

```
BEGIN
    ctx_ddl.create_preference('EXPERT_STORAGE', 'BASIC_STORAGE');
    ctx_ddl.set_attribute('EXPERT_STORAGE',
                    'I_TABLE_CLAUSE',
                    'tablespace TEXT_TS storage (
                            initial 4K
                            next 8M
                            maxextents unlimited
                            pctincrease 0)');
    ctx_ddl.set_attribute('EXPERT_STORAGE',
                    'K_TABLE_CLAUSE',
                    'tablespace TEXT_TS storage (
                            initial 4K
                            next 8M
                            maxextents unlimited
                            pctincrease 0)');
```

```
    ctx_ddl.set_attribute('EXPERT_STORAGE',
                          'R_TABLE_CLAUSE',
                          'lob (data) store as (cache)
                           tablespace TEXT_TS storage (
                                  initial 4K
                                  next 8M
                                  maxextents unlimited
                                  pctincrease 0)');
    ctx_ddl.set_attribute('EXPERT_STORAGE',
                          'I_INDEX_CLAUSE',
                          'COMPRESS 2
                           tablespace TEXT_TS storage (
                                  initial 4K
                                  next 8M
                                  maxextents unlimited
                                  pctincrease 0)');
END;
/
```

If this preference is provided at index creation, the index and tables will be created according to the storage parameters.

## Index Types

Oracle provides four Oracle Text index types. The CONTEXT index is quite powerful, and is the type most frequently used. CTXCAT is primarily for catalog applications, and was introduced in Oracle 9*i*. The CTXRULE index is great for library and knowledge repository applications. Finally, the CTXXPATH index, which works with the XMLTYPE data type, is for XML document indexing.

The next two sections provide examples of the CONTEXT and CTXCAT indexes. These indexes are also used in the PL/SQL Server Page example discussed later.

**CONTEXT Index**    The CONTEXT index is the most commonly used type of index because of its power and flexibility. Using this index type, it's possible to index multiple languages and use wordlists, thesauri, stoplists, and datastores, just to name a few features. The following example creates an Oracle Text index on a table called DOCUMENT_REPOSITORY. The document column is a BFILE, and the files being indexed are those that are in the directory that was created with the create_user.sql script.

The create index syntax is as follows:

```
CREATE INDEX index_name ON table_name(column_name)
      INDEXTYPE IS CTXSYS.CONTEXT
      [ONLINE] [PARAMETERS('parameter_name parameter_value')]
      [PARALLEL y/n] [UNUSABLE];
```

## Why Would I Use This?

We use the CONTEXT index more than any other. It's great for search applications where there's infrequent DML against the data source. Using this index, results can be ranked, multiple languages can be easily indexed, and thesauri, wordlists, and stoplists can be used. In addition, indexing XML documents and searching within sections is possible.

The following example creates an index called EXPERT_INDEX.

```
--Available online as part of create_text_indexes.sql

CREATE INDEX EXPERT_IDX ON document_repository(document)
INDEXTYPE IS CTXSYS.CONTEXT
PARAMETERS (
  'LEXER EXPERT_LEXER
  WORDLIST EXPERT_WORDLIST
  STOPLIST EXPERT_STOPLIST
  DATASTORE CTXSYS.DEFAULT_DATASTORE
  SYNC (ON COMMIT)'
    )
/
```

Until Oracle 10g Release 1, CONTEXT indexes had to be manually synchronized whenever there were any DML commands run against the data source. Now we have a SYNC parameter available to make this process automatic. SYNC offers the following three options:

- **ON COMMIT**   This option forces an index synchronization whenever a transaction against the data source is committed.

- **EVERY _interval_**   This follows the same format as that used to specify intervals for jobs.

- **MANUAL**   This default sync option requires manual synchronization.

**TIP**
_Use SYNC (ON COMMIT) only when the data change must be made available right away, and when the changes are infrequent. If there are frequent changes, the ON COMMIT setting will cause performance problems for your application, so specify the EVERY interval parameter._

On creation of the index, the following tables are automatically generated:

```
DR$EXPERT_IDX$I
DR$EXPERT_IDX$K
DR$EXPERT_IDX$N
DR$EXPERT_IDX$P
DR$EXPERT_IDX$R
```

Notice that the name of the index is always placed between the dollar signs ($...$). This makes querying for the tables against USER|ALL|DBA_TABLES easy as long as you know the index name.

The last example used a DIRECT_DATASTORE to index a single source column. It isn't possible to index two columns in a CREATE INDEX statement, but using a MULTI_COLUMN_DATASTORE, multiple columns can be concatenated so that by indexing a single source, multiple columns are included. The "Datastore" section earlier in this chapter demonstrated how to create a concatenated datastore. To use the datastore, include the EXPERT_CONCAT_DATASTORE name in the list of parameters as follows:

**--Available online as part of create_text_indexes.sql**

```
CREATE INDEX concat_idx
ON document_repository(short_description)
INDEXTYPE IS CTXSYS.CONTEXT
PARAMETERS('
   DATASTORE EXPERT_CONCAT_DATASTORE
   WORDLIST EXPERT_WORDLIST
   LEXER EXPERT_LEXER
   STOPLIST EXPERT_STOPLIST
   SYNC (ON COMMIT)'
   )
/
```

In addition to indexing documents for full text searching, it's possible to index XML documents using section groups so the documents can be searched within specific tags in the document. The following index uses AUTO_SECTION_GROUP as the section group for the index.

**--Available online as part of create_text_indexes.sql**

```
CREATE INDEX xml_idx
ON document_repository(xml_doc)
INDEXTYPE IS CTXSYS.CONTEXT
PARAMETERS ('
```

```
SECTION GROUP CTXSYS.AUTO_SECTION_GROUP
DATASTORE CTXSYS.DEFAULT_DATASTORE
WORDLIST EXPERT_WORDLIST
LEXER EXPERT_LEXER
STOPLIST EXPERT_STOPLIST')
/
```

The `AUTO_SECTION_GROUP` section group used in the example identifies begin and end tags in the XML documents. It's possible to search between these tags using the `WITHIN` operator. Section group searching is discussed in greater detail later in this chapter in the section titled "Section Searching."

**CTXCAT Index**     The `CTXCAT` index is better for basic Text queries against small amounts of data than the `CONTEXT` index. The basic index creation syntax is as follows:

```
CREATE INDEX index_name ON table_name(column_name)
     INDEXTYPE IS CTXSYS.CTXCAT
     [PARAMETERS('parameter_name parameter_value')];
```

The following example creates an index called `EXPERT_TITLE_IDX` of type `CTXSYS.CTXCAT`. The stoplist, lexer, and wordlist are the same as the `CONTEXT` index created in the last section.

`--Available online as part of create_text_indexes.sql`

```
CREATE INDEX expert_title_idx ON document_repository(title)
INDEXTYPE IS CTXSYS.CTXCAT
PARAMETERS (
   'LEXER EXPERT_LEXER
    WORDLIST EXPERT_WORDLIST
    STOPLIST EXPERT_STOPLIST'
      )
/
```

The biggest difference in the index creation has to do with the parameters. There is no need for a `MULTI_COLUMN_DATASTORE`, for example, since `CTXCAT` supports the concept of an index set; an index can be made up of subindexes. For more details on all available parameters, refer to the *Oracle Text Reference* on the OTN web site.

The `CTXCAT` index creation also created the following tables automatically:

```
DR$EXPERT_TITLE_IDX$I
DR$EXPERT_TITLE_IDX$P
```

**Why Would I Use This?**
The CTXCAT index is best for catalog applications. It has fewer features than the CONTEXT index, but is great for applications requiring frequent updates. Where the CONTEXT index requires the SYNC parameter to tell Oracle when to synchronize DML changes, the CTXCAT index synchronized on commit by default.

Since the table structure is different from that of the CONTEXT index, one would expect the query processing to be different as well. This is discussed in the next section titled "Query Processing."

# Query Processing

In this section, we discuss basic query processing against CONTEXT and CTXCAT indexes. Both use basic SQL syntax to select the data, but there are significant differences behind the scenes. The query processing has not been documented very well to this point. Here we use SQL trace to see some of the details though, and shed some light on how basic Text queries are executed.

## Standard SELECT

As a baseline, let's first examine a basic SELECT statement execution. A basic SELECT statement involves three macro steps: PARSE, EXECUTE, and FETCH. On execution, Oracle attempts to get the required data from the database buffer cache. If not found there, it goes to disk. If there is an index available, and the cost (according to the cost-based optimizer) determines that using it is cheaper than another access method, the data is retrieved using the index. Although not simple, there are very few surprises during the execution.

## SELECT Using CONTAINS

To use the CONTEXT index, add the CONTAINS predicate to the WHERE clause. A simple SELECT is shown in the following example:

--Available online as part of queries.sql

```
SELECT score(1), title
FROM document_repository
WHERE CONTAINS(document, 'constitution', 1) > 0
ORDER BY 1 DESC;
```

The query against the `DOCUMENT_REPOSITORY.DOCUMENT` column with the `CONTAINS` predicate forces the use of the `EXPERT_IDX` index created in the earlier index creation example. To really see what is happening though, use a level 4 trace and examine the raw (not `tkprof`) trace.

**SQL Trace**    By default, the Extensible Query Optimizer is enabled. When enabled, the Extensible Query Optimizer can determine the I/O and CPU cost associated with the `CONTAINS` predicate, find the cost of each call to the `CONTAINS()` function, and determine the selectivity of the `CONTAINS` predicate.

To see this in action, we ran the basic `SELECT` earlier. Examining the SQL trace shows the steps.

### Step 1: Determine the I/O and CPU cost of the `CONTAINS()` function

```
--Available online as part of contains_trace.doc
...
"CTXSYS"."TEXTOPTSTATS".ODCIStatsFunctionCost(
          sys.ODCIFuncInfo('CTXSYS',
            'CTX_CONTAINS',
            'TEXTCONTAINS',
            2),
          cost,
          sys.ODCIARGDESCLIST(
            sys.ODCIARGDESC(
               2, 'DOCUMENT_REPOSITORY', 'PLSQL',
               '"DOCUMENT"', NULL, NULL, NULL),
            sys.ODCIARGDESC(3, NULL, NULL, NULL, NULL, NULL, NULL)),
          NULL,
          'constitution',
          sys.ODCIENV(0,0,0,1));
...
```

### Step 2: Determine the selectivity of the `CONTAINS` predicate

```
-- Available online as part of contains_trace.doc
...
"CTXSYS"."TEXTOPTSTATS".ODCIStatsSelectivity(
          sys.ODCIPREDINFO('CTXSYS',
            'CTX_CONTAINS',
            'TEXTCONTAINS',
             32),
          sel,
          sys.ODCIARGDESCLIST(
            sys.ODCIARGDESC(3, NULL, NULL, NULL, NULL, NULL, NULL),
```

```
                    sys.ODCIARGDESC(5, NULL, NULL, NULL, NULL, NULL, NULL),
                    sys.ODCIARGDESC(2, 'DOCUMENT_REPOSITORY', 'PLSQL',
                         "DOCUMENT"', NULL, NULL, NULL),
                    sys.ODCIARGDESC(3, NULL, NULL, NULL, NULL, NULL, NULL)),
                0,
                NULL,
                NULL,
                'constitution',
                sys.ODCIENV(0,0,0,1));
    ...
```

## Step 3: Determine the I/O and CPU cost of the CONTAINS predicate

```
-- Available online as part of contains_trace.doc
    ...
"CTXSYS"."TEXTOPTSTATS".ODCIStatsIndexCost(
                sys.ODCIINDEXINFO('PLSQL',
                    'EXPERT_IDX',
                    sys.ODCICOLINFOLIST(
                        sys.ODCICOLINFO('PLSQL', 'DOCUMENT_REPOSITORY',
                                        '"DOCUMENT"', 'BFILE', NULL, NULL)),

                    NULL,
                    0,
                    0),
                50.00000000,
                cost,
                sys.ODCIQUERYINFO(
                    2,
                    sys.ODCIOBJECTLIST(sys.ODCIOBJECT('SCORE', 'CTXSYS'))),
                sys.ODCIPREDINFO('CTXSYS', 'CONTAINS', NULL, 0),
                sys.ODCIARGDESCLIST(
                    sys.ODCIARGDESC(3, NULL, NULL, NULL, NULL, NULL, NULL),
                    sys.ODCIARGDESC(5, NULL, NULL, NULL, NULL, NULL, NULL),
                    sys.ODCIARGDESC(2, 'DOCUMENT_REPOSITORY', 'PLSQL',
                                    '"DOCUMENT"', NULL, NULL, NULL),
                    sys.ODCIARGDESC(3, NULL, NULL, NULL, NULL, NULL, NULL)),
                1,
                NULL,
                'constitution',
                sys.ODCIENV(0,0,0,1));
    ...
```

**NOTE**
*The 50.00000000 in this last call is the selectivity retrieved from step 2.*

Only after these three steps are completed does the query actually get executed:

-- Available online as part of contains_trace.doc

```
SELECT score(1), title
FROM document_repository
WHERE CONTAINS(document, 'constitution', 1) > 0
ORDER BY 1 DESC;
```

This is not the end of the processing though. To retrieve the records, the $I table (the index data table) is queried as follows:

-- Available online as part of contains_trace.doc

```
SELECT /*+ INDEX(i) */ TOKEN_FIRST,TOKEN_LAST,TOKEN_COUNT,ROWID
FROM "PLSQL"."DR$EXPERT_IDX$I" i
WHERE TOKEN_TEXT = 'CONSTITUTION'
AND TOKEN_TYPE = 0
ORDER BY TOKEN_TEXT, TOKEN_TYPE, TOKEN_FIRST;
```

**NOTE**
*The search term is UPPERCASE when querying against the DR$EXPERT_IDX$I table because all of the tokens are stored in uppercase by default. The original SELECT was in lowercase. This automatic conversion to uppercase allows the Text index to provide case-insensitive searching.*

This query returns the following result:

```
TOKEN_FIRST TOKEN_LAST TOKEN_COUNT ROWID
----------- ---------- ----------- ------------------
          1          2           2 AAAN54AAEAAAOvEAAo
```

Finally, the $R table (the rowid table) is queried.

-- Available online as part of contains_trace.doc

```
SELECT data
FROM "PLSQL"."DR$EXPERT_IDX$R"
WHERE row_no = 0;
```

Only now do we see the results of our query:

```
SCORE(1) TITLE
---------- ---------------------------
      55 United States Constitution
       8 Bill of Rights
```

Keep in mind that modifications to the query, such as the addition of other columns in the where clause or the addition of operators, will result in a different trace.

**NOTE**
*To read more about the Extensible Query Optimizer, see the Oracle Text Reference for your version of the data server.*

## SELECT Using CATSEARCH

Query processing using CATSEARCH against a CTXCAT index is quite different from the CONTAINS query shown earlier. CTXCAT allows the use of subindexes, and only includes two DR$ tables. The following example uses CATSEARCH:

 -- **Available online as part of queries.sql**

```
SELECT title, short_description
FROM document_repository
WHERE CATSEARCH(title, 'bill', null) > 0;
```

The query against the DOCUMENT_REPOSITORY.TITLE column with the CATSEARCH predicate forces the use of the EXPERT_TITLE_IDX index created in the earlier index creation example. Unless you use query templates to mimic a CONTEXT query, CATSEARCH queries are Boolean. To really see what's happening during query execution, use a level 4 trace and examine the raw (not tkprof) trace.

**NOTE**
*Query templates are beyond the scope of our discussion here. Please see the Oracle Text Reference available at http://otn.oracle.com for more details on this feature.*

**SQL Trace**     The first thing you might notice in the trace is that it's shorter than the trace using CONTAINS. For starters, there are no calls to "CTXSYS"."TEXTOPTSTATS" like there were with the CONTAINS search. Instead, I/O and CPU cost, as well as selectivity, is drawn from `ASSOCIATIONS$` (see `catsearch_trace.doc`). This is followed by query execution, and two `SELECT`s against the `DR$..$I` table before the results are returned.

**TIP**
*RCH queries are typically faster in execution than their `CONTAINS` counterparts, though the indexing operation takes longer for `CTXCAT` indexes than for `CONTEXT` indexes. Choose your index based on required functionality first, but if the limitations with `CTXCAT` indexes are not an issue, consider this type of index to see performance gains for your searches.*

# Building a Search Application Using PL/SQL

PL/SQL is a natural choice when designing an information retrieval application. Tight integration with the data server and a mature development language makes PL/SQL-based IR systems fast and reliable. In addition to using traditional PL/SQL objects like procedures, functions, and packages, PL/SQL Server Pages are an excellent choice for web-based IR systems.

## PL/SQL Search and Retrieval

Search capabilities with Oracle Text include exact match, wildcard, stemming, theme-based searching, and section searching. The next few sections demonstrate these types of searches, as well as the generation of the document gist.

### Exact Match

Exact match searches for the term(s) in the text, and does so literally. There's no interpretation, and if multiple terms are included in the search, it takes them just as they are typed. For example, if the terms `DEFENCE CONSTITUTION` are typed, `DEFENCE` must be followed by `CONSTITUTION` in the text for a document to be returned. Searches are case-insensitive by default.

**--Available online as part of plsql_queries.sql**

```
SET SERVEROUTPUT ON
/* To get an exact match, pass the string without modification.*/
```

```
BEGIN
   DBMS_OUTPUT.PUT_LINE('EXACT MATCH SEARCH USING FOR LOOP');
   DBMS_OUTPUT.PUT_LINE('=================================');

   FOR c IN (SELECT SCORE(1) "RANK", title
         FROM document_repository
         WHERE CONTAINS(document, 'defence', 1) > 0
         ORDER BY 1 DESC)
   LOOP
      DBMS_OUTPUT.PUT_LINE('-');
      DBMS_OUTPUT.PUT_LINE('Score: '||c.rank);
      DBMS_OUTPUT.PUT_LINE('Title: '||c.title);
   END LOOP;
END;
/
```

This anonymous block returns the following:

```
EXACT MATCH SEARCH USING FOR LOOP
=================================
-
Score: 4
Title: United States Constitution
-
Score: 4
Title: The US Bill of Rights
```

The term DEFENCE occurs in the U.S. Constitution and Bill of Rights once per document, and the scores are identical.

## Wildcard

Wildcard queries use a % either before or after the search term(s). Wildcard queries can be very expensive, but there are a few ways to improve the performance. The first is to set the PREFIX_INDEX attribute to TRUE for the index wordlist. It's possible to set the minimum and maximum length of the prefix to control the size of the Text index. A second wordlist attribute with performance implications is the SUBSTRING_INDEX attribute.

The following example performs a wildcard search on the term DEFEN%. The indexed documents include both DEFENCE and DEFENSE, and this returns documents containing either.

**--Available online as part of plsql_queries.sql**

```
SET SERVEROUTPUT ON
/* Wildcard uses a % before and/or after the search string */
```

```
BEGIN
   DBMS_OUTPUT.PUT_LINE('WILDCARD SEARCH USING FOR LOOP');
   DBMS_OUTPUT.PUT_LINE('==============================');

   FOR c IN (SELECT SCORE(1) "RANK", title
           FROM document_repository
           WHERE CONTAINS(document, 'defen%', 1) > 0
           ORDER BY 1 DESC)
   LOOP
      DBMS_OUTPUT.PUT_LINE('-');
      DBMS_OUTPUT.PUT_LINE('Score: '||c.rank);
      DBMS_OUTPUT.PUT_LINE('Title: '||c.title);
   END LOOP;
END;
/
```

The results are as follows:

```
WILDCARD SEARCH USING FOR LOOP
==============================
-
Score: 13
Title: United States Constitution
-
Score: 4
Title: The US Bill of Rights
```

Since wildcard queries are not very precise, scores are typically lower than other types of searches that use complete terms. Remember that by expanding the number of matching terms, relevance in the document set becomes more difficult to determine.

## Stemming

If a document contains the word MICE, would a search on MOUSE return the document? No. Would a wildcard help? No. The terms come from the same root (stem), but the spelling is different enough that any kind of wildcard search is completely useless. Stemming matches search terms to their root, and associates them with documents whose tokens map to the same root. Oracle uses $ as the stemming operator.

The following query searches for $DEFENSE:

**--Available online as part of plsql_queries.sql**

```
SET SERVEROUTPUT ON
/* Stemming uses a $ preceding the search term(s) */
```

```
BEGIN
   DBMS_OUTPUT.PUT_LINE('STEMMING SEARCH USING FOR LOOP');
   DBMS_OUTPUT.PUT_LINE('==============================');

   FOR c IN (SELECT SCORE(1) "RANK", title
          FROM document_repository
          WHERE CONTAINS(document, '$defense', 1) > 0
          ORDER BY 1 DESC)
   LOOP
      DBMS_OUTPUT.PUT_LINE('-');
      DBMS_OUTPUT.PUT_LINE('Score: '||c.rank);
      DBMS_OUTPUT.PUT_LINE('Title: '||c.title);
   END LOOP;
END;
/
```

The anonymous block returns the following

```
STEMMING SEARCH USING FOR LOOP
==============================
-
Score: 8
Title: United States Constitution
-
Score: 4
Title: The US Bill of Rights
```

The Constitution contains both DEFENSE and DEFENCE. Using stemming, the scores reflect a higher match for Constitution than what was returned earlier using Exact Match.

## Multiple Keyword

Use the Accumulate operator (,) to search for multiple terms where results should include documents that contain one or more of the terms. This operator ensures that if any of the terms exist in a document, they will be returned even if none of the others exists.

The following anonymous block takes a search string of two terms, and replaces the white-space delimited string with a comma (the Accumulate operator):

**--Available online as part of plsql_queries.sql**

```
SET SERVEROUTPUT ON
/* Use REPLACE to change space to comma delimited */
DECLARE
   v_search_string VARCHAR2(100 CHAR);
```

```
BEGIN

   -- original search string is made of two words
   v_search_string := 'defence congress';

   -- replace the white space with a comma
   v_search_string := REPLACE(v_search_string, ' ', ', ');

   DBMS_OUTPUT.PUT_LINE('MULTI-TERM SEARCH USING FOR LOOP');
   DBMS_OUTPUT.PUT_LINE('==================================');

   FOR c IN (SELECT SCORE(1) "RANK", title
          FROM document_repository
          WHERE CONTAINS(document, v_search_string, 1) > 0
          ORDER BY 1 DESC)
   LOOP
      DBMS_OUTPUT.PUT_LINE('-');
      DBMS_OUTPUT.PUT_LINE('Score: '||c.rank);
      DBMS_OUTPUT.PUT_LINE('Title: '||c.title);
   END LOOP;
END;
/
```

The results are as follows:

```
MULTI-TERM SEARCH USING FOR LOOP
==================================
-
Score: 76
Title: United States Constitution
-
Score: 52
Title: The US Bill of Rights
-
Score: 50
Title: Amendments to the Constitution of the United States
```

The more terms that exist in the source document, the higher the score.

## Themes

Themes generation uses a knowledge base (one is provided with your Oracle installation). Themes are generally nouns that provide meaning to the documents, and they can be searched on. To see what themes are in the indexed documents, run the following anonymous block:

```
-- Available online as part of themes.sql
```

```
SET SERVEROUTPUT ON
```

```
DECLARE
   v_themes ctx_doc.theme_tab;
   v_rowid ROWID;
BEGIN
   SELECT rowid
   INTO v_rowid
   FROM document_repository
   WHERE document_id = 2;

   CTX_DOC.THEMES('expert_idx', v_rowid, v_themes, num_themes =>10);
   DBMS_OUTPUT.PUT_LINE('        THEMES        ');
   DBMS_OUTPUT.PUT_LINE('====================');
   FOR c IN 1..v_themes.count
   LOOP
      DBMS_OUTPUT.PUT_LINE('Theme:  '||v_themes(c).theme);
      DBMS_OUTPUT.PUT_LINE('Weight: '||v_themes(c).weight);
      DBMS_OUTPUT.PUT_LINE('-');
   END LOOP;
END;
/
```

The results show the following themes:

```
THEMES
====================
Theme:  law
Weight: 12
-
Theme:  government
Weight: 12
-
Theme:  support
Weight: 2
-
Theme:  freedom
Weight: 26
-
Theme:  security
Weight: 14
...
```

In this redacted list of themes, the freedom theme was the most prominent.

## ABOUT Queries

The ability to search on what a document is about rather than on specific keywords is an unusual concept if you are new to information retrieval. Document themes were generated using the CTX_DOC.THEMES built in. In addition to listing themes, it's possible to search on them. Theme-based searching adds a degree of intelligence to the search that can turn a good search application into excellent IR applications.

The following example uses the ABOUT operator with the theme being searched in parentheses:

**--Available online as part of plsql_queries.sql**

```
/* Use the ABOUT operator to search themes */
SET SERVEROUTPUT ON
BEGIN
   DBMS_OUTPUT.PUT_LINE('ABOUT SEARCH USING FOR LOOP');
   DBMS_OUTPUT.PUT_LINE('===========================');

   FOR c IN (SELECT SCORE(1) "RANK", title
         FROM document_repository
         WHERE CONTAINS(document, 'ABOUT(law)', 1) > 0
         ORDER BY 1 DESC)
   LOOP
      DBMS_OUTPUT.PUT_LINE('-');
      DBMS_OUTPUT.PUT_LINE('Score: '||c.rank);
      DBMS_OUTPUT.PUT_LINE('Title: '||c.title);
   END LOOP;
END;
/
```

The results should appear as follows:

```
ABOUT SEARCH USING FOR LOOP
===========================
-
Score: 46
Title: The US Bill of Rights
-
Score: 31
Title: United States Constitution
-
Score: 4
Title: Amendments to the Constitution of the United States
```

All other aspects of theme-based searching are the same as other queries.

## Section Searching

Using section searching, it's possible to search in only portions of documents rather than the entire document. An XML document is a perfect example of when section searching is handy. The following example searches between the *begin* and *end* tags labeled <TEXT> and </TEXT> in an XML document:

--Available online as part of plsql_queries.sql

```
SET SERVEROUTPUT ON
/* Search an XML document using section searching and the WITHIN operator */
BEGIN
    DBMS_OUTPUT.PUT_LINE('SECTION SEARCH USING FOR LOOP');
    DBMS_OUTPUT.PUT_LINE('==================================');

    FOR c IN (SELECT SCORE(1) "RANK", title
            FROM document_repository
            WHERE CONTAINS(xml_doc, 'President within TEXT', 1) > 0
            ORDER BY 1 DESC)
    LOOP
        DBMS_OUTPUT.PUT_LINE('-');
        DBMS_OUTPUT.PUT_LINE('Score: '||c.rank);
        DBMS_OUTPUT.PUT_LINE('Title: '||c.title);
    END LOOP;
END;
/
```

The results should appear as follows:

```
SECTION SEARCH USING FOR LOOP
==================================
-
Score: 100
Title: Amendments to the Constitution of the United States
```

For documents where section groups and section searching are appropriate, higher levels of relevance can be had with this method.

## Gist

A gist is essentially a summary of the source text or document. The gist extraction identifies the paragraphs that seem to represent the document as a whole. The gist output is made up of paragraphs from the document.

For gist extraction, the index lexer must have the INDEX_THEMES attribute set to TRUE. The following examples do this:

-- Available online as part of create_text_indexes.sql

```
BEGIN
    CTX_DDL.CREATE_PREFERENCE('EXPERT_LEXER', 'BASIC_LEXER');
```

```
CTX_DDL.SET_ATTRIBUTE('EXPERT_LEXER', 'INDEX_THEMES', 'YES');
   CTX_DDL.SET_ATTRIBUTE('EXPERT_LEXER', 'THEME_LANGUAGE', 'ENGLISH');
END;
/
```

After indexing, the gist of a document can be extracted using the CTX_ DOC.GIST procedure as follows:

--**Available online as part of gist.sql**

```
SET SERVEROUTPUT ON
DECLARE
   v_gist CLOB;
   v_offset PLS_INTEGER := 1;
   v_amount PLS_INTEGER := 32767;
   v_buffer VARCHAR2(32767);
   v_rowid   ROWID;
BEGIN
   EXECUTE IMMEDIATE('truncate table expert_gist');

   SELECT rowid
   INTO v_rowid
   FROM document_repository
   WHERE document_id = 1;

   CTX_DOC.GIST(
      index_name => 'EXPERT_IDX',
      textkey => v_rowid,
      restab => 'EXPERT_GIST',
      query_id => 1,
      glevel => 'P',
      pov => 'GENERIC');

   SELECT gist
   INTO v_gist
   FROM expert_gist;

   BEGIN
      LOOP
         DBMS_LOB.READ(
            lob_loc => v_gist,
            amount => v_amount,
            offset => v_offset,
            buffer => v_buffer);
```

```
            DBMS_OUTPUT.PUT_LINE(SUBSTR(v_buffer, 1, 255));
            v_offset := v_offset + v_amount;
            v_amount := 32767;
        END LOOP;
    EXCEPTION
    WHEN NO_DATA_FOUND
    THEN
        NULL;
    END;
END;
/
```

The output in this case is only the first 255 characters to limit the result. This anonymous block can be modified to output the entire text if desired. Running this block against the `plsql` schema with data and indexes in place, the following is returned:

```
We the People of the United States, in Order to form a more perfect
Union, establish Justice, insure domestic Tranquility, provide for the
common defense, promote the general Welfare, and secure the Blessings
of Liberty to ourselves and our Posterity, do
```

For a browser-based example using PL/SQL Server Pages (PSPs) see the "Theme and Gist Display" section later in this chapter.

# PSP Search

A simple, yet very effective way to create a web-based IR application is to use PL/SQL Server Pages (PSP). PSPs are a mix of HTML and PL/SQL, so we can embed the same anonymous blocks used in the last section (with some minor changes) to an HTML page.

**NOTE**
*PSPs are discussed in greater detail in Chapter 11.*
*We use them in this chapter to demonstrate Oracle*
*Text with PL/SQL.*

### Building a Search Page

To illustrate PSPs, we have an example called `psp_search.psp`. The following list of requirements is met with this page:

- Provide a text search against multiple data sources.

- The default search type should use commas to separate terms (accumulate).

■ Exact match, stemming, wildcard, and fuzzy must be possible.

■ When documents are searched, provide a method of displaying the documents with keyword highlighting.

■ When documents are searched, provide a method of displaying the document themes and weights.

■ When documents are searched, provide a method of displaying the document gist.

■ Change the result set depending on the data source being searched.

This example has to do a lot to meet these requirements, but it's not terribly complex. Figure 9-5 shows what the page will look like before a search.

The first part of the `psp_search.psp` page includes the cursors. See the following example:

**NOTE**
*Refer to the* Chapter9/PSP_Example/PSP_
README.txt *file for installation instructions.*

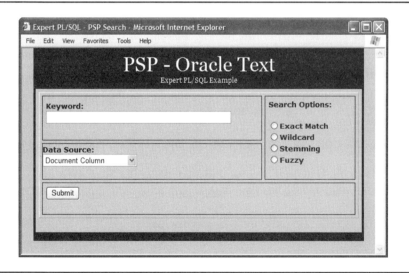

**FIGURE 9-5.** *The PSP search format*

--**Available online as part of psp_search.psp**

```
/* Cursor to search the documents for the specified search string */
CURSOR document_cur (cp_search_string VARCHAR2) IS
   SELECT SCORE(1) rank, document_id, title
   FROM document_repository
   WHERE CONTAINS(document, cp_search_string, 1) > 0
   ORDER BY 1 DESC;

/* Cursor to search the titles for the specified search string */
CURSOR title_cur (cp_search_string VARCHAR2) IS
   SELECT title, short_description
   FROM document_repository
   WHERE CATSEARCH(title, cp_search_string, null) > 0;

/* Cursor to search a concatenated datastore */
CURSOR concat_cur (cp_search_string VARCHAR2) IS
   SELECT score(1), title, short_description
   FROM document_repository
   WHERE CONTAINS(short_description, cp_search_string, 1) > 0
   ORDER BY 1 DESC;
```

All three cursors retrieve records in different ways:

- The first cursor searches a column of type BFILE where the documents are stored on your data server file system. It uses CONTAINS to perform the search.

- The second cursor is searching a column with a CTXCAT index created on it. It uses CATSEARCH to carry out the search.

- The third cursor uses CONTAINS to search like the first cursor, but it's actually searching a concatenated Datastore.

Note also that the SELECT list for the second and third cursors differs from the first.

If the HTML page were to display a result table when opened, it would be null and pointless. To avoid this, after the search form is created, the following is included:

--**Available online as part of psp_search.psp**

```
IF p_keyword IS NOT NULL
   THEN
```

p_keyword is the search string parameter. If there's no text passed to the parameter, then no results are displayed. This way, when a page is first loaded, only the search form is shown. After a keyword is entered by the user and the Submit button is clicked, the parameter is no longer NULL, and the results table is shown.

One of the requirements was to provide for exact match, wildcard, stemming, and fuzzy searching, and for the default search mode to be *accumulate*. For the `psp_search.psp` page, radio buttons named `psp_search_type` are used. The following section of the page uses `CASE` to set the search string based on the value of parameter `psp_search_type`:

--**Available online as part of psp_search.psp**

```
/* Set the search string according to the chosen search type */
CASE
    WHEN p_search_type = 'exact' THEN v_search_string := p_keyword;
    WHEN p_search_type = 'wildcard' THEN v_search_string := p_keyword||'%';
    WHEN p_search_type = 'stemming' THEN v_search_string := '$'||p_keyword;
    WHEN p_search_type = 'fuzzy' THEN v_search_string := 'FUZZY('
                            ||p_keyword||', 70, 6, weight)';
    ELSE v_search_string := REPLACE(p_keyword, ' ', ', ');
END CASE;
```

The multiple data source requirement is implemented with a drop-down box named `p_data_source`. The value of the drop-down determines the cursor used, as well as the structure of the table generated. The following redacted code shows the `IF-THEN` followed by the loop through the `document_cur` cursor:

--**Available online as part of psp_search.psp**

```
IF p_data_source = 'document'
    THEN
        ...
    FOR c IN document_cur(v_search_string)
        LOOP
            ...
        END LOOP;
```

If the data source is title, the `title_cur` cursor is used.

--**Available online as part of psp_search.psp**

```
ELSIF p_data_source = 'title'
    THEN
        ...
    FOR c IN title_cur(v_search_string)
        LOOP
            ...
        END LOOP;
```

Finally, the only option remaining uses the `concat_cur` cursor.

**--Available online as part of psp_search.psp**

```
ELSE
   ...
   FOR c IN concat_cur(v_search_string)
      LOOP
         ...
      END LOOP;
END IF;
```

This doesn't yet satisfy the requirements to provide a method to display documents with keyword highlighting, generate the gist, and show the themes when the data source is `Document`. `Document`, `Gist`, and `Theme` buttons are displayed when the data source is `Document Column`.

Figure 9-6 shows what the page looks like after searching for the term `constitution`.

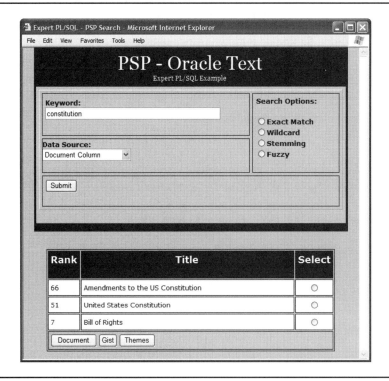

**FIGURE 9-6.** *A PSP search with document results*

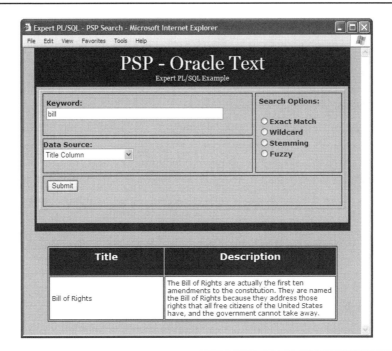

**FIGURE 9-7.** *A PSP search with title results*

The results section differs when a different data source is used. Figure 9-7 shows the screen when the `Title Column` is chosen as the data source, and the term `bill` is entered.

Not only is the table different, but the buttons are no longer available.

## Theme and Gist Display

The method used to generate the gist in this example requires a table to store data while processing. The `PLSQL` schema (created using the `create_user.sql` script) includes a table called `EXPERT_GIST` for this purpose. The following section of code truncates the `EXPERT_GIST` table as soon as the `psp_theme_gist.psp` page is opened.

**--Available online as part of psp_theme_gist.psp**

```
/* Truncate the table that is used to store the gist */
   EXECUTE IMMEDIATE('truncate table expert_gist');
```

The p_select parameter (indicating whether a record was selected) is tested to ensure a value is available. If there is no value for p_select, the user is prompted to return to the search page. The following code tests the p_select parameter:

--Available online as part of psp_theme_gist.psp

```
IF p_select IS NULL
   THEN
%>
   <center>
   <h2>You must select a document.  Use your browser's back button,
       select a record, and click the button again.</h2>
   </center>
<%  ELSE  %>
<%  IF p_theme_gist = 'Gist'
    THEN
        ...
```

If the Gist button is pressed, CTX_DOC.GIST generates the gist as follows:

--Available online as part of psp_theme_gist.psp

```
CTX_DOC.GIST(
   index_name => 'EXPERT_IDX',
   textkey => v_rowid,
   restab => 'EXPERT_GIST',
   query_id => 1,
   glevel => 'P',
   pov => 'GENERIC');

   SELECT gist
   INTO v_gist
   FROM expert_gist;
BEGIN
   LOOP
     DBMS_LOB.READ(
        lob_loc => v_gist,
        amount => v_amount,
        offset => v_offset,
        buffer => v_buffer);
%>
     <%= v_buffer %>
<%
     v_offset := v_offset + v_amount;
     v_amount := 32767;
   END LOOP;
```

```
EXCEPTION
   WHEN NO_DATA_FOUND
   THEN
      NULL;
END;
/
```

To see what this looks like in the page, search on Constitution, click Bill of Rights, and click Gist in the psp_search.psp screen. The page in Figure 9-8 will be displayed.

Returning to the search screen (click your browser's Back button), click the Theme button, and a list of themes and weights for the document is shown. The following code uses CTX_DOC.THEMES:

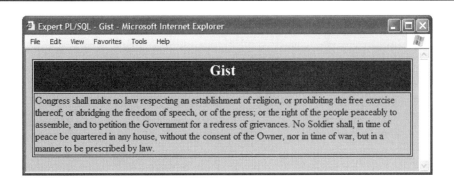 **--Available online as part of psp_theme_gist.psp**

```
ELSIF p_theme_gist='Themes'
THEN
   ...
   ctx_doc.themes('expert_idx', v_rowid, v_themes, num_themes =>10);
   FOR c IN 1..v_themes.count
   LOOP
      ...
   END LOOP;
END IF;
```

The call to CTX_DOC.GIST and CTX_DOC.THEMES requires the rowid of the record being processed. It's possible to switch this from rowid to primary key using CTX_DOC.SET_KEY_TYPE.

---

Expert PL/SQL - Gist - Microsoft Internet Explorer

File   Edit   View   Favorites   Tools   Help

## Gist

Congress shall make no law respecting an establishment of religion, or prohibiting the free exercise thereof; or abridging the freedom of speech, or of the press; or the right of the people peaceably to assemble, and to petition the Government for a redress of grievances. No Soldier shall, in time of peace be quartered in any house, without the consent of the Owner, nor in time of war, but in a manner to be prescribed by law.

---

**FIGURE 9-8.**   *The Gist screen*

## Keyword Highlighting

Return to the search screen and search on constitution again. Select Amendments and click the Document button. The following ELSIF tests for this condition:

**--Available online as part of psp_theme_gist.psp**

```
<% ELSIF p_theme_gist = 'Document'
   THEN%>
```

The BFILE is retrieved, highlighting the term that was searched as follows:

**--Available online as part of psp_theme_gist.psp**

```
<%
CTX_DOC.MARKUP( index_name => 'EXPERT_IDX',
                textkey => v_rowid,
                text_query => p_keyword,
                restab => 'EXPERT_MARKUP',
                query_id => 1,
                starttag => '<font style="background-color:#FFFF00">',
                endtag => '</font>');

      SELECT document
      INTO v_document
      FROM expert_markup;

      BEGIN
         LOOP
            DBMS_LOB.READ(
               lob_loc => v_document,
               amount => v_amount,
               offset => v_offset,
               buffer => v_buffer); %>
         <%= v_buffer %>
         <%
         v_offset := v_offset + v_amount;
         v_amount := 32767;
         END LOOP;
      EXCEPTION
         WHEN NO_DATA_FOUND
         THEN NULL;
      END;
%>
```

The results appear as shown in Figure 9-9.

The markup tag can be changed. Just modify the starttag and endtag in the call to CTX_DOC.MARKUP.

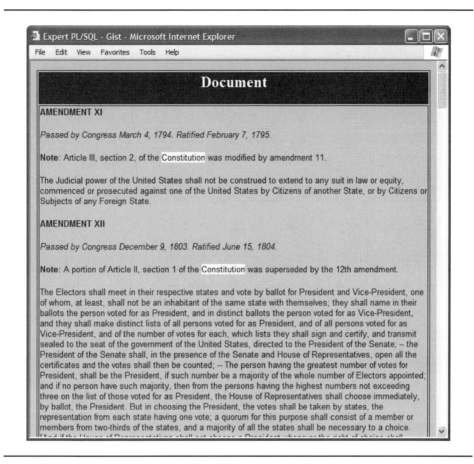

**FIGURE 9-9.** *Keyword highlighting*

# Summary

Oracle Text and PL/SQL provide a fully integrated IR solution for the relational database. Oracle Text supports the indexing of more than 150 different document types using the INSO or Verity filters, and can do theme/gist extraction, keyword and theme highlighting, and stemming, fuzzy, wildcard searching, and more. The globalization features are unparalleled in the industry, and PL/SQL Server Pages provide an IR interface that is both flexible, and easy to develop and use.

# CHAPTER
# 10

## Introduction to
## Regular Expressions

egular expressions were introduced in Oracle 10*g* Release 1, much to the delight of UNIX/Perl programmers everywhere. If you know regular expressions like the back of your hand, this chapter will show you Oracle's implementation, and how your knowledge can be leveraged with PL/SQL. If you aren't familiar with regular expressions, we'll show you what they are, how they work, and what you can do with them.

The chapter begins with an overview of regular expressions, their history, and some typical applications. We discuss the features available with Oracle, including metacharacters and built-in functions. Finally, we demonstrate how regular expressions combined with PL/SQL are a powerful combination that can transform your applications, and make common labor-intensive tasks simple and elegant.

# Foundations of Regular Expressions

A regular expression, abbreviated *regex*, is a string that describes the structure of some text. A regex string is composed of literals and metacharacters. For example, a regex string that represents either Georgian or George can be expressed as:

```
Georg(e|ian)
```

The characters for both names are present, but are represented in a single string using group (..) and alternate | metacharacters. Carry this example out to some of your business applications. Perhaps you want to extract all e-mail addresses from web pages. E-mail addresses follow a distinct pattern of *string@string.com/net/edu/ you_get_the_idea*. If a pattern can be established, then a regex string can be formed to represent it. Knowing the pattern allows the programmer to extract all e-mail addresses from all web sites. The following regex pattern finds all e-mail addresses:

```
[[:alnum:]](([_\.\-\+]?[[:alnum:]]+)*)@([[:alnum:]]+)(([\.-]?
[[:alnum:]]+)*)\.([[:alpha:]]{2,})
```

While this example is substantially longer than the `Georg(e|ian)` example that preceded it, it's really no more complex when broken into its individual components. We'll return to this example later and examine what each component does.

## History

Even if you think you've never used regular expressions before, chances are you have. For example, have you ever used the grep utility on UNIX? The following example uses grep to find the smon background process for the Oracle instance:

```
ps -ef | grep smon
```

which results in:

```
oraprd    21342    1    0    May  07  ?            2:57   ora_smon_SID
```

Okay, so what does grep have to do with regular expressions? GREP = Global *Regular Expression* Print.

Regex is a language that's supported by Perl, Java, .NET, Sed, Awk, Python, and PL/SQL, among others. The extent to which each language mentioned here supports regex differs. On one hand, Perl relies heavily on regular expressions. In fact, without the tight integration between Perl and regular expressions, Perl's usefulness would diminish significantly. Other languages, such as Java, .NET, or PL/SQL, have a more loosely coupled relationship with regular expressions. The languages use regular expressions as a way to extend the core of the language, but they are not a central component of it.

## POSIX

Not only do different languages offer different levels of regex integration, but they also support various flavors of regular expressions. It can be quite frustrating to write a regex solution for Perl and have the same string fail to work with Java. It was because of this that the Portable Operating System Interface (POSIX) standard was established. This standard can be broken into two types of regular expressions: a Basic Regular Expression (BRE) and an Extended Regular Expression (ERE).

**BREs**    Basic Regular Expressions support most of the same metacharacters that Extended Regular Expressions do. The most obvious feature that BREs support and EREs don't is backreferencing. Backreferences provide the ability to match part of the last expression in memory—essentially going back in time, if you will, to a prior pattern.

**EREs**    Extended Regular Expressions provide support for alternation, something BREs don't support. Alternation is the ability to match alternate versions of a term, just like how the Georg(e|ian) example from earlier in the chapter matches both George and Georgian.

# Oracle and Regular Expressions

Oracle added support for regular expressions in Oracle 10*g* Release 1. They adhere to the POSIX ERE standard, but also provide limited support for backreferencing, as well as some common non-POSIX metacharacters. The list of non-POSIX metacharacters that are supported grew with Oracle 10*g* Release 2. (Please see Appendix A for details about all of the metacharacters currently supported.)

Prior to the formal introduction of regular expression support, the OWA_ PATTERN built-in package delivered pattern-matching capabilities. The current implementation of regex extends the capabilities further, and has fewer restrictions placed on it than their OWA_PATTERN predecessor though.

**TIP**
*It's a good idea to convert any programs using OWA_PATTERN to simulate regex to the new regex syntax.*

## Features Overview

Oracle's regular expression support is loose, meaning it's not actually core to Oracle. We cannot simply pass strings at the SQL prompt and have Oracle understand what we're saying. Instead, Oracle provides functions that interpret the metacharacters supplied to them, and acts according to POSIX ERE standards. This method of support is common among most programming languages, with the distinct difference being Perl whose regex support is fully integrated.

The next two sections demonstrate the metacharacters and regex built-ins supported by Oracle. These sections reflect features available through Oracle 10*g* Release 2.

## Metacharacters

Regular expression syntax is made up of constants, bracket expressions (also called character classes), and metacharacters. Constants are simply characters that are interpreted literally. They have no special meaning to Oracle beyond the character itself. Bracket expressions are essentially shortcut characterizations of a type of string. For example, the [[:alnum:]] bracket expression matches any alphanumeric string. Lastly, metacharacters are characters that have special meaning when used with the supplied regex functions (discussed in the next section). They are similar to the & or % characters in SQL in that, unless escaped prior to using, Oracle reacts differently to these characters than other nonspecial characters. The combination of constants, bracket expressions, and metacharacters determines the pattern the regex will match.

Table 10-1 lists the bracket expressions available as of Oracle 10*g* Release 2. Refer to Appendix A for a complete list, including examples using each bracket expression.

| Bracket Expression | Description |
|---|---|
| *[[:alnum:]]* | Alphanumeric characters |
| *[[:alpha:]]* | Alphabetic characters |
| *[[:cntrl:]]* | Control characters |
| *[[:digit:]]* | Numeric digits |
| *[[:graph:]]* | Graphical characters |
| *[[:lower:]]* | Lowercase characters |
| *[[:print:]]* | Printable characters |
| *[[:punct:]]* | Punctuation characters |
| *[[:space:]]* | Space characters |
| *[[:upper:]]* | Uppercase characters |
| *[[:xdigit:]]* | Hexadecimal characters |

**TABLE 10-1.**   *Bracket Expressions*

Metacharacters can be broken into POSIX ERE–supported characters, and non-POSIX ERE characters. Table 10-2 lists many of the characters supported by the POSIX ERE standard. A complete list of characters is available in Appendix A along with examples using each.

These metacharacters and bracket expressions don't mean much of anything without the functions provided by Oracle. They are discussed in the next section.

# Regex Operator and Functions

Oracle provides three regex functions and one regex operator. While you may not be familiar with the regex versions, you should know their SQL counterparts quite well. They are

- SUBSTR
- INSTR
- REPLACE
- LIKE

| Metacharacter | POSIX ERE | Description |
| --- | --- | --- |
| *? | | Matches if there are zero or more occurrences of the prior string. |
| +? | | Matches if there are one or more occurrences of the prior string. |
| {m} | ✓ | m is an integer. When provided with a subexpression, it finds EXACTLY m occurrences of it in the text. |
| {n}? | | Matches exactly one occurrence of the prior string. |
| {m,} | ✓ | m is an integer. When provided with a subexpression, it finds AT LEAST m occurrences of it in the text. |
| {n,}? | | Matches the prior string at least n times. |
| {m,n} | ✓ | m and n are integers. When provided with a subexpression, it finds AT LEAST m occurrences of it in the text, but no more than n. |
| {n,m}? | | Matches the prior string at least n times, but no more than m times. |
| c | ✓ | The search should be case-sensitive. |
| i | ✓ | The search should be case-insensitive. |
| m | ✓ | The search is over a multiline string. This allows beginning of line (^) pattern matching when the source string contains multiple lines. |
| n | ✓ | The period, which normally matches a single character, can match a new line. |
| x | ✓ | White space in a regular expression is ignored when x is used. |

**TABLE 10-2.** *Metacharacters*

| Metacharacter | POSIX ERE | Description |
|---|---|---|
| \A | | Matches patterns from the beginning of a string, rather than just the beginning of a line, so multiline strings will not have the pattern matched once per line. |
| \d | | Matches any digit. |
| \D | | Matches any nondigit. |
| \s | | Matches any white space character. |
| \S | | Matches any non–white space character. |
| \w | | Matches any character or number. The difference between this metacharacter and [:alnum:] is that \w includes an underscore. |
| \W | | Matches any nonword character. |
| * | ✓ | Wildcard. When provided with a subexpression, finds zero or more occurrences of it in the text. |
| + | ✓ | When provided with a subexpression, finds one or more occurrences of it in the text. |
| ? | ✓ | When provided with a subexpression, finds zero or one occurrences of it in the text. |
| . | ✓ | Corresponds to any character in the text. |
| ^ | ✓ | Anchor. Finds a match for the expression if it is at the beginning of the line. |
| $ | ✓ | Anchor. Finds a match for the expression if it is at the end of the line. |
| / | ✓ | Separate alternates. Use is similar to an OR. |
| (...) | ✓ | Group subexpressions. |

**TABLE 10-2.** *Metacharacters* (cont.)

Usage for the regex versions of the operator and functions is quite similar, though the support for regular expression syntax takes some getting used to.

### REGEXP_SUBSTR

REGEXP_SUBSTR matches a portion of a supplied string with the regular expression that's provided. The syntax is as follows:

```
REGEXP_SUBSTR(source_string,
        pattern,
        start_position,
        occurrence,
        match_parameter)
```

SOURCE_STRING is required, and can be either a quoted string or variable. PATTERN is the regular expression and is included in single quotes. START_POSITION allows for exact positioning in a string, and is 1 by default. OCCURRENCE is optional, and specifies which string, relative to other matching strings in the source, should be matched. Finally, MATCH_PARAMETER, which is optional, provides for case-sensitive or -insensitive matching.

The following simple SELECT pulls the ZIP code from the string that was passed to the function:

**NOTE**
*Use the* create_user.sql *script followed by the* seed_data.sql *script before running any other examples. They are required for the example scripts to be successful. All scripts can be found online.*

```
-- Available online as part of sql_examples.sql
COLUMN REGEXP_SUBSTR FORMAT A13
SELECT REGEXP_SUBSTR('The ZIP code 80831 is for Falcon, CO',
    '[[:digit:]]{5}') "REGEXP_SUBSTR"
FROM dual;
```

This returns the following:

```
REGEXP_SUBSTR
-------------
80831
```

**Why Would I Use This?**

We've used the `REGEXP_SUBSTR` function to extract text from large HTML pages, pulling e-mail addresses and phone numbers, and inserting them into other columns. It's possible to use this function anywhere the traditional `SUBSTR` function is used though. The advantage of `REGEXP_SUBSTR` over `SUBSTR` is its ability to find text based on patterns instead of literal characters. Another advantage is the ability to specify whether you want the search to be case-sensitive or -insensitive.

Of course, we're not telling `REGEXP_SUBSTR` to return the ZIP code. We supplied the [[:digit:]] bracket expression so only numbers would be matched. We followed this with the {m} metacharacter, which matches *m* occurrences of the preceding expression (see Table 10-2). The English version of this regular expression is the following:

Find exactly five digits in the string 'The ZIP code 80831 is for Falcon, CO'. The ZIP code is the only set of characters that can match.

We can extend this example a bit by using a different bracket expression. The following example finds the third string that includes three or more characters:

```
-- Available online as part of sql_examples.sql
COLUMN REGEXP_SUBSTR FORMAT A13
SELECT REGEXP_SUBSTR('The ZIP code 80831 is for Falcon, CO',
    '[[:alpha:]]{3,}', 1, 3) "REGEXP_SUBSTR"
FROM dual;
```

This example includes the following regex:

```
[[:alpha:]]{3,}
```

`[[:alpha:]]` matches only alphabetic characters. The metacharacter {m,} is used to specify that the matching string should be made up of three or more characters. The remainder of the arguments passed to `REGEXP_SUBSTR` includes the position, which is set to 1, and the occurrence, which is set to 3.

The query results in the following:

REGEXP_SUBSTR
--------------
code

Now to bring in the example shown at the beginning of the chapter as a way to match most e-mail addresses. The following SELECT extracts the e-mail address from the source string:

```
-- Available online as part of sql_examples.sql
COLUMN REGEXP_SUBSTR FORMAT A30
SELECT REGEXP_SUBSTR('Comments or questions - email feedback@plsqlbook.com',
    '[[:alnum:]]((([_\.\-\+]?[[:alnum:]]+)*)@'
    ||'([[:alnum:]]+)((([\.-]?[[:alnum:]]+)*)\.([[:alpha:]]{2,})')
    "REGEXP_SUBSTR"
FROM dual;
```

This returns the following:

REGEXP_SUBSTR
------------------------
feedback@plsqlbook.com

This regular expression can be broken into individual metacharacters, or groups of metacharacters to see how it works.

The string will contain alphabetic characters and/or numbers. This is indicated by the bracket expression [[:alnum:]] shown here:

**[[:alnum:]]**((([_\.\-\+]?[[:alnum:]]+)*)@([[:alnum:]]+)(([\.-]?[[:alnum:]]+)*)\.([[:alpha:]]{2,})

The question mark following the last bracket in the highlighted text shown in the next illustration indicates that zero or more occurrences of the preceding expression will be found. In this case, the preceding expression finds an underscore (_), period (.), hyphen (-), or plus symbol (+). Notice that the backslash (\) was not mentioned. This is because the backslash here is used to escape the special characters. If we wanted to include the backslash, we would have to do a double backslash (\\). If there were additional special characters allowed, this is where they would be placed.

[[:alnum:]](((**[_\.\-\+]?**[[:alnum:]]+)*)@([[:alnum:]]+)(([\.-]?[[:alnum:]]+)*)\.([[:alpha:]]{2,})

The `[[:alnum:]]`+ shown next tells Oracle to match at least one alphanumeric character.

[[:alnum:]](([_\.\-\+]?**[[:alnum:]]+**)*)@([[:alnum:]]+)(([\.-]?[[:alnum:]]+)*)\.([[:alpha:]]{2,})

Two subexpressions are grouped together by parentheses and are followed by an * (asterisk), as shown in the next illustration. The asterisk says that there can be zero or more occurrences of it in the text. This is important since the regex started off with a `[[:alnum:]]` already, which matches any string that doesn't contain special characters. Some e-mail addresses do not have periods or underscores, but we are allowing for the possibility with this optional grouping. Also, if there is a hyphen, for example, it must have one alphanumeric character following it. The string *feedback_@plsqlbook.com* would not be matched because the regex requires an alphanumeric character following the underscore (_).

[[:alnum:]]**((**[_\.\-\+]?[[:alnum:]]+**)***)@([[:alnum:]]+)(([\.-]?[[:alnum:]]+)*)\.([[:alpha:]]{2,})

The next illustration adds the @ symbol, which is required once, and only once, for the string to match.

[[:alnum:]](([_\.\-\+]?[[:alnum:]]+)*)**@**([[:alnum:]]+)(([\.-]?[[:alnum:]]+)*)\.([[:alpha:]]{2,})

The @ symbol is followed by one or more alphanumeric characters:

[[:alnum:]](([_\.\-\+]?[[:alnum:]]+)*)@**([[:alnum:]]+)**(([\.-]?[[:alnum:]]+)*)\.([[:alpha:]]{2,})

The metacharacters shown in the following illustration tell Oracle that zero or more periods (.) or hyphens (-) are allowed in the text.

[[:alnum:]](([_\.\-\+]?[[:alnum:]]+)*)@([[:alnum:]]+)((**[\.-]?**[[:alnum:]]+)*)\.([[:alpha:]]{2,})

One or more alphanumeric characters will follow the period or hyphen in this part of the e-mail address:

[[:alnum:]](([_\.\-\+]?[[:alnum:]]+)*)@([[:alnum:]]+)(([\.-]?**[[:alnum:]]+**)*)\.([[:alpha:]]{2,})

The grouping expression shown in the next illustration indicates that there can be zero or more combinations of the preceding subexpression. It also makes certain that the domain name does not end with a period. While *feedback@mail .plsqlbook.com* is valid, *feedback@plsqlbook-.com* is not.

[[:alnum:]]((_\.\-\+]?[[:alnum:]]+)*)@([[:alnum:]]+)**(([\.-]?[[:alnum:]]+)*)**\.([[:alpha:]]{2,})

The domain is followed by a period. Again, the backslash (\) is used to escape the special character (period in this case).

[[:alnum:]]((_\.\-\+]?[[:alnum:]]+)*)@([[:alnum:]]+)(([\.-]?[[:alnum:]]+)*)**\.**([[:alpha:]]{2,})

The next illustration shows how the regex matches .com, .net, .jp, and any other extension. We're using `[[:alpha:]]` instead of `[[:alnum:]]` since we only want alphabetic characters, not numbers. This is followed by {2,}, which tells Oracle that there must be two or more occurrences of the preceding subexpression. So a two-character `jp` will match, as will a three-character `com` or `net`.

[[:alnum:]]((_\.\-\+]?[[:alnum:]]+)*)@([[:alnum:]]+)(([\.-]?[[:alnum:]]+)*)\.**([[:alpha:]]{2,})**

## REGEXP_INSTR

REGEXP_INSTR returns the position of the character or string that matches the regular expression. Using the same string and regular expression we did for REGEXP_SUBSTR, it's possible to find out where the ZIP code is relative to the entire string. The following SELECT shows this:

```
-- Available online as part of sql_examples.sql
SELECT REGEXP_INSTR('The ZIP code 80831 is for Falcon, CO',
    '[[:digit:]]{5}') "REGEXP_INSTR"
FROM dual;
```

This returns the following:

```
REGEXP_INSTR
------------
          14
```

Syntax for REGEXP_INSTR is similar to the INSTR function.

```
REGEXP_INSTR(
        source_string,
        pattern,
```

      start_position,
      occurrence,
      return_option,
      match_parameter)

SOURCE_STRING is either a literal string, as was the case in the preceding example, or a variable or column containing some string. PATTERN is the regex you're looking for. START_POSITION indicates the character starting position. The default START_POSITION is 1. OCCURRENCE is optional, and specifies which string, relative to other matching strings in the source, should be matched. RETURN_OPTION determines which character position is actually returned. The default is zero (0), which means the value returned indicates the position of the first character matching the regex. If this is changed to 1, the value returned is the character after the first character matching the regex. Finally, MATCH_PARAMETER, which is optional, provides for case-sensitive or -insensitive matching.

## REGEXP_REPLACE

REGEXP_REPLACE, like the REPLACE function, provides a way to modify a string that matches the supplied regular expression. The syntax is shown next:

   REGEXP_REPLACE(
      source_string,
      pattern,
      *start_position*,
      *occurrence*,
      *match_parameter*)

### Why Would I Use This?

The uses of the REGEXP_REPLACE function range from correcting spelling to formatting text for input or output. One of the best examples of its use is to format currently unstructured phone numbers. Phone numbers can be supplied in formats such as 999-999-9999, or (999)999-9999, or 999.999.9999, or +99 999 999 9999...well, you get the idea. REGEXP_REPLACE provides an easy way to match all of these variations using a regular expression, and then replace them with a single format.

SOURCE_STRING is either a literal string, as was the case in the preceding example, or a variable or column containing some string. PATTERN is the regex you're looking for. START_POSITION indicates the character starting position. The default START_POSITION is 1. OCCURRENCE is optional, and specifies which string, relative to other matching strings in the source, should be matched. Finally, MATCH_PARAMETER, which is optional, provides for case-sensitive or -insensitive matching.

To illustrate this function, the following example formats a phone number:

```
-- Available online as part of sql_examples.sql
COLUMN REGEXP_REPLACE FORMAT A50
SELECT REGEXP_REPLACE('Reformat the phone number 719-111-1111 ...',
         '[1]?[- .]?(\(?[[:digit:]]{3}\)?)+[- .]?'
         ||'([[:digit:]]{3})[- .]?([[:digit:]]{4})',
         ' (\1) \2-\3') "REGEXP_REPLACE"
FROM dual;
```

The original phone number is formatted as 719-111-1111. The value returned after using REGEXP_REPLACE is

```
REGEXP_REPLACE
-------------------------------------------
Reformat the phone number (719) 111-1111 ...
```

The phone number is now formatted differently, but only for display. If we had a table with phone numbers of different types, however, it would be possible to include the same REGEXP_REPLACE with an UPDATE statement.

## REGEXP_LIKE

The REGEXP_LIKE operator is similar to the LIKE operator, but is more powerful since it supports the use of regular expressions to match text. Use the following syntax:

```
REGEXP_LIKE(
        source_string,
        pattern,
        match_parameter)
```

SOURCE_STRING is either a literal string, as was the case in the preceding example, or a variable or column containing some string. PATTERN is the regex you're looking for. MATCH_PARAMETER can be either case-sensitive or -insensitive.

To illustrate its use, the following example searches the PLANTS table for a plant species, but provides two possibilities:

```
-- Available online as part of sql_examples.sql
COLUMN common_name FORMAT A30
COLUMN species FORMAT A30
SELECT common_name, species
FROM plants
WHERE REGEXP_LIKE (species,
          'parthenocissus (quinquefolia|tricuspidata)', 'i');
```

This returns the following result:

```
COMMON_NAME                     SPECIES
------------------------------  ---------------------------
Virginia Creeper                Parthenocissus quinquefolia
Boston Ivy                      Parthenocissus tricuspidata
```

It matched both Parthenocissus quinquefolia and Parthenocissus tricuspidata and was case-insensitive.

# PL/SQL and Regular Expressions

PL/SQL fully supports the regex functions demonstrated in the last example. The ability to use conditional logic and other PL/SQL programming constructs makes regular expression use in Oracle truly powerful. Consider the ability to loop through a collection, using REGEXP_REPLACE to modify the string in the array, and passing it back for further use. It is possible to use regular expressions in cursors so the records selected match a pattern rather than a literal string. Regular expressions can be used in triggers to verify or modify data being inserted, which opens the possibility of allowing free-form data entry and extracting only the data required, and then formatting it according to requirements without the user even knowing.

## Common Uses

While the uses are virtually limitless, we wanted to provide code to help you with some of the most common uses for regular expressions in PL/SQL. The following four sections demonstrate how regex and PL/SQL can verify text input, format output, provide case-insensitive searches, and mine web pages.

## Verifying Input with Triggers

If your application code does not enforce a specific format for data entry, it's possible to use regular expressions in a trigger on the destination table for this task. In the following example, we create a trigger on the BUYERS table that verifies the format of the e-mail address being added:

```
-- Available online as part of triggers.sql
SET SERVEROUTPUT ON
CREATE OR REPLACE TRIGGER buyer_trig
BEFORE INSERT OR UPDATE ON buyers
FOR EACH ROW
DECLARE
    v_email VARCHAR2(50 CHAR);
    v_verify BOOLEAN;
BEGIN
  IF :NEW.email IS NOT NULL
    THEN
    v_verify := REGEXP_LIKE(
                    :NEW.email,
'                   ^[[:alnum:]](([_\.\-\+]?'
                ||'[[:alnum:]]+)*)@([[:alnum:]]+)'
                ||'(([\.-]?[[:alnum:]]+)*)\.'
                ||'([[:alpha:]]{2,})$');
    IF NOT v_verify
    THEN
      DBMS_OUTPUT.PUT_LINE('email address: '||:NEW.email);
      RAISE_APPLICATION_ERROR( - 20001, HANDLE_ERRORS.GET_CODE(1));
    END IF;
  END IF;
END;
/
```

To test the trigger, try and insert a valid e-mail address into the BUYERS table and verify that it's successful.

```
-- Available online as part of triggers.sql
INSERT INTO buyers
VALUES (100, 'Ron', 'Hardman', 'ron.hardman@plsqlbook.com',
'2918804554');
```

The row is successfully added. Now try and insert an invalid e-mail address and verify that the application error is raised.

```
-- Available online as part of triggers.sql
INSERT INTO buyers
VALUES (101, 'Michael', 'McLaughlin', 'm@mclaughlin@plsqlbook.com', '3392081098');
```

This returns the following message:

```
ORA-20001: Unless you operate under a completely separate set of
Internet rules than the rest of the world, the e-mail address you
provided is not valid
```

It's possible to apply this same logic to any text or number that requires a specific format. For instance, by applying this logic to a phone number insertion, it's possible to resolve the entry to any known format, and then use REGEXP_REPLACE to alter the format. If it can't be matched (doesn't fit any known format), return a message to the user.

## Format Output

This example does the reverse of the phone number scenario we mentioned at the end of the last section. Instead of using a trigger to validate and reformat input, this procedure reformats phone numbers for display.

```
-- Available online as part of display_phone_numbers.sql
CREATE OR REPLACE FUNCTION display_phone_numbers (
    i_buyer_id IN buyers.buyer_id%TYPE)
    RETURN VARCHAR2
IS
    v_phone_number VARCHAR2(30 CHAR);
    v_error VARCHAR2(30 CHAR);
BEGIN
    --Retrieve the phone number from the buyers table
    SELECT phone
    INTO v_phone_number
    FROM buyers
    WHERE buyer_id = i_buyer_id;

    --Format the number
    v_phone_number :=
        REGEXP_REPLACE(v_phone_number,
            '^([[:digit:]]{3})([[:digit:]]{3})([[:digit:]]{4})$',
            '(\1) \2-\3');
```

```
      RETURN v_phone_number;
EXCEPTION
   WHEN OTHERS
   THEN
      DBMS_OUTPUT.PUT_LINE(DBMS_UTILITY.FORMAT_ERROR_STACK);
END;
/
```

To test this, run the following anonymous block to show all buyer names and formatted phone numbers:

`-- Available online as part of display_phone_numbers.sql`

```
SET PAGES 9999 SERVEROUTPUT ON
DECLARE
   CURSOR buyer_cur IS
   SELECT buyer_id, first_name, last_name,
          phone AS "Phone"
   FROM buyers;
BEGIN
   FOR buyer_rec IN buyer_cur
   LOOP
      DBMS_OUTPUT.PUT_LINE(buyer_rec.last_name
                           ||', '||buyer_rec.first_name
                           ||CHR(9)
                           ||display_phone_numbers(buyer_rec.buyer_id));
DBMS_OUTPUT.PUT(CHR(10));
   END LOOP;
END;
/
```

This returns the following result:

```
Packer, Blenda    (123) 234-3456
Cloud, June       (192) 837-4650
Hardman, Patricia     (498) 123-7465
Cronk, Kevin      (883) 399-2201
Haehn, Dave       (987) 123-9812
Eldridge, Scott (312) 777-4948
Henss, Ruth       (446) 572-8367
Kooser, Shelley (719) 335-2278
Zimmerman, Judy (719) 327-3948
Hardman, George (719) 332-7658
Doebler, Tom      (719) 334-2556
Stoddard, Roy     (223) 918-2736
```

All phone numbers have the new format.

## Case-Insensitive Searches

In this example, we use a case-insensitive search with REGEXP_LIKE in a cursor. The anonymous block selects plants that have a common name like Clematis or Clematus and matches regardless of case.

```
-- Available online as part of cursor.sql
DECLARE
    v_common_name PLANTS.COMMON_NAME%TYPE;
    v_first_name BUYERS.FIRST_NAME%TYPE;
    v_last_name BUYERS.LAST_NAME%TYPE;
    v_order_date ORDERS.ORDER_DATE%TYPE;

    CURSOR order_cur IS
        SELECT p.common_name, b.first_name, b.last_name, o.order_date
          FROM orders o, buyers b, plants p
         WHERE o.buyer_id = b.buyer_id
         AND o.plant_id = p.plant_id
         AND REGEXP_LIKE(p.common_name, 'clemat(is|us)', 'i');
BEGIN
OPEN order_cur;
LOOP
  FETCH order_cur INTO v_common_name,
  v_first_name,
  v_last_name,
  v_order_date;
  EXIT WHEN order_cur%NOTFOUND;
  DBMS_OUTPUT.PUT_LINE('=============================');
  DBMS_OUTPUT.PUT_LINE(v_first_name ||' '|| v_last_name
                       ||' ordered '|| v_common_name
                       ||' on '|| v_order_date);
END LOOP;
DBMS_OUTPUT.PUT_LINE('=============================');
CLOSE order_cur;
EXCEPTION
  WHEN OTHERS
  THEN
  DBMS_OUTPUT.PUT_LINE(DBMS_UTILITY.FORMAT_ERROR_STACK);
  CLOSE order_cur;
END;
/
```

This returns the following records:

```
============================
Kevin Cronk ordered Clematus on 19-MAR-05
============================
June Cloud ordered Niobe Clematis on 19-MAR-05
============================
Dave Haehn ordered Jackman Clematis on 19-MAR-05
============================
```

Both spellings were found, and three different common names that included those spellings were returned.

## Mining Web Pages

Mining web pages is a common task, depending on what you are after. Spammers mine for e-mail addresses, phone numbers, and for ways to exploit the target. This isn't what we're referring to here, however. We're talking about extracting text that is useful for "real" business purposes, such as pulling only data in certain sections of the document.

In this example, we create a procedure that takes a tag name as input and returns only that section of the document.

```
-- Available online as part of web_page_extract.sql
SET SERVEROUTPUT ON
CREATE OR REPLACE PROCEDURE html_extract (
    p_tag IN VARCHAR2)
IS
    CURSOR section_cur IS
        SELECT REGEXP_SUBSTR(page, '<'
            ||p_tag||'>(.*?)</'
            ||p_tag||'>', 1, 1, 'i') AS "TAG_TEXT"
        FROM web_pages;
BEGIN
    FOR text IN section_cur
    LOOP
        DBMS_OUTPUT.PUT_LINE(text.tag_text);
    END LOOP;
END;
/
```

The tag is passed to the procedure, and is included in the cursor. `MATCH_PARAMETER` is set to ‘`i`’ so it is case-insensitive. To test the procedure, run the following:

```
EXEC html_extract('title');
```

This returns the following result:

```
<title>html and regular expressions</title>
```

Change the call to look for the contents of the `BODY` as follows:

```
EXEC html_extract('body');
```

The result changes accordingly:

```
<body>Expert PL/SQL</body>
```

This procedure can be used to strip sections of the HTML document apart for insertion into their own columns for instance. If you wish, it’s possible to match the tags without printing them as well. Use `REGEXP_REPLACE` to strip out any tags.

# Development Tools

In our Oracle Press book, titled *Oracle 10g PL/SQL Programming*, we included a chapter (Chapter 2) that showed how to use JDeveloper for PL/SQL development. While there are other tools on the market for doing development, JDeveloper is a common tool in most Oracle shops.

At the time of this writing, JDeveloper does not include any help for regex developers. If you’re new to regular expressions, or you would like the assistance that a development environment can provide, there’s a utility available that can plug in to JDeveloper as an external tool. It’s called Regexbuddy.

## Regexbuddy

Regexbuddy (www.regexbuddy.com), developed by JGSoft, includes a development interface, a library with some common regular expressions already available, and a tutorial. To add Regexbuddy to JDeveloper, open your JDeveloper IDE and navigate to Tools | External Tools, as shown in Figure 10-1.

Click Add, and click the Browse button next to the Program Executable field. Navigate to the installation directory for Regexbuddy, and select Regexbuddy.exe, as shown in Figure 10-2.

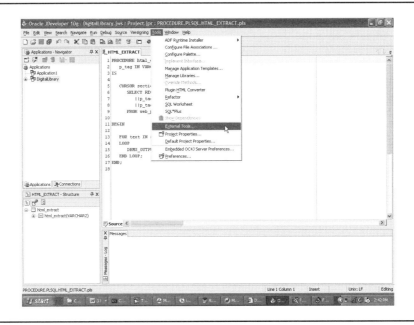

**FIGURE 10-1.** *Add external tools.*

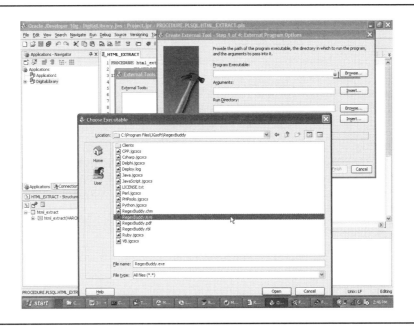

**FIGURE 10-2.** *Select Regexbuddy.exe.*

Click Next through the remaining windows, leaving the defaults, and Regexbuddy will be added to the Tools menu, as shown in Figure 10-3.

Select Regexbuddy from the menu to launch it and we'll take a quick tour.

**Simple Regexbuddy Example**      The following example goes through the step-by-step creation of a simple regular expression. With your Regexbuddy open, select the Create tab, and click the Insert Token button, as shown in Figure 10-4.

Select Literal Text from the menu and type **Georg** in the text box. Click OK. Notice the text is added to the text window, as shown in Figure 10-5.

Once again, click Insert Token and select Capturing Group from the menu, as shown in Figure 10-6. This inserts a set of parentheses in the text window with the cursor between the open and close parentheses.

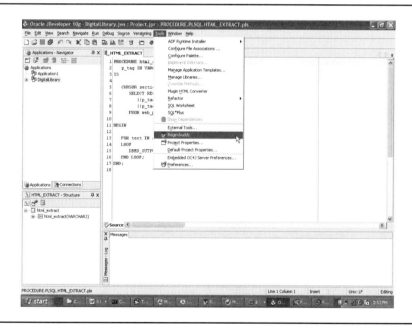

**FIGURE 10-3.**    *Regexbuddy is now on the menu.*

**FIGURE 10-4.** *Insert Token*

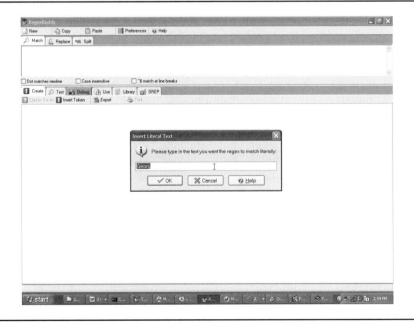

**FIGURE 10-5.** *Literal Text*

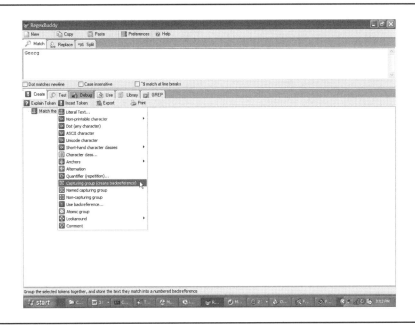

**FIGURE 10-6.** *Grouping*

With the cursor between the open and close parentheses, select Insert Token and Literal Text, and enter **e** into the text field. Click OK and you will see the "e" added to the string. Select Insert Token again, and choose Alternation. A pipe ( | ) is added to the string. Select Insert Token again, choose Literal Text, and add **ian** to the text field, as shown in Figure 10-7.

Notice that the bottom pane provides a description for each part of the regular expression. This is helpful especially when first learning, or when debugging a regex.

Now, it's a bit excessive to use it as we just did. Enter literals where you need them directly to the string, and if you know the syntax, just type it; it's faster that way. But for complex regular expressions, it's handy to have the explanation right there until you become proficient.

**NOTE**
*One word of caution when using Regexbuddy. It's not specific to POSIX ERE, so some of the features you see won't work with Oracle's functions and operator. When in doubt, refer to the metacharacter and bracket expression (character class) list in this chapter, or in the Oracle documentation.*

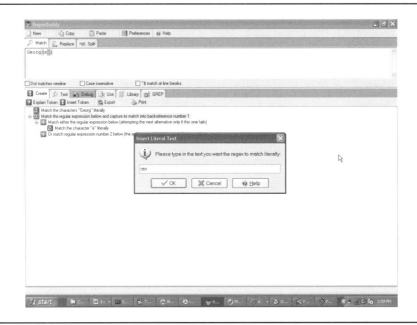

**FIGURE 10-7.** *Alternation*

# Summary

Regular expressions have been a long time coming in Oracle, and now that they are here, take advantage of what they can offer you in your PL/SQL development. The three functions (REGEXP_SUBSTR, REGEXP_INSTR, and REGEXP_REPLACE) and operator (REGEXP_LIKE) provide full-featured support for the POSIX ERE standard. For novices, or developers who find the assistance of a regex development tool to be of benefit, try Regexbuddy from JGSoft. It provides an easy-to-use interface, and can be added to JDeveloper as an external tool that launches from the JDeveloper IDE.

# PART
## V

# PL/SQL Server Pages and Database Management

# CHAPTER
## 11

# Leveraging the PL/SQL Toolkit

he PL/SQL Toolkit actually means the PL/SQL Web Toolkit. It was added in Oracle 7 and has been expanded and stabilized in subsequent releases. The PL/SQL Toolkit enables developers to render dynamic web pages based on business logic embedded in stored procedures. Oracle PL/SQL Server Pages (PSPs) were introduced in Oracle 8*i* (8.1.6 and later), which enabled you to write complete web pages and store them in the database. We'll be covering the following topics:

- Criteria for selection between PL/SQL Toolkit and PSPs

- Describing the Oracle HTTP Server (OHS) architecture

- Describing and configuring the standalone HTTP server

  - Describing the `mod_plsql` cartridge

  - Configuring the Oracle HTTP Server

    - Configuring the Oracle 9*i* HTTP Server

    - Configuring the Oracle 10gR1 HTTP Server

    - Configuring the Oracle 10gR2 HTTP Server

- Building and accessing PL/SQL Toolkit stored procedures

  - Developing no formal parameter procedures

  - Developing formal parameter procedures

  - Understanding advantages and limitations

- Building and accessing PL/SQL Server Pages (PSPs)

  - Developing no formal parameter procedures

  - Developing formal parameter procedures

  - Understanding advantages and limitations

## Why Would I Use This?

We use the PL/SQL Toolkit or PSPs to simplify the development of dynamic web pages. Understanding this enables us to consider, configure, and select approaches to building web pages.

We find the PL/SQL Toolkit extremely useful in building models that directly interact with the database. Whether you like traditional stored objects or PSPs is a matter of preference, but we believe PSPs will grow because of the similarities to JSPs.

This chapter introduces you to the big picture of using the PL/SQL Toolkit and PSPs as dynamic web pages to Oracle databases. We'll discuss when to use the PL/SQL Toolkit versus PSPs, the architecture and configuration of the HTTP server and mod_plsql cartridge, and then examine uses of the PL/SQL Toolkit and PSPs. If you understand the architecture well, you may skip to points of interest, but each section in the chapter is dependent on earlier discussions.

# Criteria for the Selection Between PL/SQL Toolkit and PSPs

There are two solutions to writing dynamic web pages using the PL/SQL programming language. One is the PL/SQL Toolkit, which is done by writing PL/SQL stored procedures. The other is using PL/SQL Server Pages (PSPs), which are similar to Java Server Pages (JSPs). PSPs may also use the PL/SQL Toolkit to support formatting of the HTML web page.

The guidelines for developing with the PL/SQL Toolkit or PSPs are compared side-by-side next:

| PL/SQL Web Toolkit | PL/SQL Server Pages |
| --- | --- |
| A large body of PL/SQL code that produces formatted output. | A large body of dynamic HTML to display in a single web page. |
| The Oracle Portal authoring tool, which uses the PL/SQL Toolkit. | Authoring tools effectively support PSPs. |
| Web pages require line-by-line formatting and control. | Web pages include JavaScript embedded tags. |
| Other server-side includes are used in the rendered page. | Other server-side includes are not used in the rendered page. |
| Migrating from static text web pages. | Migrating from Java Server Pages (JSPs) because they use the same syntax. |
| | Migrating Active Data Object (ADO) pages because Active Server Pages (ASPs) have a similar syntax. |

These two approaches require the Oracle HTTP Server (OHS) to work. The next section describes and demonstrates how to configure the OHS application.

# Describing and Configuring the Standalone HTTP Server

The OHS provides an HTTP listener to receive and process Uniform Resource Locator (URL) requests. It is based on the Apache HTTP server. The Apache and OHS server support the Common Gateway Interface (CGI), which enables running server-side include programs. Perl is programming language that runs as a server-side include. Server-side include programs are located on the server or application server tier in n-tier application computing solutions. Perl uses a `mod_perl` module that embeds a Perl interpreter inside the Apache server and reduces the overhead needed to relaunch Perl programs.

Oracle implements a `mod_plsql` module that does the same thing for PL/SQL programs. OHS defines the relationship between incoming requests based on a virtual mapping that links by a Data Access Descriptor (DAD). The DAD contains the connection information to affect an HTTP pipelined connection to the Oracle database. Information received in the URL by the OHS listener is mapped against possible DAD values. The DAD values then map the connections to the database. The DAD is in the `Apache/modplsql/conf/dads.conf` physical file, which resides in the OHS home.

**NOTE**
*The OHS home must be separate from the Oracle database home when they are on the same tiers.*

There are two approaches to implementing OHS. One includes the Oracle Application Server 9*i*/10*g*, which is delivered in the standard product release. The other approach is as a smaller standalone component with the Oracle 9*i*/10*g* Database. Configuration of the Oracle Application Server 9*i*/10*g* can be found in Chapter 4 of the *Oracle Application Server 10*g *Administration Handbook* by

## Why Would I Use This?

You need to understand the OHS architecture to configure and use it. We need to explain this because the Oracle documentation is rather extensive and spread across several reference manuals.

We have provided these steps to jump-start your ability to use the technology. If you are using this without installing the Oracle 9*i*/10*g* iAS product, these steps will save you a lot of configuration time. Also, we feel you will benefit from understanding the detail of the architecture that is often not explored.

Oracle Press. This chapter demonstrates the configuration of the smaller solution shipped with the Oracle Database product.

The general architecture is displayed in Figure 11-1.

As you can see from the figure, the following is the process:

1. OHS receives a PL/SQL Toolkit procedure or PL/SQL Server Page request from a client browser.

2. OHS routes the request to the mod_plsql module.

3. The request is forwarded by mod_plsql to the Oracle Database, which is done by using the DAD mapping information on the file system.

4. The mod_plsql module prepares the call parameters and runs the PL/SQL procedure or stored PSP procedure.

5. The PL/SQL procedure generates an HTML page based on the definitions and logic in the stored object.

6. The Oracle Database returns the response to the mod_plsql module.

7. OHS forwards the return HTML page to the client browser where it is rendered.

You have covered the general architecture for the OHS product. The next sections will describe and configure OHS.

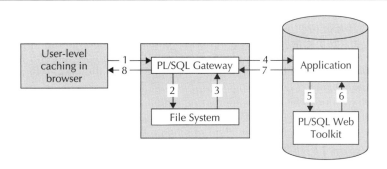

**FIGURE 11-1.**   *Overview of the Oracle HTTP Server (OHS)*

# Describing and Configuring the Standalone Oracle HTTP Server

The OHS product changes with each release of the Oracle Database server. How it works in Oracle 9*i* and 10*g* is covered in the chapter. A brief new feature description is provided in Oracle 10gR2 and more will be added to the stage programming code as notes.

This section will describe and demonstrate how to configure the mod_plsql DAD and the standalone Oracle HTTP Server shipped with the Oracle Database 9*i*/10*g*.

**NOTE**
*The Oracle Database 10g ships the OHS product on the companion CD, so you'll need to install it. The companion disk also contains critical components for the Oracle Call Interface (OCI) discussed in Chapter 5.*

## Describing and Configuring the mod_plsql Cartridge

The mod_plsql module or cartridge is a framework that provides essential services. It was originally defined as a cartridge in the Common Object Request Broker Architecture (CORBA). You probably know it better as a module. The Oracle PL/SQL Gateway is delivered by mod_plsql, which provides the following services:

- Accelerates your PL/SQL dynamic content.

- Enables your PL/SQL programs to become part of OHS, which is an implementation of the Apache HTTP server.

- Monitors access throughout the HTTP cycle from the URL to the HTML page return.

### Why Would I Use This?
You need to know how to configure the Oracle HTTP Server to make PL/SQL Toolkit and PSPs work without using the Oracle 9*i*/10*g* iAS product. The Oracle 9*i*/10*g* iAS product provides you with some neat tools as a developer but migrating those skills to your DBA and the server is not always straightforward.

If you attempt these examples without installing the Oracle 9*i*/10*g* iAS product, these steps will save you some configuration time. Also, we feel you will benefit from understanding the detail of the Oracle HTTP Server architecture that is often not explored.

In UNIX, the key to configuring mod_plsql is the DAD file. You'll find the DAD file in the $OHS_HOME/Apache/modplsql/conf/dads.conf file. The minimum configuration is noted next:

```
<Location /pls>
   SetHandler pls_handler
   Order deny,allow
   Allow from all
   AllowOverride None
   PlsqlDatabaseUsername          <oracle_user_name>
   PlsqlDatabasePassword          <oracle_password>
   PlsqlDatabaseConnectString     <hostname>.<domain_name>:<port>:<sid>
   PlsqlAuthenticationMode        Basic
</Location>
```

The Windows platform will require different changes. For instance, the Oracle and OHS home in Oracle 9*i* are in the same folder on Windows. You do not modify the dads.conf file, but rather the $ORACLE_HOME\Apache\modplsql\cfg\plsql.conf file.

The syntax is very rigid and you can explore additional parameters by referring to the *Oracle HTTP Server* mod_plsql *User's Guide*. You can create multiple PL/SQL DADs in this configuration file. Also, you should read and understand the following before configuring the dads.conf file:

■ **Location**   Defines the URL component that will point to a specific DAD. This location marker enables you to define multiple DADs for any given Oracle Database instance.

■ **PlsqlDatabaseUsername**   Defines the Oracle instance user name.

■ **PlsqlDatabasePassword**   Defines the Oracle instance user's password. It is defined in clear text but may be obfuscated by running the dadTool .pl program.

■ **PlsqlDatabaseConnectString**   Defines the connection string to the instance. It requires the hostname domain name separated by a dot or period. Then, there is a colon that is followed by the port number for the Oracle Database listener, which is followed by a colon and the Oracle TNS service name used by the listener.

When you have configured your dads.conf file, you are ready to configure OHS. In case something goes wrong and you fail to connect with a ubiquitous error like a 503 from your web browser, you should enable logging. You enable logging by editing the following line in the $OHS_HOME/conf/plsql.conf file:

```
PlsqlLogEnable Off
```

You should change it to the following:

```
PlsqlLogEnable On
```

Log files will be generated for each URL attempt to connect to the database. The log files will be found in the $OHS_HOME/Apache/modplsql/logs/_pls directory. The last directory name in the path statement is generated automatically based on the location value used in the dads.conf file.

The most often encountered problem is a failure to connect to the database. If you get an error like the following, you have a connection problem between your dads.conf file and the Oracle Database listener:

```
<2749636625 ms>[ReqStartTime: 3/May/2005:12:49:26]
<2749636625 ms>Request ID ReqID:3758_1115146166
<2749636625 ms>Connecting to database with connect string : "CODE"
<2749748861 ms>ORA-12154 LogOn ORA-12154: TNS:could not resolve service name
<2749748862 ms>Stale Connection due to Oracle error 12154
<2749748862 ms>Logoff: Closing connection due to stale connection
<2749748862 ms>[ReqEndtime: 3/May/2005:12:51:18]
<2749748862 ms>[ReqExecTime: 112237 ms]
```

If you receive a connection error, please check all the related values and map them to your listener.ora and tnsnames.ora files. The potential errors in your dads.conf file are PlsqlDatabaseUsername, PlsqlDatabasePassword, and PlsqlDatabaseConnectString values.

Unfortunately, OHS changes between releases. The specifics of configuration will be covered in the next sections.

# Configuring the Oracle HTTP Server

All the Oracle HTTP Server versions require you to configure an environment file. The generic environment file requirements are noted next:

## UNIX

```
ORACLE_HOME=/<mnt_point>/<directories>
export ORACLE_HOME
PATH=$ORACLE_HOME/Apache/modplsql/conf:$PATH
export PATH
PATH=$ORACLE_HOME/perl/bin:$PATH;export PATH
LD_LIBRARY_PATH=$ORACLE_HOME/lib
export LD_LIBRARY_PATH
```

### Windows

```
set ORACLE_HOME=<logical_drive>\<directories>
set PATH=%ORACLE_HOME%\Apache\modplsql\conf;%PATH%
set PATH=%ORACLE_HOME%\perl\bin;%PATH%
set LD_LIBRARY_PATH=%ORACLE_HOME%\lib
```

The next sections cover the configuration of Oracle 9*i* and 10*g* environments.

## Configuring the Oracle 9*i* HTTP Server

Once you have a correct environment file, you should source the file into your environment. Then, you will be able to start, stop, and check the status for the Oracle 9*i* OHS.

UNIX requires that you build an environment file with the following entry in order to start the services:

```
PATH=$ORACLE_HOME/Apache/Apache/bin:$PATH
export PATH
```

You start and stop OHS with the `apachectl` utility. The options are start, status, and stop. When you change the DAD configuration files, you need to stop and start OHS for the changes to take effect. You may find this behavior familiar since this is how the Oracle listener works.

**NOTE**
*The actual environment is defined for you in Windows in the startJSV and stopJSV batch files. The `%ORACLE_HOME%\Apache\Apache\bin` folder contains these files.*

### Why Would I Use This?

You need to know how to start, stop, and check the OHS service shipped with Oracle Database 9*i*. Oracle has changed the method of controlling the Apache services in subsequent releases but Oracle 9*i* uses the `apachectl` utility.

## Configuring the Oracle 10gR1 HTTP Server

Once you have a correct environment file, you should source the file into your environment. Then, you will be able to start, stop, and check the status for the Oracle 10g OHS.

UNIX requires that you build an environment file to start the service. The environment file should contain the following:

```
PATH=$ORACLE_HOME/opmn/bin:$PATH
export PATH
```

Oracle 10g ships with a new feature called the Oracle Process Management and Notification (OPMN) utility. It provides you with a dashboard view of the database instance. As a result, the OHS product can no longer be started with the `apachectl` utility because it may cause unexpected behavior in the OPMN utility.

In Oracle 10g, you start and stop OHS with the `opmnctl` utility. The options are start, status, and stop. When you change the DAD configuration files, you need to stop and start OHS for the changes to take effect. Again, you may find this behavior familiar since this is how the Oracle listener works.

> **NOTE**
> *OHS configuration in 10g Release 2 is identical to that in 10g Release 1. Release 2 does add a new embedded gateway feature, which is the `DBMS_EPGC` package. Employing the embedded gateway, web applications can use an HTTP listener to call PL/SQL procedures without using the Apache HTTP listener.*

### Why Would I Use This?

You need to know how to start, stop, and check the OHS service shipped with Oracle 10gR1 and 10gR2 databases. We think Oracle 9i users will be surprised to find that Oracle put the Oracle Process Management and Notification (`opmnctl`) utility as the primary interface to the `apachectl` utility. You will need to modify any scripts that you had in an Oracle 9i environment that referenced `apachectl` to point them to `opmnctl`.

You will find this crucial in Oracle 10gR1 and progressively critical with future releases because of web caching. We have provided the syntax to jump-start your migration to Oracle 10g.

You have now learned how to configure the OHS product. The balance of the chapter will illustrate building stored PL/SQL Toolkit or PSP procedures.

# Building and Accessing PL/SQL Toolkit Stored Procedures

The ability to build PL/SQL Toolkit–enabled procedures is a powerful tool that's been available since Oracle 7. The following example demonstrates how to develop and run procedures with and without formal parameters and then discuss their advantages and limitations.

The three most used PL/SQL Toolkit packages are the HTF, HTP, and OWA_UTIL packages. They provide many standard HTML tag functions. A complete list of PL/SQL Toolkit packages are shown in Table 11-1.

The packages are introduced in Appendix C of the *Oracle Database Application Developer's Guide* and covered in more detail in the *Oracle PL/SQL Packages and Type Reference*. Check them for further details on these packages.

## Why Would I Use This?

You need to understand the basics of the packages in the PL/SQL Toolkit to build dynamic web pages. We think that you'll agree that it's helpful to know where the packages are and what they do without digging through Oracle's online documentation.

## Developing and Running No Formal Parameter Procedures

Building a PL/SQL Toolkit stored procedure that renders a Hello World web page is done by using the HTP and OWA_UTIL package procedures to build a standard stored procedure. If you have not run the create_user.sql script for this chapter you may encounter unanticipated problems. You should run create_user.sql now.

| Package | Description |
|---|---|
| HTP | Hypertext procedures package provides code to generate HTML tags. For example, the procedure HTP.ANCHOR tag generates the HTML anchor tag, <A>. |
| HTF | Hypertext functions package provides code to generate HTML tags. The difference between the HTF and HTP packages is that the former returns the HTML tags as a result of a standard function. You will use functions when you need to nest calls. |
| OWA_CACHE | Functions and procedures that enable the PL/SQL Gateway to *cache* and improve the performance of your PL/SQL web application. You can use this package to expire and validate caching when using the PL/SQL Gateway file system. |
| OWA_COOKIE | OWA_COOKIE enables you to send and retrieve HTTP cookies with a client web browser. Cookies are strings that browsers use to maintain state between HTTP calls. They limit the duration of the transaction state by setting a client session cookie expiration date. |
| OWA_CUSTOM | OWA_CUSTOM authorizes file download and upload functions used by cookies. |
| OWA_IMAGE | OWA_IMAGE gets the coordinates where a user clicks an image. You use the package when you have images that map to links invoking the PL/SQL Gateway. |
| OWA_OPT_LOCK | OWA_OPT_LOCK implements an optimistic locking strategy to prevent lost data updates. Lost updates can happen when a user selects, alters, and attempts to update a row whose values have been changed. The values changed because another user or process accessed the same data but submitted the DML operation to change the data first. |
| OWA_PATTERN | OWA_PATTERN delivers string matching and string manipulation based on regular expression functionality. |
| OWA_SEC | OWA_SEC authenticates requests through the PL/SQL Gateway. |
| OWA_TEXT | OWA_TEXT enables you to manipulate strings. You can also manipulate the strings directly. |

**TABLE 11-1.** *PL/SQL Toolkit Packages*

| Package | Description |
|---|---|
| `OWA_UTIL` | The utility catchall package does the following: It supports dynamic SQL utilities, which produce pages with dynamically generated SQL code. It supports HTML utilities retrieving the values of CGI environment variables and performs URL redirects. It supports date utilities to manage and correct date-handling. Date values are ordinary strings in HTML that must be cast to an Oracle Database `DATE` data type. |
| `WPG_DOCLOAD` | A utility that downloads documents from a document repository defined by your DAD configuration. You can download or upload binary or text files in accordance with the RFC 1867 specification, "Form-Based File Upload in HTML" (IETF). |

**TABLE 11-1.**   *PL/SQL Toolkit Packages* (cont.)

The following script builds a Hello World web page:

```
-- Available online as part of create_helloworld1.sql

-- Create a PL/SQL Toolkit generated web page.
CREATE OR REPLACE PROCEDURE HelloWorldProcedure1 AS

BEGIN

  -- Set an HTML META tag.
  owa_util.mime_header('text/html');   -- <META Content-type:text/html>

  -- Set HTML page rendering.
  htp.htmlopen;                        -- <HTML>
  htp.headopen;                        -- <HEAD>
  htp.htitle('HelloWorldProcedure1');  -- <TITLE>HelloWorldProcedure</TITLE>
  htp.headclose;                       -- </HEAD>
  htp.bodyopen;                        -- <BODY>
  htp.line;                            -- <HR>
  htp.print('Hello world.');           -- Hello world.
  htp.line;                            -- <HR>
  htp.bodyclose;                       -- </BODY>
  htp.htmlclose;                       -- </HTML>

END HelloWorldProcedure1;
/
```

---

**Why Would I Use This?**

We find it helpful to build a "Hello World" program to understand a new programming approach because it provides us with an uncluttered look at how to write it. We like the simplicity of "Hello World" programs in illustrating a basic beginning program. We hope you agree with us.

---

The procedure is stored in the database by using standard SQL Data Definition Language (DDL) commands. Once stored in the database, you access it by using a URL and your web browser. The following URL assumes you've defined the DAD Location as /pls, as done earlier in this chapter:

```
http://<hostname>.<domain_name>:<port>/pls/HelloWorldProcedure1
```

The web browser renders the image shown in Figure 11-2.

This illustrates how to develop a static page without any arguments. In the next example, you'll see how to build a dynamic page that accepts formal arguments.

# Developing Formal Parameter Procedures

Web pages are dynamic when they have the ability to display different information from a data source, like a database or file system. Passing parameters to a web page enables dynamic behavior and content.

**FIGURE 11-2.** *Rendered HelloWorldProcedure1 web page*

**Why Would I Use This?**

You need to know how to pass parameters to enable you to submit and process dynamic content because passing arguments determines dynamic web page components. We know writing programs that don't accept arguments are only useful in learning fundamentals. The approaches to passing formal parameters are not trivial. We hope this simplifies learning the approaches.

There are two approaches to passing actual parameters to web pages. One is using HTML form tags to collect input selections or data entry that are then submitted to the data source to render a new page. The other is to hard-code values in the URL statement.

PL/SQL Toolkit procedures support formal parameters just as they do in stored functions or procedures. You define the procedure with a formal parameter list, which is also known as the signature for the function or procedure. PL/SQL web pages only support the following native types as formal parameters:

- A NUMBER data type

- A VARCHAR2 data type

- A PL/SQL collection, which is limited to a table of NUMBER or VARCHAR2 data types. These are implemented by using the OWA_UTIL.IDENT_ARR type, which is an Oracle 9*i* index-by table or Oracle 10*g* associative array of NUMBER or VARCHAR2 native PL/SQL types.

You can overload procedures in PL/SQL procedures but mod_plsql will raise an exception in some cases. For example, mod_plsql raises an exception if you use the same formal parameter name in overloaded procedures and only change the data type from NUMBER to VARCHAR2 or vice versa. However, you can use the same formal parameter name and change the data type to PL/SQL collections without raising an exception. The mod_plsql module can see the difference between a NUMBER or VARCHAR2 native type and PL/SQL collection.

The basic example of passing a single parameter is found in `create_helloworld2.sql`, which creates the following stored procedure:

**-- Available online as part of create_helloworld2.sql script.**

```
-- Create a PL/SQL Toolkit generated web page.
CREATE OR REPLACE PROCEDURE HelloWorldProcedure2
( who VARCHAR2) AS

BEGIN

  -- Set a HTML META tag.
  owa_util.mime_header('text/html');        -- <META Content-type:text/html>

  -- Set HTML page rendering tags.
  htp.htmlopen;                             -- <HTML>
  htp.headopen;                             -- <HEAD>
  htp.htitle('HelloWorldProcedure2');       -- <TITLE>HelloWorld...</TITLE>
  htp.headclose;                            -- </HEAD>
  htp.bodyopen;                             -- <BODY>
  htp.line;                                 -- <HR>
  htp.print('Hello '||who||'''s world.');   -- Hello world.
  htp.line;                                 -- <HR>
  htp.bodyclose;                            -- </BODY>
  htp.htmlclose;                            -- </HTML>

END HelloWorldProcedure2;
/
```

Like the earlier `HelloWorldProcedure1`, this is stored in the database by using a standard SQL DDL command. Once stored in the database, you access it by using a URL and your web browser. The following URL assumes you have defined the DAD location as `/pls`, as done earlier in this chapter:

`http://<hostname>.<domain_name>:<port>/pls/HelloWorldProcedure2?who=Sarah`

The URL appends a question mark and a list of variable assignments. The `who` is the defined variable name for the single formal parameter defined for the stored procedure, `HelloWorldProcedure2`. The variable name uses an equal sign to assign the next string to the value. The URL is parsed by the OHS and the argument is managed by the `mod_plsql` module. The web browser renders the image shown in Figure 11-3.

**FIGURE 11-3.**   *Rendered HelloWorldProcedure2 web page*

The preceding example illustrated how you could build a dynamic PL/SQL Toolkit procedure with native types. You'll now learn how to pass a PL/SQL collection variable to the PL/SQL Toolkit procedure. The `create_president1.sql` script creates a president table sequence and seeds the table to support the passing of a PL/SQL collection variable to a dynamic web page. The president table and sequence are defined as:

-- **Available online as part of create_president1.sql script.**

```
-- Create table for dynamic web page display.
CREATE TABLE president
( president_id       NUMBER
, last_name          VARCHAR2(20 CHAR)
, first_name         VARCHAR2(20 CHAR)
, middle_name        VARCHAR2(20 CHAR)
, term_start         NUMBER
, term_end           NUMBER
, party              VARCHAR2(24 CHAR)
, CONSTRAINT pk_p1   PRIMARY KEY (president_id));


-- Create sequence for primary key numbering.
CREATE SEQUENCE president_s1
  INCREMENT BY    1
  START WITH      1
  ORDER;
```

There are two approaches to managing a PL/SQL collection against the PL/SQL Toolkit. One approach is to use a single collection variable and pass it multiple times in the URL, while the other is to use flexible parameter passing. The following example, found in the `create_president1.sql` script, uses a single parameter passed multiple times in the URL:

**-- Available online as part of create_president1.sql script.**

```
-- Create a PL/SQL Toolkit generated web page.
CREATE OR REPLACE PROCEDURE President1
( years    OWA_UTIL.IDENT_ARR ) AS

  CURSOR get_presidents
  ( term_start_in NUMBER
  , term_end_in   NUMBER ) IS

    SELECT   president_id pres_number
    ,        first_name||' '||middle_name||' '||last_name pres_name
    ,        term_start||'-'||term_end tenure
    FROM     president
    WHERE    term_start BETWEEN term_start_in AND term_end_in
    OR       term_end BETWEEN term_start_in AND term_end_in;

BEGIN

  -- Set HTML page rendering tags.
  htp.htmlopen;
  htp.headopen;
  htp.htitle('President1');
  htp.headclose;
  htp.bodyopen;
  htp.line;

  -- Use PL/SQL Toolkit to format the page.
  htp.tableopen(cborder      => 2
              ,cattributes => 'style=background-color:feedb8');
    htp.tablerowopen;
      htp.tabledata(cvalue       => '#'
                   ,calign       => 'center'
                   ,cattributes  => 'style=color:#336699
                                           background-color:#cccc99
                                           font-weight:bold
                                           width=50');
      htp.tabledata(cvalue       => 'NAME'
                   ,calign       => 'center'
                   ,cattributes  => 'style=color:#336699
```

```
                                        background-color:#cccc99
                                        font-weight:bold
                                        width=200');
        htp.tabledata(cvalue       => 'TENURE'
                     ,calign       => 'center'
                     ,cattributes  => 'style=color:#336699
                                        background-color:#cccc99
                                        font-weight:bold
                                        width=100');
    htp.tablerowclose;

  -- Use a loop to collect the data.
  FOR i IN get_presidents(years(1),years(2)) LOOP

    htp.tablerowopen;
      htp.tabledata(cvalue       => i.pres_number
                   ,calign       => 'center'
                   ,cattributes  => 'style=background-color:#f7f7e7');
      htp.tabledata(cvalue       => i.pres_name
                   ,calign       => 'left'
                   ,cattributes  => 'style=background-color:#f7f7e7');
      htp.tabledata(cvalue       => i.tenure
                   ,calign       => 'center'
                   ,cattributes  => 'style=background-color:#f7f7e7');
    htp.tablerowclose;

  END LOOP;

  -- Close the table.
  htp.tableclose;

  -- Print a line and close body and page.
  htp.line;
  htp.bodyclose;
  htp.htmlclose;

END president1;
/
```

You call this by using the following URL:

```
http://<hostname>.<domain_name>:<port>/pls/President1?years=1880&years=1893
```

The URL appends a question mark and a list of variable assignments. The first `years` actual parameter becomes element one in the PL/SQL collection, and the next actual parameter the second, and so on. This is simple and easy-to-use syntax and renders the following `HTP` formatted web page shown in Figure 11-4.

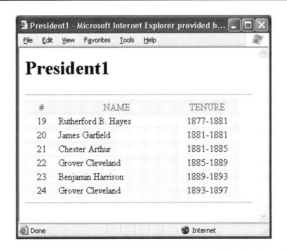

**FIGURE 11-4.** *Rendered President1 web page*

The preceding example illustrated how you can build a dynamic PL/SQL Toolkit procedure with a PL/SQL collection type. There is also the approach using flexible parameter passing, which has two alternatives. The Oracle recommended alternative uses two PL/SQL collection types, one as the index set and the other as the values set. They both should use either OWA_UTIL.ident_arr or OWA.ident_arr for variable length strings less than 30 characters, or OWA_UTIL.vc_arr or OWA.vc_arr for larger variable length strings.

Flexible parameter passing is demonstrated in create_president2.sql, but only the signature of the procedure changes from the prior example. The code is unchanged except for variable names. Flexible parameter passing requires specific variable names because they are managed by an Oracle HTTP API. The signature for the president2 procedure follows:

**-- Available online as part of create_president1.sql script.**

```
-- Create a PL/SQL Toolkit generated webpage.
CREATE OR REPLACE PROCEDURE President2
( name_array     OWA.VC_ARR
, value_array    OWA.VC_ARR ) AS
…
END president2;
/
```

**NOTE**
*There is no discretion on the naming convention of variables when you have chosen flexible parameter naming. These are the expected names by the mod_ plsql module. They must be name_array and value_array. If you make any variation to the naming convention, the Apache log will show a PLS-00306 error. Flexible parameter naming uses these names in the signature and will fail without them.*

The URL necessary to create a connection with flexible parameter naming is a departure from typical web pages. The following runs the `president2` procedure:

 `http://<hostname>.<domain_name>:<port>/pls/!President2?1880&2=1893`

The URL includes an exclamation mark (also called a bang symbol) before the PL/SQL procedure name. You may then use an index system for entries to be passed to the procedure, where item one equals element 1880 and item two equals element 1893. If you find this clearer, then it may help you build web pages. However, you can only use one set of values when you use flexible parameter naming.

**TIP**
*When you want to have more than one set of PL/SQL collections passed to your PL/SQL Toolkit enabled procedure, you should avoid flexible parameter naming. The flexible parameter passing mechanism is tied to the implementation of the mod_plsql module and may change from release to release.*

# Understanding Advantages and Limitations

Advantages of PL/SQL Toolkit procedures include the ability to pass PL/SQL collections or tables of VARCHAR2 data types. Also, you can build small units called from other Java Server Pages (JSPs), PSPs, or as links within static web pages. Calling them "static" is a misnomer, but physical files that contain links are known as static web pages.

Disadvantages are that you have a complex partial solution. PSPs offer a more flexible, intuitive, and consistent approach to dynamic page development.

Having learned how to use the PL/SQL Toolkit to build dynamic web pages in this section, it's now time to explore PL/SQL Server Pages (PSPs) procedures.

# Building and Accessing PL/SQL Server Pages (PSPs)

The ability to build PL/SQL Server Pages (PSPs) procedures is a powerful tool that's been available since Oracle 8*i*, Release 8.1.6. The following demonstrates how to develop and run PSP procedures with and without formal parameters, and then discusses their advantages and limitations.

PSPs can include JavaScript or other client-side script code natively in the stored procedure. PSPs use the same scripting syntax as Java Server Pages (JSPs), which makes the skills readily transferable between web development solutions. PSPs push the processing to the server and present the client browser with a plain HTML text file for rendering.

PSPs can contain text, tags, PSP directives, declarations, and scriptlets. They typically have the .psp file extension. Text and tags in PSPs are typical of HTML pages. PSPs have directives that enable controlling the page behaviors as noted in Table 11-2.

PSP procedures are loaded into the database by the `loadpsp` utility. However, there is no `droppsp` utility like `dropjava`. You drop PSP procedures by using a standard DDL DROP command from the SQL*Plus environment. The `-replace` option first removes the prior copy before attempting to load the new one. If you do not have a backup copy of your working PSP procedure, you should make one before running the `loadpsp` utility. The general syntax for the utility is

```
Loadpsp [-replace] -user username/password[@connect_string]
        < [ include_file_name … ] [ error_file_name ] >
        psp_file_name.psp_file_extension
```

### Why Would I Use This?

We use PSPs to create a complete dynamic web page that uses native Oracle types. PSPs have an advantage because they contain a similar programming structure to JSPs. We think that you'll find PSPs provide a more natural solution to web programming than standard PL/SQL stored objects.

You will lose one feature of standard PL/SQL web page programming, which is the flexible parameter passing feature. We don't think you'll miss that feature too much but you should know it can't be used in PSPs.

Another feature of PSPs is that including native JavaScript has a more natural syntax. We like that feature because it lets us leverage any JSP scripting logic that doesn't fit into a library by cutting and pasting it into our PSPs.

| Directive | Description |
|---|---|
| PAGE | What scripting language it uses.<br>What type of information (MIME type) it produces.<br>What code to run to handle all uncaught exceptions. This might be an HTML file with a friendly message, renamed to a `.psp` file. You must specify this same filename in the **loadpsp** command that compiles the main PSP file. You must specify exactly the same name in both the errorPage directive and in the **loadpsp** command, including any relative path name such as `../include/`.<br><br>Syntax:<br>`<%@ page [language="PL/SQL"]`<br>`            [contentType="content type string"]`<br>`            charset="encoding"`<br>`            [errorPage="file.psp"] %>` |
| PROCEDURE | Specifies the name of the stored procedure produced by the PSP file. The name is the filename without the `.psp` extension by default.<br><br>Syntax:<br>`<%@ plsql procedure="procedure_name" %>` |
| PARAMETER | Specifies the name, and optionally the type and default, for each parameter expected by the PSP stored procedure. The parameters are passed using name-value pairs, typically from an HTML form. To specify a default value of a character type, use single quotes around the value, inside the double quotes required by the directive.<br><br>Syntax:<br>`<%@ plsql parameter="parameter name"`<br>`   [type="PL/SQL type"]`<br>`   [default="value"] %>` |

**TABLE 11-2.** *PL/SQL Server Page Directives*

| Directive | Description |
|---|---|
| INCLUDE | Specifies the name of a file to be included at a specific point in the PSP file. The file must have an extension other than `.psp`. It can contain HTML, PSP script elements, or a combination of both. The name resolution and file inclusion happens when the PSP file is loaded into the database as a stored procedure, so any changes to the file after that are not reflected when the stored procedure is run.<br><br>Syntax:<br>`<%@ include file="path name" %>` |
| DECLARATION BLOCK | Declares a set of PL/SQL variables that are visible throughout the page, not just within the next `BEGIN`/`END` block. This element typically spans multiple lines, with individual PL/SQL variable declarations ended by semicolons.<br><br>Syntax:<br>`<%! PL/SQL declaration;`<br>`[ PL/SQL declaration; ] ... %>` |
| CODE BLOCK SCRIPTLET | Executes a set of PL/SQL statements when the stored procedure is run. This element typically spans multiple lines, with individual PL/SQL statements ended by semicolons. The statements can include complete blocks, or can be the bracketing parts of `IF/THEN/ELSE` or `BEGIN/END` blocks. When a code block is split into multiple scriptlets, you can put HTML or other directives in the middle, and those pieces are conditionally executed when the stored procedure is run.<br><br>Syntax:<br>`<%! PL/SQL statement;`<br>`[ PL/SQL statement; ] ... %>` |
| EXPRESSION BLOCK | Specifies a single PL/SQL expression, such as a string, arithmetic expression, function call, or combination of those things. The result is substituted as a string at that spot in the HTML page that is produced by the stored procedure. You do not need to end the PL/SQL expression with a semicolon.<br><br>Syntax:<br>`<%! PL/SQL expression %>` |

**TABLE 11-2.** *PL/SQL Server Page Directives* (cont.)

The next two sections show you how to develop and run PSP procedures with, and without, arguments. You will see they are very much like the PL/SQL Toolkit server-side includes that were covered earlier in the chapter.

## Developing and Running No Formal Parameter PSP Procedures

You'll now build a PSP stored procedure that renders a Hello World web page. This PSP takes no formal parameters and acts much like a static web page.

The following script builds a HelloWorld1 PSP:

```
-- Available online as part of HelloWorld1.psp script.

<%@ plsql language="PL/SQL"  %>
<%@ plsql procedure="HelloWorld1" %>

<HTML>
<TITLE>Expert PL/SQL - HelloWorld1</TITLE>
<HEAD>
</HEAD>
<BODY>
<! Print a plain string. >
Hello World!
<BR><BR>
<! Print using the PL/SQL Toolkit >
<% htp.print('Hello World!'); %>
</TD></TR></TABLE>
</BODY>
</HTML>
```

You use the following syntax to put the PSP procedure into the database:

```
loadpsp -replace -user plsql/plsql HelloWorld1.psp
```

### Why Would I Use This?
As discussed previously, we like the "Hello World" program because it provides an uncluttered look at a basic program. The "Hello World" program lets us see how to do it without formal parameters and provides a nice simple test case.

After the procedure is stored in the database by using the `loadpsp` utility, you can see that the `loadpsp` utility does some text conversion of the file. You can set the SQL*Plus `PAGESIZE` to 999 and see those modifications by using the following query:

```
SELECT   text
FROM     user_source
WHERE    name = 'HELLOWORLD1';
```

You can see that the procedure has been modified by running the `loadpsp` utility. The following is the stored source for the `HelloWorld1` procedure:

```
PROCEDURE HelloWorld1  AS
  BEGIN NULL;
htp.prn('
');
htp.prn('

<HTML>
<TITLE>Expert PL/SQL - HelloWorld1</TITLE>
<HEAD>
</HEAD>
<BODY>
<! Print a plain string. >
Hello World!
<BR><BR>
<! Print using the PL/SQL Toolkit >
');
 htp.print('Hello World!');
htp.prn('
</TD></TR></TABLE>
</BODY>
</HTML>
');
 END;
```

The `loadpsp` utility takes the PSP file and builds a standard PL/SQL procedure. It puts a `BEGIN` in front and appends an `END` to create proper block structure. It also inserts a `NULL` statement in the event you have uploaded only a shell. All HTML tags are encapsulated by using the HTP package from the PL/SQL Toolkit.

Once stored in the database, you access it by using a URL and your web browser. The following URL assumes you have defined the DAD Location as /pls, as done earlier in this chapter:

```
http://<hostname>.<domain_name>:<port>/pls/HelloWorld1
```

The web browser renders the image shown in Figure 11-5.

**FIGURE 11-5.** *Rendered HelloWorld1 PSP*

This example demonstrated how to build a PSP without any formal parameters. The next section explores formal parameters.

## Developing Formal Parameter PSP Procedures

Dynamic content works by passing parameters that determine changing output. Developing PSPs that accept formal parameters is necessary to build real web applications. This section will review how to build a PSP to accept parameters, and how to run the PSP from a URL and also dynamically from a static web page using JavaScript components.

As covered earlier, the parameter directives are enclosed between <%@ and %> brackets. When you define parameters, they may have a PL/SQL type but not a size. Physical size will be managed in your code blocks because if you manage

### Why Would I Use This?

You need to know how to use formal parameters to be able to submit and process dynamic content because passing arguments determines dynamic PSPs. We know you can't really write very useful programs unless we show you how to use formal parameters in your PSPs.

We think you'll like the type casting used in the PSPs. We like it and the default substitution feature.

them in the declaration section, you can't effectively trap errors. The following `HelloWorld2.psp` script enables you to build a PSP that accepts a single parameter:

**-- Available online as part of HelloWorld2.psp script.**

```
<%@ plsql language="PL/SQL" type="PL/SQL type" %>
<%@ plsql procedure="HelloWorld2" %>
<! -- Defines a parameter in a PARAMETER block.
<%@ plsql parameter="who" type="VARCHAR2" default="NULL" %>

<HEAD>
<TITLE>Expert PL/SQL - HelloWorld2</TITLE>
<%!
  -- Defines a cursor in a DECLARATION block.
  CURSOR get_user
  ( requestor VARCHAR2) IS
    SELECT  'Hello '|| USER ||' schema, this is '||requestor||'!' line
    FROM    dual;
%>
</HEAD>
<BODY>
<%
  -- Defines a for-loop in a CODE or SCRIPTLET block.
  FOR i IN get_user(who) LOOP
%>

<%=
  -- Defines a value returned to the web page in an EXPRESSION block.
  i.line
%>
<%
  -- Defines an end-loop in a CODE or SCRIPTLET block.
  END LOOP;
%>
</BODY>
</HTML>
```

This PSP does the following:

- It defines a page directive.

- It defines a procedure directive.

- It defines a parameter directive with a single parameter of a `VARCHAR2` data type and sets the default value for the parameter to a null value.

- It defines a standard header section of an HTML page and puts a declaration block in the header. PSPs do not require DECLARE, BEGIN, or END blocks and will fail parsing in the loadpsp utility if they are present.

- It defines a standard body section of an HTML page and uses a scriptlet or code block to start a for-loop. Then, it uses an expression block to write the value returned by the for-loop to the web page. Lastly, it closes the for-loop in another code block.

**NOTE**
*You must enclose all expressions in scriptlet or code blocks because they terminate the line like the semicolon in PL/SQL programs.*

You use the following syntax to put the PSP procedure into the database:

```
loadpsp -replace -user plsql/plsql HelloWorld21.psp
```

After the procedure is stored in the database by using the loadpsp utility, you can see that the loadpsp utility does some text conversion of the file. You can set the SQL*Plus PAGESIZE to 999 and see those modifications by using the following query:

```
SELECT    text
FROM      user_source
WHERE     name = 'HELLOWORLD2';
```

Note that the procedure has been modified by running the loadpsp utility. The following is the stored source for the HelloWorld2 procedure, which will append a BEGIN and END into the file (as seen previously in the chapter) as well as a single null statement. A DECLARE statement is unnecessary since it's defined in the scope of a stored procedure.

After putting it in the database, you access it by using a URL and your web browser. The following URL assumes you've defined the DAD Location as /pls, as done earlier in this chapter:

```
http://<hostname>.<domain_name>:<port>/pls/HelloWorld2
```

The web browser renders the image shown in Figure 11-6.

Now that you've seen a small example program, we'll present a more real-world example file. This program is a reimplementation of the President1 and President2 PL/SQL Toolkit procedures seen earlier in this chapter, except the program is now a PSP.

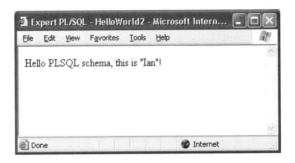

**FIGURE 11-6.** *Rendered HelloWorld2 PSP*

This script is dependent on running `create_president1.sql` before attempting to put it in the database. If you have not done so, please run `create_president1.sql` now. The `President3.psp` script follows:

-- **Available online as part of President3.psp script.**

```
<%@ plsql language="PL/SQL" type="PL/SQL type" %>
<%@ plsql procedure="President3" %>
<! -- Defines a parameter in a PARAMETER block.
<%@ plsql parameter="year1" type="NUMBER" default="NULL" %>
<%@ plsql parameter="year2" type="NUMBER" default="NULL" %>
<HEAD>
<TITLE>President3 PSP</TITLE>
  <%!
    -- Defines a cursor in a DECLARATION block.
    CURSOR get_presidents
    ( term_start_in NUMBER
    , term_end_in   NUMBER ) IS

      SELECT   president_id pres_number
      ,        first_name||' '||middle_name||' '||last_name pres_name
      ,        term_start||'-'||term_end tenure
      FROM     president
      WHERE    term_start BETWEEN term_start_in AND term_end_in
      OR       term_end BETWEEN term_start_in AND term_end_in;
  %>
</HEAD>
<BODY>
<! -- Set HTML page rendering tags. >
<HR>
```

```
<! -- Use PL/SQL Toolkit to format the page. >
<TABLE cborder=2 style=background-color:feedb8>
  <TR>
    <TD align="center"
        style="color:#336699;
               background-color:#cccc99;
               font-eight:bold;width=50">
      #
    </TD>
    <TD align="center"
        style="color:#336699;
               background-color:#cccc99;
               font-weight:bold;width=200">
      NAME
    </TD>
    <TD align="center"
        style="color:#336699;
               background-color:#cccc99;
               font-weight:bold;width=100">
      TENURE
    </TD>
  </TR>
  <TR>
    <%
      -- Use a loop to collect the data.
      FOR i IN get_presidents(year1,year2) LOOP
    %>
    <TD align="center"
        style="color:#336699;
               background-color:#f7f7e7">
      <%= i.pres_number %>
    </TD>
    <TD align="center"
        style="color:#336699;background-color:#f7f7e7">
      <%= i.pres_name %>
    </TD>
    <TD align="center"
       style="color:#336699;background-color:#f7f7e7">
      <%= i.tenure %>
    </TD>
  </TR>
  <%
    -- Defines an end-loop in a CODE or SCRIPTLET block.
    END LOOP;
  %>
```

```
<! -- Close the table. >
</TABLE>
<! -- Print a line and close body and page. >
<HR>
</BODY>
</HTML>
```

This PSP does the following:

- It defines a page directive.

- It defines a procedure directive.

- It defines a parameter directive with a single parameter of a VARCHAR2 data type and sets the default value for the parameter to a null value.

- It defines a standard header section of an HTML page and puts a declaration block in the header. As mentioned previously, PSPs do not require DECLARE, BEGIN, or END blocks and will fail parsing in the loadpsp utility if they are present.

- It defines a standard body section of an HTML page and uses a scriptlet or code block to start a for-loop. Then, it uses an expression block to write the value returned by the for-loop to the web page. Lastly, it closes the for-loop in another code block.

**NOTE**
*You should note that the parameter directives use native PL/SQL types and not the OWA.VC_ARR type employed as a PL/SQL Toolkit procedure. If you attempt to use OWA.VC_ARR or other mod_plsql type, the loadpsp utility will raise an ORA-00382 error. You must use supported database schema types.*

Use the following syntax to put the PSP procedure into the database:

```
loadpsp -replace -user plsql/plsql President3.psp
```

As covered earlier in the chapter, the loadpsp utility does some text conversion of the file. If you would like to see it, set the SQL*Plus PAGESIZE to 999 and use the following query:

```
SELECT    text
FROM      user_source
WHERE     name = 'HELLOWORLD2';
```

After putting it in the database, access it by using a URL and your web browser. The following URL assumes you have defined the DAD Location as /pls, as done earlier in this chapter:

```
http://<hostname>.<domain_name>:<port>/pls/President3?year1=1787&year2=1836
```

The web browser renders the first seven presidents of the United States (shown in Figure 11-7).

You have now learned how to build PSPs. They are powerful tools and can only be developed with the Oracle Database and Oracle HTTP Server (OHS). Using the Oracle 9i/10g iAS server makes some development steps easier. All examples in this chapter were tested with the database standalone OHS product.

## Understanding Advantages and Limitations

As mentioned earlier in the chapter, PSPs are great solutions when you have a large body of HTML that includes dynamic database content. Java Server Pages (JSPs) and PSPs are complex documents and easier solutions when using an authoring tool.

The limitations of PSPs are that they work as standalone complete solutions. You cannot leverage them as modules elsewhere in your web-enabled applications.

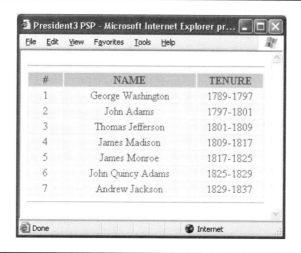

**FIGURE 11-7.** *Rendered President3 PSP*

# Summary

You should now have an understanding of how to implement and troubleshoot server-side PL/SQL Toolkit web pages and PL/SQL Server Pages (PSPs). With these skills, you can build robust web application solutions in native PL/SQL, and leverage the tight integration that PL/SQL enjoys with the data server in your development.

# CHAPTER
## 12

## Managing the Database

L/SQL is not just for developers. Database administrators (DBAs) use and are impacted by PL/SQL every day, and rely on scripts, supplied packages, and utilities to manage the database. In this chapter, we focus on Oracle supplied packages that are of particular interest to DBAs. The following topics are discussed:

■ Database performance management

■ Moving OS files from within the database

■ File compression

■ Exporting and importing data while using filters

■ Securing your applications with encryption

You will want to download this chapter's code, including the user creation script and seed data, from the Oracle Press web site, or from www.PLSQLBook .com.

# Database Performance

Performance tuning is an area looked upon by many as part art and part science. While it is true that tuning techniques differ from one application/database to another, the strategies that are employed remain fairly constant. In this section, we focus our attention on the DBMS_STATS built-in package, and how DBAs can best make use of it.

## DBMS_STATS: Table and Index Statistics

Oracle deprecated the Rule-Based Optimizer (RBO) in Oracle 10g Release 1 of the data server, and now supports only cost-based optimization. The Cost-Based Optimizer (CBO) relies on init.ora parameters, along with table and index statistics, to accurately determine the cost associated with different executions plans. When the cost of several execution plans (also called explain plans) is determined, Oracle chooses the lowest cost plan. While it's possible to override some of the CBO's choices using query hints, the init.ora parameter settings and accurate table and index statistics are required to provide fast SQL processing.

The built-in package named DBMS_STATS enables the DBA to perform the following tasks:

■ Gather statistics for database objects, the schema, or the database, and store the statistics in user-defined tables, or push them to the data dictionary.

■ Move statistics from one system to another.

- Restore or import statistics to the data dictionary.

- Create user-defined statistics.

In Oracle 10g Release 2, there are 98 procedures and functions in the DBMS_
STATS package. We won't examine all of them here. Instead, we'll use the package
to help with a common tuning scenario, and show how it can help you work more
effectively with Oracle support should they need to be involved.

## A Performance Issue in Production
## That Can't Be Replicated in a Test

It is quite common to see a performance problem in production that can't be
reproduced in other internal environments. One of the main reasons is a difference
in the amount of data stored between the two systems. In many environments, *test* is
only a fraction of the size of *production*. This in turn impacts the statistics on the
tables and indexes, resulting in different optimal execution plans between otherwise
identical systems.

If you have discovered that the poor performance is due to SQL, and the execution
plan is not consistent across instances, follow these steps to troubleshoot:

1. Generate statistics for the table, index, schema, or database in both
   production and the test, as shown next:

   ```
   -- Available online as part of dbms_stats.sql
   -- Generate statistics based on a 10-percent sample size
   BEGIN
       DBMS_STATS.GATHER_SCHEMA_STATS('PLSQL', 10);
   END;
   /
   ```

2. Verify your TIMED_STATISTICS parameter is set to TRUE, and that MAX_
   DUMP_FILE_SIZE is set large enough to accommodate a full trace.

3. Trace the poor performing process in both *production* and *test* instances
   using SQL trace.

4. Use the TKPROF utility (see Chapter 8 for complete instructions) with an
   explain plan to identify the poor performing SQL.

   ```
   $ tkprof <<trace.trc>> <<output.txt>> /
   > explain=<<username>>/<<password>> sort=exeela,prsela,fchela
   ```

5. Compare the execution plan from both instances. If the execution plans from the two instances match, then retest the poor performing system. Gathering statistics may have corrected the problem. If the execution plans are different, proceed to step 6.

6. Create a table to the schema's statistics as follows:

```
-- Available online as part of dbms_stats.sql
BEGIN
    DBMS_STATS.CREATE_STAT_TABLE(null,
                                 'STATISTICS',
                                 null);
END;
/
```

7. Export statistics from the data dictionary in production (or your poor performing environment) to the table created in step 6.

```
-- Available online as part of dbms_stats.sql
BEGIN
    DBMS_STATS.EXPORT_SCHEMA_STATS ('PLSQL',
                                    'STATISTICS',
                                    NULL, NULL);
END;
/
```

8. Export the STATISTICS table created in step 5.

```
-- Available online as part of dbms_stats.sql
$ exp userid=plsql/oracle tables=STATISTICS \
> file=statistics.dmp log=statistics_export.log
```

9. Import statistics into your test instance (or your good performing environment).

```
$ imp userid=plsql/oracle tables=STATISTICS file=statistics.dmp \
> log=statistics_import.log ignore=y
```

10. Load the statistics to the data dictionary in the test environment.

```
-- Available online as part of dbms_stats.sql
BEGIN
    DBMS_STATS.IMPORT_SCHEMA_STATS (
        'PLSQL',
        'STATISTICS',
        NULL, NULL, NULL, NULL);
END;
/
```

11. Rerun the SQL identified in step 3 in test and generate the execution plan.

The execution plan will now be the same in both test and production. You can tune the SQL or PL/SQL in the test instance since you have a reproducible test case. The ability to reproduce a poor execution plan is not limited to only internal instances. If an issue needs to go to Oracle support, upload the statistics dump file so they can reproduce the issue as well. It will lead to faster resolution times since it is much easier for Oracle to debug the problem using a local instance.

**NOTE**
*If you're still finding that the execution plans differ, compare database parameters between the two instances, and confirm both are on the same database patch levels. Also, closely examine the SQL statements. It may be that you are comparing similar, but not identical statements, causing the execution plans to be different.*

# Moving Data

How can data be efficiently moved from one database to another? How about metadata, or files that the database points to, but that are actually stored on the file server? Moving data in Oracle, especially large amounts of it, is not a trivial task. Data integrity is the number one concern of DBAs, so any time it's moved from one location to another it needs to be done using a reliable and efficient tool or method.

In this section we demonstrate the main features of three packages that were introduced in Oracle 10g. The first package, called DBMS_DATAPUMP, offers the same basic features of the traditional IMPORT and EXPORT utilities, but includes a number of enhancements as well. The second package reviewed here is the DBMS_FILE_TRANSFER package that provides an easy way to move files on the operating system from within Oracle. The third package discussed is the UTL_COMPRESS package that compresses data, similar to the *gunzip* utility on the operating system.

## DBMS_DATAPUMP: Import and Export Data

The IMPORT and EXPORT utilities have been mainstays of the Oracle DBA arsenal, but there have always been some significant limitations related to portability of dump files that they generated. Oracle provides a built-in package that fulfills the same need as the aforementioned utilities, while eliminating those quirks that made them cumbersome to use.

Data Pump was introduced in Oracle 10g Release 1. Its purpose is to allow for the transfer of data between databases, even in cases where the operating system, tablespace and datafile names and locations, and character sets in source and destination data sources are inconsistent. Performance was a major consideration for Oracle when they developed this utility. Data Pump can be run in parallel and data can be processed in bulk. As a result, export is estimated to be two to three times faster with Data Pump than with the export utility. Import is estimated to be 5 to 40 times faster, but the times are somewhat dependent on the degree of parallelism your environment can support.

Data Pump's engine, so to speak, is the DBMS_DATAPUMP package. All methods of running Data Pump involve this package. Options for performing exports and imports include execution through an API directly, through Enterprise Manager, or through command-line utilities (expdb and impdp). This high degree of flexibility is yet another advantage over export and import utilities.

When a Data Pump job is started, it creates a Master process. From the Master process, one or more child processes are spawned. We say one or more because the number of parallel processes is determined by the DBMS_DATAPUMP.SET_PARALLEL procedure. A master table is also created during the run, and is dropped when the job is complete. It is possible to preserve this table beyond the completion of the job as you will see in a later example. It is this master table that allows us to stop and restart a job, and have DBMS_DATAPUMP pick up where it left off.

Table 12-1 shows the procedures and functions available in the DBMS_DATAPUMP package.

To test out some of these, download the examples from the Oracle Press web site or www.PLSQLBook.com. Inside the code directory is a folder called Data_Pump. Follow the directions in the DATAPUMP_README.txt to run this in your environment.

## Exporting

After creating the users per the README's instructions, generate the following table in the PLSQL schema:

```
-- Available online as part of dbms_datapump_objects.sql
CREATE TABLE test_datapump AS
    SELECT * FROM dba_users;
```

A SELECT COUNT on the new table shows 26 records.

```
SQL> SELECT COUNT(*) FROM TEST_DATAPUMP;
  COUNT(*)
----------
        26
```

| Name | Description |
|------|-------------|
| ADD_DEVICE | Dump files, log files, and SQL files are created as part of export, import, and SQL_FILE operations. ADD_DEVICE adds a sequential device for this set. |
| ADD_FILE | Dump files, log files, and SQL files are created as part of export, import, and close SQL_FILE operations. ADD_FILE specifies the filename, location, size, and type of the file, and adds it to the dump file set. |
| ATTACH | It is possible to detach your session from a Data Pump job and then reattach to it later using this function. When the job name and owner are specified, this function returns the handle that can be used for other operations. |
| CREATE_JOB_VIEW | This overloaded procedure creates a view of the metadata. It is available in Oracle 10g Release 2. |
| DATA_FILTER | Applies any one of the following row filters to the specified table:<br>INCLUDE_ROWS<br>PARTITION_EXPR<br>PARTITION_LIST<br>SAMPLE<br>SUBQUERY<br>The filter settings will determine what data is exported or imported. |
| DETACH | The handle is released, detaching the user session from the Data Pump job. See ATTACH for reattaching the session to the Data Pump job. |
| ESTABLISH_REMOTE_CONTEXT | Provided with a remote link, this procedure readies Data Pump to work with a remote database. |
| GET_DUMPFILE_INFO | Requests information for a named dump file. It is available in Oracle 10g Release 2. |

**TABLE 12-1.**   *DBMS_DATAPUMP Procedures and Functions*

| Name | Description |
|------|-------------|
| GET_STATUS | This overloaded procedure returns the status of a job, and returns any error conditions that occur. |
| HAS_PRIVS | Determines whether or not a given user has the privilege passed to the function. For example, if user PLSQL has exp_full_database privileges, then the following call would return a value of 1:<br>DBMS_DATAPUMP.HAS_PRIVS(oper=> 'EXPORT'); |
| LOG_ENTRY | Inserts a message into the specified log file. |
| LOG_ERROR | Adds an error to the log file, and notifies all users through GET_STATUS that there is an error condition. |
| METADATA_FILTER | Allows the restriction of metadata to be included in a Data Pump job. The following filters are available:<br>NAME_EXPR<br>NAME_LIST<br>SCHEMA_EXPR<br>SCHEMA_LIST<br>TABLESPACE_EXPR<br>TABLESPACE_LIST<br>INCLUDE_PATH_EXPR<br>INCLUDE_PATH_LIST<br>EXCLUDE_PATH_EXPR<br>EXCLUDE_PATH_LIST |
| METADATA_REMAP | Remaps objects from one schema, tablespace, or datafile to another on import. This procedure is only available for import and SQL_FILE operations. |
| METADATA_TRANSFORM | Available for import and SQL_FILE operations, this procedure specifies the transformations applied during processing. Transformations include<br>PCTSPACE<br>SEGMENT_ATTRIBUTES<br>STORAGE<br>OID |

**TABLE 12-1.** *DBMS_DATAPUMP Procedures and Functions* (cont.)

| Name | Description |
|------|-------------|
| OPEN | The OPEN function returns a handle for a new job. The handle is used for most other procedures and functions in the DBMS_DATAPUMP package. |
| SET_DEBUG | Turns debugging on or off. To set debug to on, set ON_OFF => 1. To turn it off again, set ON_OFF => 0. |
| SET_PARALLEL | Data Pump supports parallel operations. Sets the DEGREE to no more than twice the number of CPUs your system has. |
| SET_PARAMETER | Sets the values for optional parameters for job processing. |
| SETUP_REMOTE_CONTEXT | Procedure to set up a remote Data Pump job. |
| START_JOB | Starts or continues a Data Pump job. |
| STOP_JOB | Halts a job, but does not necessarily permanently terminate it. It may be restarted again. |
| WAIT_FOR_JOB | Using this procedure, a job runs until it completes, returning either a *completed* or *stopped* status. Available in Oracle 10g Release 2. |

**TABLE 12-1.**   *DBMS_DATAPUMP Procedures and Functions* (cont.)

These 26 records have two distinct values for ACCOUNT_STATUS as can be seen in the following SELECT:

```
SQL> SELECT account_status, count(1)
  2   FROM test_datapump
  3   GROUP BY account_status;

ACCOUNT_STATUS                    COUNT(1)
------------------------------- ----------
OPEN                                     8
EXPIRED & LOCKED                        18
```

The following procedure uses DBMS_DATAPUMP to export the tables in the PLSQL schema:

**NOTE**
*If you run this more than once, you must change the name of the job and dump file. Submitting a duplicate Data Pump job name will result in the following:*

```
ERROR at line 1:
ORA-31634: job already exists
```

*Dump files are not overwritten when the same name is supplied twice. Supplying a duplicate dump file name will result in the following:*

```
ERROR at line 1:
ORA-39001: invalid argument value
```

```
-- Available online as part of dbms_datapump_objects.sql
CREATE OR REPLACE PROCEDURE export_tables (
    i_job_name VARCHAR2,
    i_dump_file_name VARCHAR2)
AS
  v_handle NUMBER;
  v_status VARCHAR2(500 CHAR);
  v_privs NUMBER;
  v_job_name VARCHAR2(30 CHAR) := UPPER(i_job_name);
  /*************************************
   * This procedure exports all tables
   * in the current schema, and returns
   * the completion status.
   *************************************/
BEGIN
  -- Use OPEN to get the handle
  v_handle := DBMS_DATAPUMP.OPEN('EXPORT',
                                 'TABLE',
                                 NULL,
                                 v_job_name,
                                 NULL);
  DBMS_OUTPUT.PUT(CHR(10));
  DBMS_OUTPUT.PUT_LINE('==================================');
  DBMS_OUTPUT.PUT_LINE('==    Data Pump table export');
  DBMS_OUTPUT.PUT_LINE('==');
  DBMS_OUTPUT.PUT_LINE('== The handle is: '||v_handle);
  DBMS_OUTPUT.PUT_LINE('==================================');
  DBMS_OUTPUT.PUT(CHR(10));
```

```
   -- Do not discard the master table after export
   DBMS_DATAPUMP.SET_PARAMETER(v_handle, 'KEEP_MASTER', 1);

   -- Limit the dump to the TEST_DATAPUMP table only
   DBMS_DATAPUMP.METADATA_FILTER(v_handle, 'NAME_EXPR',
                                 'IN (''TEST_DATAPUMP'')');

   -- The dump file will be placed in the OS directory
   --    associated with EXPORT_DIR
   DBMS_DATAPUMP.ADD_FILE(v_handle, i_dump_file_name, 'EXPORT_DIR');

   -- Start the job associated with the handle
   DBMS_DATAPUMP.START_JOB(v_handle);

   -- Wait until the job completes, and then get the status
   DBMS_DATAPUMP.WAIT_FOR_JOB(v_handle, v_status);
   DBMS_OUTPUT.PUT_LINE('Final status: '||v_status);

   -- Detach from the job
   DBMS_DATAPUMP.DETACH(v_handle);

END export_tables;
/
```

This procedure performs the following steps:

■ It executes DBMS_DATAPUMP.OPEN and receives the handle. As part of this call it specifies that the operation will be EXPORT, it will export TABLE, and the name of the job is passed in to the procedure.

■ After the handle is received and printed to the screen, it calls the DBMS_ DATAPUMP.SET_PARAMETER procedure, and then tells Oracle to keep the master table that is created as part of the Data Pump export.

■ It limits the export to a single table using DBMS_DATAPUMP.METADATA_ FILTER.

■ It specifies the directory and filename for the export file using DBMS_ DATAPUMP.ADD_FILE. The filename is then passed to the procedure.

■ It starts the job using DBMS_DATAPUMP.START_JOB. Only the handle is required.

■ It detaches the session from the job.

**NOTE**
*DBMS_DATAPUMP.WAIT_FOR_JOB was a nice addition to this package. It does not return until the job is finished, either successfully, or in error status. It returns the status of the completed job.*

**TIP**
*If you are exporting a large amount of data, you might want to remove the call to DBMS_DATAPUMP .WAIT_FOR_JOB, and instead detach from the job right away. It will still run, and you can attach to it later, or simply monitor it using DBA_DATAPUMP_ JOBS.*

To execute this procedure, simply pass a name for the job and a name for the file.

```
-- Available online as part of dbms_datapump_export.sql
SQL> SET SERVEROUTPUT ON
SQL> exec export_tables('job1', 'plsql_table_export.dmp')
```

It will take just a few moments, and then return the following:

```
=================================
==    Data Pump table export
==
==    The handle is: 27
=================================
Final status: COMPLETED
PL/SQL procedure successfully completed.
```

Check your directory and verify that the PLSQL_TABLE_EXPORT.DMP file was created, and that the size is greater than zero.

**NOTE**
*If this fails to create the dump file, go back to your user creation script and verify the directory created is valid. If it is not a valid directory, or if it failed to create for some reason, then this procedure will not create the dump file. An alternative to defining the directory in the create_user.sql script is to set the DATA_PUMP_DIR environment variable on your operating system to the proper directory.*

Since we kept the master table that was created on export, you will find a table called `JOB1` in your schema. Do a `describe` on this table to see the master table's structure. Also note that we never named this table—we named the job. The master table is created with the same name as the job.

## Importing

Now that we have a dump file, we can import the tables into the `PLSQL2` schema (created per the README's instructions from the online code). The export filtered for a specific table name. The import example goes one step further in filtering for specific rows.

```
-- Available online as part of dbms_datapump_objects.sql
CREATE OR REPLACE PROCEDURE import_tables (
   i_job_name VARCHAR2,
   i_dump_file_name VARCHAR2)
AS
  v_handle NUMBER;
  v_status VARCHAR2(500 CHAR);
  v_privs NUMBER;
  v_job_name VARCHAR2(30 CHAR) := UPPER(i_job_name);

  /**************************************
   * This procedure exports all tables
   * in the current schema, and returns
   * the completion status.
   **************************************/

BEGIN
  -- Use OPEN to get the handle
  v_handle := DBMS_DATAPUMP.OPEN('IMPORT',
                                 'TABLE',
                                 NULL,
                                 v_job_name,
                                 NULL);
  DBMS_OUTPUT.PUT(CHR(10));
  DBMS_OUTPUT.PUT_LINE('==================================');
  DBMS_OUTPUT.PUT_LINE('==    Data Pump table import');
  DBMS_OUTPUT.PUT_LINE('==');
  DBMS_OUTPUT.PUT_LINE('== The handle is: '||v_handle);
  DBMS_OUTPUT.PUT_LINE('==================================');
  DBMS_OUTPUT.PUT(CHR(10));

  -- Specify the dump file to import
  DBMS_DATAPUMP.ADD_FILE(v_handle, i_dump_file_name, 'EXPORT_DIR');
```

```
     -- The log file will be placed in the OS directory
     --   associated with EXPORT_DIR
     DBMS_DATAPUMP.ADD_FILE(v_handle, 'import.log',
                            'EXPORT_DIR', NULL,
                            DBMS_DATAPUMP.KU$_FILE_TYPE_LOG_FILE);

     -- Map the object owned by user PLSQL to user PLSQL2
     DBMS_DATAPUMP.METADATA_REMAP(v_handle,'REMAP_SCHEMA','PLSQL','PLSQL2');

     -- Skip the table if it already exists
     DBMS_DATAPUMP.SET_PARAMETER(v_handle,'TABLE_EXISTS_ACTION','SKIP');

     -- Limit the rows imported to only those that have an
     --   ACCOUNT_STATUS value of OPEN
     DBMS_DATAPUMP.DATA_FILTER(v_handle, 'SUBQUERY',
     'WHERE ACCOUNT_STATUS = ''OPEN''');

     -- Start the job associated with the handle
     DBMS_DATAPUMP.START_JOB(v_handle);

     -- Wait until the job completes, and then get the status
     DBMS_DATAPUMP.WAIT_FOR_JOB(v_handle, v_status);
     DBMS_OUTPUT.PUT_LINE('Final status: '||v_status);

     -- Detach from the job
     DBMS_DATAPUMP.DETACH(v_handle);
END import_tables;
/
```

This breaks down as follows:

- The handle is retrieved using DBMS_DATAPUMP.OPEN.

- DBMS_DATAPUMP.ADD_FILE's default filetype is a dump file, so it is left at NULL when pointing to the import file. The next call to this procedure, however, is for the log file creation. The filetype is specified as DBMS_DATAPUMP.KU$_FILE_TYPE_LOG_FILE.

- Since the import is going into a different schema than the original, the METADATA_REMAP procedure is used to change ownership of the object from the original owner to the new one.

- The SET_PARAMETER procedure makes sure that, if the table being imported already exists, it is skipped on import.

■ Next, DATA_FILTER is used to restrict rows being imported to the new schema to only those who have an ACCOUNT_STATUS of OPEN.

■ Finally, START_JOB is used to run the job.

To see how this works, run the following:

```
-- Available online as part of dbms_datapump_import.sql
SET SERVEROUTPUT ON
exec import_tables('job2', 'plsql_table_export.dmp');
```

This returns the following:

```
=================================
==    Data Pump table import
==
==    The handle is: 110
=================================
Final status: COMPLETED
```

A COUNT of the records in the table reveals that only eight records are present, while there were 26 in the original table.

```
SQL> SELECT COUNT(*) FROM TEST_DATAPUMP;
   COUNT(*)
----------
         8
```

The reason for the change in record count is the DATA_FILTER that was applied on import. The following SELECT shows that only OPEN records remain:

```
SQL> SELECT account_status, count(1)
  2  FROM test_datapump
  3  GROUP BY account_status;

ACCOUNT_STATUS                     COUNT(1)
-------------------------------- ----------
OPEN                                    8
```

DBMS_DATAPUMP can be extended beyond these examples to work with encrypted data, perform actions such as import/export over network connections to remote databases, import/export schemas, databases, and metadata, and do it in parallel.

## DBMS_FILE_TRANSFER: Move Binary Files

The DBMS_FILE_TRANSFER package extends Oracle's file manipulation beyond the traditional UTL_FILE. There are three procedures in this package that copy, get, and put files on the operating system. Table 12-2 shows these procedures and the arguments they take.

| Procedure and Function Details | Description |
| --- | --- |
| PROCEDURE **COPY_FILE**<br>Argument Name<br>SOURCE_DIRECTORY_OBJECT<br>SOURCE_FILE_NAME<br>DESTINATION_DIRECTORY_OBJECT<br>DESTINATION_FILE_NAME | Copies a file on a local file system to another filename or location. |
| PROCEDURE **GET_FILE**<br>Argument Name<br>SOURCE_DIRECTORY_OBJECT<br>SOURCE_FILE_NAME<br>SOURCE_DATABASE<br>DESTINATION_DIRECTORY_OBJECT<br>DESTINATION_FILE_NAME | Used when working with a remote database, it creates a copy of a remote file on the local file system. |
| PROCEDURE **PUT_FILE**<br>Argument Name<br>SOURCE_DIRECTORY_OBJECT<br>SOURCE_FILE_NAME<br>DESTINATION_DIRECTORY_OBJECT<br>DESTINATION_FILE_NAME<br>DESTINATION_DATABASE | The opposite of GET_FILE, this puts a file on the local file system of a remote database. |

**TABLE 12-2.** *DBMS_FILE_TRANSFER Procedures*

The following example shows how the DBMS_FILE_TRANSFER.COPY_FILE procedure works:

```
-- Available online as part of dbms_file_transfer.sql
BEGIN
  DBMS_FILE_TRANSFER.COPY_FILE (
                    source_directory_object => 'IMAGE_DIR',
                    source_file_name => 'File_Transfer.txt',
                    destination_directory_object => 'IMAGE_DIR',
                    destination_file_name => 'File_Transfer_Copy.txt');
END;
/
```

The only difference between COPY_FILE, GET_FILE, and PUT_FILE is that for the GET and PUT procedures a database link must be specified.

## UTL_COMPRESS: Compress Database Files

The UTL_COMPRESS package uses the Lempel-Ziv (LZ) compression algorithm to compress data of type RAW, BFILE, or BLOB. LZ is a dictionary-based algorithm that works well when there is a fair amount of redundancy in the data. It follows that the larger the amount of data being compressed, the greater the redundancy. With greater redundancy, the opportunities for compression expand. Other common compression utilities that use the LZ algorithm are gunzip, WinZip, gzip, and the UNIX compress/uncompress.

The compress and uncompress procedures and functions are the heart of this package. The procedures and functions related to compression are listed in Table 12-3.

### Why Would I Use This?

We use this package primarily for binary files that are accessed infrequently. While the uncompress utility is efficient, it is still one more step to perform for delivering data to a user, so we don't use it when the demand for the data is high. We use this package, just like in the example presented here, for compressing digital images that are part of an archive to reduce space used by the archive.

| Procedure and Function Details | Description |
|---|---|
| FUNCTION **LZ_COMPRESS** <br><br> Argument Name / Type <br> SRC / RAW \| BLOB \| BFILE <br> QUALITY / BINARY_INTEGER | Compresses data to the level of quality specified (1–9, with a default value of 6), returning the compressed result as type RAW and BLOB. If SRC is BFILE, the function returns a BLOB. |
| PROCEDURE **LZ_COMPRESS** <br><br> Argument Name / Type <br> SRC / BLOB \| BFILE <br> DST / BLOB <br> QUALITY / BINARY_INTEGER | Compresses data to the level of quality specified (1–9, with a default value of 6). The compressed data is output to DST. |
| FUNCTION **LZ_COMPRESS_OPEN** <br><br> Argument Name / Type <br> DST / BLOB <br> QUALITY / BINARY_INTEGER | Initializes the destination lob for the addition of piecewise compressed data. Quality can be integers 1–9, and the default is 6. |
| PROCEDURE **LZ_COMPRESS_ADD** <br><br> Argument Name / Type <br> HANDLE / BINARY_INTEGER <br> DST / BLOB <br> SRC / RAW | Adds compressed data to an already compressed LOB. HANDLE is the returned value from the LZ_COMPRESS_OPEN function. |
| PROCEDURE **LZ_COMPRESS_CLOSE** <br><br> Argument Name / Type <br> HANDLE / BINARY_INTEGER <br> DST / BLOB | Closes the destination LOB that was opened for piecewise manipulation of data. HANDLE is the value returned by the LZ_COMPRESS_OPEN function. |

**TABLE 12-3.** *Compression Procedures and Functions*

Notice that some of the procedures and functions have a QUALITY parameter. The integer range accepted here is from 1 to 9, with a default value of 6. QUALITY determines how thorough you wish the compression to be. If the value is set close to 1, compression will be less complete than if closer to 9, but it will be much faster. Oracle describes it on a sliding scale from *fast* to *best*, 1 being the quickest (and poorest quality), and 9 being the best quality (and slowest).

What gets compressed can also be uncompressed. Table 12-4 lists all procedures and functions related to uncompressing data.

## How Does That Work?

Named after inventors Abraham Lempel and Jacob Ziv, the LZ compression algorithm is a dictionary compression method. The following is a description of how this compression works in a nutshell. Prior to encoding a file, there is a blank dictionary. As compression occurs, the dictionary is built so that terms, or parts of terms, can be replaced with dictionary code words that offer more efficient storage. The larger the file size being compressed, the more complete the dictionary becomes. As the size of the dictionary increases, the likelihood of new terms matching dictionary terms increases, and so it follows that the rate of compression will increase.

| Procedure and Function Details | | Description |
| --- | --- | --- |
| FUNCTION **LZ_UNCOMPRESS** | | Uncompress data, returning it in either RAW or BLOB format. If SRC is BFILE, the function returns a BLOB. |
| Argument Name | Type | |
| SRC | RAW \| BLOB \| BFILE | |
| PROCEDURE **LZ_UNCOMPRESS** | | Uncompress data output to the destination determined by DST. |
| Argument Name | Type | |
| SRC | BLOB \| BFILE | |
| DST | BLOB | |
| FUNCTION **LZ_UNCOMPRESS_OPEN** | | Initializes the source LOB for piecewise uncompression. It returns the handle used by LZ_ UNCOMPRESS_EXTRACT and LZ_UNCOMPRESS_CLOSE. |
| Argument Name | Type | |
| SRC | BLOB | |
| PROCEDURE **LZ_UNCOMPRESS_EXTRACT** | | Pulls a piece of uncompressed data to the destination. HANDLE is the return value from the LZ_ UNCOMPRESS_OPEN function. |
| Argument Name | Type | |
| HANDLE | BINARY_INTEGER | |
| DST | RAW | |
| PROCEDURE **LZ_UNCOMPRESS_CLOSE** | | Closes the LOB that was opened for piecewise extraction. HANDLE is the value returned by the LZ_ UNCOMPRESS_OPEN function. |
| Argument Name | Type | |
| HANDLE | BINARY_INTEGER | |

**TABLE 12-4.** *Uncompress Procedures and Functions*

The following example demonstrates how to compress and uncompress an image stored as a BFILE, verify the size has changed, and then uncompress it again. It shows the use of COMPRESS and UNCOMPRESS procedures, and displays the size of the LOB at each step of the way.

```
-- Available online as part of compression.sql
SET SERVEROUTPUT ON
DECLARE
    v_bfile_original BFILE;
    v_blob_compress BLOB := TO_BLOB('a');  -- initialize the blob
    v_blob_uncompress BLOB := TO_BLOB('a'); -- initialize the blob
    v_length PLS_INTEGER;
BEGIN
  -- Get the length of the image prior to compression
  SELECT DBMS_LOB.GETLENGTH(image)
  INTO v_length
  FROM compress_images;

  -- Display the length
  DBMS_OUTPUT.PUT(CHR(10));
  DBMS_OUTPUT.PUT_LINE('Before compression length: '|| v_length);

  -- Get the pointer
  SELECT image
  INTO v_bfile_original
  FROM compress_images;

  -- Open the bfile for read
  DBMS_LOB.OPEN(v_bfile_original);

  -- Compress the image
  UTL_COMPRESS.LZ_COMPRESS (src => v_bfile_original,
                            dst => v_blob_compress);
  -- Display the length
  v_length := DBMS_LOB.GETLENGTH(v_blob_compress);
  DBMS_OUTPUT.PUT(CHR(10));
  DBMS_OUTPUT.PUT_LINE('Compressed length: '|| v_length);

  -- Uncompress the blob
  UTL_COMPRESS.LZ_UNCOMPRESS (v_blob_compress,
                              v_blob_uncompress);
  -- Display the length
  v_length := DBMS_LOB.GETLENGTH(v_blob_uncompress);
  DBMS_OUTPUT.PUT(CHR(10));
  DBMS_OUTPUT.PUT_LINE('Uncompressed length: '|| v_length);
```

```
    -- Close the bfile and free temporary lobs
    DBMS_LOB.CLOSE(v_bfile_original);
    DBMS_LOB.FREETEMPORARY(v_blob_compress);
    DBMS_LOB.FREETEMPORARY(v_blob_uncompress);
END;
/
```

The results of this anonymous block are as follows:

```
Before compression length: 27342
After compression length: 18585
After uncompression length: 27342
```

The before length matches the byte size of the file as shown on the operating system:

```
27342 book_cover.jpg
```

Compression for this file reduced the size by almost 9K, and uncompressing it restored it to the original size.

# Data Security

Cryptography is often thought of as a black art, understood by organizations like the NSA or CIA. Although much of the work in cryptography stems from agencies like this, businesses now make the greatest use of current crypto techniques to protect their data from malicious hackers.

Oracle provides encryption utilities to protect data, and utilities that hide PL/SQL source code. In this section, we introduce cryptography, and Oracle's encryption support using DBMS_CRYPTO. We also look at the WRAP utility, and show how it can be used to hide PL/SQL source code.

## Etarvqitcrja

This heading is encrypted using an extraordinarily simple form of substitution cryptography called a shift cipher, or Caesar cipher. It is an encryption technique known to have been used by Julius Caesar to communicate secretly with his military, hence the name Caesar cipher. The heading uses a shift of 2, substituting each letter in the term *Cryptography* with the character two positions to the right of it in the English alphabet, as shown in Figure 12-1.

| C | r | y | p | t | o | g | r | a | p | h | y |
|---|---|---|---|---|---|---|---|---|---|---|---|
| E | t | a | r | v | q | i | t | c | r | j | a |

**FIGURE 12-1.**   *The shift cipher*

Of course, you should never use this kind of cryptography for anything you truly wish to hide. It can be easily deciphered with current techniques. It does illustrate though how long cryptography has been in use by governments and military to guard national secrets.

Today, cryptography is highly valued by businesses, not just governments. The amount of sensitive data, for both customers and the businesses themselves, requires highly secure forms of cryptography to protect it from misuse. The algorithms available for cryptography are much more varied and complex than the shift/Caesar cipher, of course. We examine the possibilities in the rest of this section.

## Cryptography Explained

Cryptography has historically been linked closely with linguistics and discrete mathematics. It deals with hiding, or encrypting data. Encryption makes data unreadable using a cipher, which is an algorithm that encodes the text in some way. The encrypted text is therefore said to be enciphered, and the text itself is called ciphertext. Decryption reverses this process, and the unencrypted text is said to be deciphered.

Ciphers can be classified as symmetric key (sometimes referred to as private key) or asymmetric key (sometimes referred to as public key) or algorithms. Symmetric key ciphers rely on a key to decipher the encrypted text. The key that's used to encrypt the message is also used to decrypt the message, so the recipient must have the same key as the sender.

This creates all kinds of logistical problems in that the key must remain absolutely secure. When the recipient is remote, or there are a number of recipients, the communication of the key is itself in need of encryption. See the problem?

Asymmetric key ciphers on the other hand do not rely on the same key to encipher and decipher text. Two keys are used (referred to as a key pair), one being made public, and the other remaining private. If one key is known, it is not possible to deduce the value of the second key, though they are related mathematically. Anyone with access to the public key can encrypt text, while only those with access to the private key can decipher it.

You see an example of asymmetric encryption with many safe deposit boxes. The public key is the one held by the bank, and is available to anyone there. The public key can lock the box, but cannot open it. The owner of the safe deposit box holds another key which is kept private. This key can only open the box. The only way someone at the bank can place something in the box is if the owner leaves it open. Once they lock it, only the owner can see the contents. They never have to exchange keys.

Just like banks, asymmetric encryption can be broken into. The stronger the bank vault, the less likely it is that an intruder can gain access to the safe deposit box contents. Similarly, the security of encrypted data is only as good as the security of its key. Cryptanalysis is the study of ways to exploit weaknesses of cryptography, and decipher encrypted materials.

In fact, there are a number of contests to do that very thing, the most well-known of which is sponsored by RSA Security. RSA, which stands for Rivest, Shamir, and Adleman, was the first public key encryption algorithm published back in the 1970s by RSA Security. RSA Security's contest is called The New RSA Factoring Challenge. It awards cash to those who can factor the challenge numbers. The largest number to be factored at this time is 576-bit (174 digits).

**NOTE**
*To learn more about the challenge, visit http:// www.rsasecurity.com/rsalabs/node.asp?id=2091. If the link is no longer valid, visit www.rsasecurity .com to learn more about the challenge.*

## Factoring

Factorization is determining the prime numbers whose product makes up the whole. The integer 14421 is the product of 3 * 11 * 19 * 23, all of which are called prime factors. Why is factoring important to cryptography? Take a large number, much bigger than 14421, and generate two large prime factors of it. This is essentially how pair keys are generated for public key encryption.

One example, taken from The New RSA Factoring Challenge, provides the following 576-bit (174-digit) number:

```
18819881292060796383869723946165043980716356337941738270076335642298885971523466548531906060650474304531738801130339671619969232120573403187955065699622130516875930765025
7059
```

The challenge was to determine all of the prime numbers (any pair) whose product totaled that number. This was successfully factored (in other words, hacked) in December, 2003. RSA published the results, showing two key pairs that are prime factors of the challenge number. They are

3980750864240649373971255005503864911990643623425 2

6708406385189575946388957261768583317

And:

4727721461074353025362230719730482246329146953020 9

7116459852171130520711256363590397527

Though no small task, they only cracked the lowest number in the challenge. The highest is 2048-bit (617 digits), which is

```
25195908475657893494027183240048398571429282126204032027 7
77137836046362020707595556264018525880784406918290641249 5
15082189298559149176184502808489120072844992687392807287 7
76735971418347270261896375014971824691165077613379859095 7
00097330459748808428401797429100642458691817195118746121 5
15172654632282216869987549182422433637259085141865462043 5
76798423387184774447920739934236584823824281198163815010 6
74810451660377306056201619676256133844143603833904414952 6
34432190114657544454178424020924616515723350778707749817 1
25772467962926386356373289912154831438167899885040445364 0
23527381951378636564391212010397122822120720357
```

Anyone who is able to factor this will get a check for $200,000. We think anyone using 2048-bit encryption can count on their secrets being as safe as RSA's $200,000 for quite some time.

## The DBMS_CRYPTO Encryption Toolkit

Oracle 10g Release 1 introduced the DBMS_CRYPTO package to replace the DBMS_ OBFUSCATION_TOOLKIT package. DBMS_CRYPTO provides cryptography support similar to DBMS_OBFUSCATION_TOOLKIT, but it is far more current in its encryption standard support. It also has a function to generate random numbers for encryption keys (DBMS_OBFUSCATION_TOOLKIT supported only RAW and VARCHAR2), reducing the temptation to use the less effective and safe DBMS_ RANDOM package.

## Oracle's Secret Decoder Ring

No, they don't actually use a ring, but the DBMS_CRYPTO supplied package essentially acts the same way. It supports various encryption and hashing ciphers, giving DBAs and developers flexibility in the design of their systems. Table 12-5 lists the different ciphers supported by DBMS_CRYPTO.

| Algorithm | Description |
| --- | --- |
| DES | DES stands for Data Encryption Standard, but is sometimes referred to as the DEA (Data Encryption Algorithm). DES is a symmetric key algorithm (also called *secret-key*) with a key length of 56 bits. |
| 3DES | 3DES (Triple DES) is more secure than its DES counterpart, and is therefore preferred when security outweighs speed of encryption. 3DES takes approximately three times as long to encrypt data than DES. |
| RC4 | RC4, developed by RSA Security, is a symmetric key cipher that is referred to as a stream cipher, and is most commonly associated with SSL, WEP, and WPA (the last two are used for wireless). |
| AES | The Advanced Encryption Standard was accepted by NIST (National Institute of Standards and Technology) as a standard in 2001. It is a symmetric key cipher called a block cipher. |
| SHA-1 | SHA stands for Secure Hash Algorithm. It is used for protocols such as SSL. SHA-1 is recommended over MD4 and MD5 for a hash algorithm. |
| MD4 | This hash function is the fourth release of the Message-Digest cipher. The 128-bit hashes are not considered very secure. Oracle recommends it not be used for new development. |
| MD5 | The Message-Digest cipher 5 corrected many of the problems with MD4. While still widely used, it's being phased out in favor of SHA-1 due to significant security concerns. Oracle recommends it not be used for new development. |
| HMAC_MD5, HMAC_SH1 | These two algorithms are Message Authentication Codes (MAC) that use a keyed hash cipher to ensure the integrity of a message. The type of hash function is shown in the name— either MD-5 or SHA-1. |

**TABLE 12-5.** *Algorithms Supported by DBMS_CRYPTO*

Although `DBMS_OBFUSCATION_TOOLKIT` is still available in Oracle 10g, it's recommended you move to `DBMS_CRYPTO` to take advantage of the higher level of encryption supported, as well as the new features that are being added to that package.

## Using DBMS_CRYPTO

The following example encrypts data using `ENCRYPT_AES`, `CHAIN_CBC`, and `PAD_PKCS5`. We use `AES_CBC_PKCS5` which combines these three in our variable definition shown in bold.

```
-- Available online as part of crypto_aes.sql
CREATE OR REPLACE PROCEDURE crypto_aes (
    i_plaintext IN VARCHAR2)
IS
    v_ciphertext RAW(500);
    v_deciphered VARCHAR2(500 CHAR);
    v_plaintext RAW(200) := UTL_I18N.STRING_TO_RAW(
                                    i_plaintext,
                                    'AL32UTF8');
    v_type BINARY_INTEGER := DBMS_CRYPTO.AES_CBC_PKCS5;
    v_key RAW(128) := UTL_I18N.STRING_TO_RAW(
            DBMS_CRYPTO.RANDOMBYTES(16),   --generates 128 bit key..128/8
            'AL32UTF8');
BEGIN
    DBMS_OUTPUT.PUT(CHR(10));
    DBMS_OUTPUT.PUT_LINE(
        'Encrypted using ENCRYPT_AES + CHAIN_CBC + PAD_PKCS5');
    DBMS_OUTPUT.PUT_LINE('================================================');
    DBMS_OUTPUT.PUT(CHR(10));
    DBMS_OUTPUT.PUT_LINE('PLAINTEXT: '||i_plaintext);
    v_ciphertext := DBMS_CRYPTO.ENCRYPT(v_plaintext,
                                        v_type,
                                        v_key);
    DBMS_OUTPUT.PUT(CHR(10));
    DBMS_OUTPUT.PUT_LINE('CIPHERTEXT: '||v_ciphertext);
    DBMS_OUTPUT.PUT(CHR(10));
    DBMS_OUTPUT.PUT(CHR(10));
    v_deciphered := UTL_I18N.RAW_TO_CHAR(
                        DBMS_CRYPTO.DECRYPT(v_ciphertext,
                                            v_type,
                                            v_key));
    DBMS_OUTPUT.PUT(CHR(10));
    DBMS_OUTPUT.PUT_LINE('Decrypt the ciphertext');
    DBMS_OUTPUT.PUT_LINE('====================');
    DBMS_OUTPUT.PUT(CHR(10));
    DBMS_OUTPUT.PUT_LINE('DECIPHERED: '||v_deciphered);
END crypto_aes;
/
```

This procedure does the following:

- Uses the `UTL_I18N.STRING_TO_RAW` function to convert the input string to `RAW` type. The `ENCRYPT` function of `DBMS_CRYPTO` requires input be a `RAW`.

- `DBMS_CRYPTO.AES_CBC_PKCS5` is used to specify the type of encryption that will be performed. This constant combines `ENCRYPT_AES`, `CHAIN_CBC`, and `PAD_PKCS5`. Alternatively, We could have listed all three of these separated by a plus (+) symbol.

- We actually used two packages to generate the key. The first is the `DBMS_CRYPTO.RANDOMBYTES` function. We passed a value of 16 bytes (128 bits / 8 = 16 bytes) to generate string. This value is used by `UTL_I18N.STRING_TO_RAW` to convert it to the `RAW` value required by the `ENCRYPT` function.

- All values are set, so the `DBMS_CRYPTO.ENCRYPT` is as easy as passing the variables.

- To decipher the ciphertext, it's first passed to the `DBMS_CRYPTO.DECRYPT` function, which returns a value of type `RAW`. This value is then passed to `UTL_I18N.RAW_TO_CHAR` to return the deciphered text.

To test this, run the following:

```
-- Available online as part of crypto_aes.sql
SET SERVEROUTPUT ON
exec crypto_aes('Expert PLSQL')
```

This returns the following result:

```
Encrypted using ENCRYPT_AES + CHAIN_CBC + PAD_PKCS5
===================================================
PLAINTEXT: Expert PLSQL
CIPHERTEXT: 2A514B2B046C5B82434EE547381034C2

Decrypt the ciphertext
======================
DECIPHERED: Expert PLSQL
```

# Summary

In this chapter, we demonstrated how to secure data using the Oracle built-in package DBMS_CRYPTO, discussed compression capabilities with UTL_COMPRESS, and showed how, with DBMS_FILE_TRANSFER, it's possible to move and copy files on local and remote file systems. Performance tuning is made easier with the DBMS_STATS package, and we showed how statistics can be moved from one system to another using this package. We also demonstrated how data can be exported and imported using DBMS_DATAPUMP, including filtering for specific objects and data.

# PART
# VI

## Appendixes

# APPENDIX

## A

# Regular Expression Metacharacters and Functions

f you have a background in Perl, you should be familiar with regular expressions added in version 10*g* of the Oracle data server. Oracle 10*g* supports the IEEE POSIX extended regular expressions standard and works with the following data types:

- CHAR
- VARCHAR2
- NCHAR
- NVARCHAR
- CLOB
- NCLOB

See Chapter 10 for more on this topic.

# POSIX Bracket Expressions

The following POSIX bracket expressions (shown in Table A-1) are available with Oracle 10*g* Release 2.

| Bracket Expression | Description | Example |
|---|---|---|
| *[[:alnum:]]* | Alphanumeric characters | ```SELECT REGEXP_SUBSTR( '3967 S. Bills Dr., Stevens Point, WI 54481', '[[:alnum:]]{4}') FROM dual;``` |
| *[[:alpha:]]* | Alphabetic characters | ```SELECT REGEXP_SUBSTR( '3967 S. Bills Dr., Stevens Point, WI 54481', '[[:alpha:]]{4}') FROM dual;``` |

**TABLE A-1.** *POSIX Bracket Expressions*

| Bracket Expression | Description | Example |
|---|---|---|
| *[[:cntrl:]]* | Control characters | ```-- Strips a tab between Stevens and Point SELECT REGEXP_REPLACE( 'Stevens     Point', '[[:cntrl:]]') FROM dual;``` |
| *[[:digit:]]* | Numeric digits | ```SELECT REGEXP_SUBSTR( '3967 S. Bills Dr., Stevens Point, WI 54481', '[[:digit:]]{5}') FROM dual;``` |
| *[[:graph:]]* | Graphical characters | ```SELECT REGEXP_SUBSTR( '3967 S. Bills Dr., Stevens Point, WI 54481', '[[:graph:]]{4}') FROM dual;``` |
| *[[:lower:]]* | Lowercase characters | ```SELECT REGEXP_SUBSTR( '3967 S. Bills Dr., Stevens Point, WI 54481', '[[:lower:]]{4}') FROM dual;``` |
| *[[:print:]]* | Printable characters | ```SELECT REGEXP_SUBSTR( '3967 S. Bills Dr., Stevens Point, WI 54481', '[[:print:]]{4}') FROM dual;``` |
| *[[:punct:]]* | Punctuation characters | ```SELECT REGEXP_REPLACE( '3967 S. Bills Dr., Stevens Point, WI 54481', '[[:punct:]]', '-') FROM dual;``` |
| *[[:space:]]* | Space characters | ```SELECT REGEXP_REPLACE( '3967 S. Bills Dr., Stevens Point, WI 54481', '[[:space:]]', '-') FROM dual;``` |

**TABLE A-1.**   *POSIX Bracket Expressions* (cont.)

| Bracket Expression | Description | Example |
|---|---|---|
| *[[:upper:]]* | Uppercase characters | `SELECT REGEXP_SUBSTR(`<br>`'3967 S. Bills Dr., Stevens Point, WI`<br>`54481', '[[:upper:]]{2}')`<br>`from dual;` |
| *[[:xdigit:]]* | Hexadecimal characters | `SELECT TO_CHAR(REGEXP_SUBSTR(`<br>`'3967 S. Bills Dr., Stevens Point, WI`<br>`54481',`<br>`'[[:xdigit:]]{4}'), 'xxxx')`<br>`FROM dual;` |

**TABLE A-1.** *POSIX Bracket Expressions* (cont.)

# POSIX Metacharacters

Additional regular expression metacharacters are shown in Table A-2. Use the following test data for the examples:

`--Available online as part of regexp_seed.sql`

```
CREATE TABLE reg_exp_tbl (
    name VARCHAR2(100 CHAR),
    address VARCHAR2(100 CHAR)
);
INSERT INTO reg_exp_tbl
    VALUES (
    'Scott Eldridge',
    '2989 Berkeley, CA  39030');
INSERT INTO reg_exp_tbl
    VALUES (
    'Tom Doebler',
    '20034 Polonia Ct., Polonia, WI 54421');
INSERT INTO reg_exp_tbl
    VALUES (
    'Darell Smith',
    '90002 Packer Fan Ct, Polonia, WI 54421');
INSERT INTO reg_exp_tbl
    VALUES (
    'Judy Zimmerman',
    '10000 Zimmer Pl., Texas City, TX 90372');
COMMIT;
```

| Metacharacter | Description | Example |
|---|---|---|
| *{m}* | *m* is an integer. When provided with a subexpression, finds EXACTLY *m* occurrences of it in the text. | ```SELECT name, address FROM reg_exp_tbl WHERE REGEXP_LIKE( address, '0{3}');``` |
| *{m,}* | *m* is an integer. When provided with a subexpression, finds AT LEAST *m* occurrences of it in the text. | ```SELECT name, address FROM reg_exp_tbl WHERE REGEXP_LIKE( address, '0{2,}');``` |
| *{m,n}* | *m* and *n* are integers. When provided with a subexpression, finds AT LEAST *m* occurrences of it in the text, but no more than *n*. | ```SELECT name, address FROM reg_exp_tbl WHERE REGEXP_LIKE( address, '0{2,3}');``` |
| *c* | The search should be case-sensitive. | ```SELECT name, address FROM reg_exp_tbl WHERE REGEXP_LIKE( address, 'polonia', 'c');``` |
| *i* | The search should be case-insensitive. | ```SELECT name, address FROM reg_exp_tbl WHERE REGEXP_LIKE( address, 'polonia', 'i');``` |
| *m* | The search is over a multiline string. This allows beginning-of-line (^) pattern matching when the source string contains multiple lines. | ```SELECT name, address FROM reg_exp_tbl WHERE REGEXP_LIKE( name||chr(10)|| address, '^20034', 'm');``` |

**TABLE A-2.** *Regular Expression POSIX Metacharacters*

| Metacharacter | Description | Example |
|---|---|---|
| *n* | The period, which normally matches a single character, can match a new line. | ```SELECT name, address FROM reg_exp_tbl WHERE REGEXP_LIKE( name||chr(10)|| address, 'Doebler.20034', 'n');``` |
| *x* | White space in a regular expression is ignored when *x* is used. | ```SELECT name, address FROM reg_exp_tbl WHERE REGEXP_LIKE( address, 'W  I', 'x');``` |
| * | Wildcard. When provided with a subexpression, finds zero or more occurrences of it in the text. | ```SELECT name, address FROM reg_exp_tbl WHERE REGEXP_LIKE( address, 'Pol*');``` |
| + | When provided with a subexpression, finds one or more occurrences of it in the text. | ```SELECT name, address FROM reg_exp_tbl WHERE REGEXP_LIKE( address, 'Ct+');``` |
| ? | When provided with a subexpression, finds zero or one occurrences of it in the text. | ```SELECT name, address FROM reg_exp_tbl WHERE REGEXP_LIKE( address, 'Ct?');``` |
| . | Corresponds to any character in the text. | ```SELECT name, address FROM reg_exp_tbl WHERE REGEXP_LIKE( address, 'Pol.nia');``` |

**TABLE A-2.** *Regular Expression POSIX Metacharacters* (cont.)

| Metacharacter | Description | Example |
|---|---|---|
| ^ | Anchor. Finds a match for the expression if it is at the beginning of the line. | ```SELECT name, address FROM reg_exp_tbl WHERE REGEXP_LIKE( address, '^2');``` |
| $ | Anchor. Finds a match for the expression if it is at the end of the line. | ```SELECT name, address FROM reg_exp_tbl WHERE REGEXP_LIKE( address, '2$');``` |
| \| | Separate alternates. Use is similar to an OR. | ```SELECT name, address FROM reg_exp_tbl WHERE REGEXP_LIKE( address, 'Polonia\|Berkeley');``` |
| ( ) | Group subexpressions. | ```SELECT name, address FROM reg_exp_tbl WHERE REGEXP_LIKE( address, 'Berk(el\|l)ey');``` |

**TABLE A-2.** *Regular Expression POSIX Metacharacters* (cont.)

# Non-POSIX Metacharacters

Oracle 10*g* Release 2 adds new metacharacters that are not part of the POSIX standard. They are supported by Perl, however, and many others. The metacharacters, descriptions, and examples are shown in Table A-3.

| Metacharacter | Description | Example |
|---|---|---|
| *? | Matches if there are zero or more occurrences of the prior string. | ```SELECT name, address FROM reg_exp_tbl WHERE REGEXP_LIKE(address, '(Polonia )*?Ct');``` |
| +? | Matches if there are one or more occurrences of the prior string. | ```SELECT name, address FROM reg_exp_tbl WHERE REGEXP_LIKE(address, '(Polonia )+?Ct');``` |
| {n}? | Matches exactly one occurrence of the prior string. | ```SELECT REGEXP_SUBSTR('e-mail     feedback@plsqlbook.com     with comments',     '(([[:alnum:]]+)*)     @(([[:alnum:]]+)*)     \.([[:alpha:]]{3}?)') FROM dual;``` |
| {n,}? | Matches the prior string at least *n* times. | ```SELECT REGEXP_SUBSTR('e-mail     feedback@plsqlbook.com     with comments',     '(([[:alnum:]]+)*)     @(([[:alnum:]]+)*)     \.([[:alpha:]]{2,}?)') FROM dual;``` |
| {n,m}? | Matches the prior string at least *n* times, but no more than *m* times. | ```SELECT REGEXP_SUBSTR('e-mail     feedback@plsqlbook.com     with comments',     '(([[:alnum:]]+)*)     @(([[:alnum:]]+)*)     \.([[:alpha:]]{2,3}?)') FROM dual;``` |

**TABLE A-3.** *Non-POSIX Metacharacters*

| Metacharacter | Description | Example |
|---|---|---|
| \A | Matches patterns from the beginning of a string, rather than just the beginning of a line, so multiline strings will not have the pattern matched once per line. | ```SELECT REGEXP_SUBSTR(     'ab'||chr(10)||'ab',     '\Aab') FROM dual;``` |
| \d | Matches any digit. | ```SELECT REGEXP_SUBSTR(     address,     '\d{5}') FROM reg_exp_tbl;``` |
| \D | Matches any nondigit. | ```SELECT REGEXP_SUBSTR(     address,     '\D{2}') FROM reg_exp_tbl;``` |
| \s | Matches any white-space character. | ```SELECT name, address FROM reg_exp_tbl WHERE REGEXP_LIKE(     address, '\s{2}');``` |
| \S | Matches any non-white-space character. | ```SELECT REGEXP_SUBSTR(     'Polonia Ct., ',     '\S{4}') FROM dual;``` |
| \w | Matches any character or number. The difference between this meta-character and [:alnum:] is that \w includes underscores. | ```SELECT REGEXP_SUBSTR(     address,     '\w{5}') FROM reg_exp_tbl;``` |
| \W | Matches any nonword character. | ```SELECT REGEXP_SUBSTR(     'Matches any     non-word character',     '\W') FROM dual;``` |

**TABLE A-3.** *Non-POSIX Metacharacters* (cont.)

# Functions

Oracle provides four regular expression functions in Oracle 10*g* Release 2. Table A-4 shows the syntax for each function. The italicized parameters are optional. The examples for REGEXP_LIKE require that the *regexp_seed.sql* seed data script be run.

| Name | Syntax | Example |
|------|--------|---------|
| REGEXP_INSTR | REGEXP_INSTR ( source_string, pattern, *start_position*, *occurrence*, *return_option*, *match_parameter*) | SELECT REGEXP_INSTR( '3967 S. Bills Dr., Stevens Point, WI 54481', '[[:digit:]]{5}') FROM dual; |
| REGEXP_SUBSTR | REGEXP_SUBSTR ( source_string, pattern, *start_position*, *occurrence*, *match_parameter*) | SELECT REGEXP_SUBSTR( '3967 S. Bills Dr., Stevens Point, WI 54481', '[[:digit:]]{5}') FROM dual; |
| REGEXP_LIKE | REGEXP_LIKE ( source_string, pattern, *match_parameter*) | SELECT name, address FROM reg_exp_tbl WHERE REGEXP_LIKE( address, 'Berk(el\|l)ey'); |
| REGEXP_REPLACE | REGEXP_REPLACE ( source_string, pattern, *start_position*, *occurrence*, *match_parameter*) | SELECT REGEXP_ REPLACE( '3967 S. Bills Dr., Stevens Point, WI 54481', '[[:space:]]', '-') FROM dual; |

**TABLE A-4.**  *Regular Expression Functions*

# APPENDIX
# B

# Oracle Text
# Supplied Packages

he user CTXSYS owns the built-in packages listed in this appendix. CTXSYS is created during database configuration when the Oracle Text option is selected for installation. In order to use them, EXECUTE permissions must be granted to your user. This list is based on the version 10.1.0.2.0 of the *Context* dictionary. To determine the version you have, run the following from the CTXSYS schema.

```
conn ctxsys/<<password>>

SELECT *
  FROM ctx_version;

VER_DICT   VER_CODE
---------- -------------
10.1.0.2.0 10.1.0.2.0
```

# Package Creation

When Oracle Text is selected as an option during database configuration, the CTXSYS schema and supplied packages are created automatically. Nothing needs to be done manually to create the schema and objects. Should you want to examine the scripts used to create the packages, however, look in the $ORACLE_HOME/ctx/admin directory. Each object creation script is stored separately, and the filenames are included with the descriptions below. Package creation scripts are separated between spec and body. Scripts for the spec end in .plh, while the body scripts have the extension .plb. The .plb files are encrypted so they can't be viewed, but the plh files are not encrypted.

# The Packages

In this section, we list the packages, the scripts that create them, and the procedures and functions in each. The section titled "Most Common Packages," which appears later in this appendix, highlights a few of the packages you'll find most useful.

## CTX_ADM

CTX_ADM is the maintenance and administration package for Oracle Text. It's evolved over time as text indexing operations moved away from the ConText cartridge and the server to built-in functionality.

### Creation Scripts
dr0adm.pkh/plb

## Public Synonym
None

## Contents

| | |
|---|---|
| *Procedure SHUTDOWN* | This procedure is obsolete in Oracle 10gR1, but exists to prevent errors in code that still calls it. It harkens back to the days of the ConText server and the separate administration of the server from the Oracle Database. |
| *Procedure RECOVER* | The recover procedure recovers the data dictionary. |
| *Procedure SET_PARAMETER* | Sets parameters for the system. |
| *Procedure TEST_EXTPROC* | Success when running this indicates that extproc can be invoked. For more information on extproc, see the Oracle Concepts Manual on the OTN web site (http://otn.oracle.com). |
| *Procedure MARK_FAILED* | This procedure is UNPUBLISHED. Use it to mark an index as FAILED if its current status is INPROGRESS. If you try to ALTER an index that is marked as INPROGRESS, it will fail. Marking the index as FAILED allows the ALTER to succeed. |
| *Procedure DROP_USER_OBJECTS* | This procedure is used when dropping a user to clean up text objects such as lexers and preferences. It is not generally called individually. |

# CTX_CLS

The CTX_CLS package provides procedures for classification and training. Classification groups similar documents together. Training performs automatic classification based on an initial set of sample documents and categories. Rules are created based on this sample documentation set, and future documents are classified automatically.

## Creation Scripts
dr0cls.pkh/plb

## Public Synonym
CTX_CLS

## Contents

| | |
|---|---|
| *Procedure CLUSTERING* | Overloaded procedure that clusters a collection of documents. |
| *Procedure TRAIN* | Automatically generates rules based on a training set, or sample set, of documents that are already classified. |

# CTX_DDL

The most used CTXSYS package, CTX_DDL maintains preferences, policies, stoplists, section groups, and attributes. It provides a means to add sublexers to the multilexer, sync CONTEXT indexes that may be out-of-sync, and optimizes indexes by reducing fragmentation.

## Creation Scripts
dr0ddl.pkh/plb

## Public Synonym
CTX_DDL

## Contents

| | |
|---|---|
| *Procedure ADD_ATTR_ SECTION* | Specifies attribute sections that should be indexed within an XML document. |
| *Procedure ADD_FIELD_ SECTION* | Adds a new field to an existing section group. Sections are detected by tags. Similar to ADD_ ZONE_SECTION. |
| *Procedure ADD_INDEX* | Adds an index to an existing index set. |
| *Procedure ADD_MDATA* | Adds mdata (metadata) values to documents. |
| *Procedure ADD_MDATA_ SECTION* | Adds a new mdata section to an existing section group. |
| *Procedure ADD_SPECIAL_ SECTION* | Adds a new special section to an existing section group. Special sections are detected in the text, not the tags. |

| | |
|---|---|
| *Procedure ADD_STOPCLASS* | Adds a new stopclass to an existing stoplist. |
| *Procedure ADD_STOP_ SECTION* | Stop sections define the sections that should not be indexed in a document (HTML or XML, for example). This adds a new stop section to an existing stoplist. |
| *Procedure ADD_STOPTHEME* | Adds a new stoptheme to an existing stoplist. Themes are words or phrases that define what a document is *about*. For example, the major theme of this book is PL/SQL. |
| *Procedure ADD_STOPWORD* | Add a new word to an existing stoplist. |
| *Procedure ADD_SUB_LEXER* | Adds a sublexer under a multilexer. Multilexers allow multiple languages to be indexed in the same index. The sublexers are the individual languages supported by the multilexer. |
| *Procedure ADD_ZONE_ SECTION* | Adds a new section to an existing section group. Sections are detected by tags. Similar to `ADD_ FIELD_SECTION`. |
| *Procedure COPY_POLICY* | Creates a new policy based on an existing policy. |
| *Procedure CREATE_ INDEX_SET* | Creates an index set that can have text indexes added to it using the `ADD_INDEX` procedure. |
| *Procedure CREATE_POLICY* | Creates a policy for use with the `ORA:CONTAINS` operator and XML documents. |
| *Procedure CREATE_ PREFERENCE* | Creates preferences that tell Oracle Text how an object is to be customized. |
| *Procedure CREATE_ SECTION_GROUP* | Creates a section group that specifies how document sections are defined (such as HTML and XML). A section group might be the header in an HTML file, for example. |
| *Procedure CREATE_STOPLIST* | Creates a stoplist, or a list of words that should not be indexed. |
| *Procedure DROP_INDEX_SET* | Drops the supplied index set. |
| *Procedure DROP_POLICY* | Drops the supplied policy. |
| *Procedure DROP_ PREFERENCE* | Drops the supplied preference. |

| | |
|---|---|
| *Procedure DROP_SECTION_GROUP* | Drops the supplied section group. |
| *Procedure DROP_STOPLIST* | Drops the supplied stoplist. |
| *Procedure OPTIMIZE_INDEX* | Allows index optimization in parallel, and supports full or partial optimization with a limit on the amount of time to devote to the optimization process. |
| *Procedure REMOVE_INDEX* | Removes an index from an index set. |
| *Procedure REMOVE_MDATA* | Removes mdata values from a document. |
| *Procedure REMOVE_SECTION* | Removes a section from a section group without removing the section group. |
| *Procedure REMOVE_STOPCLASS* | Removes a stopclass from a section group without removing the section group. |
| *Procedure REMOVE_STOPTHEME* | Removes a stoptheme from a section group without removing the section group. |
| *Procedure REMOVE_STOPWORD* | Add a new word to an existing stoplist. |
| *Procedure REMOVE_SUB_LEXER* | Removes a sublexer without removing the multilexer preference. |
| *Procedure REPLACE_INDEX_METADATA* | Removes mdata values from a document. Similar to `REMOVE_MDATA`. |
| *Procedure SET_ATTRIBUTE* | Defines attributes for preferences at preference creation time. The types of attributes available are dependent on the type of preference being created. |
| *Procedure SYNC_INDEX* | Synchronizes a `CONTEXT` index without rebuilding the index. Oracle 10*g* now supports automatic synchronization of `CONTEXT` indexes. |
| *Procedure UNSET_ATTRIBUTE* | Removes an attribute setting from a preference without removing the preference. |
| *Procedure UPDATE_POLICY* | Updates the preferences of the supplied policy. |

# CTX_DOC

The CTX_DOC package is used for specialty text indexing and display features such as theme and gist creation, and the highlighting of keywords in a search. All POLICY procedures can perform their tasks without an index.

## Creation Scripts

dr0doc.pkh/plb

## Public Synonym

CTX_DOC

## Contents

| | |
|---|---|
| *Procedure FILTER* | Overloaded procedure that takes a document, or document reference as input, and returns the filtered text. The results are returned either to a physical table (the text is stored as a CLOB), or as a CLOB locator. The ability to filter certain documents is controlled by the type of filter you use. The default INSO filter can extract text from more than 150 different document types. |
| *Procedure GIST* | Overloaded procedure that generates the theme and gist of a document and then returns the results to either a physical table or a CLOB locator. |
| *Procedure HIGHLIGHT* | Overloaded procedure that returns offset terms for a document based on the query specified. The results are returned either in-memory or to a physical table. |
| *Procedure IFILTER* | Filters binary data to plain text. |
| *Procedure MARKUP* | Overloaded procedure that returns the markup of a document to a table, or as a CLOB locator. The output can be HTML or a text document. |
| *Function PKENCODE* | Used in conjunction with other CTX_DOC procedures. This function creates a composite key based on list of PK strings. |
| *Procedure POLICY_ FILTER* | Overloaded procedure that filters policies and then returns the text to a CLOB locator. It accepts documents as VARCHAR2 or any type of LOB. |

| | |
|---|---|
| *Procedure POLICY_GIST* | Overloaded procedure that generates the theme and gist of a document and then returns the results to a CLOB locator. The document can be VARCHAR2 or any type of LOB. |
| *Procedure POLICY_HIGHLIGHT* | Overloaded procedure that returns offset terms for a document based on the query specified. It allows you to make the terms used in the search stand out from the rest of the text. It accepts documents as VARCHAR2 or any type of LOB, and returns the results to a PL/SQL table. |
| *Procedure POLICY_MARKUP* | Overloaded procedure returns the CLOB locator of markup text. It takes documents as VARCHAR2 or any LOB type. |
| *Procedure POLICY_THEMES* | Overloaded procedure that takes documents either as VARCHAR2 or any type of LOB value and returns themes to a PL/SQL table. |
| *Procedure POLICY_TOKENS* | Overloaded procedure that returns tokens to a PL/SQL table of a document. The document can be VARCHAR2 or any type of LOB. |
| *Procedure SET_KEY_TYPE* | Changes the value of parameter `CTX_DOC_KEY_TYPE`. |
| *Procedure THEMES* | Overloaded procedure. One version generates themes for documents in the specified index, while the other returns the themes to a PL/SQL table. |
| *Procedure TOKENS* | Overloaded procedure that returns tokens for a document to either a PL/SQL table or a physical table. |

# CTX_OUTPUT

CTX_OUTPUT provides output services including log files and trace files for Oracle Text.

## Creation Scripts
dr0out.pkh/plb

## Public Synonym
CTX_OUTPUT

## Contents

# CTX_QUERY

CTX_QUERY returns information regarding the query terms you specify. It allows for storage of text query expressions, and returns count information when provided with a query expression. One of the more interesting procedures is HFEEDBACK which gives detailed hierarchical information related to the search terms specified. The results are based on the knowledge base of your system.

## Creation Scripts
dr0query.pkh/plb

## Public Synonym
CTX_QUERY

## Contents

| | |
|---|---|
| *Procedure BROWSE_WORDS* | Returns the words before, after, or around the word passed to the procedure. It also returns the count of the documents that include each word. |
| *Function CHK_ TXNQRY_DISBL_ SWITCH* | Returns a 0 or 1 based on the current system value. The function is a subprogram called by other procedures and functions. |
| *Function CHK_XPATH* | Oracle Text must process an XPATH expression in a particular format. This function takes an XPATH expression and returns results in a format understood by Oracle. |
| *Function COUNT_HITS* | Function that returns the number of hits for a specified query. |
| *Procedure EXPLAIN* | Returns the explain plan for a text query. |
| *Function FCONTAINS* | Returns the score of a query using the CONTAINS operator. Works with POLICIES. |
| *Procedure HFEEDBACK* | When given a text query, this procedure writes information from the knowledge base to a results table that shows terms and categories related to the terms you specified in your call to the procedure. The results are dependent on your knowledge base. |
| *Procedure REMOVE_SQE* | Removes a stored query. |
| *Procedure STORE_SQE* | Stores query expressions under the name supplied. |

# CTX_REPORT

CTX_REPORT is a very useful package that retrieves information to assist in both the maintenance and tuning of Oracle Text indexes. It retrieves statistical information about existing indexes including storage and fragmentation details. It delivers summary reports for query logs to determine how frequently certain queries are run, highlighting ways in which we can improve application queries for improved results.

## Creation Scripts
dr0repor.pkh/plb

## Public Synonym
CTX_REPORT

## Contents

| | |
|---|---|
| *Procedure/Function* <br> *CREATE_INDEX_* <br> *SCRIPT* | Overloaded. This report output includes a script to fully create an index and all preferences, stoplists, and section groups. |
| *Procedure/Function* <br> *CREATE_POLICY_* <br> *SCRIPT* | Overloaded. Identical to CREATE_INDEX_SCRIPT, but the focus is on POLICIES rather than INDEXES. |
| *Procedure/Function* <br> *DESCRIBE_INDEX* | Overloaded. Use this when troubleshooting indexes. It provides metadata regarding the index, including the type of Lexer used, storage clauses, and stoplists. In 10*g*R1, output can be in XML format or formatted text. |
| *Procedure/Function* <br> *DESCRIBE_POLICY* | Overloaded. Identical to DESCRIBE_INDEX, but for POLICIES rather than INDEXES. In 10*g*R1, output can be in XML format or formatted text. |
| *Procedure/Function* <br> *INDEX_SIZE* | Overloaded. Useful for DBAs in monitoring space usage of indexes and index tables. The report displays primarily information about tablespace usage for text components. In 10*g*R1, output can be in XML format or formatted text. |
| *Procedure INDEX_* <br> *STATS* | One of the most useful reports for tuning text index performance. It includes statistics about index fragmentation, the number of documents indexed, and more. In 10*g*R1, output can be in XML format or formatted text. |

| Procedure QUERY_ LOG_SUMMARY | Analyze the effectiveness of your indexes with this report. You can determine the most common queries made, the most common unsuccessful queries, query frequency, and so on. In 10gR1, output can be in XML format or formatted text. |
| --- | --- |
| Procedure/Function TOKEN_INFO | Overloaded. Provides information to determine if an index is corrupt. In 10gR1, output can be in XML format or formatted text. |
| Function TOKEN_ TYPE | Function that returns a number. This function is used with other procedures and functions that have a TOKEN_TYPE parameter, like TOKEN_INFO. |

# CTX_THES

The CTX_THES package provides a way to manage thesauri. Oracle Text allows for the creation of thesauri for improved search capabilities. For example, if a term is commonly referred to as a "widget," but the contents are stored as a "gadget" and it means the same thing, a thesaurus can link the two terms together. Search on "widget" and results containing "gadget" are returned.

### Creation Scripts
dr0thes.pkh/plb

### Public Synonym
CTX_THES

### Contents

| Procedure ALTER_PHRASE | This procedure alters a phrase in a thesaurus. |
| --- | --- |
| Procedure ALTER_ THESAURUS | Truncate or rename a thesaurus using this procedure. |
| Procedures/Functions BT | Overloaded. BT stands for Broader Terms. This procedure/function returns the broader terms as defined in the thesaurus. Terms or phrases are related to each other in hierarchical fashion. This procedure allows you to specify the hierarchy level to drill down to. |

| | |
|---|---|
| *Procedure/Function BTG* | Overloaded. BTG stands for Broader Terms Generic. Similar to BT. |
| *Procedure/Function BTI* | Overloaded. BTI stands for Broader Terms Instance. Similar to BT. |
| *Procedure/Function BTP* | Overloaded. BTP stands for Broader Terms Partitive. Similar to BT. |
| *Procedure CREATE_ PHRASE* | This procedure adds phrases to existing thesauri. |
| *Procedure CREATE_ RELATION* | This procedure creates a relationship between two phrases in a thesaurus. If a phrase does not exist in the thesaurus, it is created. |
| *Procedure CREATE_ THESAURUS* | This procedure creates an empty thesaurus. |
| *Procedure CREATE_ TRANSLATION* | This procedure creates a relationship between two phrases in different languages. If a translation is not present already, it is added to the thesaurus. |
| *Procedure DROP_PHRASE* | This procedure drops the specified phrase from a thesaurus. |
| *Procedure DROP_ RELATION* | This procedure drops the specified relationship from a thesaurus. |
| *Procedure DROP_ THESAURUS* | This procedure drops the specified thesaurus. |
| *Procedure DROP_ TRANSLATION* | This procedure drops the specified translation of a phrase. |
| *Function HAS_RELATION* | The HAS_RELATION function tests whether a phrase has the specified relationship. It returns a Boolean value. |
| *Procedure/Function NT* | Overloaded. This is the reverse of BT. NT stands for Narrower Terms, and returns the narrower terms of a phrase. |
| *Procedure/Function NTG* | Overloaded. NTG stands for Narrower Terms Generic. NTG is similar to NT. |
| *Procedure/Function NTI* | Overloaded. NTI stands for Narrower Terms Instance. NTI is similar to NT. |

| | |
|---|---|
| *Procedure/Function NTP* | Overloaded. NTP stands for Narrower Terms Partitive. NTP is similar to NT. |
| *Procedure OUTPUT_STYLE* | This procedure sets the type of output shown in expansion functions. |
| *Procedure/Function PT* | Overloaded. PT stands for Preferred Term. It returns the preferred term from the thesaurus based on the specified term or phrase. |
| *Procedure/Function RT* | Overloaded. RT stands for Related Terms. It returns the related terms from the thesaurus based on the specified term or phrase. |
| *Function SN* | SN stands for Scope Note. This function returns the scope note, or comment. |
| *Procedure/Function SYN* | Overloaded. SYN stands for SYNonym. This function returns the synonyms from the thesaurus based on the specified term or phrase. |
| *Procedure THES_TT* | TT stands for Top Term. This procedure finds all top terms, or terms that have narrower, but not broader terms. It finds all top terms, not specific to any term or phrase. |
| *Procedure/Function TR* | Overloaded. TR stands for TRanslation. Provided a phrase, this procedure/function finds the foreign language translation based on the language relationships defined in the thesaurus. |
| *Procedure/Function TRSYN* | Overloaded. TR stands for TRanslation and SYN stands for SYNonym. This procedure/function returns the foreign language translation of a given phrase, and the foreign language synonym of that phrase. |
| *Procedure/Function TT* | Overloaded. TT stands for Top Term. This differs from THES_TT in that TT returns the top terms based on a specific term or phrase. |
| *Procedure UPDATE_TRANSLATION* | Procedure to update an existing translation in a thesaurus. |

# The Most Common Packages

Of all of these packages, there are two that will be used more than the others. CTX_
DDL has to do with the creation and maintenance of index structures, while CTX_
REPORT generates Oracle Text object re-creation scripts, analyzes log files, and
helps optimize the index by reporting various statistics about them.

## CTX_DDL Examples

The CTX_DDL package is used in nearly every situation where Oracle Text is
employed. To create preferences for indexes, CTX_DDL.CREATE_PREFERENCE is
used. To add stopwords to a stoplist, use CTX_DDL.ADD_STOPWORD. The following
example uses CTX_DDL to create BASIC_LEXER as the preferred lexer and set the
attribute BASE_LETTER as YES.

```
-- Available online as part of CTX_DDL.sql
BEGIN
    CTX_DDL.CREATE_PREFERENCE('MY_LEXER', 'BASIC_LEXER');
    CTX_DDL.SET_ATTRIBUTE('MY_LEXER', 'BASE_LETTER', 'YES');
END;
/
```

Another use for CTX_DDL is to synchronize CONTEXT indexes using the CTX_
DDL.SYNC_INDEX procedure. The following code example checks the CTX_
USER_PENDING view for indexes that need to be synchronized, loops through the
results, and then calls the CTX_DDL.SYNC_INDEX procedure for each record.

```
-- Available online as part of CTX_DDL.sql
SET SERVEROUTPUT ON
CREATE OR REPLACE PROCEDURE index_sync
IS
    CURSOR index_cur
    IS
        SELECT pnd_index_name
        FROM ctx_user_pending;

    v_index_name VARCHAR2(30);
BEGIN
    OPEN index_cur;
    LOOP
        FETCH index_cur INTO v_index_name;
        EXIT WHEN index_cur%NOTFOUND;

        DBMS_OUTPUT.PUT_LINE('Index: '||v_index_name||' is pending');
```

```
               -- Sync any indexes returned by the cursor
               CTX_DDL.SYNC_INDEX(v_index_name);

               DBMS_OUTPUT.PUT_LINE('Index: '
                                  ||v_index_name
                                  ||' has been synchronized');
      END LOOP;
      CLOSE index_cur;

EXCEPTION
      WHEN OTHERS
      THEN
         DBMS_OUTPUT.PUT_LINE(SQLERRM);
END index_sync;
/
```

After running this procedure, you can select CTX_USER_PENDING to return no rows. Replace CTX_USER_PENDING with CTX_PENDING in the cursor to check all indexes in the database.

## CTX_REPORT Examples

CTX_REPORT has two primary purposes at the time of this writing. The first is to generate scripts to re-create the objects, essentially reverse-engineering them from an existing install. The second is to report index statistics to assist with index optimization.

The following select statement uses CTX_REPORT.CREATE_INDEX_SCRIPT to reverse-engineer an index:

```
--Available online as part of CTX_REPORT.sql
SET PAGES 9999 LONG 64000
SELECT ctx_report.create_index_script('MY_INDEX', null)
FROM dual;
```

The output from this select appears as follows:

```
CTX_REPORT.CREATE_INDEX_SCRIPT('MY_INDEX',NULL)
-----------------------------------------------------------------
begin
  ctx_ddl.create_preference('"MY_INDEX_DST"','DIRECT_DATASTORE');
end;
/
begin
  ctx_ddl.create_preference('"MY_INDEX_FIL"','NULL_FILTER');
end;
/
...
```

The script outputs all index dependencies, even ones that weren't specified with the original index creation when defaults were used.

In this next example, we generate index statistics for the MY_INDEX Oracle Text index. Before being able to report the statistics though, we need to log them somewhere. The INDEX_REPORT table is all we need.

**Available online as part of CTX_REPORT.sql**
```
CREATE TABLE index_report (
   id number(10),
   report CLOB);
```

Now that the table is present to log the report to, we can use CTX_REPORT.

**--Available online as part of CTX_REPORT.sql**
```
DECLARE
   v_report CLOB := null;
BEGIN
   CTX_REPORT.INDEX_STATS(
                  index_name => 'MY_INDEX',
                  report => v_report,
                  part_name => NULL,
                  frag_stats => NULL,
                  list_size => 20,
                  report_format => NULL);

   INSERT INTO index_report (id, report)
     VALUES (1, v_report);

   COMMIT;
   DBMS_LOB.FREETEMPORARY(v_report);
END;
/
```

The report is now in the INDEX_REPORT table, so we need to retrieve it. We can do this with a simple SELECT.

**--Available online as part of CTX_REPORT.sql**
```
SET PAGES 9999 HEAD OFF
SPOOL index_stats.txt

SELECT report
FROM index_report
WHERE id = 1;

SPOOL OFF
```

The output appears as follows:

```
=========================================================================
                    STATISTICS FOR "QNXO"."MY_INDEX"
=========================================================================
indexed documents:                                                      3
allocated docids:                                                       3
$I rows:                                                                7
-------------------------------------------------------------------------
                           TOKEN STATISTICS
-------------------------------------------------------------------------
unique tokens:                                                          7
average $I rows per token:                                           1.00
tokens with most $I rows:
  UNITED (0:TEXT)                                                       1
  STATES (0:TEXT)                                                       1
...
```

Using this report and the others available with CTX_REPORT, it's possible to fine-tune Oracle Text–based applications, and optimize the searches for optimal efficiency.

# APPENDIX
# C

## PL/SQL Web Toolkit Packages

he collection of packages in this appendix is referred to by different names depending on the version of Oracle you are running. Regardless of their names, they all provide developers an easy way to integrate PL/SQL and web development. They can work with the Oracle Application Server and/or Apache using `mod_plsql`, as well as directly from the command line.

**NOTE**
*See Chapter 11 for more information on*
`mod_plsql.`

# The Packages

In this section we list packages that are part of the PL/SQL Toolkit, and the procedures and functions in each. The list is from Oracle 10*g* Release 1, so if you have a different release, you will have slightly different package contents. Chapter 11 contains a full discussion about the PL/SQL Toolkit, as well as examples showing their implementation.

## HTF

Hypertext Functions (HTFs) return HTML tags to the program(s) that called them. If you wish to have the HTML tags generated directly to the web page, look at the HTP package as an alternative. You might have guessed by its name that this package exclusively contains functions. The HTP package contains each function's procedure counterpart.

### Contents

| | | |
|---|---|---|
| ADDRESS | BLOCKQUOTEOPEN | DIV |
| ANCHOR | BODYOPEN | DLISTDEF |
| ANCHOR2 | BOLD | DLISTOPEN |
| APPLETOPEN | BR | DLISTTERM |
| AREA | CENTER | EM |
| BASE | CITE | EMPHASIS |
| BASEFONT | CODE | ESCAPE_SC |
| BGSOUND | COMMENT | ESCAPE_URL |
| BIG | DFN | FONTOPEN |

| | | |
|---|---|---|
| FORMAT_CELL | HTITLE | PLAINTEXT |
| FORMCHECKBOX | IMG | PREOPEN |
| FORMFILE | IMG2 | S |
| FORMHIDDEN | ISINDEX | SAMPLE |
| FORMIMAGE | ITALIC | SCRIPT |
| FORMOPEN | KBD | SMALL |
| FORMPASSWORD | KEYBOARD | STRIKE |
| FORMRADIO | LINE | STRONG |
| FORMRESET | LINKREL | STYLE |
| FORMSELECTOPEN | LINKREV | SUB |
| FORMSELECTOPTION | LISTHEADER | SUP |
| FORMSUBMIT | LISTITEM | TABLECAPTION |
| FORMTEXT | MAILTO | TABLEDATA |
| FORMTEXTAREA | MAPOPEN | TABLEHEADER |
| FORMTEXTAREA2 | META | TABLEOPEN |
| FORMTEXTAREAOPEN | NEXTID | TABLEROWOPEN |
| FORMTEXTAREAOPEN2 | NL | TELETYPE |
| FRAME | NOBR | TITLE |
| FRAMESETOPEN | OLISTOPEN | ULISTOPEN |
| HEADER | PARAGRAPH | UNDERLINE |
| HR | PARAM | VARIABLE |

# HTP

The Hypertext Procedures package contains procedures that mirror the function in the HTF package, plus a number of additional procedures for generating HTML. The major difference between HTP and HTF is that HTP generates tags directly to the web page whereas HTF returns tags to the calling program.

## Contents

| | |
|---|---|
| FORMSELECTOPTION | KBD |
| FORMSUBMIT | KEYBOARD |
| FORMTEXT | LINE |
| FORMTEXTAREA | LINKREL |
| FORMTEXTAREA2 | LINKREV |
| FORMTEXTAREACLOSE | LISTHEADER |
| FORMTEXTAREAOPEN | LISTINGCLOSE |
| FORMTEXTAREAOPEN2 | LISTINGOPEN |
| FRAME | LISTITEM |
| FRAMESETCLOSE | MAILTO |
| FRAMESETOPEN | MAPCLOSE |
| GET_DOWNLOAD_FILES_LIST | MAPOPEN |
| GET_LINE | MENULISTCLOSE |
| GET_PAGE | MENULISTOPEN |
| GET_PAGE_CHARSET_CONVERT | META |
| GET_PAGE_RAW | NEXTID |
| HEADCLOSE | NL |
| HEADER | NOBR |
| HEADOPEN | NOFRAMESCLOSE |
| HR | NOFRAMESOPEN |
| HTITLE | OLISTCLOSE |
| HTMLCLOSE | OLISTOPEN |
| HTMLOPEN | P (overloaded) |
| IMG | PARA |
| IMG2 | PARAGRAPH |
| INIT | PARAM |
| ISINDEX | PLAINTEXT |
| ITALIC | PRECLOSE |

| | |
|---|---|
| PREOPEN | SUB |
| PRINT (overloaded) | SUP |
| PRINTS | TABLECAPTION |
| PRINT_HEADER | TABLECLOSE |
| PRN (overloaded) | TABLEDATA |
| PS | TABLEHEADER |
| PUTRAW | TABLEOPEN |
| S | TABLEROWCLOSE |
| SAMPLE | TABLEROWOPEN |
| SCRIPT | TELETYPE |
| SETHTTPCHARSET | TITLE |
| SET_TRANSFER_MODE | ULISTCLOSE |
| SHOWPAGE | ULISTOPEN |
| SMALL | UNDERLINE |
| STRIKE | VARIABLE |
| STRONG | WBR |
| STYLE | |

# OWA_CACHE

Improve performance of PL/SQL-based applications by using the OWA_CACHE package. This package enables the caching of database-generated web content on the application server.

## Contents

| | |
|---|---|
| DISABLE | SET_CACHE |
| GET_ETAG | SET_EXPIRES |
| GET_LEVEL | SET_NOT_MODIFIED |
| INIT | SET_SURROGATE_CONTROL |

# OWA_COOKIE

Send, remove, and read cookies from a client browser using the PL/SQL OWA_
COOKIE package. Cookies are small text files that store information about a user's
visit to a particular web page. The cookie can track session-specific information, or
remain on the client machine for subsequent visits to the same web site so
information can be persistent across sessions.

## Contents

| | |
|---|---|
| GET | REMOVE |
| GET_ALL | SEND |
| INIT | |

# OWA_CUSTOM

The OWA_CUSTOM package contains a single function that returns a Boolean value.
The package is used for custom authentication. For example, when a DAD
connection is established in the Oracle Application Server, there is an option to
select the authentication mode. When custom or global authentication is selected
for the DAD, the Global PL/SQL Agent connects to the data server using the DAD
connection string, and control is passed to the application code for final authentication.

## Contents

OWA_CUSTOM contains a single function called AUTHORIZE.

# OWA_IMAGE

Provided with a POINT, the OWA_IMAGE package can return the *x* and *y* coordinates
for an image. POINT is a type defined by the following:

```
TYPE POINT IS TABLE OF VARCHAR2(32767)
    INDEX BY BINARY_INTEGER
```

The POINT is passed to the two function listed next.

## Contents

| | |
|---|---|
| GET_X | GET_Y |

# OWA_OPT_LOCK

The name of this package is a bit misleading. The OWA_OPT_LOCK package employs *optimistic locking*, which in reality is not a database lock at all. Instead of locking the records (HTTP is stateless, so traditional database locks cannot be used), OWA_OPT_LOCK determines if a record has been modified by someone else since it was last retrieved. If the database record *has* been modified since it was last retrieved, the current user's modification is rejected. The record must be re-queried before the modification is allowed.

## Contents

| | |
|---|---|
| CHECKSUM (overloaded) | STORE_VALUES |
| GET_ROWID | VERIFY_VALUES |

# OWA_PATTERN

The OWA_PATTERN package was available in Oracle prior to the introduction of regular expressions (regex) in Oracle 10g, and has a similar purpose (though one that's less elegant than the current regex implementation). See Chapter 10 for more information about regular expressions.

## Contents

| | |
|---|---|
| AMATCH (overloaded) | GETPAT |
| CHANGE (overloaded) | MATCH (overloaded) |

# OWA_SEC

OWA_SEC works with OWA_CUSTOM to provide custom authentication for web applications. It is called by OWA_CUSTOM during authorization.

## Contents

| | |
|---|---|
| GET_CLIENT_HOSTNAME | GET_USER_ID |
| GET_CLIENT_IP | SET_AUTHORIZATION |
| GET_PASSWORD | SET_PROTECTION_REALM |

# OWA_TEXT

Used primarily by OWA_PATTERN for string manipulation and pattern matching, OWA_TEXT provides procedures, functions, and types that hold and print text.

## Contents

| | |
|---|---|
| ADD2MULTI | PRINT_MULTI |
| NEW_MULTI (overloaded) | PRINT_ROW_LIST |
| NEW_ROW_LIST (overloaded) | STREAM2MULTI |

# OWA_UTIL

The OWA_UTIL package provides a wide variety of subprograms designed to make the developer's life easier. One example of this is the date conversion function that takes the date string (not a date datatype) from an HTML field and formats it as a DATE data type for PL/SQL processing. Other utilities provide convenient database-to-HTML table operations, as well as the ability to retrieve a single CGI environment variable, or print the entire list along with their values.

## Contents

| | |
|---|---|
| BIND_VARIABLES | ITE |
| CALENDARPRINT (overloaded) | LISTPRINT (overloaded) |
| CELLSPRINT (overloaded) | MIME_HEADER |
| CHOOSE_DATE | NAME_RESOLVE |
| COMMA_TO_IDENT_ARR (overloaded) | PATH_TO_ME |
| DESCRIBE_COLS | PRINT_CGI_ENV |
| GET_CGI_ENV | PRINT_VERSION |
| GET_OWA_SERVICE_PATH | REDIRECT_URL |
| GET_PROCEDURE | RESOLVE_TABLE |
| GET_VERSION | SHOWPAGE |
| HTTP_HEADER_CLOSE | SHOWSOURCE |

| | |
|---|---|
| SHOW_QUERY_COLUMNS | TABLEHEADERROWOPEN (overloaded) |
| SIGNATURE (overloaded) | TABLENODATA |
| STATUS_LINE | TABLEOPEN |
| TABLECAPTION | TABLEPRINT |
| TABLECLOSE (overloaded) | TABLEROWCLOSE |
| TABLEDATA | TABLEROWOPEN |
| TABLEHEADER (overloaded) | TODATE |
| TABLEHEADERROWCLOSE (overloaded) | WHO_CALLED_ME |

# WPG_DOCLOAD

The `WPG_DOCLOAD` package works with the PL/SQL Gateway to download files, including LOBs.

## Contents

| | |
|---|---|
| DOWNLOAD_FILE (overloaded) | GET_DOWNLOAD_BLOB |
| GET_CONTENT_LENGTH | GET_DOWNLOAD_FILE |
| GET_DOWNLOAD_BFILE | IS_FILE_DOWNLOAD |

# APPENDIX
# D

## Basic Primer on Java and Java Database Connectivity (JDBC)

he Basic Primer on Java and the Java Database Connectivity (JDBC) model is provided to assist PL/SQL developers working the examples found in Chapter 5 of this book. This appendix covers the following:

- Java and JDBC architecture

- Configuring the Oracle Java environment

- Testing a client-side or thin-driver JDBC connection

# Java and JDBC Architecture

Java is a robust Object-Oriented (OO) programming language that employs a Java virtual machine (JVM). A virtual machine creates a self-contained environment that mimics services like an operating system. The JVM runs as a process in the Windows, Apple, and UNIX operating systems, while Java programs run inside the JVM with all the rights and privileges granted to the JVM by the operating system. These permissions are found in the `java.policy` and `java.security` files.

Java also provides robust networking capabilities, which are likewise controlled within the scope of the same two configuration files. Java communicates with databases by using the Java Database Connectivity (JDBC) utilities. Oracle provides three JDBC drivers: the client-side or thin driver, the Oracle Call Interface (OCI) or thick driver, and the server-side internal driver.

The drivers have specific roles in the Java communication model. The OCI and server-side internal drivers are targeted for use with Oracle database or application server file systems and libraries. The client-side or thin driver is not dependent on the Oracle database or application server file systems and libraries. The thin driver is frequently used to connect remotely to the Oracle instance, and connects by sending a signal to the Oracle listener, which then brokers a connection to the database.

Testing your Java environment and ability to connect to the Oracle instance is important before attempting to develop stored Java static and instantiable class files. If you cannot connect with the `PATH` and `CLASSPATH` environment variables, you may have a problem with your configuration or the Oracle listener. The following sections discuss configuring and testing your Java environment and the ability to connect to the Oracle database instance.

# Configuring the Oracle Java Environment

The Oracle 9*i* and 10*g* software is delivered with a Java Software Development Kit (JSDK or Java SDK). It contains the current supported version for the release of the database file system. You need to set your `PATH` and `CLASSPATH` variables to work with the Java programming language and JVM environment.

Multiple ways exist to configure Java, which are dependent on where you've positioned the Java SDK files. The following assumes you're using the Java SDK shipped with the Oracle database for the Windows and UNIX platforms.

## WINDOWS

```
C:> set PATH=%PATH%;C:%ORACLE_HOME%\jdk\bin
C:> set CLASSPATH=%CLASSPATH%;C:%ORACLE_HOME%\jdbc\lib\classes12.zip
```

## UNIX

```
# export PATH=$PATH:/<mount>/$ORACLE_HOME/jdk/bin
# export CLASSPATH=$CLASSPATH:/<mount>/$ORACLE_HOME/jdbc/lib/classes12.zip
```

You should now be able to test a basic Java program. Java programs are called class files. They are written in plain text files adhering to the syntax rules of the Java programming language, which you can find at the Sun Microsystems web site. A robust tutorial is available at http://java.sun.com/docs/books/tutorial/index.html.

There are two core executables to run Java programs, which you'll use in the examples. They are

- **javac** Compiles your text file Java programs into Java byte code

- **java** Runs your compiled Java byte code programs

The file-naming convention in Java is case-sensitive and you should ensure you name files consistent with the web-based code example files. If you attempt to compile a Java file when the file name and class name are different, you'll receive an error. Also, the file extension for Java programs is always a lowercase `.java`.

The `javac` executable compiles the text file into a Java byte file, which is interpreted at runtime by the JVM. Java class files are run using the `java` executable.

Java uses a `main()` method to start a program. The `main()` method acts as the launching pad for the program when called by the `java` executable, which launches a JVM process to interpret and run the Java program. The smallest footprint for a Java program is a Java class with only a `main()` method definition. The following illustrates that basic program and validates that you've correctly configured your Java environment:

**-- Available online as part of HelloWorld.java file.**

```
// Class definition.
public class HelloWorld
{
```

```
// Static main to print Hello World.
public static void main(String args[])
{
  // Print the message to console.
  System.out.println("Hello World.");

} // End of static main.

} // End of HelloWorld class.
```

Assuming you're at the command line in the same directory as the Java program, use the following syntax to compile the file:

```
javac HelloWorld.java
```

You may then execute the Java program class file with the Java executable:

```
java HelloWorld
```

If executed successfully, you will see the following output:

```
Hello World.
```

The Java class files require you to configure the env parameter in your `listener.ora`. You will need to set `LD_LIBRARY_PATH` in the `listener.ora` file. You set it as follows:

```
LD_LIBRARY_PATH=C:\oracle\ora92\lib;C:\oracle\ora92\jdbc\lib
```

You have now verified your configuration. The next section provides you with a utility to test the JDBC connection.

# Testing a Client-Side or Thin-Driver JDBC Connection

The following Java program enables you to test your JDBC connection by soliciting input for the necessary arguments to connect to an Oracle instance. It will simply query the `DUAL` table for a "Hello World." string. You will be prompted for the following input parameters by the program when run by the Java executable:

```
----------------------------------------------------------------
Enter User [UID/PASSWD]:
Enter Host Name: <hostname.domain_name>
Enter Port Name: <Oracle listener port>
Enter Database Name: <Oracle SID>
```

You can use this file to test your ability to connect through any Oracle listener to the Oracle Database instance:

**-- Available online as part of HelloWorldThin.java file.**

```java
// Class imports.
import java.sql.*;
import java.io.*;
import java.util.*;

// Oracle class imports.
import oracle.jdbc.driver.*;

// ------------------------- Begin Class ----------------------------/

// Class definition.
public class HelloWorldThin
{
  // Define a static class String variable.
  private static String user;

  // --------------------- Begin Constructor -------------------------/

  /*
  || The constructors of the class are:
  || ===================================================================
  ||  Access       Constructor Type  Constructor
  ||  ---------     ----------------  ------------------------------------
  ||  public        Default           ThinJDBC()
  */

  // Default constructor.
  public HelloWorldThin()
  {
    // Null constructor.

  } // End of default constructor.

  // ---------------------- End Constructor --------------------------/
  // ---------------------- Begin Methods ----------------------------/

  /*
  || The static main instantiates a test instance of the class:
  || ===================================================================
  ||  Return Type  Method Name                    Access    Parameter List
  ||  -----------  ---------------------------     --------  --------------
  ||  void         printLine()                     private
  ||  void         printLine()                     private   String s
  ||  String       readEntry()                     private
  */

  // ------------------------------------------------------------------/
```

```java
    // Print line only method.
    private static void printLine()
    {
      // Call overloaded method with a null String.
      printLine(null);

    } // End of printLine() method.

    // ----------------------------------------------------------------------/

    // Print String with a line method.
    private static void printLine(String s)
    {
      if (s != null)
      {
        // Print the String to console.
        System.out.println(s);

      } // End of if String length is zero.

      // Print a line.
      System.out.print  ("----------------------------------------");
      System.out.println("----------------------------------------");

    } // End of printLine(String s) method.

    // ----------------------------------------------------------------------/

    // Method to read a line from standard input.
    private static String readEntry()
    {
      // Use try-catch to raise exception for an IO exception.
      try
      {
        // Define an int to read a stream.
        int c;

        // Define and intialize a StringBuffer.
        StringBuffer buffer = new StringBuffer();

        // Read first character.
        c = System.in.read();

        // Use a loop to increment and read all characters.
        while (c != '\n' && c != -1)
        {
          // If the character is not an EOL marker, append it to the buffer.
          buffer.append((char)c);
```

```java
      // Read next character.
      c = System.in.read();

    } // End of while character not EOL marker.

    // Return trimmed buffer.
    return buffer.toString().trim();

  } // End of try block.
  catch (IOException e)
  {
    // Return a null if input is a null.
    return null;

  } // End of catch block.

} // End of readEntry() method.

// ------------------------ End Methods ----------------------------/

// --------------------- Begin Static Main -------------------------/

// Static main to test JDBC connection, with exceptions thrown.
public static void main(String args[]) throws SQLException, IOException
{
  // Define and initialize Boolean control variables.
  boolean debug = false;

  // Define String variables.
  String userIn;
  String password;
  String host;
  String port;
  String database;
  String debugString = new String("DEBUG");

  // Define int variable.
  int slashIndex;

  // Print line for console output.
  printLine();

  // Validate whether connection is run in debug mode.
  if (args.length > 0)
  {
    // Is the argument a debug instruction.
    if (args[0].toUpperCase().equals(debugString))
    {
      // Enable debug.
      debug = true;
```

```java
    // Print debug mode enabled.
    printLine("Debug mode is enabled.");

  }
  else
  {
    // Send message on argument.
    for (int i = 0;i < args.length;i++)
    {
      // Print submitted arguments.
      System.out.println("Incorrect argument(s): [" + args[i] + "]");

    } // End of loop to print submitted arguments.

    // Print line break after for-loop because may run more than once.
    printLine();

    // Print valid arguments.
    printLine("Valid case insensitive argument is: DEBUG.");

  } // End of if to validate argument instruction.

} // End of if to manage any arguments.

// Load Oracle JDBC driver.
DriverManager.registerDriver(new oracle.jdbc.driver.OracleDriver());

// Prompt the user for connect information.
System.out.print("Enter User [UID/PASSWD]: ");

// Get user input.
userIn = readEntry();

// Parse user input for token between UID and password.
slashIndex = userIn.indexOf("/");

// Check for token in String.

if (slashIndex != -1)
{
  // Assign the substring to the left of the token for user.
  user = userIn.substring(0, slashIndex);

  // Assign the substring to the right of the token for password.
  password = userIn.substring(slashIndex + 1);

}
else // Token missing from the String.
{
  // Assign the first entry as user.
  user = userIn;
```

```
  // Get user input for password.
  System.out.print("Enter Password: ");

  // Assign the second entry as password.
  password = readEntry();

} // End of if for token in String.

// Get user input for password.
System.out.print("Enter Host Name: ");

// Assign entry to database name.
host = readEntry();

// Get user input for password.
System.out.print("Enter Port Name: ");

// Assign entry to database name.
port = readEntry();

// Get user input for password.
System.out.print("Enter Database Name: ");

// Assign entry to database name.
database = readEntry();

// Print message advising progress.
printLine("Connecting to the database ...");

// Print JDBC connect string.
printLine("jdbc:oracle:oci8:@" +
          host + ":" + port + ":" + database + "," +
          user + "," + password);

// Attempt Oracle8i connection.
try
{
  // Define and initialize a JDBC connection.
  Connection conn = DriverManager.getConnection("jdbc:oracle:thin:@" +
                    host + ":" + port + ":" + database, user,
                    password);

  // Print connected.
  printLine("Connected.");

  // Define metadata object.
  DatabaseMetaData dmd = conn.getMetaData();

  // Print database metadata.
  printLine("Driver Version: [" + dmd.getDriverVersion() + "]\n" +
            "Driver Name:    [" + dmd.getDriverName() + "]");
```

```
  // Create a statement.
  Statement stmt = conn.createStatement();

  // Execute and return statement.
  ResultSet rset = stmt.executeQuery("SELECT 'Hello World.' FROM dual");

  // Enter a loop for the return set.
  while (rset.next())
  {
    // Print result set.
    printLine(rset.getString(1));

  } // End of loop to read return set.

  // Close the result set.
  rset.close();
  stmt.close();
  conn.close();

  // Print line and acknowledgment.
  printLine("The JDBC Connection worked.");

} // End of try to establish a connection.
catch (SQLException e)
{
  // Print the meaningful error or stacktrace for debug mode.
  if (debug)
  {
    // Use print() because the String returned has a postpended "\n".
    e.printStackTrace();
    printLine();
  }
  else
  {
    // If a mistyped host name, port number or database name.
    if (e.getSQLState() == null)
    {
      // Provide SQL state error message since detail is missing in
      // the classes12.zip archive for SQLException.getErrorCode()
      // returns a 17002.
      System.out.println(
        new SQLException("Oracle Thin Client Net8 Connection Error.",
                  "ORA-" + e.getErrorCode() +
                  ": Incorrect Net8 thin client arguments:\n\n" +
                  "  host name      [" + host + "]\n" +
                  "  port number    [" + port + "]\n" +
                  "  database name  [" + database + "]\n",
                  e.getErrorCode()).getSQLState());
    }
    else
```

```
    {
      // Trim the postpended "\n".
      printLine(e.getMessage().substring(0,e.getMessage().length()-1));

    } // End of if mistyped host name, port number or database name.

  } // End of if to print message or StackTrace.

  // Print line and acknowledgment.
  printLine("The JDBC Connection failed.");

  } // End of SQLException catch.

  } // End of static main.

  // ----------------------- End Static Main --------------------------/

} // End of ThinJDBC class.
```

Before introducing the program, you saw the program output to collect arguments to connect your Oracle instance. The balance of the output is shown next:

**-- This is output from the HelloWorldThin.java file.**

```
Connecting to the database ...
-----------------------------------------------------------------
jdbc:oracle:oci8:@<hostname.domain_name>:<port>:<SID>,<UID>,<PSSWD>
-----------------------------------------------------------------
Connected.
-----------------------------------------------------------------
Driver Version: [9.2.0.1.0]
Driver Name:    [Oracle JDBC driver]
-----------------------------------------------------------------
Hello World.
-----------------------------------------------------------------
The JDBC Connection worked.
-----------------------------------------------------------------
```

**NOTE**
*You should check the management of the 17002 error in the SQL connection catch block. It can be very useful in writing Java programs that use distributed Java architectures like Enterprise Java Beans (EJBs).*

Any error messages or failures to print to the console indicate that there's an error in the setup of the environment. You'll need to revisit the instructions and troubleshoot the problem.

# Index

## S

## U

# GET YOUR FREE SUBSCRIPTION
# TO ORACLE MAGAZINE

*Oracle Magazine* is essential gear for today's information technology professionals. Stay informed and increase your productivity with every issue of *Oracle Magazine*. Inside each free bimonthly issue you'll get:

IF THERE ARE OTHER ORACLE USERS AT YOUR LOCATION WHO WOULD LIKE TO RECEIVE THEIR OWN SUBSCRIPTION TO ORACLE MAGAZINE, PLEASE PHOTOCOPY THIS FORM AND PASS IT ALONG.

- Up-to-date information on Oracle Database, Oracle Application Server, Web development, enterprise grid computing, database technology, and business trends
- Third-party vendor news and announcements
- Technical articles on Oracle and partner products, technologies, and operating environments
- Development and administration tips
- Real-world customer stories

## Three easy ways to subscribe:

### ① Web
Visit our Web site at otn.oracle.com/oraclemagazine. You'll find a subscription form there, plus much more!

### ② Fax
Complete the questionnaire on the back of this card and fax the questionnaire side only to +1.847.763.9638.

### ③ Mail
Complete the questionnaire on the back of this card and mail it to P.O. Box 1263, Skokie, IL 60076-8263

# FREE SUBSCRIPTION

○ **Yes, please send me a FREE subscription to *Oracle Magazine*.**  ○ **NO**

To receive a free subscription to *Oracle Magazine*, you must fill out the entire card, sign it, and date it (incomplete cards cannot be processed or acknowledged). You can also fax your application to +1.847.763.9638.
**Or subscribe at our Web site at otn.oracle.com/oraclemagazine**

○ From time to time, Oracle Publishing allows our partners exclusive access to our e-mail addresses for special promotions and announcements. To be included in this program, please check this circle.

○ Oracle Publishing allows sharing of our mailing list with selected third parties. If you prefer your mailing address not to be included in this program, please check here. If at any time you would like to be removed from this mailing list, please contact Customer Service at +1.847.647.9630 or send an e-mail to oracle@halldata.com.

signature (required)                               date

X

name                               title

company                            e-mail address

street/p.o. box

city/state/zip or postal code      telephone

country                            fax

---

YOU MUST ANSWER ALL TEN QUESTIONS BELOW.

**① WHAT IS THE PRIMARY BUSINESS ACTIVITY OF YOUR FIRM AT THIS LOCATION?** (check one only)
- ☐ 01 Aerospace and Defense Manufacturing
- ☐ 02 Application Service Provider
- ☐ 03 Automotive Manufacturing
- ☐ 04 Chemicals, Oil and Gas
- ☐ 05 Communications and Media
- ☐ 06 Construction/Engineering
- ☐ 07 Consumer Sector/Consumer Packaged Goods
- ☐ 08 Education
- ☐ 09 Financial Services/Insurance
- ☐ 10 Government (civil)
- ☐ 11 Government (military)
- ☐ 12 Healthcare
- ☐ 13 High Technology Manufacturing, OEM
- ☐ 14 Integrated Software Vendor
- ☐ 15 Life Sciences (Biotech, Pharmaceuticals)
- ☐ 16 Mining
- ☐ 17 Retail/Wholesale/Distribution
- ☐ 18 Systems Integrator, VAR/VAD
- ☐ 19 Telecommunications
- ☐ 20 Travel and Transportation
- ☐ 21 Utilities (electric, gas, sanitation, water)
- ☐ 98 Other Business and Services

**② WHICH OF THE FOLLOWING BEST DESCRIBES YOUR PRIMARY JOB FUNCTION?** (check one only)
*Corporate Management/Staff*
- ☐ 01 Executive Management (President, Chair, CEO, CFO, Owner, Partner, Principal)
- ☐ 02 Finance/Administrative Management (VP/Director/ Manager/Controller, Purchasing, Administration)
- ☐ 03 Sales/Marketing Management (VP/Director/Manager)
- ☐ 04 Computer Systems/Operations Management (CIO/VP/Director/ Manager MIS, Operations)
*IS/IT Staff*
- ☐ 05 Systems Development/ Programming Management
- ☐ 06 Systems Development/ Programming Staff
- ☐ 07 Consulting
- ☐ 08 DBA/Systems Administrator
- ☐ 09 Education/Training
- ☐ 10 Technical Support Director/Manager
- ☐ 11 Other Technical Management/Staff
- ☐ 98 Other

**③ WHAT IS YOUR CURRENT PRIMARY OPERATING PLATFORM?** (select all that apply)
- ☐ 01 Digital Equipment UNIX
- ☐ 02 Digital Equipment VAX VMS
- ☐ 03 HP UNIX

- ☐ 04 IBM AIX
- ☐ 05 IBM UNIX
- ☐ 06 Java
- ☐ 07 Linux
- ☐ 08 Macintosh
- ☐ 09 MS-DOS
- ☐ 10 MVS
- ☐ 11 NetWare
- ☐ 12 Network Computing
- ☐ 13 OpenVMS
- ☐ 14 SCO UNIX
- ☐ 15 Sequent DYNIX/ptx
- ☐ 16 Sun Solaris/SunOS
- ☐ 17 SVR4
- ☐ 18 UnixWare
- ☐ 19 Windows
- ☐ 20 Windows NT
- ☐ 21 Other UNIX
- ☐ 98 Other
- 99 ☐ None of the above

**④ DO YOU EVALUATE, SPECIFY, RECOMMEND, OR AUTHORIZE THE PURCHASE OF ANY OF THE FOLLOWING?** (check all that apply)
- ☐ 01 Hardware
- ☐ 02 Software
- ☐ 03 Application Development Tools
- ☐ 04 Database Products
- ☐ 05 Internet or Intranet Products
- 99 ☐ None of the above

**⑤ IN YOUR JOB, DO YOU USE OR PLAN TO PURCHASE ANY OF THE FOLLOWING PRODUCTS?** (check all that apply)
*Software*
- ☐ 01 Business Graphics
- ☐ 02 CAD/CAE/CAM
- ☐ 03 CASE
- ☐ 04 Communications
- ☐ 05 Database Management
- ☐ 06 File Management
- ☐ 07 Finance
- ☐ 08 Java
- ☐ 09 Materials Resource Planning
- ☐ 10 Multimedia Authoring
- ☐ 11 Networking
- ☐ 12 Office Automation
- ☐ 13 Order Entry/Inventory Control
- ☐ 14 Programming
- ☐ 15 Project Management
- ☐ 16 Scientific and Engineering
- ☐ 17 Spreadsheets
- ☐ 18 Systems Management
- ☐ 19 Workflow

*Hardware*
- ☐ 20 Macintosh
- ☐ 21 Mainframe
- ☐ 22 Massively Parallel Processing
- ☐ 23 Minicomputer
- ☐ 24 PC
- ☐ 25 Network Computer
- ☐ 26 Symmetric Multiprocessing
- ☐ 27 Workstation
*Peripherals*
- ☐ 28 Bridges/Routers/Hubs/Gateways
- ☐ 29 CD-ROM Drives
- ☐ 30 Disk Drives/Subsystems
- ☐ 31 Modems
- ☐ 32 Tape Drives/Subsystems
- ☐ 33 Video Boards/Multimedia
*Services*
- ☐ 34 Application Service Provider
- ☐ 35 Consulting
- ☐ 36 Education/Training
- ☐ 37 Maintenance
- ☐ 38 Online Database Services
- ☐ 39 Support
- ☐ 40 Technology-Based Training
- ☐ 98 Other
- 99 ☐ None of the above

**⑥ WHAT ORACLE PRODUCTS ARE IN USE AT YOUR SITE?** (check all that apply)
*Oracle E-Business Suite*
- ☐ 01 Oracle Marketing
- ☐ 02 Oracle Sales
- ☐ 03 Oracle Order Fulfillment
- ☐ 04 Oracle Supply Chain Management
- ☐ 05 Oracle Procurement
- ☐ 06 Oracle Manufacturing
- ☐ 07 Oracle Maintenance Management
- ☐ 08 Oracle Service
- ☐ 09 Oracle Contracts
- ☐ 10 Oracle Projects
- ☐ 11 Oracle Financials
- ☐ 12 Oracle Human Resources
- ☐ 13 Oracle Interaction Center
- ☐ 14 Oracle Communications/Utilities (modules)
- ☐ 15 Oracle Public Sector/University (modules)
- ☐ 16 Oracle Financial Services (modules)
*Server/Software*
- ☐ 17 Oracle9i
- ☐ 18 Oracle9i Lite
- ☐ 19 Oracle8i
- ☐ 20 Other Oracle database
- ☐ 21 Oracle9i Application Server
- ☐ 22 Oracle9i Application Server Wireless
- ☐ 23 Oracle Small Business Suite

*Tools*
- ☐ 24 Oracle Developer Suite
- ☐ 25 Oracle Discoverer
- ☐ 26 Oracle JDeveloper
- ☐ 27 Oracle Migration Workbench
- ☐ 28 Oracle9i AS Portal
- ☐ 29 Oracle Warehouse Builder
*Oracle Services*
- ☐ 30 Oracle Outsourcing
- ☐ 31 Oracle Consulting
- ☐ 32 Oracle Education
- ☐ 33 Oracle Support
- ☐ 98 Other
- 99 ☐ None of the above

**⑦ WHAT OTHER DATABASE PRODUCTS ARE IN USE AT YOUR SITE?** (check all that apply)
- ☐ 01 Access
- ☐ 02 Baan
- ☐ 03 dbase
- ☐ 04 Gupta
- ☐ 05 IBM DB2
- ☐ 06 Informix
- ☐ 07 Ingres
- ☐ 08 Microsoft Access
- ☐ 09 Microsoft SQL Server
- ☐ 10 PeopleSoft
- ☐ 11 Progress
- ☐ 12 SAP
- ☐ 13 Sybase
- ☐ 14 VSAM
- ☐ 98 Other
- 99 ☐ None of the above

**⑧ WHAT OTHER APPLICATION SERVER PRODUCTS ARE IN USE AT YOUR SITE?** (check all that apply)
- ☐ 01 BEA
- ☐ 02 IBM
- ☐ 03 Sybase
- ☐ 04 Sun
- ☐ 05 Other

**⑨ DURING THE NEXT 12 MONTHS, HOW MUCH DO YOU ANTICIPATE YOUR ORGANIZATION WILL SPEND ON COMPUTER HARDWARE, SOFTWARE, PERIPHERALS, AND SERVICES FOR YOUR LOCATION?** (check only one)
- ☐ 01 Less than $10,000
- ☐ 02 $10,000 to $49,999
- ☐ 03 $50,000 to $99,999
- ☐ 04 $100,000 to $499,999
- ☐ 05 $500,000 to $999,999
- ☐ 06 $1,000,000 and over

**⑩ WHAT IS YOUR COMPANY'S YEARLY SALES REVENUE?** (please choose one)
- ☐ 01 $500,000,000 and above
- ☐ 02 $100,000,000 to $500,000,000
- ☐ 03 $50,000,000 to $100,000,000
- ☐ 04 $5,000,000 to $50,000,000
- ☐ 05 $1,000,000 to $5,000,000

100103